THE CLINICIAN'S HANDBOOK

THE CLINICIAN'S HANDBOOK

THE PSYCHOPATHOLOGY OF ADULTHOOD AND ADOLESCENCE

SECOND EDITION

ROBERT G. MEYER
University of Louisville

ALLYN AND BACON
Boston, London, Sydney, Toronto

Series Editor: John-Paul Lenney
Production Administrator: Annette Joseph
Production Coordinator: Lisa M. Mosca
Editorial-Production Service: Harkavy Publishing Service
Text Designer: Harkavy Publishing Service
Cover Administrator: Linda K. Dickinson
Cover Designer: Christy Rosso

Library of Congress Cataloging-in-Publication Data

Meyer, Robert G.
    The clinician's handbook : the psychopathology of adulthood and
adolescence / Robert G. Meyer.—2nd ed.
        p.   cm.
    Bibliography: p.
    Includes indexes.
    ISBN 0-205-11922-0
    1. Mental illness–Diagnosis.   2. Psychodiagnostics.
3. Psychotherapy.   I. Title.
RC469.M46 1989   88-8129
616.89–dc19   CIP

Printed in the United States of America
10 9 8 7 6 5 4 3 2 1   94 93 92 91 90 89

CONTENTS

Preface ix
Introduction 1

The Rationale for Inclusion of Certain Tests 5   The Information
Evolution in This Book 8   DSM-III-R 10

1. Clinical Correlates of the MMPI and 16 PF Scales 17

MMPI 17   The ? Scale 22   MMPI Interrelationship Interpretations 36
The Cattell 16 PF Test 53   Cattell 16 PF Factors 54   16 PF Scale
Interrelationship Interpretations 60

2. Substance Use Disorders 63

MMPI 63   16 PF 64   Other Test-Response Patterns 64   Treatment
Options 65   Alcohol Use Disorder 65   Prescription Drug
Abuse 72   Polysubstance Abuse 74   Amphetamine Use Disorder 77
Cocaine Abuse 80   Opioid Use Disorder 81

3. The Schizophrenic and Paranoid Disorders 85

Schizophrenia 85   Undifferentiated Schizophrenia 94   Disorganized
Schizophrenia 94   Catatonic Schizophrenia 96   Residual Schizophrenic
Disorder 98   Schizophreniform Disorder 100   Brief Reactive
Psychosis 101   Psychotic Disorder NOS (Atypical Psychosis) 102
Paranoid Schizophrenia 103   The Paranoid (Delusional) Disorders 106
Delusional (Paranoid) Disorder 108   Shared Paranoid and Induced Psychotic
Disorders 111

4. Mood (Affective) Disorders 113

Treatment Options 113   Manic Episode 114   Major Depressive
Episode 118   Dysthymia (Depressive Neurosis) 122   Bipolar

Disorder 126   Cyclothymia 126   Atypical Mood Disorders 127
Schizoaffective Disorder 127   Late Luteal Phase Dysphoric Disorder
(LLPDD) 129

5. Anxiety Disorders 135

MMPI 135   16 PF 136   Other Test-Response Patterns 136
Treatment Options 137   Agoraphobia 137   Overanxious Disorder 140
Separation Anxiety Disorder 141   Social Phobia 143   Simple
Phobia 145   Panic Disorder 147   Generalized Anxiety Disorder 149
Obsessive-Compulsive Disorder 151   Post-Traumatic Stress Disorder
and Adjustment Disorder 156   Anxiety Disorder NOS 159

6. Somatoform Disorders 161

Treatment Options 162   Somatization Disorder 162   Conversion
Disorder 166   Somatoform Pain Disorder 168   Hypochondriasis 171
Body Dysmorphic Disorder 174   Undifferentiated Somatoform Disorder
and Somatoform Disorder NOS 175

7. Dissociative and Sleep Disorders 177

Diagnostic Considerations 177   Psychogenic Amnesia 178   Psychogenic
Fugue 180   Multiple Personality 181   Depersonalization Disorder 183
Sleep Disorders 185

8. The Sexual Disorders 189

Transsexualism 189   Paraphilias 192   Fetishism 194   Transvestic
Fetishism 196   Pedophilia 197   Exhibitionism 200   Voyeurism 204
Frotteurism 205   Sexual Masochism 207   Sexual Sadism 209
Zoophilia 210   Male Psychosexual Dysfunction 211   Female
Psychosexual Dysfunction 216

9. The Personality Disorders 219

Treatment Options 220   Paranoid Personality Disorder 221   Schizoid
Personality Disorder 223   Schizotypal Personality Disorder 226
Histrionic Personality Disorder 228   Narcissistic Personality
Disorder 231   Antisocial Personality Disorder 234   Conduct
Disorder 238   Borderline Personality Disorder 242   Identity
Disorder 245   Avoidant Personality Disorder 247   Dependent
Personality Disorder 249   Obsessive-Compulsive Personality Disorder 252
Passive-Aggressive Personality Disorder 254   Oppositional-Defiant
Disorder 257   Sadistic Personality Disorder 258   Self-Defeating
Personality Disorder 262

10. The Criminal Personality 265

Megargee's Ten Criminal Subtypes 266   Summary 270

11. Disorders of Impulse Control 271

Overall Test-Response Patterns 271   Pathological Gambling 272
Kleptomania 274   Pyromania 276   Trichotillomania 278
Intermittent-Explosive Disorder 279   Rape 282   Anorexia Nervosa
and Bulimia Nervosa 285

12. Malingering and the Factitious Disorders 289

Malingering 289   Factitious Disorders 303

13. Aggression Potential, Child Abuse, and Suicide Potential 307

Aggression Potential 307   Child Abuse 311   Suicide Potential 314

**14. Central Nervous System Impairment, Attention-Deficit
    Hyperactivity Disorder, and Retardation** 323

Central Nervous System Impairment 323   Attention-Deficit
Hyperactivity Disorder 334   Mental Retardation 340

**15. Criminal Responsibility (Insanity), Civil Commitment, and
    Competency** 343

Criminal Responsibility (Insanity) 343   Civil Commitment 349
Competency 350

**16. Professional Case Preparation and Presentation: For Office or
    Courtroom** 355

Malpractice 355   General Principles for Case Preparation 356
A Model Report Format 357   Expert Witness Case Preparation 361
Deposition Preparation and Presentation 362   Courtroom
Presentation 363   Anticipating Cross-Examination 365
The Clinician's Role in Court 367

Appendix A: The Meyer Information Battery 371

**Appendix B: Major Groups of Psychotropic Chemotherapeutic
Agents** 381

Bibliography 383

Name Index 409

Subject Index 415

PREFACE

As early as my graduate training and internship, I looked for a book that had not only integrated discussion of coverage of the common symptoms, personality styles, test patterns, and treatment recommendations but had also linked these with the various major psychodiagnostic categories that clinicians use every day. These data were available, but they were not incorporated in a practical handbook. Later, books such as Graham's *The MMPI: A Practical Guide* and Zimmerman and Woo-Sam's *Clinical Interpretation of the WAIS* took steps in this direction. Yet these books have each dealt with only a single test. Also, such texts—as well as others that do deal with a number of tests, for example, Newmark (1985)—only occasionally link general behavior patterns to particular test results, but such results are not related clearly to specific diagnostic classifications. Finally, there is seldom any link with the next step, treatment recommendations.

The Clinician's Handbook is an attempt to integrate these distinct, but necessarily related, considerations. This book presents updated correlates for the most commonly used objective psychological test, the Minnesota Multiphasic Personality Inventory (MMPI), as well as complementary personality information from the IPAT's (Institute of Personality and Ability Testing) Cattell Sixteen Personality Factor Questionnaire (16 PF) Test (and, analogously, IPAT's High School Personality Questionnaire, the HSPQ, for adolescents and young adults ages 12–18, because virtually the same factors are measured in each). It links this information with data from the other psychological tests most commonly used with adults and adolescents, primarily the Wechsler Adult Intelligence Scale-Revised (the WAIS-R), the Millon Clinical Multiaxial Inventory (MCMI), and the Rorschach Ink Blot Technique, but also to the Thematic Apperception Test (TAT) and drawing tests. The next steps are to integrate common behavioral features (and *Diagnostic and Statistical Manual of Mental Disorders* descriptors in most instances) and the most valid treatment recommendations. This synthesis is based on the assumptions that virtually all theories and schools are useful to some degree and that the biggest challenge to modern treatment is determining the best fit of client type with treatment type. Moreover, the eclecticism (in the best sense of that word) of this view dovetails with a multimodal approach to treatment recommendations. That is, it rarely appears that a single treatment approach is sufficient to treat clusters of disordered behaviors comprehensively, and the use of only one technique is seldom the best approach with any one client.

The Clinician's Handbook was designed first for practitioners, since they are likely to encounter the broadest variety of emotional disorders in their work. Even practitioners who do not regularly administer the tests noted above should find this book useful, as test responses are tied to various functional aspects of each disorder and to treatment options that might be used. The practitioner can assess this information in several ways. Generally, it is most useful to begin with common initial diagnoses and to examine the book's behavioral descriptors, DSM-III-R requirements, and various personality indices that are detailed for each. The relevant treatment recommendations can then be checked and incorporated into a report or overall treatment program.

Clinicians who prefer to look at MMPI data before making a tentative diagnosis can use this book by going to Chapter 2 to locate the particular high score (or two-point code) that is obtained and then, if desired, use Table 1.1 at the end of Chapter 1. The table presents a list of probable diagnoses associated with virtually all of the two-point MMPI codes. These probable diagnoses can then be checked as described above.

Although originally designed for the practitioner—including clinical, counseling, educational, forensic, and industrial psychologists; psychiatrists; clinical social workers; psychiatric nurses; family and marital therapists; and pastoral counselors—The Clinician's Handbook is also useful as a text in graduate-level courses. The breakdown of the disorder patterns follows the same schema as that of DSM-III-R and adds material about important allied topics, such as the criminal personality, acting-out potential, malingering, central nervous system dysfunction, and legal concepts (insanity, incompetency) as they relate to diagnostic categories. Thus, a full spectrum of adult and adolescent psychopathology can be studied. Numerous instructors have used this book as a primary text, which they supplemented with readings on research relevant to the various disorder patterns and with other textbooks. The Clinician's Handbook can also be used to supplement a standard text of abnormal psychology or in clinical courses and practicums as an adjunct to books on specific tests, test research, or test administration.

As noted in the Introduction, this book incorporates most modern research available on the relationship of disorder patterns to diagnostic indicators and treatment options. Table A (in the Introduction) lists the many standard sources for the general and developing tradition of research studies noted throughout. The Introduction details the long process by which this book evolved; the bedrock was the available research.

It is clear that this material, like any other body of information, will change with time. It is hoped that many of these changes will be spurred on by this book itself—that is, that researchers will refine, through more practical and precise studies, the clusters of diagnostic features, test results, and treatment options that are offered in the following pages. Reports of research and feedback from clinicians as they use these formulations would be most welcome. Please send any information to the author, Department of Psychology, University of Louisville, Belknap Campus, Louisville, KY 40292.

I am grateful to the American Psychiatric Association for its permission to convey generally the essence of the DSM-III-R categories seen in this book. Readers who want a more detailed description of the behavioral and statistical correlates of these categories should consult the DSM-III-R itself. Those wishing a narrative and amplified analysis of the major categories and subcategories of psychopathology can consult *Case Studies in Abnormal Behavior* (Meyer and Osborne, 1987).

This book has been significantly aided by the contributions of the many teachers, colleagues, and students whom I have known over the years; each has in some way been helpful. A particular debt is owed to professors Albert I. Rabin and Bertram Karon at Michigan State University, as well as to many other clinicians and colleagues, such as Norman Abeles, Curtis Barrett, Vytautas Bieliauskas, Patricia Carpenter, Mary Clarke, David Connell, Dan Cox, Herb Eber, Will Edgerton, Ray Fowler, Sam Fulkerson, Carleton Gass, Phil Johnson, Rhett Landis, Peter Mayfield, Ken McNiel, Lovick Miller, Irene Nolan, Steve Riggert, Paul Salmon, Harvey A. Tilker, and Wilfred Van Gorp, all of whom have been helpful and instructive throughout the years. Thanks is also owed to three reviewers who read the entire manuscript and made comments that helped to improve its quality and usefulness. They are: Diane R. Follingstad of the University of South Carolina, Columbia; Wilfred Van Gorp of the Veterans Administration Medical Center in Los Angeles; and Harrison Voigt of the California Institute of Integral Studies.

A special thanks is due my editor at Allyn and Bacon, John-Paul Lenney. A major acknowledgment and thank-you goes to Sandy Hartz, Suzanne Paris, and Sharon Mills, who contributed significantly to this book, and also to Daril Bentley for editorial assistance.

R.G.M.

Introduction

It would be unreasonable to expect that any one treatment approach or single pattern of test responses will be specifically relevant to one and only one diagnostic grouping and, conversely, that individual clients in any one category are going to respond to only one type of treatment or show a single pattern on diagnostic tests. Cumulative experience of clinicians bears out these statements. Psychological tests have been a substantial improvement over interview data alone. This is true even when the interview data are obtained in a controlled format, such as the Mental Status Examination, which includes assessment of the following: (1) physical appearance; (2) motor activities; (3) speech activity and patterns; (4) mood and affect; (5) alertness and attention; (6) content and organization of thoughts; (7) perception; (8) the general areas of memory, abstract thinking, and the client's fund of knowledge; and (9) the client's attitude toward the examination and toward his or her condition (Melton et al., 1987; Grisso, 1986).

Some of the questions that commonly appear in the Mental Status Examination are the following: What is this place? Who am I? What day is it? Who are you? Who is the President? Who was the President before he was? What does "Don't cry over spilled milk" mean?

Even though there is structure provided to the interview by the Mental Status Examination, the examination contains the weakness of all data obtained from interviews. There are few or no statistical or normative standards for the obtained responses on which to base a communicable inference and an eventual diagnosis. Examiners are too often left to develop their own idiosyncratic notions of what a certain response means. While this procedure may be helpful in developing beginning inferences, these are strengthened significantly (or called into question) when the more objective data of psychological testing are considered as well.

The author saw the potential of idiosyncratic error in the first case conference examination of a patient that he ever witnessed. The senior clinician who was examining the client proceeded with the questions of the Mental Status Examination. The client did generally well on most questions, except that he did not remember what date it was, he had some trouble counting backward from 100 by 7s after he got to 86, and he gave a rather concrete interpretation to the "spilled milk" question. After the client left the room, the examining clinician suggested the diagnosis of schizophrenia, pointing out that the client's lack of awareness of what date it was suggested a global disorientation, the problem in counting backward from 100 by 7s suggested general confusion, and the difficulties with the proverb suggested concreteness.

By this time, I was uncomfortable since I also had missed the date by a full seven days. In actuality, a simpler and better explanation for the client's behavior is available. A lack of knowledge of the exact date, even being off by a number of days, is common. In addition, people who have been in an institution for any period of time easily become confused about, if not indifferent to, the date. The problems with the other two pieces of data are explainable by the fact that this client was not very bright.

There are trends, probabilities, and even some hard data to link the categories typically used by clinicians to various patterns. This book presents these relationships to the extent they are known at this time. In that regard, it is hoped that this book will result in more research that relates patterns of responses on several tests (which is what most clinicians use in an individual case) to various syndromes. As in any other area of scientific knowledge, subsequent research may supplant little, much, or all of what is now known.

This book is based on research results that have been melded with reported consensual clinical experience. The extent of the research data and the clinical experience naturally varies, depending on the particular syndrome being discussed.

If a single author or study is the source of material leading to a diagnostic or therapeutic recommendation, it will be directly referenced. If the recommendation is the speculation of the author alone, it will be so labeled. Where two or more different sources have provided information on which a recommendation is either directly based or inferred, it will be stated in ways such as, "The evidence shows . . ." or "The classic profile for . . . ," or it will be put in a direct statement, such as "Clients who are low on scale 8 are. . . ." The primary sources for the inferences for each of the four major tests used in this book—Minnesota Multiphasic Personality Inventory (MMPI), Cattell Sixteen Personality Factor (16 PF) Questionnaire, Wechsler Adult Intelligence Scale-Revised (WAIS-R), and Rorschach—are presented in Table A.

In the second chapter, the clinical correlates of the MMPI and 16 PF scales are examined. Many researchers and clinicians have carried out similar work in this area, and much is owed to them. This chapter will attempt to integrate and update previous efforts so that the reader has an up-to-date body of information along traditional lines—that is, the various behavior patterns that are associated with the scale patterns. For some readers, much of this information will be new. For others, it will be at least a short refresher and a handy section to which to refer on occasion while using the rest of the book.

The remainder of this book will proceed in a standard sequence for each syndrome, with a number of related syndromes grouped together under an appropriate chapter heading. An overview of the material relevant to the specific diagnostic syndrome being discussed is presented first for each syndrome. This is then usually followed by a synopsis of what the *Diagnostic and Statistical Manual-III-R* (DSM-III-R) requires so that the clinician can apply this diagnosis to a client. In some cases, where there is little detail in the DSM-III-R requirements, I incorporate it into the first general subsection rather than having a specific DSM-III-R subsection for that syndrome.

The next subsection presents the MMPI code types and scale patterns one might expect with a client who exhibits this specific disorder. In most cases, the disorder can manifest itself in a variety of ways, so the text attempts to detail the major possibilities. This same approach is used in the next subsection, the presentation of 16 PF correlates. Following the subsection on the 16 PF, corresponding information from other relevant test sources will be presented, notably from the Wechsler Adult Intelligence Scale-Revised (WAIS-R) and the Rorschach. When referring to the WAIS-R, it should be understood that the research and data from the WAIS research are integrated as the primary sources (the WAIS being the earlier version of the WAIS-R).

For some of the syndromes, little information is available. If so, only a short subsection is included based on this limited information, and, combined with consensual speculation, it is presented under the heading of Diagnostic Considerations, a designation that supplants the categories usually used—for example, MMPI, 16 PF, and Other Test Response Patterns.

The last subsection, usually entitled Treatment Options, will succinctly present a number of possible treatment methods appropriate for the particular disorder, since the clinician often faces this question. An important point is that I will not consistently mention psychotherapy, chemotherapy, or general schools of therapy as treatment options for the various syndromes. There is good reason to believe that psychotherapy is an appropriate treatment for virtually every syndrome mentioned here, either as the major component or as an adjunct to other techniques (Zeig, 1987; Landman and Dawes, 1982; Smith and Glass, 1977; Olbrisch, 1977). Hence, it would be redundant to mention it continually as an option. On those occasions when psychotherapy is specifically mandated, this fact will be noted. Similarly, the proponents

MMPI

Archer (1987)
Boerger et al. (1974)
Butcher (1979)
Butcher and Graham (1988)
Carson (1969)
Colligan et al. (1983)
Dahlstrom and Dahlstrom (1960)
Dahlstrom and Welsch (1960)
Dahlstrom et al. (1972)
Dahlstrom et al. (1975)
Dahlstrom et al. (1986)
Duckworth (1979)
Fowler (1976, 1981)
Gilberstadt and Duker (1965)
Golden (1979)
Graham (1977, 1987)
Greene (1980)
Gynther et al. (1973a)
Gynther et al. (1973b)
Hedlund (1977)
Holland and Watson (1980)
Hsu and Betman (1986)
Kelly and King (1979c)
Lachar (1974)
Lane and Lachar (1979)
Lorr et al. (1985)
Marks et al. (1974)
Megargee (1966)
Megargee and Bohn (1979)
Morey et al. (1988)
Newmark (1979)
Webb et al. (1981)

WAIS

Allison et al. (1988)
Anastasi (1987)
Blatt and Allison (1981)
Gilbert (1978, 1980)
Golden (1979)
Guertin et al. (1962)
Holland and Watson (1980)
Kaufman et al. (1988)
Klinger and Saunders (1975)
Matarazzo (1972)
Newmark (1985)
Rabin (1964, 1968)
Rapaport et al. (1968)
Shafer (1948)
Swiercinsky (1985)
Wechsler (1981)
Zimmerman and Woo-Sam (1973)

RORSCHACH

Allison et al. (1988)
Anastasi (1987)
Aronow and Reznikoff (1976)
Beck (1951)
Beck and Beck (1978)
Beck and Molish (1952)
Cooper et al. (1988)
Exner (1974, 1978, 1986)
Gilbert (1978, 1980)
Goldfried et al. (1971)
Klopfer and Davidson (1962)
Klopfer and Taulbee (1976)
Lanyon (1984)
Lerner (1975)
Levitt (1980)
Megargee (1966)
Newmark (1985)
Ogdon (1977)
Peterson (1978)
Phillips and Smith (1953)
Piotrowski (1979)
Rabin (1964, 1968, 1972, 1981)
Rapaport et al. (1968)
Rickers-Ovsiankina (1960)
Rorschach (1951)
Shafer (1948, 1954)
Siegel (1987)
Swiercinsky (1985)
Wagner and Wagner (1981)
Wiggins (1969)
Wiggins et al. (1971)

16 PF

Burger and Kabacoff (1982)
Cattell (1965, 1973, 1979, 1986)
Cattell and Warburton (1967)
Cattell et al. (1970)
Eber (1975, 1987)
Golden (1979)
IPAT Staff (1963, 1972)
Karson (1959, 1960)
Karson and O'Dell (1976)
Krug (1978, 1980, 1981)
Krug and Johns (1986)
Lanyon (1984)
Lorr and Suziedelis (1985)
Lorr et al. (1985)
Megargee (1966)
Reuter et al. (1985)

of psychoanalysis and the other major therapy schools often assert that their techniques are valid for the majority of syndromes noted here. Where the literature indicates that a particular theoretical approach is especially efficient, it will be noted. Also, chemotherapy may be a useful adjunct in many of the categories. It will be mentioned only where it is specifically warranted, with no implied assertion that it may be inappropriate in those groupings where it is not specifically listed.

The reader will also note that specific secondary or derived MMPI or 16 PF scales for the diagnosis of a pattern or type of disorder are seldom mentioned. For example, many secondary scales have been derived on the MMPI for almost everything from depression to potential for happiness in marriage (Fowler, 1976; Graham, 1987). In fact, there are secondary scales derived by researchers for almost every type of personality or affect pattern imaginable. The problem is that these scales are not routinely given in standard clinical assessments, and many are not well validated and/or do not measure what the scale title suggests they do (Fowler, 1981). Two major exceptions are the Ego Strength Scale, which is useful in measuring personal resiliency and potential for response to psychotherapy, and the MacAndrew Alcoholism Scale (MacAndrew, 1965; Wolfson and Erbaugh, 1984). Several others are fine for research purposes, and they may be helpful in assessing a population for a specific concern. However, in the majority of assessments, the clinician may neither score for these scales nor administer any special questionnaires. The reader is referred to the many other sources that provide commentary about these derived scales and specific tests.

■   ## The Rationale for Inclusion of Certain Tests

The reader might ask why the primary emphasis is on the MMPI, 16 PF, WAIS-R, and Rorschach. (See also, immediately following, discussion of the MCMI.) The reason is obvious with the MMPI and WAIS-R: They are the most commonly used and researched objective psychological tests (Allison et al., 1988; Newmark, 1985; Piotrowski et al., 1985). Virtually every clinician, regardless of theoretical orientation or type of training, has some familiarity with the MMPI and WAIS-R. There also has been such an extensive amount of normative data gathered on the MMPI that it is by far the most useful standard objective test among the clinician's diagnostic options. As many readers are aware, a revised version of the MMPI has been developed, with alternate forms for adolescents and adults. In general, the interpretations derived from the original MMPI are expected to hold for the revised form (Butcher and Graham, 1988). (Since the Supreme Court has recently upheld the validity of the University of Minnesota and National Computer Systems copyright on the MMPI, costs for computer interpretation may rise.)

In using the WAIS-R, variables such as sex, race, and education have to be taken into account (Kaufman et al., 1988). Some may find the WAIS-SAM version to reduce testing time, and it appears to retain good validity (Cargonello and Gurekas, 1988).

Although certain clinicians question the validity of projective tests, there are data to support their usefulness in many situations, and the Rorschach has become one of the most commonly used and well known of these tests (Piotrowski et al., 1985). The TAT is also commonly used (Bellak, 1986; Piotrowski et al., 1985), and many of the observations on the TAT in this book apply equally well to other, newer thematic tests (Caine et al., 1986).

The Cattell 16 PF test also is commonly used. While the MMPI is particularly good at assessing severe patterns of pathology, the 16 PF is used more commonly as a measure of personality patterns (Lorr et al., 1985; Reuter et al., 1985). Thus, they dovetail nicely and provide the practitioner with an effective overview of the client. This is not to say that other tests, such as the Edwards Personal Preference Test, would not be useful as an adjunct to the MMPI as well. However, the validity data on the 16 PF are certainly as impressive as the data on these other tests (Cattell, 1979; Krug, 1981; Krug and Johns, 1986). The Cattell group has also formulated tests (using virtually the same scales) for persons in the lower age ranges. Thus, if practitioners use these tests with adults, they begin to develop some facility with a related set of children's tests, and vice versa. Also, it is felt that the motivational distortion scores derived for the 16 PF are more useful (Winder et al., 1975; Krug, 1978; Krug and Johns, 1986) than those in other available tests, when they have them at all. Finally, from a personal standpoint, I have worked with both the childhood and adult forms of the Cattell test since internship and have gathered a great deal more data regarding this test. Like numerous clinicians, I have continually used it in conjunction with the MMPI and have found the combination to be especially effective.

The MCMI (Millon Clinical Multiaxial Inventory) is included in this edition because of its increasing popularity with clinicians. It was designed primarily by Theodore Millon and first published in 1976 by National Computer Systems (NCS). The advantages of the MCMI, in addition to simply being "new," are (1) its brevity—175 items, (2) its coordination of scales with the DSM diagnostic system, (3) its evolution from a clinical theory (which may be a minus, depending upon your view of the theory), (4) the selection of test items by contrasting responses of a diagnostic group with undifferentiated psychiatric patients rather than normals, (5) the conversion of MCMI scores into base rates rather than normalized standard score transformations, and (6) a three-step validation procedure: theoretical-substantive, internal-structural, and external-criterion.

The disadvantages of the MCMI are (1) the problem of applying scores from one set of databases to new ones, (2) the scoring of twenty scales from a very small number of questions, (3) the large variance in one factor, termed a neuroticism-distress-maladjustment factor, a problem further compounded by the small number of questions, (4) the penchant for the MCMI to indicate pathology where there is none, (5) the fact that the MCMI may be more of a direct measure of Millon's personality theories about a category than the DSM-III-R formulation of that category, (6) a lack of correspondence between individual MCMI correlations and DSM-III-R categories, even though the MCMI scale and DSM-III-R disorder may share the same name, and (7) the absence of clearly interpretable validity scales or scores and the definite problems in assessing "faking good" with the MCMI (Millon, 1985, 1986; Widiger et al., 1985; Widiger and Sanderson, 1987; Cantrell and Dana, 1987; Moreland and Orstad, 1987; McNiel and Meyer, 1988; Van Gorp and Meyer, 1986; Retzlaff and Gibertini, 1987; Choca et al., 1986; Patrick, 1988). Thus, in this book the suggested MCMI correlates for overall diagnostic patterns—especially for specific patterns, for example, Cocaine Abuse rather than Substance Abuse—are less data based and more speculative than those listed for the MMPI and 16 PF.

In addition, there is one other flaw with the MCMI. It is the most serious of all, and it stems from the private and proprietary evolution of this instrument. For the most part, one must take the word of NCS and Dr. Millon that their generation, selection, and, in many instances, analysis and interpretation of the data, all of which seem to make the MCMI look "good," were carried out in the best fashion. In a related vein, it is often financially prohibitive to do research with the MCMI, since the profile should be computer scored. While the MCMI can be hand scored, it is difficult to do research at times because of lack of access to certain sets of base rates, or the exact research results used by NCS. After encountering some red tape, one may be able to obtain a discount to do research using computer scoring. Yet it's hard to imagine that there wouldn't be even more red tape if one kept getting results pointing to problems with the MCMI. Therefore, we'll just have to keep taking the word of NCS that the MCMI is good and that the best way to get up-to-date information on it is to write National Computer Systems, P.O. Box 1416, Minneapolis, MN 55440. The results on the MCMI break down as follows:

BASIC PERSONALITY SCALES		CLINICAL SYMPTOM SYNDROMES	
Scale 1:	Schizoid (Asocial)	Scale A:	Anxiety
Scale 2:	Avoidant	Scale H:	Somatoform
Scale 3:	Dependent (Submissive)	Scale N:	Hypomanic
Scale 4:	Histrionic (Gregarious)	Scale D:	Dysthymic
Scale 5:	Negativistic	Scale B:	Alcohol Abuse

Scale 6:	Antisocial (Aggressive)	Scale T:	Drug Abuse
Scale 7:	Compulsive (Conforming)	Scale SS:	Psychotic Thinking
		Scale CC:	Psychotic Depression
Scale 8:	Passive-Aggressive (Negativistic)	Scale PP:	Psychotic Delusions

PATHOLOGICAL PERSONALITY DISORDERS

Scale S: Schizotypal (Schizoid)

Scale C: Borderline (Cycloid)

Scale P: Paranoid

■ **The Information Evolution in This Book**

Before proceeding to a discussion of DSM-III-R, and then to the description of the correlates of the MMPI and 16 PF in behavior in the next chapter, I would like to point out the procedure by which the information in this book was gathered and integrated. The following stages were followed to bring research information into coordination with consensual clinical experience.

1. For about fifteen years (up to the publication of the 1983 edition of this handbook), I continually used these tests, especially the MMPI, 16 PF, and WAIS-R, in a wide-ranging diagnostic practice and kept written records that were cross-checked and compared to the research literature to develop correlations of test patterns with various syndromes and the syndromes with the most appropriate treatments. This is in keeping with Arkes's (1981) admonition that too much dependence on memory quickly leads to error in clinical inference. These patterns also were used as a teaching tool in graduate courses in diagnostic testing and clinical psychopathology. Thus, the developing concepts were again continually checked against available clinical research literature and within the case itself.

2. A thorough formal review of the literature was instituted, and from this and the information collected in step 1, a first draft was written that correlated the patterns on the 16 PF and MMPI and appropriate treatments with the diagnostic categories in the initial DSM-III.

3. Graduate students in sequential clinical psychopathology courses were each assigned a subset of DSM-III categories. They were asked, independent of the information in the first draft, to find correlates of the DSM-III draft categories on the MMPI, 16 PF, WAIS-R, and Rorschach in the research and clinical literature. Another review of the most recent literature was coordinated with the corrections and suggestions gleaned from the production of these graduate students.

4. As soon as the final DSM-III was published, the work that emerged from step 3 was coordinated with changes from the earlier versions to produce a polished draft.

5. The information derived up to that point was presented to a continuing-education seminar of twenty practicing clinical psychologists. These people responded via formal feedback procedures about the applicability and accuracy of the findings in this draft. There was substantial agreement between the views of these practicing clinicians and the draft that was produced by the end of step 4, but corrections were noted, and some interesting suggestions were incorporated.

6. After integrating this information, the latest draft was presented to five of the most respected practicing clinical psychologists in the region, all of whom regularly used these tests in their practice. Each carried out a thorough review of the book, and again, although there was general agreement with the material as presented to them, they did offer much helpful commentary.

7. After this material was integrated and amplified in accordance with the publisher's reviewers, there was a last check with the relevant research literature, and the manuscript was again considered and put into a final state.

8. After the publication of the 1983 edition of this book, it was used each year as the primary text in a graduate course on psychopathology and psychological testing. At various junctures, students were asked to critique and/or update subsections of the book, including new diagnostic categories proposed for and then included in DSM-III-R. More diagnostic categories specific to adolescence were added. Taking cues and new points of view from the work of these students, the author carried out similar continuing updates and critiques himself, using all of this material to keep reworking the manuscript.

9. The MCMI was incorporated into this edition because of its increasing popularity with a number of clinicians. MCMI diagnostic correlates of the major syndromes are now included throughout the book. After being initially generated, they were critiqued and updated by several graduate students and local clinicians who had worked extensively with the MCMI; they were later thoroughly critiqued and reworked by Wilfred Van Gorp, Kenneth McNiel, and John Boles, all of whom not only have extensive clinical experience with the MCMI but also have carried out research on the instrument.

10. A chapter on professional practice (Chapter 16), relevant to the courtroom as well as the office, was developed.

11. For each chapter, at least two (and often more) experienced practicing clinicians, each of whom is recognized as having substantial expertise in the areas covered, contributed a thorough critique and update of that chapter to aid in finalization of the manuscript.

12. A final reworking of the manuscript incorporated the changes from DSM-III to DSM-III-R, as well as the publisher's reviews and a thorough check on the relevant literature.

Throughout this process, as much research information as possible was gathered and integrated and then complemented by consensual clinical experience.

In addition to the standard DSM-III-R categories, this book examines several other topics of interest to practitioners: the issues of Acting-Out Potential (for example, Aggression and Suicide Potential); the Criminal Personality; Rape; and the legal concepts and psychological correlates of Insanity, Involuntary Civil Commitment, and Competency to Stand Trial. Malingering is included in the DSM-III-R, but it receives relatively little notice, as it does in most diagnostic texts. I consider it to be of considerable importance to the diagnostician, so it will be dealt with in some depth in a separate chapter.

Following the main text is Appendix A, a set of paper-and-pencil test materials that I have revised and integrated over the past fifteen years. The reader can use the material as a classroom handout with the text without written permission, so long as it is not sold or reproduced for any other reason. You may want to insert a drawing test different from the Draw-A-Group Test, add some Bender-Gestalt-like figures (see the section on Central Nervous System Impairment), or otherwise modify it. The four proverbs included were selected because Johnson (1966) found these to be the most efficient in discriminating between cases of central nervous system impairment and schizophrenia. The validated short form of the Marlowe-Crowne Social Desirability Scale would also be a useful addition, in order to get a quick estimate of the client's response set (Zook and Sipps, 1985).

Aside from the overall chart of DSM-III-R categories already presented, the following summary of certain aspects of the DSM-III-R may be useful to those readers who do not yet regularly use the DSM-III-R.

■   ## DSM-III-R

The DSM-III-R (American Psychiatric Association, 1987) is the revised form of the third edition of the *Diagnostic and Statistical Manual of Mental Disorders* that was published in 1980. The predecessors of DSM-III were DSM-II (1968) and DSM-I (1952). A new edition, DSM-IV, is expected in 1993, timed to coincide with the anticipated publication of the tenth edition of the *International Classification of Diseases* (ICD-10) (Spitzer, 1988). Compatibility with the ICD codes was markedly increased in the DSM-III-R and is expected to be furthered in DSM-IV.

As to the definition of "mental disorder," it is conceptualized in DSM-III-R (p. xxii) as

a clinically significant behavioral or psychological syndrome or pattern that occurs in a person and that is associated with present distress (a painful symptom) or disability (impairment in one or more important areas of functioning) or with a significantly increased risk of suffering death, pain, disability, or an important loss of freedom. In addition, this syndrome or pattern must not be merely an expectable response to a particular event, e.g., the death of a loved one. Whatever its original cause, it must currently be considered a manifestation of a behavioral, psychological, or biological dysfunction in the person. Neither deviant behavior, e.g., political, religious, or sexual, nor conflicts that are primarily between the individual and society are mental disorders unless the deviance or conflict is a symptom of a dysfunction in the person, as described above. There is no assumption that each mental disorder is a discrete entity with sharp boundaries (discontinuity) between it and other mental disorders, or between it and no mental disorder.

The actual process of making that diagnosis is governed by two principles (pp. xxiv–xxv):

1. When an Organic Mental Disorder can account for the symptoms, it preempts the diagnosis of any other disorder that could produce the same symptoms (e.g., Organic Anxiety Disorder preempts Panic Disorder).
2. When a more pervasive disorder, such as Schizophrenia, commonly has associated symptoms that are the defining symptoms of a less pervasive disorder, such as Dysthymia, only the more pervasive disorder is diagnosed if both its defining symptoms *and* associated symptoms are present. For example, only Schizophrenia (not Schizophrenia and Dysthymia) should be diagnosed when the defining symptoms of Schizophrenia are present along with chronic mild depression (which is a common associated symptom of Schizophrenia).

Also, current severity of disorder *may* now be indicated, by adding in parentheses the following terms after a diagnosis: mild, moderate, severe, in partial remission (or residual state), or in full remission. With some diagnoses, specific criteria for these severity levels are provided.

There were numerous changes in the categories from DSM-III to DSM-III-R. Many are semantic or not especially noteworthy, but the following are the more important category changes.

DSM-III	DSM-III-R
Attention deficit disorder with hyperactivity	Attention-deficit hyperactivity disorder
Attention deficit disorder without hyperactivity	Undifferentiated attention-deficit disorder

DSM-III (cont.)	DSM-III-R (cont.)
Conduct disorder undersocialized, aggressive undersocialized, nonaggressive socialized, aggressive socialized nonaggressive atypical	*Conduct disorder* isolated, aggressive type group type undifferentiated type
Oppositional disorder	Oppositional defiant disorder
Bulimia	Bulimia nervosa
Infantile autism and Childhood onset pervasive developmental disorder	Autistic disorder

Addition of: Developmental expressive writing disorder

Developmental language disorder	"Expressive" and "receptive" subcategories

Addition of: Inhalant intoxication

Addition of: "dependence" subcategory for Cocaine and Hallucinogens

Addition of: Polysubstance dependence

Deletion of: Requirement that schizophrenia begin before age 45 to warrant the diagnosis.

Paranoia	Delusional (paranoid) disorder, with specification of subtype: erotomanic, grandiose, jealous, persecutory, somatic, or unspecified
Shared paranoid disorder	Induced psychotic disorder (for the "receiver")

Acute paranoid Disorder now subsumed under Psychotic Disorders not elsewhere classified

Schizoaffective disorder to be specified as bipolar or depressive type

Major depression to be specified as chronic, melancholic, or seasonal types

Dysthymic disorder	Dysthymia
Cyclothymic disorder	Cyclothymia
Agoraphobia with panic attacks	Panic disorder with agoraphobia

DSM-III (cont.)	**DSM-III-R (cont.)**
Panic disorder	Panic disorder without agoraphobia
Psychogenic pain disorder	Somatoform pain disorder

Body dysmorphic disorder, to be added—was Dysmorphophobia, which was subsumed under Atypical Somatoform Disorder

Addition of: Gender identity disorder of adolescence or adulthood, non-transexual type

Transvestism	Transvestic Fetishism
Deletion of: Zoophilia	
Addition of: Frotteurism	
Inhibited sexual desire	Hypoactive sexual desire disorder

Addition of: Sexual Aversion Disorder

Deletion of: Ego-dystonic homosexuality

Addition of: Trichotillomania

Compulsive Personality Disorder	Obsessive Compulsive Personality Disorder

Provisional consideration is allowed for three patterns (they are not official categories, but they may be used by individual clinicians): Late luteal phase dysphoric disorder; Self-defeating personality disorder; Sadistic personality disorder. Another controversial category, Paraphilic Coercive Disorder, essentially compulsive rapists, was eventually withdrawn because, although it was felt to be valid, it was doubted that it would be useful.

One important format shift from DSM-III to DSM-III-R, and a trend that will likely continue into DSM-IV, is from a "monothetic" to a "polythetic" model for qualifying a diagnosis. In the monothetic model, criteria A, B, and C, for example, are specified, and *all* are required to make the diagnosis. In the polythetic model, a certain number within an array of possible diagnostic indicators, e.g., five of nine for Obsessive Compulsive Personality Disorder are required to make the diagnosis. In a few instances, e.g., Conduct Disorder, the symptoms are ranked by discriminating power, as determined by research. Spitzer (1988) is candid in observing that in some cases the required number of symptoms, or even the actual symptoms themselves, were arrived at by a relatively casual consensual model. This essentially boils down to "Well, three would seem about right for that diagnosis," and Spitzer emphasizes that more research is needed for many categories. The polythetic model is favored because, overall, it attains greater reliability and yet has more flexibility.

Even though the DSM has been criticized for a number of reasons (Shacht and Nathan, 1977; Garmezy, 1978; Zubin, 1978), it is the official document of the American Psychiatric Association, it has received approval from the American Psychological Association, and it has received wide international acceptance. For several reasons, the DSM-III (and now the DSM-III-R) has had more influence than its predecessors, and it will continue to do so. It has a more thorough and extensive description of categories and criteria for diagnosis; there is an increasing demand of third-party payers for a full diagnosis, and its influence on the types and number of health service providers is increasing. Another major reason is that there is simply no alternative system that has reached even a minimal level of usage and acceptability.

A major change in the DSM-III – continued and refined in the DSM-III-R – is the use of a multiaxial diagnostic system, which allows the clinician to provide several different types of information. Though there are five axes that can be potentially used, the first three make up the official DSM-III-R diagnostic categories. A client may receive a diagnosis on each of the first three axes:

Axis I: Clinical Syndromes and V Codes

Axis II: Personality Disorders and Developmental Disorders

Axis III: Physical Disorders or Conditions

Axis IV is used to denote the Severity of Psychosocial Stressors that preceded the disorder. The stressor should be noted, and it should be rated on the basis of its impact on an "average" person. Thus, it should not be influenced by the vulnerability of the individual being rated. The specific stressor should be further specified as either a "predominantly acute event" (less than six months) or "predominantly enduring circumstances" (more than six months duration). They are coded from number 1, which designates no psychosocial stressor, through 7, which is a catastrophic psychosocial stressor, with 0 referring to an unspecified stressor.

A second optional scale, Axis V, the Global Assessment of Functioning (GAF) Scale refers to the highest level of adaptive functioning noted for both the year previous to the disorder and for one's condition at the time of evaluation. The rating is on a 1-to-90 scale (DSM-III-R, p. 12) that is an integrated judgment of psychological, social, and occupational functioning (though not for physical limitations). Hence, a person could receive a high rating of 80 for the present (Current GAF: 80) and a lower rating of 70 for the past year (Highest GAF past year: 70). Most clinicians will not regularly use Axes IV and V, their predominant use being in research situations.

According to Spitzer (1988), the criteria for inclusion on Axis II is that the condition be lifelong, reasonably stable, and handicapping. Yet it is interesting that the only conditions that are appropriate for listing on Axis II are the Personality Disorders and the Developmental Disorders. This limits the potential disorders for this axis to fewer than thirty different categories, as opposed to the substantial number of categories possible for Axis I. However, personality traits (and defense mechanisms, a list of which is supplied in a DSM-III-R Appendix) rather than disorders may also be listed on Axis II. For example, if the clinician felt the client should be considered paranoid, yet did not feel a formal diagnosis of paranoid personality disorder was warranted, the paranoid trait would be put on Axis II and no code number would be used along with it, since a code number indicates a formal diagnosis of disorder.

If there is no evidence of disorder on an axis, the clinician should write, "V71.09, no diagnosis on Axis I (or II)," or one of the Conditions Not Attributable to a Mental Disorder (the V Codes) may be recorded. There may also be occasions when it is felt that the principal diagnosis—the one mainly responsible for the diagnosis and treatment—is on the second axis. In that case, the diagnosis listed on the second axis should be followed up with the phrase "Principal Diagnosis." Otherwise, it is assumed that the principal diagnosis is the one listed on Axis I. When multiple diagnoses are made on any one axis, they are to be listed in the order of importance for attention or treatment. A number of DSM-III-R diagnoses are followed by a small x, indicating a place for a further qualifying phrase (see DSM-III-R).

The clinician should take note of several categories that are available to indicate a questionable level of diagnostic certainty. For example, the clinician may put the term "Provisional" after a diagnosis to indicate a tentative formulation while more data are gathered. The designation 300.90 is used where the clinician has obtained enough data to rule out a psychotic disorder but has concluded that further diagnostic specification is not available. The diagnosis number 799.90 can be used on either Axis I or II when there is not adequate information to make a diagnostic judgment, and it is thus deferred. Most categories contain a term that is qualified by the code NOS (Not Otherwise Specified), which is used to indicate that the disorder does not fully meet the required specifications of a more refined categorization.

CHAPTER 1

Clinical Correlates of the MMPI and 16 PF Scales

The task of collecting the classical descriptors and correlates of the MMPI and 16 PF scales has been carried out by numerous authors throughout the years, mainly through an accrual process. Those authors and I owe much to those who came before us. I have taken material from my own experience and integrated it with both the classical and recent sources of clinical interpretation of the MMPI, primarily those noted earlier, in Table A.

■ ## MMPI

The Minnesota Multiphasic Personality Inventory (MMPI) is composed of 556 self-reference statements that cover topics from physical condition through social history, emotional states, social attitudes, and moral belief systems. Clients are encouraged to answer every question, though they often skip a few, and their only option is a true or false answer.

The MMPI test was derived by Starke Hathaway, a medical psychologist, and Jovian McKinley, a neuropsychiatrist, who, at the time, were working at the University of Minnesota Hospitals. They hoped that they could develop a test that would substantially aid in the routine psychological examinations given there. Their efforts culminated in the publication of the MMPI in 1943 by the Psychological Corporation. Hathaway and McKinley accumulated a large collection of self-reference statements from textbooks, psychological reports, and other tests. They eventually limited their pool of statements to the 504 they thought were relatively independent of one another. Some of the items not used are now being reconsidered for inclusion in the anticipated revision of the MMPI. A number of items are repeated on the standard MMPI form, but these may be eliminated in the revised MMPI (Butcher and Graham, 1988).

Hathaway and McKinley first administered the test to groups of normals and to patients in the following clinical groups: Hypochondriasis, Depression, Hysteria, Psychopathic Deviant, Paranoia, Psychasthenia, Schizophrenia, and Hypomania. They performed an item analysis in order to detect which items significantly differentiated these groups. In the second stage, the scales derived from that item analysis were administered to groups of normals and patients who had those specific clinical diagnoses already assigned, and after adequate cross-validation, the scales were accepted into the test. It was only later that the Masculinity-Feminity (Mf) scale was added, with the original purpose of differentiating heterosexual males from homosexual males. The final addition included the Social Introversion (Si) scale, which was initially used to distinguish female college students who were socially retiring from those who were active in a number of extracurricular activities; only later was this scale generalized to males.

The MMPI can be administered individually or in a group and can be hand or machine scored. There are a number of short versions of the MMPI-168 (Vincent et al., 1984), but they have many drawbacks as regards reliability and validity. Many groups provide a computerized interpretation and scoring service; the reader is referred to the excellent introduction to that area by Fowler (1976) and by Butcher (1987). A number of clinicians use a computer terminal. The client may take the test at the terminal or the answer sheet can be directly fed into the terminal; in either case, the results are quickly provided to the clinician. (See also the comments on computer-generated reports in Chapter 16.) Any computerized interpretation of an MMPI protocol should always be first routed through a clinician who has had substantial training in MMPI interpretation, since that clinician can consider the profile in light of the many and often subtle particulars of an individual case that are not fed into the computer. Also, in the great majority of diagnostic cases, making a report or diagnostic decision based only on one test would be a questionable practice.

After any initial scoring, a K correction is added to the raw scores obtained for scales Hs (1), Pd (4), Pt (7), Sc (8), and Ma (9), though there is some evidence that this leads to more false positives and fewer false negatives in diagnosis (Hsu, 1986). In addition to the four validity scales and ten basic clinical scales, there are a number of derived scales that require special scoring and that vary widely in their validity and reliability (Colligan and Offord, 1988). Colligan and Offord provide updated norms for the use of the Wiggins scales, the most popular group of derived scales.

The raw data from the MMPI are translated into T scores. These are the scores that are eventually coded onto the profile sheet, and they were based originally on the responses of the Minnesota normal group (Hathaway and McKinley, 1967). T scores have a mean of 50, the middle black line on the profile sheet, and a standard deviation of 10 (for the Minnesota normal group; most populations average at least a bit higher on most scales). The T score is printed on each side of the profile sheet so that it can be obtained visually from the raw data. Separate norms are available for males and females.

Most clinicians refer to profiles in two-point-code phraseology (e.g., a 4-9). This only indicates that 4 is the highest scale and 9 is the second highest scale in T scores. Three- and even four-point codes can be useful in some instances. There are also methods by which the whole profile can be coded. Though using this book does not depend on knowing how to code an MMPI fully or read these latter codes, they are occasionally found in the literature. Since some clinicians find it very useful to code their profiles, they are noted here.

There are two major coding systems for use with the MMPI. Hathaway's (1947) was the original system, although the more complete system developed by Welsh (1948) is more commonly used. The reader is referred to Graham (1977, 1987) for a detailed discussion of these methods. As an example of the Welsh code, the following profile has been coded from the T scores:

7* 2" 1' 8- 46/ /:35# 0 to the right of #9

What this actually says is that

7*   Scale 7 is 90 T or greater
2"   Scale 2 is between 80 and 89
1'   Scale 1 is between 70 and 79
8-   Scale 8 is between 60 and 69
46/ Scales 4 and 6 are between 50 and 59

/:   The juxtaposition of two break symbols (/ and :) indicates no score was in the T range of the one to the right—in this case, 40–49 range

35# # indicates scales 3 and 5 are between 30 and 39 T; the underlining states that they are within one T-score point of each other

To the right of 9 indicates that scale 9 is 29 T or less

Streiner and Miller (1979) find that acceptable interpretations from MMPI single scales and the two- and three-point code types can be made if only 300 items of the MMPI are completed, using a conversion factor from the tables in their article (p. 475). The only marked exception is scale 6, which appears to require 350 items before an adequate interpretation can be made.

While there is no inherent upper age-level limit for the MMPI, it has been traditionally accepted that only individuals with at least a sixth-grade reading level and sixteen years of age can validly complete the MMPI. However, there is some indication that the test can be properly scored for individuals under sixteen if they can read adequately and can maintain attention properly.

Those with less than a sixth-grade reading level take the test by having someone read the items to them or by listening to an audiotape. Yet there is some indication that the estimate of the need for a sixth-grade reading ability is a bit low. Ward and Ward (1980) assert that an actual grade level of 6.7 is necessary for the overall MMPI and that several scales clearly require a seventh-grade reading level.

Ward and Selby (1980) suggest that the readability problem with the MMPI can be helped by the use of what they term the Improved Readability Form (IRF), a 167-item short form of the MMPI. They provide data that suggest the form is more readable than the overall form or other short forms. It is effective with those clients who are on the edge of the ability to read and perform on the MMPI. The authors also assert that the IRF can be orally administered with effectiveness to adults with an IQ of 65–85, the group that has the greatest problems with the standard MMPI. Readers who are interested in obtaining the items that make up the IRF can request a reprint of the article and the listing of the IRF items from Dr. L. Charles Ward, Department of Psychiatry, Medical College of Georgia, Augusta, GA 30901.

Both the normal and abnormal profiles of adolescents differ from those of adults, and when dealing with adolescents, the norms for that group in Archer (1987) and Marks et al. (1974) should be consulted. Fowler (1981) advises using such norms until the time when persons have started to drop an adolescent lifestyle and are beginning to accept some primary responsibility for taking care of themselves. Thus, adolescent norms would be appropriate for a nineteen-year-old living at home under significant parental controls, whereas adult norms could be used for a street-wise seventeen-year-old who lives away from home. Adolescent norms bring the mean profile of an adolescent clinical population down from one with very high scores on F, 4, and 8 and scores around 70 T on 6 and 9 to a mean profile with F around 70, 4 and 2 as the highest scores, though they are below 70, and 8 and 9 as the next highest scores (Marks et al., 1974; Fowler, 1981).

Clinicians have often used "critical items" on the MMPI. These are usually single items whose content is used to cue the clinician to further inquiry in that area or to indicate a problem because of the face validity of the item. A number of sets of these critical items have been used historically, but most have not consistently predicted the behavior they seem to reflect. Additionally, most of them are loaded with items to which the deviant response is "true," which leaves them open to a "yes-saying" bias. In addition, many of them overlap too highly with the F scale and may reflect a tendency to "fake-bad."

At present, two sets of critical items have overcome most of these criticisms, though there still is little predictability from the items to their face-valid content. If the clinician is interested in using these critical items, he or she is referred to Koss and Butcher (1973) and Lachar and Wrobel (1979). At the very least, a perusal of critical items marked by the client is worthwhile. For one thing, clients who admit to these face-valid items usually feel that they have communicated directly to the clinician and may be quite surprised if the later content of a therapy contact indicates a lack of awareness about these issues. An extremely high level of endorsement of critical items may be indicative of malingering.

Readers who need more familiarity with the administration and scoring of the MMPI are referred to the books of Graham (1977, 1987) or Dahlstrom and Welsh (1980), which contain detailed discussions. In proceeding through the individual scales of the MMPI here, there will be descriptions of each scale, along with overall behavior correlates, correlates of high and low scores on each scale, and some patterns the clinician can expect from the scale interrelationships.

In the traditional clinical-interpretation approach to the MMPI, authors referred to the scale name rather than its number. As the years passed, however, it became clear that the actual behavioral correlates of a scale have not always matched the originally applied scale name. Therefore, the scale numbers, rather than names, will be used throughout this text. The traditional names are listed here for the sake of convenience.

SCALE NUMBER	TRADITIONAL SCALE NAME
1	Hypochondriasis (Hs)
2	Depression (D)
3	Hysteria (Hy)
4	Psychopathic Deviant (Pd)
5	Masculinity-Femininity (Mf)
6	Paranoia (Pa)
7	Psychasthenia (Pt)
8	Schizophrenia (Sc)
9	Hypomania (Ma)
0	Social Introversion (Si)

It is common to hear persons experienced in the use of MMPI referring to individuals as, say, "a high 4" or "4-8." These shorthand descriptors are helpful as an abbreviated communication of various behavioral descriptions. In general, a high score on the MMPI is one above 70 T; moderately high is a score of from 60 to 70 T; moderately low is from 40 to 50 T; and low is below 40 T.

Although there is good evidence that various groups (blacks versus Hispanics, males or females, younger or older persons) differ in their average scores on various MMPI scales, it has been asserted that this is not evidence of bias, but simply reflects actual differences or response-set differences in those persons being tested that can be accounted for in interpretation (Montgomery and Orozco, 1985; Pritchard and

Rosenblatt, 1980; Wadsworth and Checketts, 1980; Graham, 1977). Wadsworth and Checketts (1980) present evidence that the religion of neither the diagnostician nor the client, or the interaction of the two, significantly influences clinical diagnoses in general. Pritchard and Rosenblatt (1980) present impressive data to support their assertion that there is no significant evidence the MMPI is racially biased, though they and others note that blacks tend to score higher on F, 4, 8, and 9 (Butcher and Graham, 1988; Dahlstrom et al., 1986). Females are more likely to show peaks on 3 and 6, and males on 1, 4, and 7.

The following traditional conceptualization of the MMPI scales gives a schema that many clinicians find useful. It should never be applied in a hard-and-fast manner, however; it should be considered a guideline, not a fact.

	SOCIAL DEPENDENCY		HOSTILITY; ACTING-OUT
Self-Blame (Neuroticism)	D (2) ← Activity Level → Ma (9)		**Self-Aggrandizement (Psychopathy)**
	Pt (7) ← Behavioral Control → Pd (4)		
Somatic and/or Self-Pity (Psychophysiological)	Hs (1) ← Compliance Trust → Pa (6)		**Reality Contact (Psychosis)**
	Hy (3) ← Attachment, Thought Clarity → Sc (8)		

■ Individual Scale Interpretations

□   THE ? SCALE

On the ?, or "cannot say," scale, not much significance is usually attached to raw scores of less than 30. This is not actually a scale, because it accounts only for the number of items to which the individual has not responded. Of course, one has to at least examine the ? scale, since skipping many items leads to lowered scores on other scales. As the number of skipped items increases to above 30, the profile is increasingly invalidated. If more than 60 items are left unanswered (a T score above 58), the validity is significantly impaired; and if more than 100 are left unanswered (a T score above 70), the profile is virtually worthless. If a client obtains a high ? score, a reading difficulty should first be considered. If this can be ruled out, gross impairment in the decision-making required to give an answer should be considered. If this is not the problem, then obsessive, paranoid, or blatant avoidance issues should be considered. Obsessive clients may feel constrained by the either-or dichotomy allowed in the MMPI; rather than commit themselves, they may skip the item. Paranoids naturally fear the self-disclosure involved in a number of items and may avoid them.

Obviously an ounce of prevention is the most logical cure for this problem. The client should be clearly instructed ahead of time to fill out all the items or leave, at most, only a few blank. One has several options in the face of a high ? score. In most instances where many items have been skipped, the client can be persuaded to answer more questions, which leads to a valid profile. As already noted, scores can also be prorated without great loss. Some clinicians score the items that have been skipped in the direction they feel the client would have answered them, while other clinicians score them in the significant direction. Such scoring reflects the finding that a nonresponse can refer to either controversial content or decisional ambiguity (Fulkerson and Willage, 1980). In either case, the profile should be compared with that obtained by the original scoring.

☐   ## THE L SCALE

The L scale is composed of fifteen items—such as, "I do not always tell the truth"—that are scored only if they are answered "false." These face-valid items identify people who, in a naive and open fashion, present an overly idealistic and perfectionistic portrayal of themselves. Interestingly, high L scores don't markedly negate the validity of the profile since they are generally independent of elevations on most other scales. L scales do tend to be a bit higher among the elderly. Sophisticated or well-educated people seldom score high on this scale, as the items are quite transparent. When well-educated clients do score high, they are likely to be repressed and rigid in their personality structure, tense and introspective, and conforming in behavior. Oddly enough, high scores actually seem to predict underachievement.

A clinician should naturally consider possible deception anytime a high score is obtained, although this is usually true only when the person is not well educated. After considering demographics, people with high scores generally are naive and defensive about their conflicts, are unable to perceive the effects of their behavior on others, are inflexible in problem solving, and have a low tolerance for stress. Persons in occupations where there is a strong demand to present a "good-person" image (e.g., a minister) score higher on this scale, whatever their educational level. A high L score is also associated with a denial of any need for help and with an unwillingness to be honest about deficiencies, admit guilt about behavior, or admit to alcohol abuse (Hedlund, 1977). Thus, the groups most likely to score high on this scale are saints, priests, ministers, rabbis, and some prisoners—the latter because they are trying to present themselves as "normals." Prisoners, however, have a poor feel for what normal is since neither they nor their associates are in that range.

Highly sophisticated individuals who are manipulative and defensive may score low on the L scale, though a low score usually indicates a fairly relaxed and independent individual who has responded openly to the items. A very low score may occasionally be associated with wariness and cynicism, but a moderately low score primarily reflects a person who is not particularly defensive, is willing to admit some deficiencies in the self, and is able to communicate reasonably well with others. Finally, an extremely high score suggests a pathological confusion that may be either organic or functional in nature.

☐   THE F SCALE

The F scale consists of sixty-four items chosen because they were answered as true by fewer than 10 percent of a normal adult population. Blacks and adolescents consistently score higher on F, and it is best to lower the T score as many as 10 points when dealing with these populations (Butcher and Graham, 1988). Very high T scores (above 80) suggest either marked confusion, significant errors in scoring, inability of the client either to read the items or to understand the directions, a false claim of negative symptoms, hostility toward the examiner, or, for other reasons, a clearly invalid profile. If a reading problem is suspected, simply having the client read the first ten items out loud may give a clue in this regard. If a reading problem is noted, the use of a tape-recorded version (one is available from the Psychological Corporation) is suggested. Extremely high T scores (above 100) may indicate that item response was random or that the client either answered true to all questions, was faking-bad, or, if an inpatient, was psychotic. The clinician should rule out organic brain dysfunction in these clients. Gynther et al. (1973a) have shown that high F scores in an adult inpatient population may warrant the term "confused psychotic." If the F is relatively high and K is low, the F score has been pulled up by the schizophrenia-scale items (8). In an outpatient population, it is more likely to indicate some form of an invalid profile. Responding with clearer instructions or a confrontation and acceptance of any hostility in an apparently intact client who produces a high F profile usually results in a subsequent valid test. Since the F scale is highly correlated with scales 6 and 8 (reflecting item overlap) a 6-8/8-6 profile with a high F score may be directly interpreted, though with some caution.

More-moderate T scores (in the range of 65–79) are associated with mild confusion, some significant emotional problems marked by moodiness or agitation, and unconventional and sometimes very deviant religious, social, or political views. Antisocial (acting-out) and withdrawn behaviors are commonly, and paradoxically, associated with these moderate scores in adolescents. But psychotics and those labeled as severe neurotics often have F-scale scores in this range, so severe psychopathology must be ruled out. If there are other indications of anxiety, a score in this range may be a plea for help.

Moderately low scores on the F scale are associated with normal response sets, a calm demeanor, and conventional behavior patterns. If the score becomes very low, a denial of psychopathology and even more rigid and conforming personality patterns are likely. Faking-good should also be considered.

In general, if one can rule out an invalid profile, the F scale is a good indication of overall psychopathology. The higher it is, the more likely it is that there is general psychopathology, although this inference is not as valid in blacks (Smith and Graham, 1981). Conversely, the lower the F scale, the more likely it is that any existing problems are focused and under control.

THE K SCALE

The K scale consists of thirty items obtained by comparing the responses of disturbed individuals who had normal profiles with normals who also had normal profiles, and it is now generally used to identify faking-good cases. These items correlate well with social-desirability scales, by measuring more subtle defensiveness than the L scale. In that sense, they function as a suppressor variable in the other scales (Meehl and Hathaway, 1980) The amount of K contributing to the T scores of other scales should always be considered. K scores are inversely related to elevations on scales 8, 7, and 0.

There is usually a negative correlation between scores on F and K, though certain clients, especially inpatients, may score high on both. These persons are likely to have a reason for avoiding responsibility for psychopathology, such as in a criminal case. At the same time, they feel the need to be honest, possibly from the urging of their attorney or from a need to use an admission of specific psychopathology to excuse behavior. Well-educated and/or sophisticated individuals score higher on this scale, although the positive deviation from the mean is not as marked as it is in the opposite direction on L.

High K scores are generally associated with attempts to deny vulnerability and psychopathology. Such persons are unwilling to admit to psychological or physiological deficit, are inclined to blame others for their problems, and as a result are not likely to cooperate in an intervention attempt. They have little insight into their own patterns and are intolerant toward deviant or disturbed behavior in others. A high K indicates resistance to intervention, whereas a moderate elevation (50–65) indicates a good prognosis for treatment change. In fact, a rise in K is often found with improvement through treatment. A high K score generally contraindicates delinquency in adolescents, especially in females, and indeed, contraindicates antisocial acting-out in general.

Low K scores indicate weak emotional-behavioral controls and that the person is hurting and/or is feeling vulnerable. Such individuals have low self-esteem, are surprisingly harsh or clumsy in dealing with others, and thus usually have marked interpersonal problems. Low scores may also represent an exaggeration of problems as a plea for help, or faking-bad, or they may indicate a confused state that may be either organic or functional.

The F-K index, a test popular with clinicians, is discussed later with regard to several of the ensuing diagnostic categories. In particular, the reader is referred to the section on malingering for qualifications of the interpretation of this index. It has been traditionally asserted that when the index (in terms of raw scores) is negative and is greater than 12, it indicates a deliberate effort by the client to be seen as emotionally healthy and without vulnerability, and when F-K is positive and more than 11, faking-bad should be considered. Most clinicians now feel that wider differences should be allowed, and that the index is more effective in assessing faking-bad than faking-good.

☐   ## SCALE 1 (HS)

Scale 1, traditionally referred to as the Hypochondriasis scale, is comprised of thirty-three items that focus on bodily functions and disorders, though in a number of ways it is more of a characterological scale. The items are reasonably obvious in content, and the complaints embedded in the items are not very specific. Symptoms, if specific, tend to be epigastric. Thus, persons with actual physical disorders are more likely with time to score higher on scale 2 as a reaction to the disorder. Scale 1 is a good indicator of overall pessimism—the higher the score, the more pessimistic the view of the world—and correlates particularly with the channeling of pessimism into somatic concerns and complaints. High scores seem to correlate negatively with intellectual ability, and those who score high on this scale are often described as dull, unambitious, unenthusiastic, and lacking ease in oral expression (Graham, 1987). Clients with high 1 scores may be using physical symptoms to focus tension, to express hostility, or to control others. As a result, it is commonly a high score in persons consulting a physician, and these individuals are often very frustrating for a physician to deal with. High scores are also associated with clinical depression (usually exogenous rather than endogenous), though this correlation or "r" with depression does not usually hold for blacks.

High scores on scale 1, unless found in the relatively rare 1-8/8-1 profile, are seldom correlated in a consistent fashion with extreme psychotic processes. T scores greater than 80, however, may indicate somatic delusions. Even moderate scores on this scale are likely to be associated with a degree of somatization, and since this is combined with the narcissism, immaturity, lack of ambition, and stubbornness that are also characteristic of this group, the clinician's patience is sorely tested. As might be expected, such individuals are demanding and critical regarding intervention attempts and are particularly resistant to psychological interpretations of their disorder. As a result, they seldom respond positively to psychotherapy, instead demanding support, attention, and concrete physical explanation for their disorder. Therapists may find it a helpful technique with such clients to contract for a set period of time in the therapy hour during which a focus on physical complaints is allowed (sometimes called an "organ recital"). This procedure can facilitate a later uninterrupted discussion of the other critical issues that are often avoided. Shorter sessions are also helpful with such clients (Fowler, 1981).

Persons who are low on scale 1 are usually adjusting adequately to their world, though they may appear moralistic and may have problems with the warmth and sharing demands of intimate interpersonal relations. Persons who are very low on scale 1 have deinvested in their bodies and may act as if they don't care what happens to them, e.g., riding a motorcycle at a high speed, which, along with the gun, is the neuropsychologist's most dependable referral source.

SCALE 2 (D)

Scale 2, subtitled the Depression scale, consists of sixty items. It is the most frequent peak scale in psychiatric clients, and it clearly measures what it purports to: the degree of contentment with the world, self-esteem, and one's view of the future. People who score high on scale 2 are clearly distressed and usually are depressed and withdrawn and show psychomotor retardation; they may be schizoid. There is a good chance they may harbor suicidal ideation if 2 is elevated above the 80-T mark. Adolescents score somewhat lower than the general population, whereas the elderly score higher on the average, probably reflecting the different range of options available in these age groups, as well as their different sense of optimism about the future. Since a spike (a marked elevation relative to all other scales) on scale 2 particularly taps symptomatic or reactive depression, it is unstable on repeat testing, compared to other scales. The spike-2 type is seldom described in clinical literature, but when found, it is likely to be a reactive depression in response to environmental stress. In some cases, it is related to an ongoing depressive process that develops out of an inability to deal effectively with aggression, with a concomitant history of rage reaction (Kelley and King, 1979a). If a person with a spike 2 denies depression, further evaluation for possible suicide risk should be made (Butcher and Graham, 1988).

Unless they are attempting to fake-bad, persons with a very high score on scale 2 do consistently show a clinical level of depression, and they likely warrant the potentially psychotic-depressive diagnosis. If the elevation is moderate, it may reflect either a depressive episode, a neurotic-depressive component, or depression from an accompanying maladaptive personality style that cannot cope with changes in the world.

People with high scale-2 scores are at least moderately withdrawn and show a low activity level, whereas persons low on scale 2 are typically comfortable with their world and are reasonably active and alert. In some cases, a very low 2 score may reflect a lack of impulse control and possible conflict with societal mores, yet this has not usually brought the person into legal difficulties. Hedlund (1977) asserts that there is no strong correlation of scale 2 with psychotic symptomatology.

Persons very high on scale 2 initially show a moderate to marked interest in therapy. However, this can be a direct result of their situational distress; when the crisis passes, they may terminate therapy, even though pathological patterns remain. Yet some elevation on 2 is a good prognostic sign for psychotherapy. Contracting for behaviors that increase activity level are helpful here.

Although there is no definitive suicidal profile on the MMPI, it appears that scale 2 is more indicative of suicidal ideation than of actual suicide attempts, and factors tapped by other scales, e.g., scale 9, appear to act as catalysts for actual behavior in this regard.

Persons low on 2 are usually reasonably well adjusted, active and alert, and even enthusiastic, though they may be perceived by others as too flamboyant and uninhibited. Healthy adolescents often show low 2 scores. Very low scores here may reflect the manic phase of a cyclothymic process.

☐   SCALE 3 (HY)

Scale 3, termed the Hysteria scale, is comprised of sixty items that tap two overall constructs: (1) a denial of problems or vulnerabilities in one's emotional or interpersonal world, and (2) complaints of reasonably specific somatic problems. Naiveté, narcissism, neurotic defensiveness, and a lack of awareness of intrapsychic issues are characteristic of persons high on scale 3. Like those with the avoidant personality disorder, they may be highly demanding of attention and caring responses, although they avoid committing themselves in this way.

Scale 3 is only moderately correlated with the development of conversion symptomatology, the initial construct that it was thought to tap, and it shows a low correlation with psychotic complaints. However, a T score above 80 is suggestive of a conversion reaction. Rather than evidencing the hypochondriasis so characteristic of scale 1, scale 3 is more likely to tap depression-generated somatic complaints, as well as ego-alien anxiety and agitation. Thus, sophistication is a factor in the score obtained on scale 3. Those who are brighter or higher in socioeconomic class tend to score higher on scale 3; women are more likely than men to be high on scale 3. Persons with a spike on 3 often show problems with authority and feel unaccepted by their social group. They often show their rebellion in passive ways or via somatic symptoms, but in some cases, will blatantly act out in a sexual or aggressive mode.

Persons high on scale 3 are usually still interpersonally adequate, though they may be rather manipulative. The naiveté, anxiety, and need for attention result in an initially high level of apparent interest in psychotherapy. In particular, they love advice; they simply do not follow it, however. When these persons realize that they cannot manipulate the therapist to feed their ego, they may stop in a huff or attempt to maneuver the therapist into a physical or medical interpretation of their difficulties. Yet they are quite suggestible and are usually responsive to hypnosis. When 3 and K are both elevated and F and 8 are low, the person is often overly conventional and affiliative, with an exaggerated need to be liked. They have problems with assertion and avoid the exercise of power.

Some persons low on scale 3 are tough minded and cynical. They usually have a relatively low need for involvement with people and may even be misanthropic. Generally, these people are conforming to social mores and show little affect.

☐   ## SCALE 4 (PD)

Scale 4, traditionally termed the Psychopathic Deviate, has fifty items that generally tap these four factors: (1) an angry rebelliousness against recognized rules and mores, (2) shallow and often hostile and manipulative interpersonal relationships, (3) inability to profit from experience or to plan effectively for long-term future contingencies, and (4) anger at family and a belief that one was victimized as a child. An examination of three content scales—AUT (authority conflict), FAM (a residue of adolescent family conflict), and HOS (a scale measuring manifest hostility and sadistic cruelty at high levels)—may give a more precise idea as to what an overall high 4 score means in an individual case (Fowler, 1976, 1981). Behaviorally, scale 4 shows a high correlation with antisocial behavior, moodiness, characterological patterns, substance abuse, and sexual immorality. A high scale 4 indicates potential for hostile and aggressive outbursts, particularly in whites (Hedlund, 1977), as well as depressive ideation (not necessarily accompanied by psychomotor retardation). Whether or not they act out their problems in some fashion depends on whether scales 8 and/or 9 are high, and K is low. Blacks, adolescents, and males score higher on this scale, on the average, which can be adjusted for by subtracting up to 10 T points when interpreting the scale. Indeed, a reasonably high scale is "normal" in many adolescents. High-scale-4 individuals are usually extroverted yet don't empathize well with others' needs; they are also impulsive and lack social poise. They do not usually have blatant psychotic symptoms or high intrapsychically generated anxiety. A spike-4 profile commonly suggests problems with the law. If both the IQ and K are high, calculated and more-clever criminal behavior can be expected, e.g., white-collar crime.

Persons who are average on scale 4 usually show adequate interpersonal relationships and are perceived by other people as sincere and concerned. If their scores are very low, they are more likely to be conforming and even rigidly responsive to the dictates of authorities, to be manipulated by others, and to lack a great deal of energy to actuate plans. Males who score very low may have a deep-seated mistrust of females, similar to the classic concept of castration anxiety.

Whereas persons who are low on scale 4 can become dependent on the therapist's advice and recommendations and will even seek out a therapist who will give such direction, persons high on scale 4 are likely to be manipulative in any quest for or response to therapy. They may seem to be good candidates because they are usually articulate and socially sophisticated. However, at their best they subtly project blame onto other persons or situations and are inclined to use therapy to avoid problems of the real world, such as coercion from legal authorities or from intimate others. They are likely to terminate therapy as soon as they have obtained the goal of their manipulation or if they perceive the therapist as either unresponsive toward that end or able to confront their manipulations effectively.

□   SCALE 5 (MF)

Scale 5, the Masculinity-Feminity scale, is composed of sixty items that tap vocational preference, esthetic interests, sexual-role interests, and an activity-passitivity dimension. In general, low scores indicate a person who fits closely with traditional role expectations of his or her sex, whereas high scores reflect a person who in some fashion has moved away from the traditional role. For both sexes, a T score above 80 suggests a serious sexual problem. Scale 5 is highly correlated with education and intelligence, with an "r" of up to .25 with intelligence often being reported.

Men who are low on scale 5 are usually perceived by others as bland, insouciant, and/or macho. They are not likely to be introspective; they are self-indulgent and independent; they disdain intellectual and artistic pursuits in favor of active outdoor interests; and they often delight in being coarse and adventurous. They may see themselves as "good-old boys." They avoid psychotherapy.

Men who are high on scale 5 may have a homosexual identification and/or show a lack of identification with activities associated with the traditional male role. High-score males tend to be more passive, dependent, and submissive in interpersonal relationships. They are peace loving and usually avoid confrontations. They are usually sensitive, sophisticated, higher socioeconomically and intellectually, and likely to have interests in the humanities and arts. They usually do well in therapy, especially group therapy. Ambitious and intrapsychically introspective individuals also tend to score higher on scale 5. A spike-5 profile is usually indicative of transient situational disturbance. If combined with a low 4, it suggests a very passive man, a Milquetoast. By contrast, low-5, high-4 males show an exhibitionistic, almost compulsive, masculinity, often as a counterphobic reaction to issues of tenderness or vulnerability.

Women who score low on scale 5 are likely to be submissive, though petulant. They prefer to be involved in dependent interpersonal relationships, and if they exert any control in the relationship, it is through passivity and stubbornness. Low-score women who are well educated are more positive and assured about themselves and their sex role. They may not be stereotypically feminine, but they often have many feminine characteristics. They may view themselves as plain (Graham, 1987). A very low 5 suggests masochism. Women high on scale 5 have rejected many aspects of the traditional female role. They perceive themselves as extroverted and content with their world, although others may see them as unfriendly or even aggressive. As a result, they easily elicit aggression in others, including therapists. Women with a high 5 more often are interested in sports and other outdoor activities than women low on this scale. A high scale-5 score in a hospitalized woman has in a number of cases been associated with underlying psychosis; such clients may exhibit hallucinations, delusions, and suspiciousness, although acting-out is uncommon (Graham, 1977, 1986).

☐   ## SCALE 6 (PA)

Scale 6, termed Paranoia, includes forty items, and a high score comes from paranoid or unusual ideas, feelings of being wronged, or complaints about others. At the same time, a low score does not rule out similar ideation. In fact, if the person is a sophisticated, integrated, and defensive paranoid individual, he or she may score quite low on this scale. In general, there are few false positives, but true positives may be missed. Very high scores are relatively uncommon, but to the extent that T is greater than 75, look for frank psychosis, clear paranoia, or paranoid schizophrenia as a possible diagnosis.

As scores drop into the moderate-to-high range, more-integrated paranoid ideation is probable and sexual deviation or preoccupation is a significant possibility. Anger toward others for a deprived or punitive childhood or toward authority also elevates this scale into at least the moderate range. However, moderate scores can also be obtained by individuals who are perceived by others as cooperative and intelligent and without any psychological disturbance. As a result, it is worthwhile to examine responses to individual items on this scale. Both adolescents and blacks tend to score higher on scale 6.

As noted, a person with a low score on scale 6 may well be a very sophisticated and guarded paranoid, although it's more likely that he or she is a generally optimistic, warm, and productive individual. In a psychiatric population, a low scale 6 is associated with subtle defensiveness and stubbornness. When a score of less than 45 T is present, frank paranoid disorder is likely, and if it is *very* low, controlled anger and suspicion are likely.

Individuals high on scale 6 seldom become meaningfully involved in psychotherapy. They are much more concerned with "Who did that to me?" than "How could I have done that?" At best, they are intellectualized and rigid. Some success can be attained over time if the therapist is able to give adequate feedback, maintain integrity as a therapist, and gradually develop in them at least a modicum of trust (Barrett, 1981).

<hr>

☐   SCALE 7 (PT)

Scale 7, called the Psychasthenia Scale, consists of forty-eight items that include factors of (1) general discontent with one's world, (2) obsessional concerns, (3) anxiety, and (4) indecision and self-devaluation. Scale 7 primarily taps the obsessional–rather than the compulsive–features of the obsessive-compulsive disorder. The primarily compulsive personality is not that consistently high on this scale, presumably because their rigidity and denial wards off feelings of insecurity or low self-esteem. People high on this scale anxiously ruminate about problems in their world and have perfectionistic standards of performance that they seldom feel they actually meet. As a result, they show feelings of inferiority in many areas and have a negative self-image. A T score over 80 suggests excessive fear and apprehension, even panic. With high T scores, generalized physical complaints, such as fatigue, exhaustion, and insomnia are common, as well as more specific complaints involving the heart or the gastrointestinal or genitourinary systems (Graham, 1987). These features not surprisingly lead them into psychotherapy, but the obsessiveness and perfectionism often cause initial problems. They are not likely to give in, so they continue to introspect and ruminate when changes in behavior would be more productive. If the therapist can be patient and keep such clients involved beyond this initial stage of resistance, the prognosis becomes more positive. An abrupt involvement in therapies that quickly knock out repression and denial, such as confrontational therapies and encounter groups, can be dangerous to high-7 clients, since they may be attempting to hold onto control of very high anxiety or self-destructive impulses.

Hedland (1977) found the presence of phobias to be correlated with a high scale-7 score for white samples only. In female patients, there is a significant negative correlation of irritability and delusions with high scale-7 scores. In general, when a high 7 is found in a psychotic client, it points to a more acute onset. Persons low on scale 7 are perceived by others as contented and satisfied with their lives, self-confident and emotionally stable, and yet also ambitious and status-seeking.

SCALE 8 (SC)

Scale 8, traditionally termed the Schizophrenia scale, is the longest subscale on the MMPI, comprising seventy-eight items that focus on factors of (1) confused thought processes, (2) hallucinations and other indications of formal thought disorder, (3) social and interpersonal alienation, and (4) depression and dissatisfaction. Scale 8 correlates most highly (approximately .75) with scale 7 and moderately (approximately .50–.55) with F, 4, and 2. Adolescents and blacks both score higher on this scale, and the clinician should subtract up to 10 points from the T score for them. Black men, in particular, score high, possibly reflecting alienation from a society that has traditionally made it difficult for them to actualize themselves as both black and male.

Persons high on scale 8 are usually significantly disturbed, though a subsample of individuals may be faking-bad, especially when the T score is over 100. As noted, confusion, bizarre thought-processes, and social alienation are characteristics of high-8 scorers. It is interesting that a very high score here is not necessarily indicative of schizophrenia, though most who have a high score feel as if they are out of phase with the world, as if they are space cadets in a new world. Schizophrenics are more likely to score between 70 and 95 on the T score. Agitated neurotics and people who are severely emotionally unstable, and yet only borderline with respect to psychosis, are more likely to score extremely high on scale 8. Persons in the T-score range of 60 to 75 are more likely to show problems in attention and staying with tasks, with accompanying agitation and anxiety. They usually have high standards that they feel unable to meet, are inclined toward guilt, and have low self-esteem. When under stress, they are prone to become irritable and stubborn.

Persons very low on scale 8 are perceived as happy and reasonably productive individuals, accepting of authority and yielding in interpersonal relationships. Yet they have rigid thought patterns and are unable to come up with abstract or creative solutions to interpersonal and vocational problems, particularly if scale M on the 16 PF is also low.

Persons with high scores on scale 8 are enigmatic for the therapist. They are often willing to discuss their problems openly, though it is hard to pin them down about concrete ways to change their behavior. They are prone to discussions that distract from the focus on the problem and are unstable in their trust of the therapist. Nevertheless, they are likely to remain in some form of contact with the therapist over a long period of time, and if a degree of trust can be generated, modest and steady progress may occur.

SCALE 9 (MA)

This scale, termed the Mania scale, includes forty-six items that focus on a propensity for (1) high energy output, (2) distractibility and lack of persistence in tasks, (3) extroversion, and (4) grandiosity. Scale 9 can be thought of as a force that drives whatever else is there, sort of a behavioral and emotional amplifier. Persons very low on scale 9 show little energy and may be depressed; most are lacking in self-confidence and a reasonable degree of optimism about the future. A high 2 with a low 9 indicates severe depression. The clinician should note that even when scale 2 is not elevated, a very low score on scale 9 is a cue for underlying depression. As 9 moves up toward the average range, the client is more likely to be quietly productive, reliable in most job situations, and possibly perceived as quiet and withdrawn.

Elderly individuals on the average score up to 10 points lower on scale 9, and adolescents average up to 10 points higher than normal adults. Blacks also tend to score a bit higher here. In some females, a high 9 may result from counterphobic attempts to deny dependency and/or passivity.

In general, people very high on scale 9 are likely to be significantly disturbed psychologically and show grandiosity and a high level of distractibility. A T score of greater than 90 may suggest a manic or psychotic episode; in some individuals, a high 9 may reflect a counterphobic attempt to avoid an anticipated (at some level of consciousness) depression. As they move into the moderate to higher ranges, these tendencies are muted, though the person still has problems organizing tasks. Although they may be creative, they need others to carry the plans to the point of actualization. They tend to be extroverted and perceived by others as gregarious, occasionally as pushy. A spike-9 profile is likely to indicate drug abuse and/or antisocial personality disorder; in males, it is also associated with aggressive acting-out (King and Kelley, 1977). Persons with T scores in the 55–65 range usually show the ability to balance their resources and productivity reasonably well and tend to manifest a pleasant, outgoing temperament.

High-9s are difficult for the therapist to work with because they are hyperactive and distractible, not inclined to view themselves as vulnerable or responsible for problems in their world, and not able to persist introspectively to connect contingencies between their behavior and the difficulties they are encountering. If confronted by the therapist, they are likely to intellectualize their problems, attempt to distract from the issue by acting-out, or simply terminate therapy. Lithium therapy should be considered here.

A low score on 9, especially when this scale is the lowest on the profile, usually suggests a lethargic individual. Depression may be present, reflected in fatigue and physical exhaustion. These clients may also be tense and anxious. But low scorers are usually reliable, dependable, and responsible and may confront their problems with perseverance and practicality. Low-scoring males often have home and family interests and are willing to settle down. The prognosis is more favorable for hospitalized low-scorers as well (Graham, 1987).

SCALE 0 (SI)

Scale 0, subtitled Social Introversion, containing seventy items, was developed later than the other scales and as a result does not have as much consensual clinical experience or data supporting it. Scores on this scale are usually quite stable over time and may represent biological and constitutional factors that contribute to an introversion-extroversion component and feelings of social discomfort. This scale was designed to assess the propensity for avoidance of social responsibilities and contact with others. While it seems to assess this factor, it also may tap psychomotor depression, particularly when associated with social insecurity. Such individuals would score high on scale 0 and are usually perceived by others as oversensitive and touchy. A T score over 70 occasionally signifies a well-socialized and controlled but basically psychotic personality who has not been identified by the other scales. Individuals scoring low on scale 0 are likely to be seen as happy-go-lucky and extroverted, though also as opportunistic and manipulative, and they may occasionally manifest problems in impulse control. Yet, a low score on 0 often mutes the pathology suggested by elevated scores on other scales; it indicates the person may be able to vent pathology in socially acceptable ways or in a reasonably non-self-destructive manner.

Both adolescents and elderly individuals score a bit higher on this scale. Persons high on scale 0 are often initially resistant in therapy because they fear rejection in interpersonal relationships and are insecure about increased vulnerability. Yet, if they can deal with this issue in the initial stages of therapy, the prognosis is reasonably positive, for they are inclined to work productively in dealing with their symptoms. Social-skills training is useful here. The spike-0 MMPI is suggestive of situational-adjustment difficulties, such as marital problems and/or a schizoid adjustment, and also may indicate religiously oriented distress, perhaps an abrupt loss of faith in God (Kelley and King, 1979c).

■   ## MMPI Interrelationship Interpretations

The 1-2/2-1 combination is consistently indicative of somatic disturbance, accompanied by a degree of irritability, agitation, and anxiety. These individuals do "hurt" in one way or another. Unfortunately, they have often learned to live with their complaints, so even when they change through intervention, a return of symptoms is probable. The 1-2 code is relatively infrequent and, without associated elevations, points to the somatoform disorders. If 7, 8, and F are also elevated, schizophrenia should be considered. The 2-1 code is a more frequent combination, particularly in males. Men here show somatic tension along with pessimism and depression, and there is usually little physical basis for their disorders. Women who score 2-1 show more classical hypochondriacal patterns, with an emphasis on restlessness and tension, while adolescents are tense and shy and often have academic problems, sometimes school phobia. When the pattern is 2-1 rather than 1-2, there is a greater emphasis on tension-anxiety and depression.

When one is assessing an inpatient sample, particularly male, alcoholism and depression should be considered, particularly episodic forms of alcoholism accompanied by somatic concerns. Persons with the 1-2/2-1 code are generally passive-dependent in interpersonal relationships and are not likely to take responsibility for their behaviors, especially if 3 and 4 are also elevated. This passivity, combined with a general avoidance of responsibility, makes them at best a moderate risk in therapy. They need very directive and structured therapy targeted at overt symptoms.

Scales 1, 2, and 3 are commonly referred to as the neurotic triad, and elevations on these scales are found in most neurotic disorders, though "chronically hypochondriacal" may be the most applicable term when all three scales are elevated. There is often an exaggerated need for affection. When scales 1 and 3 are elevated, with a valley (10 T score points or more) on scale 2 (the conversion V), the client is prone to use somatic disorder as a projection channel for personal difficulties. The function is hysteroid and/or hypochondriacal rather than classically psychophysiological in nature. Persons with an acute illness tend to have high scale-2 scores, often without remarkable elevations on other scales. Persons with a 1-2-3 code (in that order) are indeed on a downward slope, that is, their functioning is often deteriorating. Acute clinical distress, with possible neurological involvement, and/or masking of depression is signaled by 1-2-9 and 2-1-9 codes. Persons with 1-2-3-4 or 2-1-3-4 codes are usually alcoholics, often with a strong hostility component.

When the 1-3/3-1 profile is accompanied by a marked elevation on scale 8 and an elevation on F, one must look for somatic delusions and/or psychotic paranoia. The 1-3/3-1 pattern is common in older people and in women, and when other scales are not particularly elevated, it reflects a combination of neurotic symptomatology and psychophysiological concerns. Consistent with the hysteric component, these persons have shallow interpersonal relationships, are narcissistic, and are somewhat Pollyanna-ish or avoidant in reaction to their problem. Males who show these patterns may be feminine in orientation, particularly if this is accompanied by an elevation on scale 5. When elevations on 1 and 3 are accompanied by a high 7, a panic disorder is quite possible. In adolescents, this profile is often accompanied by somatic problems and attention-seeking behaviors, and they are often referred because of school problems.

The 1-3/3-1 codes are common, and if 1 is greater than 3, there is more irritability, whining, and pessimism. When 3 is higher, there is more optimism, so a more long-suffering martyrlike complex may be in evidence. To the degree that scale 1 is close to the height of scale 3 and scale 2 is somewhat lower, conversion reactions are more likely. Such complaints as hypertension, low-back pain, eating disorders (such as anorexia nervosa and obesity), and gastrointestinal disorders are common. These individuals are seldom truly incapacitated by their symptoms, and there is usually a neurotic component. Persons who show a multiple personality are also likely to obtain a 1-3/3-1 code. The combination of passivity, resistance to responsibility in a psychological disorder, preference for medical explanations, and the suggestibility and high need for structure all predict problems in psychotherapy with the 1-3/3-1 client. They prefer powerful and magical cures and are inclined to terminate the therapy relationship prematurely if signs of concern by the therapist are not forthcoming. When a 1-3/3-1 is associated with a high K, and especially if F, 2, 7, and 8 are low, the person is very defensive, almost "overly normal," helpful, and sympathetic. They cannot tolerate the role of "patient" and resist any interpretation of unconventionality or vulnerability (Butcher and Graham, 1988).

Types under the 1-3-8 code are usually diagnosed as schizophrenic disorder, paranoid type, or paranoid personality disorder. They may appear as delusional, with bizarre symptomatology. Depression and suicidal ideation or behaviors may be present, and such individuals often are preoccupied with religion or sex. They are prone to substance abuse; are often loud, angry, anxious, restless, or bored; and aren't particularly interested in forming personal relationships. Types under the 1-3-9 code are most often diagnosed as having organic brain syndrome or somatoform disorder. If the organic brain syndrome is present, they will likely show spells of aggressiveness (Graham, 1987).

The 1-4/4-1–code type is relatively infrequent with inpatient groups, yet it occurs at least moderately often in outpatient clinical settings. In either case, it occurs far more often in men; commonly indicates consistent problems in meeting the responsibilities of life, with resultant self-pitying and antiauthoritarian attitudes; is correlated with hypochondriasis; and is possibly focused on low-back pain or headaches. With inpatients, it is more often associated with a combination of somatization symptoms, narcissism, and alcohol problems, and there are correlated problems with the vocational and interpersonal areas, particularly with the opposite sex. The 1-4/4-1 adolescent is provocative, defiant, and pessimistic, with problems at both home and school, and may even make manipulative suicide attempts.

Persons of this type are most responsive to short-term symptomatic treatment, and even here, the response is up and down at best. There is often a high associated score on the L scale, and if so, such persons do poorly in psychotherapy because of their resistance, somatization, and possible problems with alcohol. A very low score on 1, combined with a high score on 4, suggests someone who has truly given up on his or her body and is likely to take high risks physically, possibly as a counterphobic reaction to early anxiety about bodily symptoms (Fowler, 1981).

The 1-6/6-1 code is also rare. It indicates somatic and hypochondriacal preoccupations, probably delusional in nature if 8 is also high. It may indicate an attempt to stave off an emerging psychotic process. Adolescents with this code are emotionally insecure, defensive, and evasive, with family problems in general and father-absence specifically occurring.

The 1-7/7-1 code, which occurs more often in males, generally reflects high somatic tension. Obsessive patterns, especially focused on somatic complaints, and feelings of inferiority are typical.

The 1-8/8-1 code may be indicative of schizophrenia, especially acute schizophrenia, particularly if 8 is markedly elevated and F is also elevated. In general, such persons often have vague and even odd medical complaints, have trouble with expression of aggression, and may alternate behaviorally within a classic passive-aggressive pattern. Types under the 1-8/8-1 code may also feel socially inadequate and lack trust in others. They become isolated and alienated from peers, which may lead to a nomadic lifestyle and its accompanying poor work history. They may show sexual-deviate patterns. They usually have some dissociative or schizoid components, especially if scale 0 is also high. Adolescents with a 1-8/8-1 code are anxious, introverted, indecisive, and appear easily distractible. Drug abuse, suicide attempts, and/or hyperactivity occur with reasonable frequency.

The 1-9/9-1 profile is a rare code, marked by a high level of anxiety and distress. Masked depression should be considered. Gastrointestinal symptoms and headaches also occur. Types under the 1-9/9-1 code may appear to be ambitious, but they often lack direction and experience and may become frustrated when their goals are not met. Such persons may be passive-dependent in actual functioning, yet maintain a gruff exterior. If a number of other scales, including F, are moderately elevated, the possibility of brain damage should be considered. Also infrequent in adolescents, males with this code are aggressive and evasive, while females are extroverted and tense.

An extremely rare code, the 1-0/0-1 pattern indicates high social discomfort, passive-avoidant patterns, and numerous somatic complaints.

The 2-3/3-2 code is marked by apathetic depression, anxiety, and over-control, with depression predominating when 2 is higher than 3 and with anxiety and accompanying neurotic and somatic symptoms predominating when 3 is higher than 2. In both codes, there is evidence of passive dependency and shyness, particularly when 2 is high and 9 is low. The emphasis here is more on inadequacy than on somatization, the latter being primary in the 1-2/2-1 code. Clients with a 2-3/3-2 profile are more likely to have accepted their psychopathology, as opposed to the 2-7/7-2 types, who are usually still struggling to cope with it. The 2-3/3-2 in females has more emphasis on depression, whereas in males there is a bit more of a dependent though driven component. When scales 4, 7, and 8 are also moderately elevated in a 2-3/3-2 type, histrionic components are probable, though actual acting-out may be muted to the degree 7 is high. The 2-3/3-2s seem to seek responsibility in vocational and interpersonal situations but then are stressed by and dislike the responsibility associated with such committments. They are achievement- and power-oriented, but they are sensitive to rejections, so they do not get into situations where actual competition could take place. In this sense, they are similar to persons with the avoidant personality disorder. Moderate elevations on scales 2, 3, and 7 are characteristic of the phobic disorders and sexual dysfunctions. In addition to these types of problems, adolescents with this code type are clearly marked by poor peer relationships, especially with the opposite sex. They are loners, except for some subgroups in the school setting.

To the degree that 2 is greater than 3, success in psychotherapy is more likely. In fact, some elevation on 2 is almost a prerequisite for success in psychotherapy because it suggests an allowance for vulnerability that the therapist can work with. When 3 is greater than 2, there is a greater tendency to avoid intrapsychic introspection and more likelihood of projection. Hence, response to psychotherapy is poorer and directive and dramatic therapies are more helpful.

The 2-4/4-2 code is relatively common in inpatient populations, though not as likely to occur in outpatients. Since 2-4/4-2s are often both depressed and consumers of stimulation (Anderson and Bauer, 1985), alcoholism or other kinds of substance abuse are common. Other types of concomitant sociolegal problems (and some situational guilt) also occur; these people are often secondary psychopaths "in trouble." If scales 2, 4, 8, and 9 are all high, there may be evidence of schizophrenic disorder, and if 6 is also elevated, a possible paranoid component may be present.

Even though 2-4/4-2 types can often present a facade of confident behavior, they easily move into manipulative and impulsive behaviors, including suicide. In that same vein, they are likely to manifest a cry for help, possibly through manipulative suicide gestures. They verbalize a need for help, then when it is proffered, they terminate therapy before fully dealing with the more basic aspects of the problem. In general, male alcoholics with these patterns show a long history of alcohol abuse that is associated with secondary psychopathic patterns. Female alcoholics in this code type are more likely to have depressive components, situational stress, and physical complaints. A disturbed family background is common (Anderson and Bauer, 1985). Adolescents with this code usually also have very disturbed families, school problems, runaway behavior, and drug abuse patterns.

The 2-4/4-2 code, when accompanied by elevations in 7, suggest a modal diagnosis of passive-aggressive personality disorder. Depression and anxiety may also be present. The 2-4-7/7-4-2/4-7-2 pattern is common among passive-aggressive personalities and male alcoholics, who tend to be fearful, worried, and high-strung, yet show anger, hostility, and immaturity. They tend toward phobic behaviors and may be ruminative or over-ideational. They may have problems with anxiety during treatment, but they seem to respond well to goal-oriented therapies (Graham, 1987).

The 2-5/5-2 code is very rare in females. Those few who do display it are usually from a lower social class, showing much interpersonal and social-role conflict. Males with this code are passive, noncompetitive, sensitive, and idealistic. Conflicts are handled via fantasy and self-awareness.

The profile type 2-6/6-2 is rare and is primarily seen in females. They are likely to complain of physical symptoms first; on further examination, they indicate a recent interpersonal stress, such as breaking up with a lover or spouse (Kelley and King, 1979c). They tend to be more flat than depressed in affect, show paranoid ideation, are likely to have had relatives who have had problems with alcohol, and are concerned about potential alcoholism in their own lives. They are inclined to be dependent and preoccupied with thoughts of suicide and have often made manipulative suicidal gestures in the past. They are significantly disturbed characterologically and thus may earn the diagnosis of borderline or paranoid personality disorder. Adolescents with a 2-6/6-2 are more inclined to be introverted and insecure, with strong conflicts over sexual feelings.

The 2-7/7-2 pattern is very common in outpatients, especially males. If both scores are very high, you can expect the presence of agitated depression, difficulty in concentration, somatic complaints, and a high probability of suicidal thoughts. When scales 4, 8, and 9 are also elevated and 1 is low, the probability of acting out suicidal thoughts is raised; 8 in particular gives a cue as to the lack of control and/or presence of psychosis. If 0 is high, interpersonal avoidance and fear of rejection can also be expected. Males who show this overall pattern are more likely to have concomitant obsessive-compulsive patterns (especially when 7 is higher than 2), as well as vague somatic complaints and insomnia. Males with some high point combinations of scales 2, 7, and 8 are more likely to be psychotic than females, who are more likely to be neurotic (Kelley and King, 1979b).

Persons with the 2-7/7-2 pattern are generally passive and dependent, often somewhat depressed, show little anger or hostility, and keep emotionally distant from most people (though adolescents show more agitation and tension and are very likely to have entertained suicidal thoughts). Further, 2-7/7-2 types may be rigid in their thinking and may be poor problem solvers. They may also be meticulous and perfectionistic and present themselves as extremely moral and religious people (Graham, 1987). The scale-7 component points more to anhedonia than to classical depression; if it is high in the 2-7/7-2 combination, it points more to a lack of ability to experience pleasure than to psychomotor retardation (Gynther and Green, 1980). As a result, the clinician should explore possible suicide ideation. When scale 1 is also elevated, the agitated anxiety of the 2-7/7-2 profile is channeled into marked somatization. A neurotic diagnosis is probable, and assertive training can be helpful. When scale 4 (rather than 1) is elevated, chronic alcoholism, family and marital problems, passive-aggressive patterns, and underachievement are probable. When 2, 7, 4, and 5 are elevated (low 5 in females), the person often appears weak and self-effacing and elicits deprecation from others. The person seen as the "clown" or "silly egghead-intellectual" is often found here.

When elevations on 2 and 7 are associated with an elevation on scale 3, one finds both high aspirations and high standards. There is often success in achievement, though with a high cost in stress; paradoxically, the tendency toward passive dependency is even more marked. Passive behaviors accompanied by underlying anger and hostility are more likely when the elevation on scale 2 is predominant, associated with high elevations on scales F, 8, and 4 and only a moderate elevation on scale 7 (Carson, 1969). Fowler (1981) notes that when a high 5 is combined with a high 2-7/7-2, there is a paradoxically high probability of sexual acting-out. In general, the prognosis for the 2-7/7-2 type in psychotherapy is positive, as they usually remain in therapy, though it is less positive when both scores are very high.

The 2-8/8-2 code occurs infrequently, particularly in outpatient groups. A sense of having been deprived or hurt as a child is typical, as if one had been raised by one of Harlow's "wire-mothers." Confusion, concreteness, social awkwardness, a high level of tension, and depression are common. Individuals may also have blackouts, nausea, or vomiting. If scale 1 is also raised, then somatic delusions are probable. If 4 is high, too, acting-out and fear of loss of control are common. Another common diagnosis is bipolar disorder: When 2 is markedly high and greater than 8, psychotic depression is likely; but when 8 is greater than 2 and particularly high, a schizophrenic or schizoaffective adjustment is more likely. In either case, there is often suicidal ideation, and it is more likely to be associated with a specific plan than in the 2-7/7-2 profile. Even where the 2-8/8-2 code is associated with only mild elevations, inefficiency and problems in carrying out plans occur, and a sense of having been rejected by others, including therapists, is common. In general, this code type is more indicative of pathology in females, and with them particularly it should be a cue to look for substance abuse (Kelley and King, 1979a). In adolescents, these same patterns equally apply, though a history of nonspecific brain disorder is common.

The 2-9/9-2 profile incorporates a true paradox, since it is the manifestation of simultaneous manic and depressive components; that is, it represents an attempt through manic defenses to cope with underlying depression, though such a coping pattern is not often successful. If both 2 and 9 are very high, a bipolar affective disorder is suggested, although the possibility of a defense against depression caused by loss from organic brain damage should also be considered. This pattern is occasionally found in male alcoholics who are agitated and also defending themselves against depression by increased alcohol abuse. Clients with the 2-9/9-2 profile may report anxiousness and somatic problems, particularly in the upper gastrointestinal tract. In adolescents, the 2-9/9-2 profile can reflect tension, narcissism, separation anxiety, and problems in developing a distinct identity.

When 2 is low, but K and 9 are elevated (the K-9 profile), the personality is organized around competitiveness and interpersonal power. These individuals are narcissistic and depend upon evidence of weakness in others for their self-enhancement—they like to "run up the score." In females, it may be evident in exhibitionistic attractiveness—the Hollywood syndrome.

The 2-0/0-2 profile is obtained by shy individuals who are insecure about their introversion and as a result have bouts of depression. It is also particularly common in women and in adolescents who are having social difficulties. In all age ranges, it may manifest itself as a mild, chronic depression. Fowler (1981) reports that this pattern is notably common in parents (especially women) who bring their children to child-guidance clinics, and that 2-0/0-2s ultimately often beget 2-0/0-2s. Any training in social skills is helpful, as is psychotherapy to help the shy person adjust to and accept the more stable components of the introverted pattern.

The 3-4/4-3 profile, a common code in outpatients, especially females, is associated with problems in impulse control, usually focused on hostility. When 4 is greater than 3, there is a higher probability of acting-out behavior; this profile is often noted in female delinquents. However, as Davis and Sines (1971) suggest, when 3 is greater than 4, the anger is more repressed and more likely to manifest itself in intermittent aggression. Diagnoses such as a dissociative reaction, intermittent explosive disorder, or passive-aggressive personality disorder are common, whereas a diagnosis that focuses on emotional instability and anger is more characteristic when 4 is greater than 3. Some 3-4/4-3 clients may exhibit sexual promiscuity. They may appear to be socially conforming, yet are inwardly rebellious. Suicidal ideation is likely following bouts of drinking and acting-out behaviors (Graham, 1987). High conflict over dependency, denial, the antisocial aspects, and the tendency to avoid responsibility for behavior make high success in psychotherapy improbable.

When this code type is found in females, it often reflects marital problems associated with sexual difficulties and, as already noted, problems in dealing effectively with anger. These persons are usually overcontrolled but occasionally fly into rages (Kelley and King, 1979c). As a 3-4 client changes to a 4-3, divorce becomes more probable (Fowler, 1981).

The 3-5/5-3 code, moderately common in males and uncommon in females, usually manifests itself in a man who *appears* to be competent and even charming. However, narcissism, denial, and essential passivity mean there is little productivity, persistence, or ultimate responsibility. The code is frequent among fathers of child clients. Adolescents of this type are moderately depressed and withdrawn, are affectively shallow, often have weight problems, and lack skills with the opposite sex.

The 3-6/6-3 code is characterized by overt anxiety, tension, and rigidity that cover blandly manifested but deeply suppressed hostility. There is a denial of this hostility, especially of any of its results as it emerges in a passive or episodic aggressive fashion. The hostility is often directed toward significant others, so marital, family, or social problems are common. Though adolescents with this code type often perform well academically, they often manifest drug abuse and/or suicide attempts and are oversensitive, evasive, and resentful.

People who score moderately high on these two scales are hypersensitive to criticism, suspicious, and hostile, yet they overtly promote themselves as naive and optimistic about the world. They have significant difficulties in interpersonal relationships and perceive their problems as emanating from others. To the degree that these two scales are high, there is more likely to be a clear paranoid disorder. If there is distinct bimodality, paranoia is common, whereas a rise on scales F and 8 suggests paranoid schizophrenia as more likely.

In contrast, the 3-8/8-3 person (an uncommon code) shows confusion and a high probability of anxiety attacks, which are occasionally then channeled into either phobias or acting-out (depending on scale 4). If both scales are very high and F is also high, consider possible cognitive dysfunction. When scores are more moderate, consider a diagnosis that includes dependency and dissociative and/or hysteroid defense mechanisms. This disturbed thinking may manifest itself in unclear thoughts, poor concentration, lapses of memory, unusual ideas, or loose and unclear ideational associations. Further, delusions and hallucinations, as well as incoherent speech, may be present. The most common diagnosis is schizophrenia, although somatoform disorder may also be present. If 2 is moderately elevated in this pattern, psychotherapy is usually effective. If it is low, a supportive and structured therapeutic orientation is more productive. When an elevation on scale 3 is accompanied by an elevation on K and concomitant low scores on scales F and 8, look for individuals who are conforming, constricted emotionally, and yet dependent on others without acknowledging their dependency because it signifies vulnerability.

The 3-9/9-3 profile is rare, usually found in women rather than men. These persons usually manifest acute medical distress and/or depression as a referral complaint, but on closer examination are likely to show evidence of a histrionic personality disorder or, less frequently, a conversion disorder. They are verbally aggressive and inclined to distort their perceptions easily, and they have particular difficulty dealing effectively with sexual relationships, especially communication in the relationship. At a secondary level, they are likely to show headaches and a number of other somatic complaints (Kelley and King, 1979c). Adolescents show similar patterns and are often embroiled in family conflict.

The 4-5/5-4 code denotes an antiestablishment and antiauthoritarian personality, but the subtlety of expression of such attitudes is modulated by parental-cultural background, IQ, and level of education. Females often show a strong "masculine protest." The modal diagnosis for the 4-5/5-4 profile is passive-aggressive personality disorder (Graham, 1987).

Men with a 4-5/5-4 profile are often bohemian characters inclined toward various types of nonconformity. They may be overtly homosexual and flaunt this in a passive-aggressive manner. Males with a high 4 and a low 5 show stereotyped macho masculinity. Females with low-5 and high-4 scores, on the other hand, lean toward social masochism. They adopt an overly feminine posture but carry a significant degree of underlying hostility. They often generate hostility and then use guilt and/or legal sanctions to punish the aggressor. To the degree 6 is also elevated, there is a transfer of blame onto others. Females with both a high 5 and a high 4 are those who have adopted behaviors that do not fit with the traditional female role. If these scores are not markedly elevated, they suggest a woman who has developed an independent and competent lifestyle. Adolescents with this code type are more likely to directly rebel and act out. They are provocative, prone to abuse drugs, and often delinquent.

The 4-6/6-4 code is mildly similar to the 3-8/8-3 code, except that there are fewer anxiety and phobic components and the emphasis is on narcissism and suspiciousness. As such, it occurs with some frequency in adolescents, where it does not signal the degree of pathology it does in adults, though they are likely to abuse drugs and have strong conflicts with parents and school. In both adolescents and adults, there is often a transfer-of-blame mechanism, and others view them as obnoxious. To the degree scale 3 is also elevated, the pattern is more one of immaturity than obnoxiousness.

A passive-aggressive diagnosis is common, though paranoid schizophrenia must be considered if scales 4 and 6 are very high and scales 8 and F are high. Women with this pattern who are also high on 5 are hostile and angry and are effective at eliciting rage reactions in others, especially males. Persons with a 4-6/6-4 pattern are usually bitter, obnoxious, and difficult to deal with, and they quickly reject responsibility for any problems and may abuse alcohol. Intermittent aggression and a prepsychotic adjustment are also probable (Fowler, 1981). They may present somatizations in the forms of asthma, hay fever, hypertension, headaches, blackouts, and cardiac problems (Graham, 1987). They avoid being involved in any therapy, if at all possible, and seldom make any significant and lasting changes even when they are involved.

The 4-7/7-4 combination presents the paradox of the insensitivity and social alienation connoted by scale 4, combined with the moodiness and excessive concern about the effects of one's behavior connoted by scale 7. As a result, such individuals, both adolescents and adults, may be involved in cyclical acting-out behavior in which damage to other people is followed by apparent regret—such as the alcoholic who goes on a spree and disrupts friends and family, then follows this with contrite pleas for forgiveness. Yet there is good reason to believe that they are truly insensitive to the feelings of others. Certain sexual-deviate patterns that are a counterphobic response to a fear of the opposite sex attain a 4-7/7-4 profile. When the profile has high scores on 2-7 and 4-9, there is often a warring between these somewhat disparate elements. With age, both 4 and 9 tend to diminish, and the more obsessive and depressive elements of the 2-7 profile emerge. Clients with a 4-7/7-4 do indicate a desire for change and will become involved in psychotherapy. At the same time, however, they are concrete in their thinking and not psychologically minded; thus, they are not easily responsive to most insight-oriented therapies and they prefer symptomatic support and structure.

The 4-8/8-4—code types are perceived by others as narcissistic or weird. They are inclined toward antisocial and schizoid behavior, yet it is usually within a family structure and reflects some underlying dependency and a deteriorating loss of control. Very often, from an early age, they develop a set to perceive others as hostile and dangerous and their consequent "striking-out" in turn reinforces their sense of alienation. In this vein, Scott and Stone (1986) found 4-8/8-4 profiles to predominate in a sample of adult and adolescent clients who had been victims of father-daughter incest as children.

They may have periods of obsessive suicidal ideations. And if both scales are very high, with 8 greater than 4, the likelihood of bizarre thinking, psychosis, and paranoid suspiciousness increases. In this case, the clinician should consider the diagnosis of paranoid schizophrenia. Usual diagnoses include schizophrenia (paranoid type), antisocial personality, schizoid personality, or paranoid personality. Persons with a 4-8/8-4 code, especially when there is also a high score on 6, usually had very destructive family backgrounds and appear to feel as if the world is a jungle. As a result, they perceive their own acting-out as a matter of survival (Fowler, 1981). When 4 and 8 are high, such individuals may continually show antisocial behaviors (e.g., rape), they are prone to violence if cornered, and they prefer a nomadic and transient existence with few responsibilities. When elevations on 4 and 8 are accompanied by a high F and a low 2, one may find a punitive and interpersonally destructive person who yet goes about in the guise of a helpful person, such as a minister or guidance counselor. Punitive aggression, almost to the point of sadism, is directed into a good cause. In spite of an apparently caring role, they are often schizoid in their personal life. Adolescents of this type are extremely miserable and unhappy, show odd or even bizarre disorder patterns, and are immature and resentful.

The 4-9/9-4 code is a very common one; when high, it is frequently found to indicate a behavior disorder, most often an antisocial personality disorder, both in adults and adolescents. These individuals do not profit from experience; are seekers of a high degree of stimulation; may appear good-natured and charming, yet often get embroiled in sociolegal difficulties; and show deficient functioning in the interpersonal and vocational areas. At the very least, they show an enduring propensity to subvert the potential "good" of self and family. They are narcissistic and impulsive, and even though they may manifest a certain degree of ambitiousness, they have many problems from their transient life-style, narcissism, and inability to follow through on plans. A history of alcohol abuse, notably episodic sprees, is common, especially if F is also high. On occasion, this pattern is indicative of a bipolar disorder (Graham, 1987). If the profile is distinctly bimodal, these persons are not so consistently aggressive, though they are inclined toward deception. To the degree 8 and 6 are elevated, they are likely to be more directly aggressive. To the degree 0 is elevated, they are more likely to be slick and effective in their manipulations of others.

It is interesting that when women obtain a 4-9 profile that is not markedly high overall, they have been characterized as having high potential for a sales position. If 4 and 9 are only moderately elevated (in men or women) and there is an indication of psychological distress via scale 2, such persons can respond positively in psychotherapy, though initial sessions are generally replete with resistance. When 4 and 9 are quite high and 6 and/or 8 are elevated, success in psychotherapy is much less probable.

Persons with a 4-0/0-4 code—usually females, as this is a rare code for males—carry much anger, but they are unable to directly express it because they are shy and evasive. They hold grudges and can be destructive to others if it does not entail any direct confrontation.

Males with a 5-7/7-5 pattern are introspective and show episodes of anxiety and/or depression, along with schizoid components if 0 is also elevated. Females show many interpersonal problems, especially with males. Similarly, males with a 5-0/0-5 code are introspective, but, unlike 5-7/7-5s, are more schizoid and anxious than they are depressed. Both females and males with a 5-0/0-5 code show problems in heterosexual relationships; females with this code often come from a lower education and/or socio-economic background and appear passive, yet they show many social-role conflicts.

The 6-7/7-6 code is uncommon, often associated with elevations on 2 or 8, and denote anxious, tense, guilt-prone (especially to the degree 2 and/or 7 is high rather than 8), hypersensitive individuals. They typically use obsessive-compulsive defenses that are no longer effective in controlling anxiety and rumination.

The 6-8/8-6 code type is closely associated with a prepsychotic or psychotic adjustment, especially if these scales are substantially elevated. There is much rebellion and anger and other persons are alienated, thereby creating a vicious cycle for their prophecy that they are persecuted. If both of these scales are quite high and 7 is low—the "paranoid valley"—Gynther et al. (1973a) suggest looking for further evidence of paranoid schizophrenia associated with auditory hallucinations. This is especially true of psychiatric patients with this distinctive profile, as a diagnosis of schizophrenic, paranoid type, is common. These individuals are likely to manifest psychotic behavior, autistic thinking, blunted affect, rapid and incoherent speech, and withdrawal into fantasy when stressed. Psychotropic medications should certainly be considered for this population. Patterns similar to the above occur with adolescents, though learning disabilities and nonspecific brain damage are also commonly noted and they often show violent temper reactions.

In general, 6-8/8-6s show underlying inferiority, fear-proneness, and low self-esteem, which seem to be counterphobically defended against by an irritable and hostile veneer. They demonstrate poor judgment in a number of areas and are emotionally unstable. They naturally do not respond well to psychotherapy and, if at all receptive, are inclined toward fad treatments. Significantly elevated 6-8/8-6 profiles, with high L and F scores and relatively low scores on scales 3 and 7, suggest markedly disturbed persons who show paranoid ideation, though organic brain syndrome should also be considered. The degree of available psychological energy, often reflected in the degree of accompanying elevation on scale 9, is the determining factor in whether the underlying hostility evidences itself.

The hallmark of the high 6-9/9-6 profile is hostile excitement, and a counterphobic response to emotional involvement, criticism, and dependency seems to underlie this hostile agitation. A diagnosis of paranoid schizophrenia is common. The clinician needs to consider the possibility of organic brain dysfunction where the manic and suspicious adjustment may be a reaction to loss of functioning in a personality that finds loss unacceptable. At more moderate levels, the 6-9/9-6 profile suggests strong dependency and affection needs that are usually not met. These individuals are overresponsive to emotional slights or threats.

The 7-8/8-7 pattern, in the moderate range, shows depressive and/or obsessive-compulsive features, though often with much inner turmoil (Butcher and Graham, 1988). If elevations are marked and accompanied by elevations on scales 0 and 2, severe depression, anxiety, and introverted behavior should be expected and deterioration into a more blatant schizophrenic adjustment is possible. If so, it is marked by the use of neologisms, bizarre speech, depersonalization, and possibly catatonic stupor. Even in the more moderate range, these individuals show a low level of social skills, and if they are not diagnosed as schizophrenic, they at least have a borderline personality (Kelley and King, 1979b). When initially seen, 7-8/8-7 clients may be confused and panicked. They may feel chronically insecure, inferior, and inadequate and have a difficult time making decisions. They will usually report problems, especially sexual ones, in interpersonal relationships, and as a result may fantasize profusely (Graham, 1987). Suicide attempts are not infrequent, and to the degree that scale 8 is high, they may have a bizarre quality. To the degree that 7 is greater than 8, the individual usually retains better control in behavior adjustment, is less likely to be blatantly psychotic, and is still fighting deterioration in functioning. Unfortunately, a high scale 7 is soluble in alcohol and other drugs.

If both scales 7 and 8 are elevated well above the 70 T mark and 8 is higher, schizophrenia is a strong probability, particularly so if scales 1, 2, and 3 are relatively low. This holds true even more for men than for women. Even if no psychosis exists, a significant, and pervasive emotional disturbance of some sort is probable.

The 0-7/7-0 code is characterized by tension, insecurity, anxiety, and low self-confidence. This group is shy and has substantial difficulties in interpersonal relationships—especially adolescents with family members—and may be agoraphobic.

The 8-9/9-8 type identifies a person who is narcissistic, hostile, and unable to relate effectively to others. It is a more common code in adolescents and young adults, where it is often associated with self-centeredness and hyperactivity. The fear of relating is handled by distractibility techniques, so psychotherapy is extremely difficult. It is very hard for them to focus on any issue for a significant period of time. Even if the scores are only moderately high, there should be much concern about long-term adjustment. Multiple-drug abusers, particularly adolescents, may show this pattern. In adults, a high 8-9/9-8 is associated with a schizophrenic adjustment with a poor prognosis, odd or pressed speech patterns, and delusions and/or hallucinations and confusion. More likely than not, the pattern represents either a disorganized or agitated catatonic schizophrenic, depending on scales 6, 3, and K. There is often a history of delinquency, or at least of behavioral problems. A high 8-9/9-8 associated with elevation on scales F, 2, and 7 may be a schizoaffective disorder, depressed type. Even moderately high 8-9/9-8 elevations are symptomatic of a significant psychopathological process (Butcher and Graham, 1988).

The 8-0/0-8 code is a relatively uncommon one, especially in males and adolescents. The 8-0/0-8 person is significantly socially avoidant and isolated. Often diagnosed as schizoid, they are not very comfortable with their adjustment and show some anxiety as well as a propensity to become lost in fantasies.

A high 9 score, associated with moderate elevations on scale 4 and 3 and a moderate or greater elevation on K, denotes narcissistic and aggressively competitive persons. They do not tolerate vulnerability or dependency, and they raise their self-esteem by denigrating others. If this pattern is bolstered by real-world support for the narcissism, such as a high level of physical attractiveness or athletic skill, the personality style is reinforced in a vicious cycle. When these people enter therapy, the therapist hears various fascinating anecdotes and may even be entertained by dramatic self-confrontations. However, marked change cannot be expected unless the cycle of narcissism is broken in some way, such as aging or trauma resulting in a forced loss of attractiveness.

To facilitate the reader's use of the two-point codes, a list of first-consideration (not exclusive) diagnoses associated with specific two-point codes is presented in Table 1.1. This table is coordinated with the material in the previous section, as well as with that discussed in the later sections on various clinical syndromes.

TABLE 1.1   First-Consideration Diagnoses and Two-Point Codes

CODE	FIRST-CONSIDERATION DIAGNOSES
1-2	Chronic Alcohol Intoxication, Anxiety Disorder, Female Psychosexual Dysfunction, Schizophrenia (rare), Somatization, Hypochondriasis, Depression, Passive-Aggressive Personality Disorder
1-3	Conversion Disorder, Hypochondriasis, Malingering, Faking-Good, Panic Disorder, Psychogenic Pain Disorder, Eating Disorders, Multiple Personality
1-4	Hypochondriasis, Social Phobia, Chronic Alcohol Intoxication, Substance Abuse, Somatization, Affective Disorder
1-6	Somatization, Paranoid Schizophrenia
1-7	Somatization, Obsessive-Compulsive Disorder, Eating Disorders

TABLE 1.1   First-Consideration Diagnoses and Two-Point Codes (cont.)

CODE	FIRST-CONSIDERATION DIAGNOSES
1-8	Pedophilia, Schizoid Personality Disorder, Acute Schizophrenia (relatively rare), Affective Disorder, Borderline Personality Disorder
1-9	Masked Depression, Post-Traumatic Stress Disorder, Central Nervous System Impairment (rare), Dependent Personality Disorder (rare), Sexual Masochism (rare)
2-1	Anxiety Disorder, Conversion Disorder, Chronic Alcohol Intoxication, Female Psychosexual Dysfunction, Somatization
2-3	Female Psychosexual Dysfunction, Depression (especially for females), Generalized Anxiety Disorder, Histrionic Personality Disorder, Panic Disorder, Affective Disorder
2-4	Acute Alcohol Intoxication, Schizophrenia, Secondary Psychopathy, Antisocial Personality Disorder, Suicidal Potential, Unsocialized Nonaggressive Conduct Disorder, Adjustment Disorder
2-5	Passive-Aggressive Personality Disorder, Dependent Personality Disorder
2-6	Paranoid Personality Disorder, Major Depression, Paranoid Schizophrenia, Histrionic Personality Disorder, Borderline Personalty Disorder (rare)
2-7	Agoraphobia, Avoidant Personality Disorder, Dependent Personality Disorder, Major Depression, Bipolar Disorder, Depressive Episode, Dysthymic Disorder, Chronic Alcohol Intoxication, Factitious Disorder, Generalized Anxiety Disorder, Identity Disorder, Obsessive-Compulsive Disorder, Psychogenic Pain Disorder, Possible Toxic Addiction to Pain Killers, Schizotypal Personality Disorder, Sexual Masochism, Stuporous Catatonic Schizophrenia, Suicidal Potential, Zoophilia
2-8	Depressive Episode, Possible Bipolar or Cyclothymic Disorder, Suicidal, Central Nervous System Impairment, Post-Traumatic Stress Disorder, Generalized Anxiety Disorder, Panic Disorder, Explosive Disorder, Schizoaffective Disorder
2-9	Bipolar Affective Disorder, Central Nervous System Impairment
2-0	Depressive Episode, Possible Bipolar or Cyclothymic Disorder, Schizoid Personality Disorder, Avoidant Disorder
3-1	Compulsive Personality Disorder, Conversion Disorder, Hypochondriasis, Malingering, Faking-Good
3-2	Depressive Episode, Possible Bipolar or Cyclothymic Disorder, Female Psychosexual Dysfunction, Histrionic Personality Disorder
3-4	Histrionic, Borderline, Passive-Aggressive and Avoidant Personality Disorders, Dissociative Disorder, Intermittent Explosive Disorder, Manic Episode (rare), Pedophilia, Psychogenic Amnesia, Voyeurism, Substance Abuse

3-6 Paranoia, Paranoid Personality Disorder, Paranoid Schizophrenia, Somatization, Affective Disorder

3-7 Depersonalization Disorder, Somatization, Anxiety Disorder

3-8 Multiple Personality, Pedophilia, Schizophrenia (rare), Somatization, Possible Psychosis, Affective Disorder

3-9 Somatization, Bipolary Disorder, Conversion Disorder, Explosive Personality Disorder (rare), Possible Psychosis, Histrionic Personality Disorder (rare), Panic Disorder, Passive-Aggressive Personality Disorder (rare), Somatization

4-1 Hypochondriasis, Social Phobia, Chronic Alcohol Intoxication, Somatization

4-2 Acute Alcohol Intoxication, Primary Psychopath, Antisocial Personality, Schiozphrenia, Secondary Psychopath, Antisocial Personality, Suicidal Potential, Unsocialized Nonaggressive Conduct Disorder

4-3 Aggression Potential, Explosive Disorder of Impulse Control, Passive-Aggressive Personality Disorder, Pedophilia, Rape, Voyeurism

4-5 Narcissistic and Passive-Aggressive Personality Dissorders. Exhibitionism, Homosexuality, Opiate Abuse, Aggression (in females)

4-6 Substance Abuse (especially Amphetamine Disorder), Oppositional Personality Disorder, Chronic Alcohol Intoxication, Paranoid Schizophrenia, Passive-Aggressive Personality Disorder, Somatization (rare), Intermittent Explosive Disorder, Depression

4-7 Chronic Alcohol Intoxication, Bipolar and Cyclothymic Disorder, Substance Abuse

4-8 Exhibitionism, Pedophilia, Primary Psychopathy, Schizoid Personality, Antisocial Personality, Borderline Personality, Pyromania, Rape, Schizophrenia, Sexual Sadism, Unsocialized Aggressive Conduct Disorder

4-9 Amphetamine Disorder, Chronic Alcohol Intoxication, Pathological Gambling, Rape, Secondary Psychopathy, Antisocial Personality, Histrionic Personality, Sexual Sadism, Socialized Nonaggressive Conduct Disorder

5-1 Transsexualism

5-3 Transvestism

5-7 Schizoid, Passive-Aggressive Personality Disorder, Anxiety Reactions

6-1 Paranoid Schizophrenia

6-2 Borderline Personality Disorder, Shared Paranoid Disorder

6-3 Paranoia, Paranoid Schizophrenia, Paranoid Personality Disorder, Somatization

6-4 Chronic Alcohol Intoxication, Paranoia, Paranoid Schizophrenia, Passive-Aggressive Personality Disorder, Shared Paranoid Disorder

TABLE 1.1 First-Consideration Diagnoses and Two-Point Codes (cont.)

CODE	FIRST-CONSIDERATION DIAGNOSES
6-7	Obsessive-Compulsive Disorder, Multiple Phobias, Anxiety Reactions, Affective Disorder, Avoidant Disorder
6-8	Aggressive Acting-Out, Polydrug Abuse, Paranoid Schizophrenia, Central Nervous System Impairment, Borderline Personality Disorder, Schizoaffective Disorder
6-9	Central Nervous System Impairment, Paranoid Schizophrenia
7-1	Somatization
7-2	Agorphobia, Avoidant Personality Disorder, Dependent Personality Disorder, Depressive Episode, Bipolar or Cyclothymic Disorder, Dysthymic Disorder, Chronic Alcohol Intoxication, Obsessive-Compulsive Disorder, Post-Traumatic Stress and Adjustment Disorder, Sexual Masochism, Suicidal Potential
7-3	Somatization
7-4	Chronic Alcohol Intoxication
7-8	Borderline Personality Disorder, Substance Abuse, Brief Reactive Disorder, Depression, Suicidal Attempts, Obsessive-Compulsive Disorder, Schizophrenia, Schizophreniform Disorder
7-0	Anxiety Disorders, Agoraphobia, Avoidant Personality Disorder
8-1	Pedophilia, Schizophrenia, Schizotypal Personality Disorder
8-2	Depression, Schizoaffective Disorder
8-3	Multiple Personality, Pedophilia, Somatization
8-4	Paranoid Schizophrenia, Pedophilia, Primary Psychopathy, Antisocial Personality, Rape, Unsocialized or Socialized Aggressive Conduct Disorder
8-6	Central Nervous System Impairment, Schizophrenia, Paranoid Schizophrenia, Primary Psychopathy, Antisocial Personality
8-7	Borderline Personality Disorder, Brief Reactive Psychosis, Depression, Obsessive-Compulsive Disorder, Schizophreniform Disorder
8-9	Acting-Out in General, Polydrug Abuse, Agitated Catatonic Schizophrenia, Central Nervous System Impairment, Depression, Schizoaffective Disorder, Disorganized Schizophrenia, Mania, Paranoid Schizophrenia
8-0	Schizoid and Avoidant Personality Disorders, Schizophrenia
9-1	Central Nervous System Impairment (rare), Dependent Personality Disorder (rare), Sexual Masochism (rare)
9-2	Central Nervous System Impairment, Bipolar Affective Disorder
9-3	Conversion Disorder, Histrionic Personality Disorder (rare), Panic Disorder, Somatization (rare)

9-4   Chronic Alcohol Intoxication, Secondary Psychopathy, Antisocial Personality

9-6   Central Nervous System Impairment, Manic Episode, Bipolar or Dysthymic Disorder, Paranoid Schizophrenia

9-8   Central Nervous System Impairment, Depression, Schizoaffective Disorder, Disorganized Schizophrenia, Mania, Schizoaffective Disorder, Bipolar or Dysthymic Disorder, Paranoid Schizophrenia

0-2   Depression

0-7   Agoraphobia

■   The Cattell 16 PF Test

The Sixteen Personality Factor Questionnaire, developed primarily by Raymond Cattell and Herbert Eber and referred to here as the 16 PF, was devised to tap a wide range of the client's ongoing personality functioning. It is designed more for personality traits and conflicts than is the MMPI, which is oriented primarily toward categories of psychopathology. The 16 PF gives scores on sixteen dimensions that Cattell derived through a factor analysis of a huge number of personality descriptors; they were then validated on a wide variety of abnormal and normal client groups.

There are six forms of the 16 PF. The first five forms are designated by the letters A through E. The sixth is a short form (128 items), which is Part 1 of the Clinical Analysis Questionnaire (Krug, 1980). As a result, it is not quite as reliable as forms A or B. Form A is the one most commonly used. It is composed of 187 items, which means there are approximately ten to thirteen items for each of the sixteen scales. The client's response to an item affects only one scale on the 16 PF, whereas in the MMPI a single response may affect more than one scale. The Institute of Personnel and Ability Testing (IPAT) (the present owners of the test) recommend that both forms A and B, which are similar in length, be administered to allow for greater validity. In practice, however, most clinicians usually administer only form A.

Forms C and D are much shorter than A and B and are useful in situations that require quick screening. It takes the average client about thirty minutes to complete forms C and D, whereas it takes about fifty minutes to complete either A or B. Form E is intended for those clients who read below the sixth-grade level. Unfortunately, the reliability and validity data on form E are not as strong as for forms A and B.

The 16 PF allows three response choices, with "undecided" commonly available as an option. This, along with the fact that it is much shorter and does not ask questions that are so personal, makes the 16 PF more acceptable to most clients than the MMPI. As with the MMPI, it is helpful to encourage the testees to give the most accurate response they can and to answer every question, if possible. They should also be warned against spending extensive time mulling over an answer and be asked to give their first clear response.

The 16 PF can be either machine- or hand-scored, and IPAT now provides a service that gives a computer-scored and -interpreted report on the 16 PF. To score the 16 PF by hand, the examiner uses two templates provided by IPAT. If the client's mark appears in the hole on the template, the appropriate number of that hole, either 2 or 1, is added to give a sum that is the raw score for that subscale. These raw data are converted into standard scores, termed "stens," a shortening of the phrase "standard ten." These stens, or standard scores, range from 1 to 10 on the answer sheet, have a mean of 5.5 (the middle of the answer sheet), and a standard deviation of 2. Thus, a sten score of 1 or 10 is considered quite extreme; scores 2, 3, 8, or 9 are significantly deviant; a score of 4 or 7 is mildly deviant from the norm; and a sten score of 5 or 6 is average. A sten score of 8, 9, or 10 is labeled "high" in this book, whereas a score of 1, 2, or 3 is "low." "Moderately high" generally refers to a score of 7 or 8, and scores of 3 or 4 are termed "moderately low." If the phrase "higher on scale" is used, it simply designates a sten score of 6 or above; "lower on scale" designates a score of 5 or lower. To convert raw data into sten scores, it is necessary to use the appropriate Tabular Supplement, based on the demographics of the client. IPAT provides tabular supplements on such groups as college students, the general population, and high school juniors and seniors. Along with the subscales, the 16 PF can be scored for faking-good or faking-bad (the reader is referred to the section in this text on malingering for more details).

Cattell 16 PF Factors

SCALE A

Scale A—which Cattell referred to as Cyclothymia versus Schizothymia—generally differentiates between people who are reserved and aloof (low on scale A) and those who are sociable and warm. High As are more gregarious and trusting, less prone to cyclical moodiness, and less vulnerable to criticism. However, very high A scores may be associated with mania and/or difficulties in impulse control.

Most of the adjectives associated with low As are fairly negative, although such persons are often more compulsive and precise and therefore more productive in certain areas. They are often more effective in tasks that require working alone and/or generating their own structure. They are self-disclosing and generate rapport only if they feel comfortable in a particular relationship. Persons who score very low are more likely to earn adjectives like "schizoid" and "introverted," as well as "obnoxious," and frequently display the "burnt-child" syndrome regarding interpersonal relationships (Karson and O'Dell, 1976).

☐   SCALE B

Scale B was originally labeled as High General Intelligence (appropriately enough, the high end of the scale) versus Mental Defectiveness. In actuality, low scores do not necessarily indicate low mental ability. For one thing, there are only thirteen items on this scale, and the scoring is binary rather than the "2, 1, or 0" scoring applied in the other scales, so any precise assertions of validity are unrealistic.

Low scores may be associated with random or distorted answering sets, attentional difficulties, impulsiveness, or a lack of ability to persist on a task. Low scores should only be a major concern if there is good reason to believe the person was trying to do well. High scores (8–10) generally indicate at least average – probably higher – intellectual ability.

☐   SCALE C

Scale C is considered to reflect dissatisfied and labile emotionality (the low end of the continuum), as opposed to emotional stability or ego strength. It taps emotional stability, maturity, and a low threshold for irritability and upset and consequent neurotic fatigue. Overall, scale C is probably the single most important predictor in the 16 PF for emotional stability. Most neurotics show low C scores; criminals are relatively higher here. Persons low on C may be faking-bad, while those scoring high may have a high motivation distortion or a faking-good score (Winder et al., 1975; Krug, 1978).

Low C scorers need to have their self-esteem improved and some control over emotional lability generated before they can make any strides with insight therapy. If there is no distortion, a higher C score offers a good prognosis for psychotherapy. There is some evidence that C will rise following a successful therapeutic intervention. In general, high Cs have learned to channel their emotionality into productive and integrated behaviors, as opposed to impulsively dissipating it.

☐   SCALE E

(The reader might wonder why there is no scale D in the 16 PF. In Cattell's original list of factors, D was referred to as Excitability, and it was not thought to be a major differentiating issue in adults, so it is only found on the Cattell tests for children.)

Scale E primarily assesses an assertive or dominance factor, as well as lesser contributions from a willingness to conform to authority. A high score on E would indicate an assertive and tough individual who has strong needs to be independent (which may mask real feelings of inferiority). However, probably because of the conflicts over role expectations, high scores in females have extra factor-loadings from attention-getting, social poise, and possible hypochondriacal aspects. High E connotes an assertive personality style, and, though it is not always associated with leadership ability, established leaders do tend to be higher on this score. Persons who are shy are low on E, whereas those who are narcissistic, chronically angry, or inappropriately assertive are higher on E.

☐   SCALE F

Scale F is denoted as Surgency versus Desurgency. This may be better described as sober introspective seriousness (the low end of the scale) versus an alert, enthusiastic, and even happy-go-lucky style. Along with scale A, scale F is an important predictor of extroversion-introversion. Persons who show bipolar affective disorders may swing markedly on this factor. Success in psychotherapy raises F, as does the initial effect of substance abuse. Hysteric individuals and those with sexual, personality, and impulsivity disorders usually score higher on this scale, whereas persons with depression, phobias, and introverted patterns score lower.

The F score drops rather markedly between the ages of eighteen and thirty-five years, and there is some indication that F rises slightly with an increased metabolic rate. Although there is a slight correlation of an above-average F score with the holding of a leadership position, this does not necessarily connote *effective* leadership because the F score may refer to impulsivity. Persons in leadership positions who are high on F often need associates who can take the plans they generate and bring them to fruition.

☐   SCALE G

Scale G denotes a person who is demanding, casual in moral standards, and potentially undependable (the low end of the continuum) versus a conscientious and responsible individual. High-G individuals are guardians of the moral order, cautious in decisions, and set in their thinking and biases. Markedly low scores are found in self-disclosing psychopaths, and even moderate scores suggest a person who is likely to disregard obligations. However, since this measures adherence to subgroup standards as well, certain criminals do score high here. Rebellious adolescents particularly score low here. Scale G measures the more overt aspects of morality, and other scores, such as an O, would further indicate whether this was a thoroughgoing personality trait. There is a definitive correlation with age and socioeconomic class; the older the person and the higher the socioeconomic status, the higher the score on scale G.

□   ## SCALE H

Scale H, termed by Cattell as Threctia vs. Parmia, denotes a person who is shy, constricted emotionally, and threat-sensitive (the low end of the continuum), versus one who is more adventurous, thick-skinned, and friendly. Cattell suggests that this is an innate (genetically determined) factor. A low H score indicates a person with an overresponsive sympathetic nervous system, whereas a higher-H person is more likely to be seen as lazy, especially during the developmental years. Very low H scores are found in introverted personalities. This is one of the factors that predict a basic schizoid temperament, as well as a chronic schizophrenic adjustment. Since H connotes threat sensitivity, it should be low in such disorders as agoraphobia and panic disorder. There is some evidence that low-H individuals are more likely to suffer ulcers.

□   ## SCALE I

Though scale I was labeled by Cattell as Harria versus Premsia, the more common connotations have to do with a person who takes a tough and realistic view of life, is inclined to be self-sufficient, and is not highly responsive to pain or conflict (the low end of the continuum), as opposed to a person who is sensitive, dependent, and possibly effeminate or demanding. Persons who are not introspective and reflective tend to score lower here. Though scale I has not been found to be highly associated with psychopathology, psychotics, on the average, are slightly lower than normals on this factor. One area of pathology in which scale I is predictive is in stress-related disorders (commonly associated with high scores on both scales E and I).

There are age and sex differences on I: Older people tend to score higher than the very young, and women consistently score higher than men. At the extreme high point, the clinician finds women who have stayed within the traditional female role, almost to a stereotypical degree. Macho men score very low on I. In general, this continuum reflects William James's traditional distinction between tough-minded and tender-minded people; those people in the tender-minded subgroup (high on I) generally wish to avoid conflict and have high esthetic interests. Being low on I does not necessarily help a person adapt to conflict, however, possibly because the tough-minded continuum is a more brittle adjustment and therefore less adaptive to certain types of stress.

☐   SCALE L

Scale L, denoted by Cattell as Protension versus Relaxed Security, is often interpreted as suspicious jealousy and emotional distancing as opposed to a relaxed trust and openness to the world (the lower end of the continuum). "Protension" is a term derived from the words "projection" and "(inner) tension," and, as is implied, paranoid concerns are often reflected here. Persons high on the scale tend to be cynical, to take elitist views, and to insist that their ideas be heard; in the latter sense, they reflect some of the dominance characteristics also attributed to scale E. Persons high on L are not primarily schizoid, though their personality easily results in rejection by others, so interpersonal isolation is secondary.

A major issue is how a person channels these traits into vocational and interpersonal interests. For example, eminent researchers often score higher on L because the characteristics of cynicism, isolation, and confidence in their intellectual superiority serve them well.

The problems of the high-L person are that they are often rejected, they may have too high a level of inner tension, their defenses may be too brittle, and they may not have enough access to other persons as emotional resources. Also, high scores predict general illness, especially coronary artery disease. On the other hand, low-L persons in general are emotionally healthy, though they are subject to interpersonal manipulation and can get heavily involved in dependency relationships.

☐   SCALE M

Scale M, originally denoted as Praxenia versus Autia, is now more commonly known as conventional practicality versus unconventional imagination (the high end of the scale). Persons high on M have well-developed imaginations, easily consider unconventional options, and more easily dissociate than others. There is some evidence that very-high-M persons alternate between outbursts of rumination-generated activity and rather placid periods when they seem to be totally wrapped up in themselves. In that sense, this scale is a measure of introversion. High M is also significantly and paradoxically correlated with both creativity and accident-proneness (e.g., the absent-minded professor).

Persons with somatoform disorders are lower on M than are those with anxiety-based disorders. The assumed explanation for this difference is that persons with anxiety-based disorders are keeping their conflicts in higher levels of consciousness, thereby experiencing anxiety, whereas the somatoform disorders reflect a denial of inner conflict.

☐   SCALE N

Scale N is termed the Artlessness (lower end of the scale) versus Shrewdness continuum. Persons on the high end are socially alert, though a bit calculating and aloof, and may show sophisticated anxiety or concerns about success in relation to high internal standards. At very high levels, individuals are Machiavellian, whereas if scores are too low, they manifest extreme naiveté about other people's motives. People on the low end are socially clumsy, overtrusting, and have rather simplistic interests. Psychotics and neurotics on the average score lower on N.

☐   ## SCALE O

Scale O is generally labeled placid confidence (the low end of the scale) versus an insecure proneness to guilt. Persons high on this scale are avoidant of stimulation, oversensitive, show a strong sense of morality and duty, and are prone to anxiety-based disorders. A high O score occasionally reflects situational depression. On the other hand, scale O is low in individuals who are psychopathic or who are more likely to act out their conflicts. Along with scale G, O taps what Freudians have referred to as "superego."

☐   ## SCALE Q_1

Scale Q_1 denotes cautious conservatism (the low end of the scale) versus a free-thinking and experimenting approach to life. Like the other Q scales, this factor has not been totally validated in all types of data collection, though most clinicians find the Q scores to be extremely helpful. The interested reader is referred to Cattell (1973) for the subtle distinctions he used to discriminate the Q scales from the previously mentioned scales.

Persons high on the Q_1 scale are rather critical of others but tend to be analytical and liberal in thought patterns. Depending on vocational and interpersonal situations, the high-Q_1 person can have difficulties with authority figures or establishment rules and hence can be disruptive in a highly structured environment. A high-Q_1 person can be viewed as an intellectualized aggressor, with an implicit potential for loss of impulse control. People quite low on this scale are colorless individuals who, rather than being rejected by others, are often simply ignored. Liberal (high Q_1) versus conservative political beliefs also affect this scale.

☐   ## SCALE Q_2

Scale Q_2 taps basic dependency (the low end of the scale) as opposed to a self-sufficient resourcefulness. Persons low on this scale show little initiative, need much more social approval, and easily move into the dependent role in relationships. In that sense, Q_2 reflects a more basic dependency factor than scale G, as G taps more of an adherence to group standards.

☐   SCALE Q_3

Scale Q_3 is denoted as low self-concept integration (the low end of the scale) versus a controlled approach to life, with an emphasis on a strong will. In clinical terms, high scores on Q_3 can reflect a great need to control conflict and anxiety that threaten to break through brittle modes of coping, or, as Karson and O'Dell (1976) so aptly state, there is a high need to bind anxiety into symptomatology or avoidance patterns. On the other hand, a low score may reflect a lack of impulse control or lack of ability to structure one's psychological world effectively. People high on scale Q_3 persist in tasks and keep their commitments, yet they are also inclined toward suppression of anger and obsessive and compulsive concerns.

☐   SCALE Q_4

Scale Q_4 is generally termed low anxiety and tension (the low end of the scale) versus high tension and anxiety. Q_4 is the best 16 PF measure of situational anxiety, and hence there is reasonable fluctuation over time. It measures a person's frustrations in attempting to cope with life. If scale O is also high, it suggests an insecure and anxious quality that persists beyond the situational parameters. Scale Q_4 is easily distorted by faking-good or -bad.

People quite high on Q_4 are likely to have experienced rejection by others, have a high level of frustrated sexuality, and are prone to both neurotic and psychosomatic disorders. Once emotional disorder crystallizes into a psychosomatic pattern, Q_4 is lower. Scale Q_4 is generally higher for the person who has continued with more conscious anxiety, such as neurosis.

■   **16 PF Scale Interrelationship Interpretations**

If a person is high on scale A, it is important also to consider the score on Q_2; if that is low, the person has a particularly high need for interpersonal feedback and may be petulant and querulous if it is not provided. High scores on both A and F show a gregarious and friendly extrovert, whereas low scores on A and F with a high score on L are central to the hostile and suspicious introvert pattern.

When a high scale B is combined with high scores on scales E and Q_3, there is likely to be much intellectualized hostility, with consequent rejection by others. It is also worthwhile to look at scale M in relation to scale B because this suggests to what degree intellectual competence is channeled into imaginative, creative activities rather than into more practical and immediate plans.

If a low scale C is found with a high H and lower G and Q_3 scores, a psychopathic quality is likely. But if the low C is associated with a high O and Q_4 and a low H, introversion and anxiety disorders are likely. When scales C, F, and A are low, particularly if associated with a moderately low H, look for a withdrawn, shy, and fearful individual. In general, a high O combined with a low C points to a deterioration in competency to adapt to environmental stressors.

As noted earlier, a high I score combined with a high E score predicts the development of stress-based disorders, especially if L and Q_4 are also high. A conflict arises in that the individual is both sensitive and dominant at the same time and is torn between the need to look assertive and yet to actuate a desire to reach out emotionally to other people. The competitiveness inherent in the high E blocks the needs of the high I. Where both E and L are quite low, a passive-aggressive personality, with passive-dependent mechanisms, is often noted.

Very low A in combination with low E is characteristic of people who have experienced rejection or abuse in interpersonal or developmental relationships and hence are avoidant of engaging in new relationships. High scores on E, L, and Q_1 particularly predict hostility, and the clinician should look to scores on scales B, M, and Q_3 to see whether this is likely to be intellectualized aggression or whether it is expected to manifest itself in controlled plans or actualized retribution.

When a high F is combined with low scores on G and Q_3, and especially if scores on N and H are high, impulsive irresponsibility is expected. A high F and low G combined with a high Q_1 and low Q_2 may indicate a young adult in severe conflict over identity development. Analogously, high O combined with low G is found in persons who portray themselves as rebellious and free-thinking but who experience much guilt whenever they act out this behavior. This is different from the pattern of low G and low O, consistently found in psychopathic individuals who show little if any guilt.

Persons with high H in combination with high Q_1 are critical in interpersonal relationships, yet avoid the risks incumbent on taking responsibility for or acting on their criticism. When the isolated suspiciousness of the high L is combined with low scores on H and A, a paranoid-schizoid component is probable and warrants further scrutiny. As noted, high I and high E are related to stress-based disorders. Conversely, low scores here predict an individual who appears passive yet may be tough at the core and able to resist stress reasonably well.

If L is low and I and M are high, look for a person who avoids interaction with the world by escaping into fantasy, whereas if I and M are low and L and N are high, look for a shrewd, cold, and pragmatically plotting individual. If a low L is accompanied by a low E, one may have an individual who is both very dependent and manipulative—a person who takes on a "poor-me" role and yet manipulates other people in a passive-dependent fashion. High Ns, particularly when they also score low on Q_1, are interpersonally provocative, and, if scale B is also high, this provocativeness may be used in an intellectual manner. Interestingly enough, a high M score generally predicts recidivism in criminal populations.

High scores on N along with a low score on G and high scores on E and H predict a con man, a person who manipulates others through a combination of assertiveness and shrewdness. The quality of the conning may be predicted by scores on M and B.

Persons high on N, E, and Q_1 and low on G are particularly difficult to work with and cause a variety of troubles in interpersonal relationships. If they are also high on B and L, their disruption is more difficult to detect. Similarly, high Q_1 and Q_3 scores, along with a moderately high G score, predict compulsiveness; this is amplified into obsessive-compulsiveness to the degree that B and M are also high.

As already noted, low scores on G and Q_3 generally indicate low impulse control and a propensity for characterological disorders; the problem is compounded if C is also low. In addition, Q_4, the measure par excellence of situational anxiety, takes on more ominous connotations if it is found along with high O and low C scores, as this predicts a more long-term disorder. When high Q_4 is associated with high M and I and low G and Q_3 scores, substance abuse is probable.

Overall, profiles that clearly slope right (low A through a high Q_4) are more indicative of psychopathology. Those that clearly slope left (higher A, B, and C down through lower Q scores) are indicative of psychological health (Krug, 1981).

Before proceeding into discussion of the diagnostic and treatment recommendations relevant to specific diagnoses, it should be noted that on occasion the 16 PF and MMPI profiles on an individual client may appear to be somewhat contradictory. It is rare that any direct contradictions occur, as the two tests do not measure exactly the same areas. However, if there is an apparent contradition, the validity scores for each test should be checked. If all is in order, the secondary adjective in the 16-PF-scale descriptors should be given more weight to see if that produces a better meld. If there is still no resolution, which is unlikely, greater weight should be given to the MMPI because it has been more thoroughly researched and has more items per scale.

CHAPTER 2

Substance Use Disorders

Modern society provides an increasing number of substances that are abused (Heath, 1986), and this is reflected in the DSM-III-R. The drugs that are commonly abused, such as heroin, barbiturates, amphetamines, cocaine, and marijuana, are given separate subcategories in the DSM-III-R. Caffeine and tobacco use disorders are also included, the latter being especially important as a precursor to other forms of chronic substance abuse (Newcomb and Bentler, 1988).

There are many narrowly defined substance use categories in the DSM-III-R, so many that it would be impossible to discuss each one here, especially since many of them are not often applied. The overall diagnoses of "abuse" and "dependence," as they are applied in the DSM-III-R to each of the various substances throughout this chapter, are detailed in the first specific substance to be discussed: alcohol. However, this section will first note some characteristics of substance use disorders in general.

■ ## MMPI

Trethvithick and Hosch (1978) have noted that persons with substance use disorders in general are typically elevated on MMPI scales 4, 8, 2, and 7, and others note that 9 is often high, too (Craig, 1988; Johnson et al., 1980; Patalano, 1980). These elevations reflect the confusion, distress, and depression that are found in addition to the sociopathic traits of drug abusers. Scores on scale 9 will vary, depending on the person's need to affiliate with others and whether they are inclined toward the use of depressants or stimulants in response to their own typical physiological patterns. The rare spike-9 profile is indicative of drug abuse associated with antisocial patterns (King and Kelley, 1977).

An MMPI content scale that is particularly useful in diagnosing substance abuse disorders, especially problems with alcohol, heroin, heavy marijuana use, and polydrug use, is the MacAndrew Alcoholism Scale (Craig, 1988; MacAndrew, 1965; Fowler, 1976, 1981; Wolfson and Erbaugh, 1984). This scale is also useful with adolescents in predicting later abuse patterns. Setting a cutoff point (raw scores) at 24 picks up about 80 percent of abusers and potential abusers; a score of 27 very strongly suggests an addiction problem of some sort; and with a score over 30, addiction is nearly certain. Since blacks and obese persons tend to score a bit higher on this scale, adjusting the cutoff two points higher is suggested for these clients; females tend to score slightly lower than males, so reducing the cutoff score by a point (with adolescent females, two points) is recommended (Wolfson and Erbaugh, 1984). Streiner and Miller (1981) provide guidelines for prorating short or incomplete MacAndrew scale protocols.

■ 16 PF

In the typical testing situation, when disposition is at least one of the considerations, individuals with substance use disorders tend to score high on the H, I, M, and Q_4 scales and low on F, which reflects their imagination and their disdain for typical societal standards, as well as their distress. They are likely to be moderately high on scale L, reflecting again their concern about arrest and the eventual disposition of their situation. They tend to be moderately low on both scales G and Q_3, reflecting again their disdain for the standard mores. They are also lower on scales B, C, and E, and if their distress is relatively high, they are also likely to show a lower score on scale F.

■ Other Test-Response Patterns

Clinicians should of course look for physical signs of substance abuse (needle marks, abscesses over veins, constriction of pupils) and make sure that adequate physiological screening, such as urinalysis, has been carried out (Craig, 1988). If the substance abuse has not been long-term or if there is little in the way of allied psychopathology, WAIS-R scores are in the normal range and do not show marked subtest deviation (Hewett and Martin, 1980). In some instances, when clients are tested after having ingested low doses of cocaine or amphetamines, they do slightly better on certain tasks, such as digit symbol, that require speed and role learning (Washton and Gold, 1987). If individuals have been abusing drugs for some time, they do poorly on tests that reflect school achievement, such as information and arithmetic, though they still do reasonably well on vocabulary. If they have begun to develop confusion, which occurs in the polydrug abuse syndrome, they are likely to do poorly on the coding and the block design test. They do best in such subtests as similarities, picture completion, and comprehension.

Scores on the MCMI of 75 or higher on B or T indicate the presence of some drug or alcohol abuse, while scores of 85 indicate a more severe abuse problem. During periods of intoxication by drugs or alcohol, the severe symptom syndromes SS and PP may become elevated and scale 5 is also high.

■   Treatment Options

A variety of treatment techniques have been used in substance use disorders (Brown, 1985; Ellis and Dryden, 1987). Common to most therapeutic situations involving substance abuse are (1) breaking through the denial, often massive denial, that there is a problem, (2) bolstering the often-wavering motivation, and (3) avoidance of manipulations and rationalizations. Aversive conditioning has been favored for working on the specific habits that form the matrix of substance abuse, as well as in helping develop an aversive response to the drug itself. It is also argued that relaxation training is helpful for substance abusers, particularly those who look toward the tranquilizers or depressant drugs. Where the disorder appears to be an escape response from fears and phobias, systematic desensitization is helpful. Analogously, assertive training may be included in the treatment package if social inadequacy is evident, as is often the case in substance dependence.

In the initial stages of treatment, when the persons are being detoxified in a controlled setting, token economies are helpful in getting them to organize their behavior in some effective fashion. With regard to the cognitive behavioral treatments, many feel that covert sensitization is especially useful for the substance abuse disorders (Cautela and Wall, 1980). Within the psychoanalytic therapies, it is felt that the Adlerian approaches have the most to offer for this particular pattern (Gedo, 1986). As the person progresses away from drug abuse, the process and existential therapies take on a particularly important role (Teyber, 1988). Certainly the critical issue in treatment success in any substance abuse pattern is the client's decision to change. Since the experience-seeking subfactor of the stimulation-seeking variable particularly characterizes the substance abuser (Zuckerman et al., 1980), the therapist needs to help the client channel this need into more legitimate and constructive pursuits. Family therapy is also usually necessary (Phares, 1988).

■   Alcohol Use Disorder

☐   DSM-III-R CONSIDERATIONS

The DSM-III-R classifies the drug use disorders either into the organic mental disorders to reflect their effect on the central nervous system or else as a psychoactive substance use disorder that emphasizes the maladaptive behavior caused by taking the substances. In an individual case, a diagnosis from both sections could be appropriate.

The subcategory diagnosis of alcoholism—the organic alcohol disorders and the substance use alcohol disorders—are very specific. The problem is that alcoholics may run the gamut of behaviors appropriate to each of several diagnostic categories in each division—and in a very short period of time. Thus, any particular observed behavior is contingent upon when the diagnostician happens to see the alcoholic. It would be absurd to try to detail these subcategories here, as it would require an inordinate amount of space. However, the important differentiation between substance abuse and substance dependence is presented.

Psychoactive Substance Abuse (e.g., Alcohol Abuse, 305.00) requires that (1) the substance be abused rather often for at least one month, (2) the criteria for Psychoactive Substance Dependence for this substance has never been met before, and (3) there be evidence of either (a) recurrent use in physically hazardous situations, e.g., driving while intoxicated, or (b) continued use despite awareness that such use is causing or increasing persistent or recurrent psychological, physical, social, or occupational problems.

Psychoactive Substance Dependence (e.g., Alcohol Dependence, 303.90) requires that this disorder has occurred for one month, or at least repeatedly over a longer period of time, and that at least three of the following possible manifestations of this disorder be evident: (1) one or more efforts, or at least a persisting desire, to cut down or stop, (2) significant time or effort spent to get, take, or recover from the substance, (3) an increase in the amount of substance taken or the time while taking it, (4) reduction or stoppage of important social, recreational, or occupational activities, (5) frequent intoxication or withdrawal symptoms that occur during important role obligations or that put one in physical danger, (6) continued use even while aware that it causes or exaggerates another significant physical, social, or psychological problem, (7) marked tolerance for (at least a 50 percent increase needed to get original effects) or lessened effects with the same amount, (8) characteristic withdrawal symptoms, or (9) use of the substance to relieve withdrawal.

☐   OTHER BEHAVIORAL CONSIDERATIONS

The psychological euphoria from alcohol is functionally a toxic response (Donovan, 1986). Alcohol is not digested, but absorbed through the stomach and intestinal walls and metabolized in the liver by the process of oxidation. In this process, alcohol fuses with oxygen, and the resulting pure grain alcohol, or ethanol, is converted by enzymes to acetaldehyde, which is further broken down to acetic acid (vinegar). The vinegar is then broken down by enzymes into water and carbon dioxide, which are passed out of the body. The liver can only break down approximately one ounce of 100 proof whiskey per hour, assuming the person is of average weight. Any excess that cannot be broken down directly affects the brain, causing intoxication. Interestingly, even when males and females are of equal weight, this process is still slower in females.

Pharmacologically, alcohol acts as a depressant that first inhibits the higher brain centers and only later depresses the lower brain centers (Donovan, 1986). The resultant decrease in control of overt behavior has led to the mistaken belief that alcohol is a stimulant. With continued alcohol intake, there is a loss of the more complex cognitive and perceptual abilities and eventually a loss in simple memory and motor coordination.

It is interesting that part of the strength of the effect depends on whether people are getting drunk or sobering up. Those who are sobering up perform better on short-term memory and perception tasks than those who have the same blood level of alcohol but who are getting high.

Long-term alcohol abuse is likely to result in central nervous system dysfunction, or organicity, especially in older alcoholics (see Chapter 14 for relevant diagnostic considerations). Also, most researchers now believe that this dysfunction is not simply a result of B-vitamin deficiencies from the poor diet that often accompanies chronic alcoholism, but at least in part is caused by the effects of alcohol per se (McKim, 1986). The reader is referred to the important work of researchers (e.g., see review by Marlatt et al., 1988) who have indicated that the *belief* that one has ingested alcohol is often more critical than whether one has actually done so. These researchers show that both aggression and sexual behavior are highly dependent on the belief system of those individuals who use alcohol, and many times the alcohol is a learned excuse for acting-out behavior in these areas (Blane and Leonard, 1987).

Fabian and Parsons (1983) addressed the question of whether cognitive deficits (decrements in problem-solving, abstracting, and spatial-perceptual skills, but with intact verbal intelligence) found in detoxified alcoholics diminish over time. Results indicated that most, but not all, cognitive deficits continued to show up, but at reduced levels, at follow-up (1.8 years later), with the greatest and perhaps the earliest improvement occurring on complex abstracting tests. Continued deficits in the four-years-sober alcoholics were most notable on perceptual-motor tasks, such as WAIS-R Digit Symbol and the Trail-Making Test. Recovery of most functions for which recovery is possible occurs roughly within the first year of sobriety. Thus, differential recovery among cognitive abilities was noted over a four-year period: Some complex cognitive abilities appear to return to normal levels, while others (perceptual-motor speed, for example) remain lower than normal.

☐   MMPI

Since chronic alcohol intoxication refers to one behavior pattern within an overall personality, and since it can be generated by diverse trains of personality development, what one might expect on various tests is even less clear than with a number of the other disorders that will be discussed later. As noted earlier, the MacAndrew Alcoholism Scale is useful here (MacAndrew, 1965; Wolfson and Erbaugh, 1984). Holland and Watson (1980) reported elevations above the 65-T level on F, 2, 4, 7, and 8 in their sample of MMPIs from inpatient alcoholics. They compared this group to neurotic, schizophrenic, and brain-damaged groups and found that the only marked differences from the other groups in general were the alcoholics' low scores on L, K, and 0. They assert that this is indicative of the introversion, somatization, and depression that are characteristic of this group. The 8-7 alcoholic is most likely to be psychotic and/or depressed (Svanum and Dallas, 1981; Conley, 1981).

The classic high 4-9 pattern that characterizes the psychopath is commonly found in outpatient alcoholics, though it is usually accompanied by a higher F score (Craig, 1988; Faulstitch et al., 1985; Svanum and Dallas, 1981). When referring to the more acute alcoholic, people like Conley (1981), Johnson et al. (1980), Gynther et al. (1973a), and Lachar (1974) have noted that the 2-4/4-2 profile is particularly common. The 2-4/4-2, also common here, reflects the depression that a person in an acute state of alcoholic disorder is likely to experience (Craig, 1988). Johnson et al. (1980) state that the 4-2 is more common than the 2-4, although the two scores are closer together here than in the 4-2 obtained with other drug disorders. This 4-2 pattern is particularly noted in those arrested for driving under the influence of alcohol.

Gynther and his colleagues have also found that the 1-2/2-1 MMPI profile is common in alcoholics, particularly for males who show an episodic pattern with numerous physical complaints. This usually represents a person who has used alcohol for a significant period of time and who primarily manifests the abuse in episodic sprees. When 3 is also elevated and 7 is one of the next highest scores, a substantial and often severe neurotic component is involved (Conley, 1981). Profiles with an elevation of 4 and 7 frequently indicate persons who manifest a cycle of alcoholic indulgence, regret and remorse, and then repetition of the acting-out, while the 2-7/7-2 is noted where remorse is more chronic and has channeled into depression.

The 4-6/6-4 profile is commonly found in alcoholics who have a long history of alcoholic problems; as the alcoholic ages, however, scales 4 and 6 decline (Faulstitch et al., 1985). They are less inclined toward episodic drinking than those with the 1-2/2-1 profile, and they are likely to avoid treatment. The 6-4/4-6 alcoholics usually have very poor work histories and have had numerous marital problems, including the tendency to get married repetitively. When the 6 scale is higher, one is more likely to have an abusive individual, with the spouse probably the main target of this abuse. The 4-9/9-4 profile with a high F scale has already been noted; such persons tend to be long-term alcoholics.

There is also the 1-4/4-1 pattern where the person is high on scale 9 and at least moderately low on the O scale: These individuals are the extroverted social alcoholics (or drug abusers in general) who do not have as severe underlying conflicts as those with other patterns.

□   ## 16 PF

Some of the early research gathered by the people who developed the Cattell 16 PF test has delineated some characteristics on the 16 PF that are common to most alcoholics (IPAT staff, 1963). They find the alcoholic to be high on the I, M, O, and Q_4 scales, as well as moderately high on the L and N scales. They expect the alcoholic to be low on the B, C, and F scales, and at least moderately low on scales E and G.

Gross and Carpenter (1971) found somewhat similar results in a study of 266 alcoholics who showed elevation on O and Q_4, with slightly elevated scales on B and M. They also found low scores on C, E, G, H, and Q_1, with a moderately low Q_3. They assert that these profiles characterize the alcoholic as having more imaginative capacity and intellectual ability than the normative group, and also indicate extroversion, passivity, emotional instability, anxiety, and interpersonal undependability.

Costello (1978) found two major subtypes of alcoholics reflected in the 16 PF. The first is characterized by high scores on L, N, O, and Q_4, with low scores on C, E, H, I, M, Q_2, and Q_3. This group, which approximates the stereotype of the alcoholic, manifests anxiety, introversion, and ambivalent dependency. The second subtype shows high scores on G, N, and Q_3, with lower scores on B, C, F, Q_1 and Q_2. This group is more aggressive, more highly socialized, and has less immediate anxiety.

The scores on the O and Q_4 scales depend in large part on the degree of anxiety the alcoholic is experiencing at the time of the test. Some alcoholics no longer have immediately intense sources of anxiety and are involved with alcohol in a large part out of habit and personality factors. They are not likely to be so high on the O and Q_4 scales and are expected to be lower on the Q_3 scale.

□   ## OTHER TEST-RESPONSE PATTERNS

In part, the response of the alcoholic to the WAIS-R is dependent on whether there has been a development of central nervous system impairment (CNSI) (Donovan, 1986) (see Chapter 14). It has generally been assumed that alcoholics do well on tests that measure vocabulary, which may be the highest score, and similarities, information, and comprehension, but do less well on tests that tap visual motor coordination and on problems in impulsivity. They occasionally miss surprisingly easy items, reflecting a lack of attention and/or CNSI.

Holland and Watson (1980) administered the WAIS-R to alcoholic inpatients, with their subjects obtaining average scores on similarities, comprehension, information, vocabulary, picture completion, and arithmetic. Scores were significantly lower on digit symbol, block design, object assembly, and picture arrangement, which suggests the decrements in visual motor coordination to which others have alluded.

Kish et al. (1980) tested four groups of alcoholics at 6, 15, 21, and 102 days of abstinence from alcohol, using the arithmetic , digit-span, block-design, similarities, and digit-symbol WAIS-R subtests. At the time of the first evaluation (6 days), the alcoholics showed scores that were deficient on all the scales used. Scores improved, however, between 6 and 21 days on digit span, block design, and similarities. This pattern continued, indicating that with reference to the degree of alcoholism they were studying (not markedly severe), "recoveries in short term memory and attention, visual, analytic and synthesizing ability, and abstracting ability" (p. 587) did occur, while the decrements in learning new material or handling arithmetic tasks continued. Others have reported the same continuing deficits in the arithmetic scale and the digit-symbol scale.

Highest elevation on scales B and T should occur on the MCMI. This may be accompanied by an elevated D, reflecting the depression often occurring in chronic alcoholics or in alcoholic withdrawal. Personality types most often associated with chronic alcohol intoxication are 2, 3, S, C, and P (Craig et al., 1985). Also, those who are schizoid should score high on scale 1. A score of at least 75 might be expected on one or more of these scales. The borderline passive-aggressive mixed-personality disorder is often seen in chronic alcoholic patients drying out (see Chapter 9). Depressed alcoholics tend to score higher on O, A, 2, 8, C, S, SS, and H than nondepressed alcoholics.

On the Rorschach, a high percentage of oral responses and anatomy responses have been reported. W responses and an increment of Dd responses have been reported by Rapaport et al. (1968) to be associated with addictive tendencies. Others (Gilbert, 1978, 1980) have found a high number of anatomy responses, a low F+ percentage, a number of aquatic-animal responses, and some color responses to be related to orality. Phillips and Smith (1953) have found an absence and/or decrement of Popular responses in the record. Bug and/or beetle responses are alleged to denote the frustrated dependency commonly associated with alcoholism.

□   TREATMENT OPTIONS

A critical first step in the treatment of alcoholics is simply getting them involved in the treatment program (Blane and Leonard, 1987). Confrontation techniques are often useful here. Another helpful approach to this problem was demonstrated by Craigie and Ross (1980): They used videotape to model self-disclosing behaviors and treatment-seeking behaviors with one group of alcoholics who were in a detoxication unit.

They compared their subsequent degree of involvement on treatment to those who had only seen general films about alcoholism and found that the modeling for self-disclosure and treatment-seeking significantly improved the probability of staying in treatment.

Many alcoholics who have been chronically imbibing will need an initial period of detoxication, especially in light of the mild confusion and memory and concentration problems commonly found as acute withdrawal symptoms in the 1–3 weeks following the cessation of drinking. In addition, a period of hospitalization or other controlled living structure keeps them from giving in to strong immediate habits that would return them to drinking (Brown, 1985). Drugs such as Antabuse can also be helpful in controlling the immediate impulse to drink, though of course the effects of the Antabuse can be bypassed in short order (Barrett, 1986). The implantation of time-release drugs similar in action to Antabuse is a future option, though there are potential legal liabilities if the client fatally overdosed with alcohol and the drug, which is possible. Aversion therapy is also helpful in giving the client additional control over impulses; aversion by electric shock can be supplemented by videotape replays of the person while he or she is drunk (Brown, 1985).

Many alcoholics, like other persons with impulse problems, are relatively unaware of their physiological reactions as they proceed in their abuse (Blane and Leonard, 1987). Analogous to obese individuals, alcoholics are less aware of how much more they drink than normal drinkers, a surprising finding in light of the alcoholic's substantial experience. Lovibond and Caddy (1970) used biofeedback to teach alcoholics to become more aware of the bodily signs associated with an increasing blood alcohol level and approaching intoxication. As a result, some of them were able to return to social drinking. Clients who are able to return to social drinking rather than to rely on total abstinence are usually better educated, have a shorter drinking history, and are more confident of their ability to avoid drinking that goes out of control (Marlatt et al., 1988; Lovibond and Caddy, 1970). In all alcoholics, there is a need for continued monitoring, supportive therapy, and work with the alcoholics' social network well beyond the point when they have stopped drinking (Newcomb and Bentler, 1988).

Continued contact is one of the advantages of Alcoholics Anonymous (AA). In addition to the group therapy support structure, AA also forces alcoholics to publicly label themselves as in need of help and gives them a new social network composed of nondrinkers. Though AA's data supporting the claim of high rates of success are highly flawed methodologically, AA is helpful to persons who have trouble with impulse drinking, who need a new social network, and who are able to work within the somewhat rigid demands of the AA belief system (Brown, 1985; Marlatt et al., 1988).

Marital and family-help therapy are important for dealing with the disruption that is usually caused in the alcoholic's family life and, most importantly, for helping the family offer positive support to the alcoholic while not subtly encouraging a return to drinking. Such approaches may be extended beyond the nuclear family to friends and associates in order to keep them from reinforcing drinking (Marlatt et al., 1988). Chemotherapy can be helpful in specific instances in weaning the person away from alcohol, though it introduces the paradoxical problems of treating drug abuse with another drug and, secondarily, the implicit message in any chemotherapy that the client's efforts to change are not the critical factor.

■ Prescription Drug Abuse

The DSM-III-R discusses a number of substance abuse patterns, and the differentiation between organic and psychological patterns mentioned in the alcoholism section is continued in this section. The DSM-III-R does not specifically discuss a pattern called prescription drug abuse. However, I feel that this is an important pattern because it focuses on the common characteristics of clients rather than making a differentiation according to the specific drug that is abused, an approach that often cuts across personality patterns. As Vogel (1985) and Meyer and Salmon (1988) point out, drug companies and physicians should openly acknowledge at least some degree of responsibility for the high level of prescription drug abuse in our society.

While the barbiturates were for many years the most commonly abused prescription drugs, amphetamines and minor tranquilizers are heavily abused in our present society. Since this book will discuss some of the ancillary patterns common to amphetamine abuse, the focus will now be on prescription drug abuse involving minor tranquilizers. This latter abuse pattern typically emerges in individuals between the ages of thirty and sixty, predominantly in middle-class and upper-class females. Female abusers are rather evenly divided between housewives and those who work outside the home. They take prescribed tranquilizers initially for nervousness or insomnia, gradually increase the dosage, and commonly compound the problem with an increased use of alcohol. The likelihood of abuse is further compounded because more than 90 percent of the mood-altering drugs taken by women have been prescribed by physicians who have no special training in psychological disorders (Vogel, 1985; Meyer and Salmon, 1988).

☐   MMPI

It has already been noted that in substance abuse in general, the clinician can expect elevations on MMPI scales 2, 4, and 8 (Craig, 1988). This would generally hold for the typical prescription drug abuses as well, though I would accentuate the depression reflected in the 2 scale. The

8 scale – and, to a lesser degree, the 7 scale – is also likely to be substantially elevated, reflecting tension, a sense of being disturbed, and allied complaints of a vague nature. At the same time, I would expect the 4 scale to be less elevated than one would find in most drug abuse patterns. It will probably be above normal, particularly since these individuals are likely to use the more simplistic defense mechanisms of denial and projection and are also narcissistic in their personality orientation (Blane and Leonard, 1987). These factors also predict moderately high scores on scales 1 and 3.

A low score on scale 5 is expected, since these individuals usually identify with the female role, and lower scores on scale 5 are typical of the standard middle-class interest pattern for females. This would vary because of age and whether the woman had a paying job. Since these individuals often feel isolated, and since many of them actually live alone, a moderately high score on scale 6 is not uncommon. The depression and the social isolation also suggest that scale 9 is likely to be lower than average.

☐　　　　16 PF

The 16 PF pattern should differ somewhat from the overall substance abuse pattern presented in the last section. Similar to that pattern, a high I score likely reflects a tender-minded and somewhat dependent individual, and the Q_4 score, reflecting anxiety, may be somewhat higher than with the standard drug abuse pattern. I expect scale A to be only moderately high, at best, and in some individuals – possibly the housewife who is bordering on agoraphobia because of her anxiety – I expect a low A.

The M score, unlike that obtained in many drug abuse patterns, should be no higher than average. In the case of the housewife, particularly the middle-class one, it may tend toward the low end of the scale. Since anxiety is not being dealt with very well, there should be a high Q_3 score. I would expect at least a moderately high L scale, in coordination with the high scale 6 on the MMPI. As in most psychological disorders, C should be low. Shyness and social isolation are likely to be reflected in a low H score and low F and E scores. Q_1 should be much lower than that of most drug abuse patterns. The B scale, measuring general intelligence, will depend on the social class and education of the individual, as well as on the degree of depression.

☐　　　　OTHER TEST-RESPONSE PATTERNS

Prescription drug abuse is likely to occur in those personality types in which anxiety and depression are major components, and this would be reflected in the MCMI by high scores on 2, 8, C, and S. Those who score high on scale 7 may be more likely to turn to prescription drugs or alcohol than illegal drugs because of the high level of conformity to social rules in these individuals. Because alcohol use is often combined with prescribed medications, elevation on B is probable.

☐   TREATMENT OPTIONS

Persons with prescription drug abuse are oriented toward medical treatment and often have a middle-class value system, so hospitalization for detoxication fits well with their concept of what should occur. After the initial stage, the clinician has to deal with the tension and depression that often underlie this pattern (Marlatt et al., 1988). The development of a relaxation response is important, particularly since it teaches clients that they can exert some control over their lives and thus do not need to be so dependent on external agents, such as drugs.

Many of these people have withdrawn socially, so assertiveness training, as well as efforts to expand their social network, are most important. Along with this, the therapist can present the issue of taking drugs as a rational and/or existential choice (McInerney et al., 1986) while emphasizing how the clients can determine many of the events that occur in their world and accept the anxieties and responsibilities concomitant with these choices.

Since insomnia and obesity are common problems that lead to prescription drug abuse, as well as to drug abuse problems in general, it is important to help the person cope with them (Higginbotham et al., 1988). With either pattern, any form of relaxation training that emphasizes deep muscle relaxation can help, though the habit control procedures are more important. With regard to weight problems, the reader is referred to the treatment options in the section on amphetamine abuse, later in this chapter.

■   **Polysubstance Abuse**

The term "polysubstance abuse" is also not included in DSM-III-R, nor was it in prior versions of the DSM. However, there is in DSM-III-R for the first time the category Polysubstance Dependence (304.90), in which a person has used at least three different substances for at least three months and no substance has predominated. The relative neglect of polysubstance abuse reflects an essential feature of our society: the belief that there is a particular remedy for virtually any physical or psychological disorder that occurs (Heath, 1986). The polysubstance abuser usually combines the expectancy that an external agent will take care of all problems with a high need for new experiences or sensation seeking (Marlatt et al., 1988; Zuckerman et al., 1980).

The use of a combination of drugs over a period of time is, of course, not new to human society (Heath, 1986), though in our present culture the pattern is magnified. The epidemic of this pattern is so recent that there are few significant data regarding how these individuals will eventually function in later life. These data are important to obtain, since polysubstance abusers appear to most clinicians to be more disturbed psychologically than those with other abuse patterns (Penk et al., 1980; Craig, 1988).

Polysubstance abusers could be described as psychotics without the loss of reality contact: They show deterioration of behavior in a wide variety of arenas—work, school performance, interpersonal relationships, and motivation—especially if they have been abusing a substantial length of time. Affect is generally flat; or, when emotion is manifest, it is quite labile. Like the alcoholic, there are many protestations of future positive change, and like the alcoholic, the promises are seldom fulfilled. This does not appear to be a manipulative deception, as the person seems intellectually committed to changing, yet the motivation and behavior necessary to actuate that change cannot be generated.

Polysubstance abusers are likely to be late adolescents or young adults (Herbert, 1987). They commonly begin ingesting some mood-altering substance in their early teens and quickly progress through the less potent substances to the point where they will use practically anything provided to them. There are some sex differences in the preferences for drugs: Males lean toward the use of alcohol, cocaine, opiates, marijuana, and hashish, and females are more prone to combine diet pills, tranquilizers, relaxants, sedatives, and, more recently, tobacco.

☐   MMPI

Older or bright adolescents can usually be tested effectively with the MMPI (Archer, 1987). As with alcoholics, scale 4 is consistently high in polysubstance abusers, as is 8, especially with late-adolescent polysubstance abusers (Craig, 1988). It is relatively lower in that subgroup of polysubstance abusers who tend to be depressed and who therefore have high 2, 7, and 8 scales as well. The more psychopathic 6-8 and 8-9-4 patterns are less likely to show depression and more likely to act out in ways other than simply drug abuse. In those individuals who are high-sensation seekers, the F scale is consistently elevated above a T score of 70. Elevations on scales 1 and 3 are not consistently found with polysubstance abusers, though when these are at least moderately elevated, some feel it is a better prediction of successful participation in treatment programs. As a person continues in the polysubstance abuse pattern, apathy increases and scores on scale 9—and, to a lesser degree, on scales 6 and 4—will be lowered. The apathy and social problems that accompany this pattern predict a high O scale, especially if depression is still present and not diluted by the drug use.

Overall, polysubstance abusers have been found to have more MMPI scores elevated over the 70-T level than do heroin abusers. The latter group on the average shows elevations above 70 T on 2, 4, and 8, whereas polysubstance abusers show them on F, 2, 4, 7, and 8 (Penk et al., 1980). As noted earlier, the MacAndrew Alcoholism Scale is useful here (MacAndrew, 1965).

☐   16 PF

Four factors consistently found in drug abusers are high F, low G, high H, and moderately high I. The high H measures their venturesomeness, more specifically their willingness to try nonapproved consciousness-altering drugs. The moderately high I, in conjunction with the other scores, reflects reliance and yet also the sensitivity and ambivalent dependency found in alcoholics. The low G measures the sociopathy to be expected here. The high F suggests extroversion and even a slightly manic quality; this primarily depends on when the individual is tested.

These persons' lack of a consistent value system, along with an imaginative though nonpersistent problem-solving approach, predicts a higher M score, and the orientation toward experimentation with drugs and disavowal of standard morality systems predicts a high Q_1 score. Similarly, emotional lability and a lack of discipline predict low scores on C and Q_3. In the early stages of the pattern, one could also expect relatively high scores on A, B, and Q_4, but with increased apathy and decreased ability to generate new behaviors, these scales should decrease. The lack of adequate social skills usually noted in this group (Herbert, 1987) would suggest at least a moderately low N score and a moderately raised Q_2 score, though the latter is then more appropriately interpreted as group avoidance rather than self-sufficiency.

☐   OTHER TEST-RESPONSE PATTERNS

A high score on the MCMI on T is indicated. If psychotic symptomatology occurs, then SS, CC, and/or PP will become elevated. The lack of concern for social rules exhibited by the narcissist and the impulsivity and stimulation-seeking of the aggressive and gregarious personalities predispose them toward polydrug abuse; elevations on scales 5 or 6 and sometimes 4 are likely.

☐   TREATMENT OPTIONS

In many instances, there is an acute toxic reaction to the drug that must be dealt with first. For example, in an acute reaction to cocaine, the standard stabilization sequence may require the use of (1) oxygen to stabilize respiration, (2) Inderal for any cardiac arrhythmias, (3) a barbiturate to reduce central nervous stimulation, or (4) benzodiazepines to control convulsive reactions (Washton and Gold, 1987). This response must be short-term and very carefully monitored in order to avoid secondary abuse patterns.

Since the typical polysubstance abuser is an adolescent or young adult who is showing a deterioration of functions in a wide array of behaviors, the broad-spectrum treatment is necessary. The clinician should be aware of the probability that such clients will attempt to obtain addicting drugs while in the detoxication phase through manipulation of their peer group (Hebert, 1987).

Group experiences that emphasize confrontive techniques are often necessary here, so rational-emotive (McInerney et al., 1986) or reality therapy (Glasser, 1980) can be an important adjunct to the treatment program. Polysubstance abusers easily verbalize promises and commitments, but they seldom tie commitments to future contingencies, and these therapies, of course, emphasize this linkage. Most importantly, clients should be forced to accept responsibility for the abuse behavior, as these persons often promote the idea that they were seduced into the drug culture. Aversive techniques can be helpful in dealing with specific habit patterns. Since family problems may have been a catalyst for the early drug abuse, this needs to be worked out via family therapy (Phares, 1988).

■ Amphetamine Use Disorder

As we have noted, the DSM-III-R lists a variety of substances for which abuse can be diagnosed, including tobacco and marijuana. For many of these substances, especially the last two, there is no consistent personality pattern. However, this book will comment on three diverse patterns—use of amphetamines, cocaine, and opiates—because they are so important in our society today.

The first synthetic amphetamine, a methamphetamine, was compounded in 1919 by the Japanese scientist Ogata (Bertinetti, 1980). Amphetamines were used to combat fatigue in World War II and are used today in treating hyperactive children. They have also been too commonly prescribed as a diet aid in the past, although there are now increasing restrictions on physicians. The use of amphetamines—or other, similarly acting sympathomimetic substances—is often the first step from abuse to dependence. Tolerance to amphetamines builds quickly, so abuse easily leads to increased intake and dependence. Continuation of an intake of amphetamines over a significant period of time leads to paranoid and other psychotic symptoms that may continue for some time after the drug is discontinued.

☐   DSM-III-R

All of the DSM-III-R diagnostic categories relevant to amphetamines include the concept "or similarly acting sympathomimetic agents," as these are thrown together in the same diagnostic category. In the section on organic diagnosis, there is the category Amphetamine Intoxication (305.70), which refers to the toxic effects of a single recent dose. Criteria include evidence of a recent use of amphetamines and two consequent (within one hour) physiological symptoms, such as tachycardia, elevated blood pressure, nausea, perspiration or chills, or pupillary dilation and such maladaptive behavioral changes as psychomotor excitement, grandiosity, or hypervigilance.

"Delirium" is the term for the syndrome that used to be called "acute brain syndrome." It involves a clouding of consciousness and memory disruption, along with evidence of two of the following: speech difficulty, perceptual problems, sleep problems, or hypo- or hyperactivity. The duration of delirium is typically short, no more than a week. In the specific instance of amphetamines (Amphetamine Delirium, 292.81), delirium lasts only about five hours, starting about an hour after ingestion of the substance, and the DSM-III-R requires evidence of onset within 24 hours of ingestion.

The Amphetamine Delusional Disorder (292.11) is the presence of rapidly developing persecutory delusions directly related to amphetamine abuse. Amphetamine Withdrawal requires evidence of one of the following three symptoms: disrupted sleep, psychomotor agitation, or fatigue, within 24 hours of the cessation of prolonged heavy use of amphetamines. Suicidal ideation and depression are also common.

Amphetamine Abuse (305.70) and Amphetamine Dependence (304.40) fit the general requirements for the abuse and dependence categories, as described in the prior section on alcohol.

□   MMPI

The elevation on scale 4 that is common to most drug abuse patterns is particularly evident in this syndrome. It is combined with an elevation on scale 9, reflecting the heightened activity and agitation associated with amphetamine use. There is also a significant elevation on scale 6, depending on the degree of abuse and whether paranoid ideation has begun. Elevations on scales 8 and 3 are also relatively common. Since amphetamine abuse is often a coping mechanism to deal with depression (Barnett and Gotlib, 1988), this will be manifest in a degree of suppression of scales 2 and 0.

□   16 PF

As with the other drug abuse patterns, low C and Q_3 scores are expected. The rejection of standard mores and the high activity level characteristic of amphetamine abuse are reflected in higher scores on E, F, M, and Q_1, and probably to a lesser degree on H. Prolonged abuse is likely to result in a higher L score, which reflects the development of a paranoid trend. Since these individuals, especially when they are still experiencing the effects of intoxication, are not likely to pay attention to a particular question for any length of time, scores on B should not be particularly high. A low score on G would be expected, as well as a moderately low score on H, the latter reflecting the autonomic over-reactivity generated by this particular drug.

OTHER TEST-RESPONSE PATTERNS

In addition to elevated T, high scores on the MCMI on N are likely to occur as a result of physiological arousal and hyperactivity. Since these individuals often show acute paranoia, an elevation on P is possible. As psychomotor activity increases, scores on D will decrease. Long periods of amphetamine use may lead to psychotic symptoms that will elevate PP and SS. Personality elevations that are likely to occur include 4, 5, and 6, along with those with whom depression was initially a factor: 2, 8, C and S. The former will be more likely after repeated amphetamine use, while the latter may be more probable in early states or preceding use.

TREATMENT OPTIONS

Since amphetamine abuse or the abuse of other similar stimulant drugs is often related to underlying anhedonia or depression, existential techniques to confront the apathy—and the cognitive behavior techniques described later for depression—are useful here. It is extremely important to teach persons that they can get involved with and control their world without the crutch of a stimulating drug (Higginbotham et al., 1988).

Covert sensitization, a subcategory of the techniques known as covert conditioning, is useful for drug disorders (Cautela and Wall, 1980). This is an imagery procedure that asks the client to imagine a highly aversive contingency or event occurring immediately on the cessation (in imagination) of the behavior that one is attempting to eliminate (in this case, involving the specific components of the amphetamine abuse sequence). This is repeated over a number of sessions and is efficient to the degree that the client can develop adequate images and that the imagery is experienced as vivid and real.

Since amphetamine abuse is often a logical extension of an abuse of other prescription or nonprescription pills for dieting, concomitant techniques to help with obesity are often useful to prevent the return to the use of amphetamines (Agras, 1987). Supportive group therapy, teaching of a relaxation response, hypnosis (in some cases), and especially behavioral control therapies are useful here. For example, it is important that the person never associate eating with other activities, such as reading or watching television; the eating has to come with independent cues. Teaching the persons to be able to interrupt meals for brief periods of time is a useful exercise. Analogously, they should be admonished to take smaller portions into the mouth, chew the food much longer, keep desirable foods out of the house as much as possible, purposely slow the pace of eating, and eat in only one spot in the house. They should keep a diary of eating behaviors so that awareness increases and therefore contingency contracting can be carried out to lower the size of the food portions (Ruderman, 1986).

■ Cocaine Abuse

Cocaine has become a favored drug in recent years. Its abuse by many sports and entertainment idols has received much media attention. Nevertheless, cocaine has been used for centuries. It is an alkaloid derivative of coca leaves, which were chewed by the Aztecs and are still used by at least four million Indians in South America. Such diverse people as Arthur Conan Doyle's character Sherlock Holmes, John Philip Sousa, and even Sigmund Freud have sung the praises of cocaine.

A number of people became inadvertently habituated to cocaine in the United States during the late 1800s by drinking Coca-Cola. John Pemberton, an Atlanta druggist, combined cocaine with sugar and kola-nut extract in a brass pot in his backyard to make the original Coca-Cola, which he advertised as a "brain medicine." When the Pure Food and Drug Law of 1906 outlawed the use of cocaine, caffeine was substituted in "the real thing." Today, refined cocaine is usually sniffed in small amounts. Most of what passes for cocaine is not pure (free-base) cocaine but cocaine hydrochloride, a salt that is approximately 85 percent cocaine by weight. Pure cocaine is sometimes smoked, a psychophysiologically more dangerous process than sniffing.

□ DIAGNOSTIC CONSIDERATIONS

The DSM-III-R diagnostic considerations that apply to substance abuse and dependence in general apply here as well. In addition, Spotts and Schontz (1984) have found that middle-class and upper-middle-class cocaine users, especially males, show an intense, narcissistic, competitive, and achievement-oriented personality, with a strong fear of intimacy and vulnerability in relationships, so diagnostic considerations for the narcissistic and obsessive-compulsive personality disorders (see Chapter 9) would also apply here. A stairstep progression on scales 1, 2, 3, 4, 7, and 8 has been noted in a population of cocaine abusers, with scores in general being significantly elevated above normal and with an inverted V on the validity scales (F being the highest score) (Spotts and Schontz, 1984). Since cocaine use will often facilitate paranoid ideation, scale 6 may be elevated (Sherer et al., 1988).

☐   TEST CONSIDERATIONS

As with other patterns of substance abuse, a high T is very likely. To the extent that alcohol abuse is involved, B will be elevated. On the scales representing the persistent personality features (1–8), expect elevation on 4 and 5. Scale 4 reveals a sociable self-image and a preference for a fast-paced life-style. Also, the immature stimulus-seeking behaviors and manipulation of others to receive attention will be evident here. A high 5 shows the interpersonal exploitiveness that typifies a cocaine abuser. As the chronicity of drug use increases, so, too, do the elevations on scales C and N. High C scores reflect the endogenous mood or other depressive components that often underlie cocaine abuse, while high N scores reflect hypomanic characteristics that also may accompany abuse.

On the Rorschach, a heightened level of defensiveness will be manifested by a small number of total responses (R), an incresed number of W, F, and Popular responses. A disproportionately high L score is also predicted, indicating that the subject has refused to process the stimuli as requested. A high number of M and Y responses may indicate a situational crisis related to the abuse condition. Because FM answers are increased under altered states of consciousness (Exner, 1986), cocaine abusers should show a higher frequency of them.

☐   TREATMENT OPTIONS

Any inpatient treatment plan should have the goals of detoxifying the person's biological system and directly and strongly confronting the destructive psychological patterns. Calcium channel blockers (e.g., nitrendipine) directly act to reverse the effects of cocaine toxicity. Confrontation techniques, pioneered with heroin abusers by group treatment centers such as Synanon and Daytop Village, are used with cocaine addicts as well. The goal is to get the addict to assume control of his or her own decisions; to plan more adaptive behaviors to satisfy vocational, interpersonal, and sexual needs; and then to look at more characterological and existential issues.

In the latter regard, Spotts and Schontz (1984) recommend intensive psychotherapy with a focus on the avoidance of dependency and unresolved spiritual and intimacy-betrayal and intimacy-avoidance crises. Such psychotherapy should take into account the often underlying depression and at the same time allow socially acceptable outlets for the commonly higher-than-average level of stimulation-seeking. As some success is attained, involvement in a group therapy modeled on AA principles can be effective (Erlich and McGeehan, 1985).

■   **Opioid Use Disorder**

Even though the opium poppy has been used as a mind-altering substance for at least 6,000 years, two events in particular spurred the increased abuse patterns noted recently. Early in the nineteenth century, morphine (ten times stronger than opium) was isolated from the opium poppy, and approximately fifty years later, Alexander Wood perfected a more effective drug delivery system: the hypodermic needle. Morphine was soon included in many patent medicines, although it was supplanted in use near the end of the century when Wright discovered heroin, a semisynthetic opioid derived from morphine. Interestingly, heroin was at one time used to cure morphine addiction, just as another addicting drug, methadone, is now used to treat heroin addiction.

Heroin induces a warm, sensual euphoria, usually followed by sleepiness and lethargy. Tolerance develops rapidly, however, and eight to twelve hours after an injection the individual is likely to experience withdrawal symptoms, the severity depending on the amount ingested and the duration of time the person has been abusing. Even so, these symptoms are seldom as severe as the mad ravings portrayed in the media. In fact, most addicts describe withdrawal as quite similar to influenza symptoms.

Perhaps no one has expressed so clearly the reinforcement from heroin as French humanist and poet Jean Cocteau:

Everything we do in life, including love, is done in an express train traveling towards death. To smoke opium is to leave the train while in motion; it is to be interested in something other than life and death. (Jarvik, 1967, p. 52)

☐   DSM-III-R

The DSM-III-R requires the same criteria for opioid abuse and dependence as it does for all the substances heretofore mentioned. In the section on organic mental disorders, the DSM-III-R lists Opioid Intoxication (305.50), which is the effects of a single dose toxic enough to produce pupillary contraction, psychomotor retardation, apathy, and the experience of either euphoria or dysphoria. Itching, flushing of the skin, nausea, and analgesia also typically occur. The diagnosis requires: (1) evidence of recent use, (2) pupillary contraction, signified by at least one sign, such as drowsiness, attention or memory problems, or slurred speech, and (3) maladaptive behavioral changes, such as psychomotor retardation or dysphoria.

Prolonged or heavy use often results in Opioid Withdrawal (292.00), in which three of the following are experienced upon cessation of use: nausea, muscle aches, craving for an opiod, lacrimation or rhinorhea, pupillary dilation, sweating, diarrhea, yawning, fever, or insomnia.

☐   MMPI

Elevations on scales 2, 4, and 8, which are generally characteristic of the drug abuse patterns, are found in opiate abuse (Penk et al., 1980).

Elevations on scales 3 and 6 are also likely, which reflects the egocentricity and problems with authority characteristic of this pattern, though it is true that the elevation on scale 6 may not be as high as it is for a person who is dependent on amphetamines. In certain opiate abusers, there is a high scale 9, indicating a person who is easily bored and has a low frustration tolerance and is in that sense narcissistic. In another subgroup, the more relaxed or bohemian opiate abuser, a 4-5 code type is common. Scores on scales 2 and 9 will vary depending on whether the person is feeling euphoric or dysphoric. Since the person is not likely to be tested while in the midst of an episode, the rise on scale 2 is more likely. It is interesting that opiate abusers seldom show a profile as pathological as most of the other significant drug abusers do. As noted earlier, the MacAndrew Alcoholism Scale is useful here (MacAndrew, 1965).

☐ 16 PF

Opiate abusers are likely to be high on scales I and M. This reflects their paradoxical indulgence in fantasy while they maintain an apathetic view of events in their world, along with their avoidance of either stress or commitment whenever possible. They are also relatively high on O, though typically not as high as alcoholics. They are relatively high on scale A, which is different from a number of other drug abuse patterns; this reflects their lack of paranoid response toward the environment, at least in relation to the amount seen in the other drug abuse patterns. They tend to be slightly above average on L, although this will vary depending on the testing situation.

Opiate abusers tend to be average on scales H, Q_1, and Q_3 and lower on N, which again differentiates them from those with other drug abuse patterns. However, like all of these patterns, they are low on scales C and E. They are also low on B, reflecting their lower socioeconomic status and educational attainment, as well as the lack of initiative found in these persons.

☐ OTHER TEST-RESPONSE PATTERNS

Keiser and Lowy (1980) present evidence that heroin addicts tend to be significantly higher on digit-span scores than on other WAIS-R subtests. This fits with the evidence that a digit-span score well above the mean of the client's other WAIS-R subtest scores is correlated with an interpersonal-detachment syndrome characterized by superficial and emotionally distant relationships.

☐ TREATMENT OPTIONS

The confrontational group experience first evolved with the opioid disorders, primarily through institutions like Synanon and Phoenix

House. These groups are effective with a number of clients, though they have been burdened by problems resulting from their resistance to any reliance on professionally trained staff. As a result, there is a lack of objectivity in assessing techniques and outcomes and a lack of awareness about the wide range of treatment techniques discussed in the professional literature. In any case, a method of providing a more therapeutic social network is critical in dealing with opioid addicts, as they easily return to their destructive peer group setting (Herbert, 1987).

Just as heroin was once used to treat morphine addiction, methadone, also an addicting drug, is now used to treat heroin addiction. It appears to be effective in certain cases, though the clinician must be aware of possible secondary abuse of the drug used for treatment, particularly in addicts who are psychopathic. Methadone can be useful at least in the initial stages of treatment. Since it does not cause the distinct euphoria of heroin, it can be taken orally and less often than heroin; also, its lower cost may allow the addict to move out of the criminal system.

CHAPTER 3

The Schizophrenic and Paranoid Disorders

■ ## Schizophrenia

Many clinicians would argue that schizophrenia is the most serious of all mental disorders (Bernstein et al., 1988; Mirsky and Duncan, 1986). Although other disorders are more common or may involve more-immediate distress, the pervasive effect of a schizophrenic disorder throughout all areas of an individual's functioning and the complexity of problems it presents in etiology and diagnosis support the assertion that it is the most serious mental disorder. About one out of every one hundred people in the United States will receive a diagnosis of schizophrenia in his or her lifetime (Myers et al., 1984). The schizophrenic who has been released after a first hospitalization unfortunately still has about a 50 percent chance of returning to the hospital within two years. It has been estimated that schizophrenics occupy approximately two thirds of our mental-hospital beds and almost one fourth of all hospital beds. These statistics reflect the long period of time that schizophrenics traditionally spend in institutions.

There are a number of premorbid predictors of schizophrenia worth assessing in a client (Meyer and Salmon, 1988):

1. A schizophrenic parent or parents, a less potent variable being the presence of other schizophrenic blood relatives. There is evidence that for daughters, the earlier their mother became schizophrenic, the higher is the likelihood that they, too, will become schizophrenic. For sons, however, this is not as critical, with a more important issue being the time of separation from a disturbed mother. The earlier separation occurs, the more damaging it is for a son.

2. A history of prenatal disruption, birth problems, viral or bacterial infections, or toxic situations during the child's pregnancy.

3. Low birth weight and/or low IQ relative to siblings.

4. Hyperactivity; cognitive slippage; any signs of central nervous system dysfunction, especially difficulties in attention tasks with distracting stimuli and/or eye-tracking, convulsions; evidence of enlarged cerebral ventricles; significant reaction time problems; or an abnormally rapid recovery rate of the autonomic nervous system.

5. An early role as the scapegoat or odd member of the family.

6. Parenting marked by emotional and/or discipline inconsistency, including double messages.

7. Rejection by peers in childhood or adolescence and perception by either teachers or peers as being significantly more irritable or unstable than other children.

8. Rejection of peers, especially if accompanied by odd thinking processes, ambivalent emotional responses, or a lack of response to standard pleasure sources.

A common cause path (Bernstein et al., 1988; Rosenbaum et al., 1988; Meyer and Salmon, 1988) for the development of a long-term schizophrenic pattern is presented in Figure 3.1.

□   DSM-III-R

To apply the diagnosis of schizophrenia, the DSM-III-R requires evidence of one of the following: either (1) two of the following: (a) delusions, (b) catatonic behavior, (c) incoherence or marked loosening of associations, (d) prominent hallucinations (throughout the day for several days or several times a week for several weeks, not just brief moments), or (2) bizarre delusions, or (3) prominent hallucinations of a voice with no depressive or elated content, or two voices, or a voice keeping up a running commentary on the person's behavior or thoughts. There must be an active phase of at least one week, and the disorder must continue for at least six months with or without a prodromal or residual phase.

Typical delusions of schizophrenics include somatic delusions, delusions of being controlled, thought broadcasting, and grandiose delusions. This symptomatology must not be directly related to a depressive or manic disorder. Schizophrenic symptomatology must precede the affective disorder, or else the affective disorder must be a relatively minor component. During the active phase of the disorder, there must be some significant impairment in areas of daily functioning, such as interpersonal relationships, school, or work.

Pathological hallucinations or delusions may sometimes be difficult to separate out from culturally sanctioned experiences that are not particularly pathological in nature. The latter experiences are usually characterized by (1) socially appropriate, productive, and adequate coping behavior before and after the experience, (2) time limitations of a few hours to a few days, (3) a reasonable degree of family and/or subgroup support, (4) a resultant gain in social prestige or self-esteem, (5) culturally congruent experiences in the delusions or hallucinations, and (6) a relative absence of psychopathological indicators (Westermeyer, 1987).

The preschizophrenic personality of individuals who later become schizophrenic can often be described as eccentric and isolated, mildly confused and disorganized, suspicious, and/or withdrawn. As a result, such individuals are likely to require the additional diagnostic qualifier of such categories as schizotypal, borderline, introverted, or paranoid personality disorder (Widiger et al., 1986).

FIGURE 3.1 A Common Developmental Path in Schizophrenia

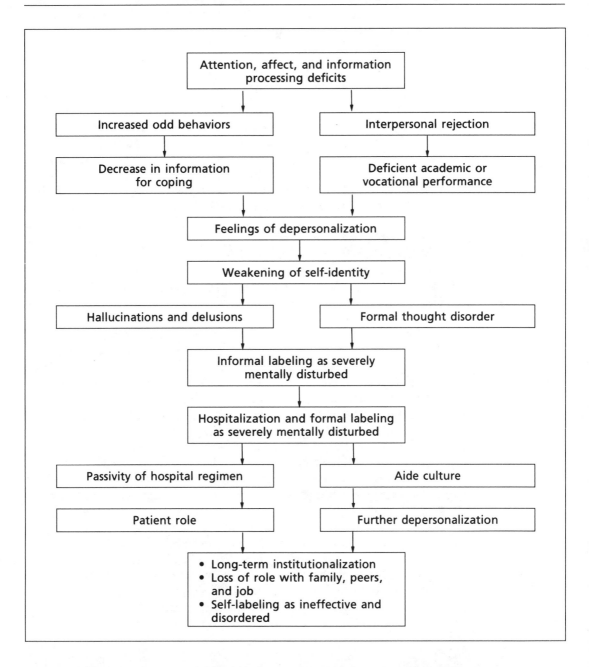

Several studies have pointed to the problems of making accurate subclassifications within the overall category of schizophrenia. Most clinicians find such classification meaningful, however, because it clarifies communications and facilitates discussions of treatment and prognosis. However, while relatives have a 5–10 percent increased risk of schizophrenia, depending upon the diagnostic criteria used, well-defined subtypes do not tend to run in families. As regards the overall diagnostic category of schizophrenia, a landmark study by the World Health Organization (1979) has demonstrated the reliability of this concept in a variety of sociocultural settings.

□   MMPI

As might be expected, most clinicians agree that scale 8 is typically elevated above 70 T in schizophrenics, since this directly reflects their tendency to escape reality through fantasy behavior and to process information inadequately (Mirsky and Duncan, 1986). Most schizophrenics tend to score in the 75–90 range, particularly as they move toward chronicity (Johnson et al., 1980). Extremely high scores are more likely to indicate severe patterns within other diagnostic categories or to reflect an attempt to fake-bad (Graham, 1987).

A variety of scale patterns have been noted (Moldin et al., 1987). Lachar (1974) points out that the 7-8/8-7 profile suggests possible chronic schizohrenia, whereas the 2-7-8 code type or a similar combination is more likely to be associated with an earlier stage of schizophrenia (Edell, 1987; Golden and Meehl, 1979). A pattern that appears especially predictive of schizophrenia is the F scale (in T scores) being in the range 70–95; scale 8, 75–100; and scale 7 less than scale 8.

When a profile is obtained where scale 8 is high and scale 1 is around 85 T and at the same time 10–20 T greater than scales 2 and 3, this suggests a schizophrenic with somatic delusions. The unusual 3-8/8-3 profile, especially when 1 is also high, also indicates an individual with high somatic concerns but with a greater tendency to dissociate (Moldin et al., 1987). A primary elevation on scale 6 is not consistently obtained in schizophrenic profiles, though it is likely in paranoid schizophrenics and occurs occasionally in some catatonic schizophrenics.

The 8-4/4-8 profile can also indicate schizophrenia, particularly when hostility and anger are major components. This individual has probably had a particularly bad childhood. When the clinician sees an 8-9/9-8 profile, it is commonly that of a schizophrenic who finds it extremely difficult to vocalize the issues at hand, is consistently problematic to work with therapeutically, and is often disruptive in functioning.

Schizophrenics are usually elevated on the F scale, and Gynther et al. (1973b) note that a very high F scale obtained in a psychiatric population is likely to indicate a confused individual rather than one who is faking-bad. Though it does occur in certain instances, a major elevation on scale 3 is not typical in schizophrenic profiles. A particularly high scale 5 in a woman who appears to fit within the traditional feminine role should alert the clinician to look for other indications of schizophrenia. In a somewhat similar vein, Holland and Watson (1980) find male schizophrenic VA-hospital inpatients to be high on F, L, 5, 6, and 8.

In this regard, Goldberg's formula (Graham, 1977) for determining psychosis using T scores should be noted. The L score must be added to the scores for scales 6 and 8, and then the scores on scales 3 and 7 must be subtracted. Using a lower cutoff point of 45, one is allegedly correct 70 percent of the time in using the label schizophrenia, though this seems to be a sign of paranoid schizophrenia more than schizophrenia in general. Newmark's formula (T on Sc > 80, < 100; total Sc raw score is no more than 35 percent of K items; T score on F > 75, < 95; on Pt> Sc) has proven to be effective, primarily with schizophrenics under 45 years of age (Newmark and Hutchins, 1980).

☐ 16 PF

On the 16 PF, schizophrenics tend to be high on I, M, O, and Q_4. This reflects their propensity to engage in fantasy as a way to control intrapsychic conflict and their tendency to withdraw and not deal in a practical fashion with the world. This pattern at the same time reflects the high level of anxiety and insecurity experienced by most of these individuals. This fits well with the concept that they are stimulation-avoidant (Nasrallah and Weinberger, 1986), as opposed to the primary psychopath who is stimulation-seeking.

Schizophrenics also tend to be low on scale C, though surprisingly often not as low as many of the other psychiatric-disorder categories. They are consistently low on scales F and H, which reflects a stimulation-avoidant pattern, as well as the depression that is likely to accompany such a high level of disturbed functioning. Though numerous schizophrenic individuals may score in the average range, in general they tend to be somewhat lower on G, Q_2 and Q_3. Along with their significant inability to cope with the world, they also tend to be low on scale B. As schizophrenia becomes chronic, C, E, F, and H tend to be lower and I and M higher.

☐ OTHER TEST-RESPONSE PATTERNS

On the WAIS-R, several patterns are commonly found in schizophrenia (Newmark, 1985; Blatt and Allison, 1981; Anastasi, 1987). First, subtest scatter is common and the verbal-scaled score tends to be higher than the performance-scaled score. Within the subtests themselves, there is a tendency to succeed on harder items while at the same time, surprisingly, to fail some of the easier items. Scores tend to be higher on block design, occasionally higher on information and vocabulary, while typically lower on arithmetic, picture arrangement, digit symbol, and comprehension. A low similarities score often includes several overinclusion responses, and a low score on comprehension is usually accompanied by evidence of irrelevant associations. A high similarities score is a good prognostic sign for schizophrenia. There are often peculiar arrangements in the picture arrangement test; and in the picture completion test, frequent reference is made to items not intended to be together. In addition, process schizophrenics do less well than reactive schizophrenics on the picture completion test, relative to their other scores.

Ogdon (1977) reviewed a wide range of studies that used the Rorschach and noted several response patterns found to be associated with psychosis in general and schizophrenia in particular: (1) poor quality and a low number of human movement responses (those in which humans are perceived as involved in at least some minimal action), (2) animal movement responses in which the organization of the response is very poor, (3) an abnormally high or low number of pure-form responses (in which the client made the response based simply on the form of the blot, without reference to any other aspect), (4) responses dictated only by the color of the blot (that is, pure-C responses), (5) an abnormally low number of responses in which all aspects of the blot are integrated into the response (whole, or W, responses), (6) a lower-than-average number of popular, or P, responses (responses perceived by most people), and/or (7) perseverating by continually seeing the same or analogous responses throughout several blots in sequence.

Exner (1978, 1986) has noted several differences between schizophrenics and normals on the Rorschach. Schizophrenics obtain more F and M responses than do either borderlines or normal persons, though there may be a high percentage of F responses. Borderline individuals average 6.4 popular responses, whereas schizophrenics average only 3.6. Not surprisingly, schizophrenics have almost twice as many unusual responses as borderline cases and certainly far more than normal individuals. Schizophrenics also give three times fewer S responses and two times fewer T determinates than normal individuals. More specifically, schizophrenics scored significantly lower than normals on R, D, DQt, Sum T, H, Xt%, Pop, and Afr and higher on Dd, (FQw)-(fQ-), Sum Y, L, Sum SP.SL (Mason et al., 1985).

Others have noted that schizophrenics are more inclined than other groups to show a massing of pure-color responses, and they occasionally show very arbitrary FC responses (for example, pink rats). Color-shock or pleasantly verbalized comments about color in the cards are considered to be favorable prognostic signs in schizophrenia (Phillips and Smith, 1953). Along with the deviant verbalizations—such as fabulized responses (two rabbits with a baseball bat), contaminations (the head of a beetle-tiger), and other incongruous combinations (a woman with a head of a horse)—schizophrenics tend to show overelaborate symbolism and absurd responses in the patterns and a number of mangled and distorted perceptions. Schizophrenics are more likely to show a perseveration of Dd responses, which reflects a high degree of overcontrol in their response patterns, combined with underactivity in the actual perceptions. They also may show a massing of sex responses, particularly referring more often to the sexual act rather than to sexual organs. As in most of the tests, there is a tendency for the quality of responses to deteriorate toward the end of the test. Not only do schizophrenics show a higher percentage of F responses, but they also show higher levels of articulation of the object as they perceive it within the F response (Ritzler et al., 1980). In essence, their ego resources are being channeled into fantasy behavior.

On the Thematic Apperception Test (TAT), schizophrenics are prone to tell rambling, confused stories or to have a very restricted response record. They are more likely to make comments of self-reference or show personal reactions, such as disgust, in response to the cards. They make bizarre comments and show less ability to concentrate on their responses. From a thematic standpoint, schizophrenics are more likely than normals to show direct sexual and aggressive themes; themes of persecution and/or omnipotence; characters changing in confused, odd, or magical ways; ideas of reference (especially linking the present card to a prior card; juxtaposition of extremes, e.g., acts of murder and tenderness; disorientation as to person, place, and time; lack of clear body boundaries; gross deviation from the stimulus properties; and grossly destructive bizarre or sexual themes (Bellak, 1986; Karon, 1981).

Proverbs have also been used to distinguish schizophrenics from other groups. Johnson (1966) found that only those proverbs that are commonly understood ("It never rains, but it pours") are consistently useful in distinguishing schizophrenics from other groups, such as persons with organic brain damage (and these are the four proverbs included in the Meyer Information Battery listed in the Appendices). Schizophrenics are more likely to give peculiar, abstract responses to these proverbs. Figures on the Bender-Gestalt are likely to be boxed, to be drawn in a confused order, and to be drawn overly large (Rossini and Kaspar, 1987).

During active phases of schizophrenia, disorientation, inappropriate affect, hallucinations, and delusions will be represented by SS scores above 84 on the MCMI. Elevations on CC and PP are likely to the extent that depression and paranoia are present. In general, elevations on 1, 2, 3, and 8 have been found to be characteristic of inpatient samples, who are often schizophrenics (McCann and Suess, 1988).

Persons with basic personality patterns encompassing traits of the schizoid, borderline, schizotypal, and avoidant personalities are more likely to use schizophrenic patterns as coping devices or to decompensate to a schizophrenic pattern (Rossenbaum et al., 1988; Mirsky and Duncan, 1986). Elevations on scales 1, 2, C, and S may be present and representative of precipitating personality styles. Scales 4 and 7 should be somewhat depressed, as these patterns are not likely to develop schizophrenic disorders. Overall, the MCMI does not appear to be as effective as the MMPI in assessing schizophrenia (Patrick, 1988).

□   TREATMENT OPTIONS

There are several prognostic indicators that point to a positive chance of remission once schizophrenia does occur (Meyer and Salmon, 1988; Kay and Lindenmayer, 1987): (1) sexual-marital status: being married or at least having a history of stable, consistent sexual-social adjustment, (2) a family history of affective disorder rather than schizophrenic disorder, (3) presence of an affective pattern (either elation or depression) in the acute stage of the schizophrenic disorder, (4) abrupt onset of the disorder and onset later than early adulthood, (5) adequate premorbid school and/or vocational adjustment, (6) evidence of premorbid competence in interpersonal relationships and a higher socioeconomic status, (7) a short length of stay in the hospital with an absence of electroconvulsive therapy (ECT) treatment, (8) nonparanoid subdiagnosis, (9) a family history of alcoholism, (10) psychomotor retardation, (11) a relatively high score on the WAIS-R similarities subscale score, and (12) evidence of clear precipitating factors at the onset of the disturbance.

More than almost any other disorder, schizophrenia warrants a multifaceted treatment plan because of its complexity. Chemotherapy— usually with the phenothiazines, the butyrophenones, or the thioxanthenes—is useful as one component in the treatment of many schizophrenics, particularly for those who are hospital-prone clients of low competence (Hersen and Breuning, 1986) (see Appendix B). Clozapine has been helpful for some schizophrenics who do not respond well to other medications. "Positive" symptoms—that is, those marked by their presence, such as hallucinations, delusions, and incoherent speech—respond more quickly to chemotherapy, while "negative" symptoms—those marked by their absence, such as social-isolation withdrawal, lack of communication skills, and poverty of speech—do not respond as well. Since there can be major problems with a schizophrenic's ability to take medication after being released from the hospital, the long-acting agents, such as the phenothiazine Prolixin, can be useful, though they have a restricted range of effectiveness and problems with side effects.

As with all the antipsychotic chemotherapies, approximately 35 percent of the clients show muscular problems and feelings of lethargy alternating with restlessness. Approximately 5 percent (up to 40 percent in the elderly) develop tardive dyskinesia, a typically irreversible syndrome that involves grimacing, lip-smacking, and involuntary neck and head movements. Also, particularly with the phenothiazines (the most commonly used drug), a significant number of deaths due to aspiration asphyxiation have been noted, since they tend to suppress the gag reflex. In addition to the side effects noted above, there is loss of creativity and spontaneity and a reinforcement of the patient role, since the client sees treatment as totally external to her- or himself. Though chemotherapy can be useful, antipsychotic drugs are no doubt prescribed too often (Hersen and Breuning, 1986; Phares, 1988).

Electroconvulsive therapy (ECT) has been used with schizophrenics since its discovery, but it has not shown marked success. Psychosurgery, dialysis, and megavitamin therapies have been tried with increasing frequency in recent years, but as yet there is little significant evidence of their success with schizophrenia (Diaz-Buxo et al., 1980; Valenstein, 1986).

Token economies have been used effectively in bringing the disrupted and institutionalized schizophrenic back to a semblance of normal functioning, and it is in this development of simple and basic behaviors that token economies are most applicable (Davey and Cullen, 1988). Milieu therapy, occasionally only a euphemism for sitting around the ward, is optimally a total treatment approach that adds the values of patient-governance and input to the concepts of group process and the "moral therapy" of the nineteenth century (Adler, 1988). Milieu therapy should also include an available combination of new and effective treatment techniques directed toward the overall improvement of schizophrenia. In this regard, occupational, activity, and art therapies can be useful adjuncts. Developing adequate vocational skills is important, and these skills should not be for obsolescent vocations, as is often the case in prison and mental hospital programs. Cognitive retraining and family and group therapy as the person moves back into the home system are also important (Jacobson and Gurman, 1986; Hersen and Breuning, 1986).

Ellsworth et al. (1979) thoroughly examined the issues in milieu therapy and advised that the milieu is much more effective when there is a mixture of both chronic and acute patients. They noted a cluster of specific factors that facilitate the positive effects of milieu therapy, notably the availability of a separate television room, recent magazines and other reading materials, music at meals, stalls separating the toilets, and pleasant pictures on the walls. This may only be a reflection of the Hawthorne Effect, wherein change per se—not necessarily positive change—acts to produce a positive effect. Whatever the reason, these changes promote a positive effect.

Liberman et al. (1986) studied the effect of teaching social skills to medicated schizophrenics who were at risk for relapse. The patients all had histories of multiple hospitalizations for schizophrenia. They were trained in such social skills as receiving (learning to identify emotional cues from a friend), processing (generating possible responses to interpersonal contacts), and responding (skills in eye contact and voice volume). The training was intensive, lasting for 90 hours, and it included daily homework assignments and nightly group sessions. Outcome measures were collected before, during, and for a follow-up period of up to two years after treatment. These measures assessed specifically trained behaviors and problem-solving skills, psychopathology, and social adjustment. The results indicated that the social-skills training was not only effective for the specific skills taught, but also had generalized to other situations outside the treatment environment. Further, the families showed increased positive responses to them.

■ Undifferentiated Schizophrenia (295.9x)

This category is marked by prominent schizophrenic symptoms; however, there are several symptoms from various subtypes, or for some reason the criteria for one of the other categories are not quite fulfilled. This category fits most clearly the above comments, testing indicators, and treatment suggestions for the overall category of schizophrenia.

■ Disorganized Schizophrenia (295.1x)

Disorganized Schizophrenia was termed Hebephrenia in earlier DSM classification systems. The DSM-III-R diagnosis of disorganized schizophrenic denotes an individual who shows incoherence, disorganized behavior or loosening of associations, and remarkably flat or inappropriate affect, often in the form of random giggling.

Delusions and hallucinations do not show the structure or pattern common to other schizophrenic disorders. Other elements commonly associated with disorganized schizophrenia include odd facial grimaces, extreme social withdrawal, and very peculiar mannerisms. As would be expected from the preceding description, social functioning is severely disrupted.

Overall, disorganized schizophrenia is characterized by very poor premorbid adjustment, slow onset (usually starting in adolescence or early adulthood), neurological problems, and chronicity of adjustment (Bernstein et al., 1988; Nasrallah and Weinberger, 1986). These individuals are likely to develop more chronic and apathetic patterns with time, and the likelihood of significant long-term remission is quite low.

☐   MMPI

Gynther et al., (1973a) note that the 8-9/9-8 profile is commonly associated with the behaviors typical of disorganized schizophrenia. This is particularly true if the affect is silly or inappropriate. When it is flat, scale 9 tends to be lower and scales 7 and 2 are likely to be higher. Disorganized schizophrenics are often so severely disturbed in functioning that they cannot adequately complete the MMPI, at least to the degree where it is suitable for scoring. The reader is referred to the section on malingering (Chapter 12), since some of that material relates to the patterns to be expected.

□   16 PF

The same problems in adequately scoring the MMPI also hold true for the 16 PF. In those individuals who are able to perform the task adequately, their 16 PF profile is likely to fit the overall schizophrenic pattern mentioned earlier, with only a few minor changes: Scale C is likely to be lower in disorganized schizophrenics than in others, as are scales N and Q_3. They also tend to be higher on scale A and lower on scale L, which reflects their willingness to interact interpersonally as expressed through fantasy, but their inability to actuate this interaction in reality.

□   OTHER TEST-RESPONSE PATTERNS

While the overall schizophrenic pattern is most likely to be reflected on the WAIS-R, this test emphasizes the very odd response patterns to an even greater degree. Proverbs are especially peculiar, and the disorganized schizophrenic is probably not able to provide even the distorted rationale that paranoid schizophrenics may volunteer if they feel comfortable enough with the tester. If the affect of the disorganized schizophrenic is silly or incongruous, there is usually an extreme scatter in the quality of responses, and this will affect the subtest patterns and the within-test scoring. They tend to do more poorly on block design, digit symbol, and object assembly than do other schizophrenic clients, reflecting the neurologic component (Nasrallah and Weinberger, 1986).

On the Rorschach, form level is very low, and although there are occasional M responses, these are likely to be of poor quality and reflective of disrupted ideation.

On the MCMI, elevations above 84 on C and S are most common, with elevation of P and 1 likely. Because PP and SS are partly defined by hallucinations and delusions, they are not likely to be very high in the disorganized schizophrenic, where these symptoms are not typically present, though moderate elevations (74–85) may occur. One personality pattern that is most likely to occur with the disorganized schizophrenic is the avoidant type; indeed, disorganization may be considered an extension of their characteristic protective maneuver in interfering with cognitive clarity (Millon, 1981). In this case, elevations above 74 may be expected on scale 2.

□   TREATMENT OPTIONS

The particularly low level of functioning of the disorganized schizophrenic warrants the use of most of the techniques noted previously in the treatment option section of the category of schizophrenic disorders. Chemotherapy is commonly required, and token economies and milieu therapy are particularly useful (Adler, 1988). Until disorganized schizophrenics can develop the basic appropriate behaviors of even the most minimally normal individual, many of the other therapy techniques—such as psychotherapy, group therapy, and occupational therapy—are virtually impossible. Since disorganized schizophrenics are likely to have a markedly poor premorbid adjustment, an emphasis on vocational training is important if they are to make any ultimate transition to normal living. Thus, rigorous training in basic social skills is necessary, first via the token economy and then later through a total-milieu approach.

In choosing a specific therapist for an extremely disturbed client, the clinician might recall the classic differentiation between A and B therapists, first studied by Whitehorn and Betz (Goldstein and Stein, 1976). They found that B therapists were significantly more successful with the extremely disturbed individual. These therapists are characterized as noncoercive problem solvers; they are able to persuade while at the same time communicate a sense of acceptance of and empathy with the schizophrenic's bizarre thoughts and fantasies.

■ Catatonic Schizophrenia (295.2x)

Severe psychomotor disturbance is the essential feature of catatonic schizophrenia (Mirsky and Duncan, 1986). The first of the two major traditional subdivisions is that of stuporous catatonia, in which movement is severely reduced and catatonic stupor, rigidity, or posturing is evident. Some may even show waxy flexibility, a condition in which the body is passively receptive to posture control. It is possible to manipulate such individuals physically just as one would move a store manikin, and they can remain in the manipulated position for extremely long periods of time.

The agitated catatonic, or excited type, is marked by uncontrollable verbal and motor behavior—apparently purposeless and not necessarily influenced by external stimuli. Individuals in this phase can be quite dangerous and may break into frenzied violence in which they hurt or kill themselves or others. This is not an outgrowth of personal hostility, but rather a response to other persons as objects in their way. Before the use of psychomotor-control drugs, agitated catatonics would sometimes drive themselves to the point where they would die from severe exhaustion.

Two different courses are typically observed in catatonic schizophrenia. The chronic form of this disorder is primarily manifested in the stuporous types, and the progression in the disorder is slow and steady. The prognosis for remission is low, and the person may eventually develop into an undifferentiated schizophrenic.

In the periodic type, an abrupt onset is usually followed by alternating periods of agitated and stuporous catatonia. Remission is more likely, though there may be recurrences. They are particularly dangerous at the point of the shift from stupor to agitation, primarily because hospital personnel have few cues as to when the shift will occur.

☐   DSM-III-R

In addition to meeting the standard criteria for schizophrenia, a diagnosis of catatonic schizophrenia requires that at some time during the active phase of the illness the symptom picture is dominated by a catatonic pattern that includes either catatonic negativity or excitement, catatonic rigidity or posturing, or catatonic stupor. Mutism is also common in this disorder. It is interesting that although the catatonic subtype was once considered to be one of the most common schizophrenic patterns, it is now relatively rare in Europe and North America, according to DSM-III-R.

☐   MMPI

The 2-7-8 pattern, with 2 most likely to predominate, is often reflective of the catatonic who is confused and yet oriented toward stuporous catatonia (Johnson et al., 1980). Agitated catatonics are more likely to show an 8-9 or 8-0 pattern (Moldin et al., 1987). If this agitation has been transferred intellectually into hostility, an elevation on scale 4 is more likely and scale 6 is usually elevated. The 0 scale is high, reflecting significant discomfort with and withdrawal from interpersonal relationships.

☐   16 PF

This pattern is similar to the prototypical pattern for schizophrenia, though it will differ on certain scales depending on whether the person tends toward stupor or agitation. This will be reflected particularly in scales F, Q_4, and, to a degree, E and Q_3. Since this pattern may border on the hostility and social isolation of the paranoid, the L scale is likely to be affected more so than for other schizophrenics; to a degree, this is also evident in a higher Q_2 score.

☐   OTHER TEST-RESPONSE PATTERNS

The schizophrenic profile would be expected on the MCMI, represented by elevations on SS along with the indicated patterns that seem to predispose toward schizophrenia (elevation on 1, 2, C, and/or S). Additionally, CC would be more prominent in this type of schizophrenia than in others, representing the catatonic and agitated types of motor activity. Scores on this scale of 85 or higher would not be uncommon. The overactivity factor of the excited type would be represented by an elevated N.

☐ TREATMENT OPTIONS

Agitated catatonic schizophrenics may force a coercive control of their behavior, so chemotherapy, the "modern straitjacket," is often necessary to bring a semblance of order into their world. Token economies and milieu therapy are also useful for ameliorating the extremes of either agitated or stuporous catatonia (Adler, 1988). The possibility of an associated manic component in the agitated catatonic must not be overlooked, so a trial period of lithium therapy can be employed.

The stuporous catatonic is not unlike the severe depressive on several continuums, so the reader might consult some of the techniques useful for moving a person out of a depressive episode (Simons et al., 1986; Beck, 1976). Direct therapy, which can be seen as a psychoanalytic analogue to implosive therapy, is useful primarily with paranoid and catatonic schizophrenics (Karon, 1976; Rosen, 1953). Through a prolonged verbal assault on the person's inner fantasies and fears, the client is goaded into at least a retaliatory response. Once this occurs, the therapist can move into more supportive and interactive roles.

■ ## Residual Schizophrenic Disorder (295.6x)

This diagnosis is applied to the individual who has already been labeled schizophrenic under the above criteria, but in whom the disorder has lessened to the point that there are no longer any prominent psychotic symptoms.

DSM-III-R requirements for the diagnosis of Residual Schizophrenic Disorder are a previously diagnosed schizophrenic episode with symptomatology that no longer includes *prominent* psychotic symptoms. However, at least two signs suggestive of schizophrenia remain, such as difficulties in social behavior or interpersonal communications, odd or peculiar mannerisms, or inappropriate or flat affect. DSM-III-R has some difficulty with the goal of making a diagnosis operational. A judgment as to whether symptoms are still prominent is quite subjective, especially in view of the potency of certain chemotherapeutic agents to mask or suppress a wide variety of behavioral responses. Nonetheless, the category is likely to be used often since it is potentially applicable to many individuals.

☐ MMPI

Since the category is residual schizophrenia, it could be debated how much psychopathology is likely to be evident in the MMPI profile. It is reasonable for the clinician to expect that in most cases the general profile of schizophrenia will be evident, but without the extremes of response. For example, a significant elevation on scale 8 would still be likely, but it should be less than in a person with active schizophrenia. Similarly, an elevation on scale F is reasonable, though on occasion this may be an individual who is trying to avoid remembering the schizophrenic episode and who becomes very defensive in that regard. As a result, scale K – and possibly L – would be high (Moldin et al., 1987). When this happens, the person is also likely to be defensive about any kind of intrapsychic exploration.

It is typical to expect a relatively low 9 score in most residual schizophrenics, particularly since many of them are still on medication to suppress behavior. Other changes will be dependent on the specific type of schizophrenia, as well as on the premorbid personality, which is likely to come to the fore as the schizophrenic symptoms are suppressed.

16 PF

Much the same suppression of extreme scales would be expected on the 16 PF. C, H, M, O, and Q_4 should still be on the negative side of the continuum, yet they will be somewhat muted from prior levels. Scale B should be somewhat higher and now more accurately reflective of the person's actual abilities. A higher score on Q_3 should reflect the fact that the individuals now have more control in their world. Other scores will be affected by the type of schizophrenia manifested, the premorbid personality, and the feelings of security about present adjustment.

OTHER TEST-RESPONSE PATTERNS

MCMI profiles of residual schizophrenic disorder may be similar to those of other schizophrenic disorders without such extreme elevations on the clinical-symptom scales CC, PP, and SS. The personality pattern elevations expected for schizophrenia – 1, 2, C, and/or S – should be more elevated relative to CC, PP, and SS, in contrast to the active phases in which clinical-symptom scales are more prominent relative to personality patterns.

TREATMENT OPTIONS

Since by definition the symptom picture of residual schizophrenia excludes pervasive and permanent psychotic symptoms, it is questionable whether any values from chemotherapy are, or could be, offset by the physical and psychological risks. It would seem that trial periods without medication should be more common for such persons than they are.

The residual symptoms are usually in the area of social and interpersonal behavior and, as such, require systems that provide adequate feedback to the schizophrenic about these behaviors. Such expatient groups as Recovery can be useful in helping previously hospitalized clients adjust, but there is the risk that mildly bizarre behaviors in the social and vocational world will be reinforced, or at least too easily tolerated, without feedback. Hence, it is important to move quickly into group therapy situations in which the predominant ethic is normality and in which feedback without inappropriate behaviors is generated in a supportive and accurate fashion. Similarly, the family can be trained to provide this feedback in a positive manner through family therapy situations (Jacobson and Gurman, 1986).

If attentional problems persist into the residual phase, which they often do (Bernstein et al., 1988), biofeedback of electroencephalographic (EEG) patterns can be employed to increase those patterns associated with attention, such as decreasing the percentage of alpha waves, the classic indicator of nonattention (Schwartz, 1987). Biofeedback of muscle patterns is potentially useful to decrease the motoric side effects of tardive dyskinesia, or even to lower the excitability level of the agitated catatonic, though the latter task would indeed be challenging.

■   Schizophreniform Disorder (295.40)

The major substantive difference between the schizophreniform disorder and schizophrenia is duration. If the disorder lasts less than six months but the symptoms are that of schizophrenia, or if the person is symptomatic but has been so for less than six months, the term "schizophreniform disorder" is appropriate. The diagnosis of schizophrenia requires symptoms for six months or more. So, even though repeated incidents of the schizophreniform disorder may account for a cumulative duration of more than six months, the diagnosis remains the same. If the duration of disorder is less than a month, the appropriate diagnosis is usually brief reactive psychosis.

The major reason for the differential diagnosis is that the schizophreniform disorder shows several characteristics that differ from schizophrenia. There is better prognosis in the schizophreniform disorder, the individual is far more likely to recover to the premorbid level of functioning.

□   DIAGNOSTIC CONSIDERATION

There is a high likelihood that the symptom picture is going to include much emotional upset and turmoil, reflecting the acute variable. This is opposed to chronic schizophrenic patterns, so scores on the MMPI, 16 PF, MCMI, and other tests are likely to be slightly accentuated. For example, on the MMPI, one is more likely to see a higher F scale than for chronic schizophrenics, but lower F, 7, 8, and 0 scales than for acute schizophrenics (Walters, 1984). This profile occurs in schizophrenia as well, although not so consistently. On the 16 PF, higher scores on scales O and Q_4 and lower scores on C and H are likely to be found more often than with schizophrenics.

☐ TREATMENT OPTIONS

Since the schizophreniform disorder is essentially a schizophrenic adjustment that has not yet lasted six months, the techniques noted as appropriate for the treatment of schizophrenia are applicable here. This is particularly so for psychological techniques, as every effort should be made to help the client avoid the patient role, and even worse, extended institutionalization. Like Rosen (1953), Hogan (1980) advises the use of an implosive technique for any brief psychotic episodes. This is possible since anxiety is high and has not yet crystallized into bizarre avoidant mechanisms.

■ Brief Reactive Psychosis (298.80)

The primary distinguishing features of this psychotic reaction are sudden onset and short duration, ranging from a few hours up to one month. Once it exceeds two weeks, the diagnosis is changed to schizophreniform disorder.

This disorder is often triggered rather suddenly by an event of extreme stress: the loss of a loved one, a traumatic war experience, or other such stress. Unable to deal with the stress, the individual withdraws into a state of mental confusion, typically characterized by extreme emotional lability, bizarre behaviors, and perceptual distortions, including hallucinations and delusions. Individuals with histrionic, schizotypal, and borderline personality disorders, as well as adolescents and young adults manifesting emotional instability of various sorts, are especially prone to this reaction.

Unlike the schizophreniform disorder and the organic mental disorders that display comparable symptoms, the brief psychotic reaction is sudden in onset and of short duration. Unlike the factitious disorder, which in some respects may be considered a stress reaction, the person with a brief psychotic reaction appears to have little or no voluntary control over his or her symptoms.

☐ DSM-III-R

The diagnosis requires evidence of at least one of the following symptoms of impaired (not socially sanctioned) reality testing: (1) distorted or incoherent thinking, (2) delusions, (3) hallucinations, or (4) severely disorganized or catatonic behavior. It also requires evidence of emotional turmoil or overwhelming perplexity or confusion, a duration of symptomatology of not more than one month, and a period of clear increase of psychopathology after the stressor.

☐ OTHER TEST RESPONSE PATTERNS

The test response patterns are similar to the schizophrenic disorders, even more so to the exaggerated patterns of the schizophreniform disorder, particularly since acute emotional distress is apparent here. Those accentuations noted in the section on test responses in schizophreniform disorder are applicable here, with some minor exceptions. Those exceptions relate to the probability of lower ego strength and indications of more-permanent disorder than are found in the other patterns. Hence, scales 4 and 6 on the MMPI would be even less likely to be elevated, and scale O is not as likely to be very different from normal in these individuals as in schizophrenia. On the 16 PF, the C and H scales are not as likely to be as low, as these are reflective of more-disturbed ongoing personality functioning. Patterns similar to schizophrenic patterns would also be expected on the MCMI, along with greater elevations on A, N, and, to a lesser degree, D. Along with the expected accompanying personality disorders, elevation on 4 is possible since this type is related to the histrionic disorder.

☐ TREATMENT OPTIONS

Since this diagnosis is warranted when the person has shown psychotic behavior only for two weeks or less, the techniques appropriate for the treatment of schizophrenia or severe affective disorder (see relevant sections) can be supplemented by the techniques of crisis intervention. Most importantly, every effort should be made to keep clients from withdrawing from their social or vocational world and adopting a patient role. If at all possible, the family should be involved in the treatment, both as a mode of cutting off pathological behaviors and as a means of providing emotional support.

In addition, the brief psychotic disorder is effectively treated with covert modeling. In this technique, clients are asked to imagine a whole set of new behaviors and imagine themselves performing these behaviors. With practice, and with contracting for gradually moving aspects of the imagery patterns into their existing world, a positive effect can be generated.

Psychotic Disorder NOS (Atypical Psychosis) (298.90)

This category is used to designate those individuals who for some reason do not fit into any of the previous categories. For example, atypical psychosis might refer to individuals with a monosymptomatic somatic delusional system or to someone with such a confusing clinical picture that a specific diagnosis would be wrong.

■ Paranoid Schizophrenia (295.3x)

This disorder is discussed here because it is a juxtaposition of concepts from both schizophrenia and the paranoid disorders, the focus of the next section. Paranoid schizophrenia shows the most fragmented thought processes of any of the paranoid disorders; for that reason, it is included under schizophrenia. At the same time, however, there is a delusional system that is the mark of a paranoid disorder. In order to warrant the DSM-III-R diagnosis of paranoid schizophrenia, the person has to fulfill the criteria for schizophrenia and present a symptom picture dominated either by preoccupation with one or more systematized delusions or with frequent auditory hallucinations related to a single theme. There should be an absence of incoherence, marked loosening of associations, catatonic behavior, grossly disorganized behavior or inappropriate affect.

A number of researchers (Zigler and Glick, 1988; Mirsky and Duncan, 1986; Lazar and Harrow, 1985; Shemberg and Levanthal, 1984) have found evidence to establish that paranoid schizophrenia is a somewhat different disorder than other forms of schizophrenia. The paranoid schizophrenic is typically brighter and more socially competent than other schizophrenics, with the first episode typically occurring later in life. They also show less anxiety, more of a counterphobic response to depressive ideation, relatively less judgment impairment, smaller deficits on most cognitive tests, and more concern with erecting boundaries in tasks and in their personal world than do other schizophrenics. There may even be differences in blood chemistry between these groups; however, these data have been contradictory to date.

Though paranoid schizophrenics are typically more adequate socially than other schizophrenics, their reactions are consistently more stilted or intense than are normal responses. This is particularly so if anger and suspicion rather than grandiosity are the focus of the symptom picture. Reasonably appropriate affective responses often exist in paranoid schizophrenia, in contrast to the other schizophrenias.

☐ MMPI

When the profile is devoid of a T-score elevation over 70, the L score is greater than or equal to 7 (absolute values), and the person is not a minister, paranoid mentation with some delusions is likely and the probability of acting-out is increased to the degree that scales 3 and 4 are high (Fjordback, 1985). Johnson et al. (1980) found that the 8-4 pattern, with high scores on 2, 6, and 7 is characteristic of paranoid schizophrenia. The 8-6/6-8 and the 6-9/9-6 profiles are also typical for paranoid schizophrenics (Moldin et al., 1987), and if the 6 is the predominant scale with 4 also raised, the person should be considered one of the more dangerous paranoid schizophrenics. If the 8 dominates in the profile, then prepsychotic schizoid traits are more likely.

A high F scale is typical, and an F − K (F minus K) ratio greater than 11 is not necessarily an indication of an invalid profile in a situation with high 4, 6, 8, and 9 scales. If the 7 scale is low, auditory hallucinations are particularly likely to occur. When the individual is more inclined toward grandiose than persecutory delusions, an 8-9/9-8 profile is more likely, with the 2 scale being lower than usual. The 1 and 3 scales are often relatively low in the protocols of paranoid schizophrenics, though Gilberstadt and Duker (1965) suggest that the 1-6/6-1 pattern with a 4 scale less than 70 T should be considered a cue to look for further evidence of paranoid schizophrenia.

☐   16 PF

The paranoid schizophrenic 16-PF profile is similar to the overall schizophrenic profile, with some significant differences. Paranoid schizophrenics, especially females, are more likely to be high on the L scale, reflecting the jealous paranoid component essential to the disorder. Paranoid schizophrenics are also more likely to be high on Q_3 because anxiety is more controlled by projecting conflict and feelings onto other agents. As a result, the O score is less, the C and E scales higher, and the Q_4 scale somewhat lower than is found in the usual schizophrenic protocol. Also, because paranoid schizophrenics on the average are more intelligent, scale B is higher.

☐   OTHER TEST-RESPONSE PATTERNS

Elevations on 1 and P are expected on the MCMI, and to a lesser extent on 2, 6, and/or C. MCMI scores of 85 and higher occur on PP, whereas the relatively less psychotic thought processes and affects exhibited by this type produce relatively lower scores on CC and SS, placing them in the 75–84 range.

On the WAIS-R, paranoid schizophrenics are likely to be higher on the similarities and picture completion subtests, while relatively lower on the digit symbol and picture arrangement subtests. This reflects the unusual interpretations they tend to make, as well as their compulsive traits, which are usually more evident premorbidly (Lazar and Harrow, 1985). On the comprehension subtest, they are occasionally lower because they tend to make peculiar and overinclusive proverb interpretations. This trait is also found in the Benjamin Proverbs (Johnson, 1966).

This is one instance when the use of more exotic proverbs can be helpful. Paranoid schizophrenics, particularly if they are bright, often understand the popular interpretation of common proverbs and sayings and will state them, even though they themselves may entertain other interpretations (Oltmanns and Maher, 1988). Exotic proverbs can bring out the delusional material more clearly.

On all tests, including the WAIS-R, paranoid schizophrenics show overconcern about the correctness of their responses and will often question the examiner as to what is the correct response. They tend to make deviant replies in response to numerous stimuli and are happy to argue about the meaning of any question presented to them (Heilbrun et al., 1985). On the Rorschach, paranoid schizophrenics are again very concerned about the meaning of the test, particularly since the ambiguous stimuli are not easily interpretable. They are more likely to look at the back of the card and to make excessive Dd responses. They show a fairly high F+ percentage, but not with the quality seen in the other paranoid disorders. If they are more oriented toward the persecutory dimension, a low number of responses is likely unless they can be made at least minimally comfortable in the testing situation.

If responsive, paranoid schizophrenics are likely to show a higher number of M responses and a low number of C responses, particularly if there is a degree of integration in their adjustment. Responses are occasionally seen as "coming at" the person, and there are more "mask" responses than usual, as well as percepts of animals or humans being attacked or surrounded. There is an overemphasis on W responses, but often with poorer form than one would expect based on their intelligence level. Content often includes grandiose or cosmic concepts as well as responses that define boundaries, such as "edge" or "border" responses (Johnson and Quinlan, 1980).

On the TAT, grandiose and pretentious stories are likely, with the person often being too negativistic to cooperate in pinning down details of the story. They are likely to use a story as a forum for making philosophical comments or moralizing about situations. Alternatively, if they feel threatened, they may refuse even to tell a story or will give very short and concrete descriptions of the pictures (Bellak, 1986). Gutters, fences, other indications of borders, castles, and similar concepts are found in the drawings of paranoids (Oster and Gould, 1987).

☐ TREATMENT OPTIONS

Several of the neuroleptic drugs have been used with the severe paranoid disorders (Shemberg and Levanthal, 1984). Although no single drug has been consistently effective, there is some evidence that chlorpromazine, haloperidol, and a trifluoperazine-amitriptyline combination may have some benefit when used as an adjunct to other treatment techniques in severe paranoid disturbance.

The significant level of disturbance and more bizarre quality of the paranoid schizophrenic, as contrasted to that of the other paranoid disorders, may warrant more intrusive methods. ECT has been used with some paranoid schizophrenics in an apparent attempt to disrupt the consistency of the belief system. However, ECT contains all the risks of any intrusive procedure, which is so important here since a fear of being intruded on in any number of dimensions is central to the paranoid disorders. In addition, there is the probability of short- and long-term memory loss, which could easily increase the sense of vulnerability so critical to many paranoids.

Chemotherapy can lessen the depression and anxiety often found in the paranoid delusional system (Zigler and Glick, 1988). But again, there are the risks of apparent intrusiveness, plus increased delusions in response to any side effects, even those that have little long-term danger.

With the more bizarre paranoid disorders, the therapist may have to crash through the defenses erected by the paranoid system rather than wait for trust to develop in a series of psychotherapy contacts. Direct analysis (Karon, 1976; Rosen, 1953) has been useful in this regard. Interpretations are forced on paranoid individuals, made necessary by their massive avoidance procedures. These interpretations usually center on what are thought to be major inner conflicts, notably in the areas of aggression, sexuality, and inadequacy. Once the person is moved into a more normal mode of functioning through any technique, approaches should then emphasize the development of trust, along with empathy for the person's distorted beliefs. (The reader is referred to the treatment techniques discussed at the end of the next section: the paranoid disorders.)

■   The Paranoid (Delusional) Disorders

The paranoid disorders are psychotic conditions in which the symptom picture is dominated by persistent persecutory delusions or delusions of jealousy. While the DSM-III-R emphasizes the "delusional" rather than "paranoid" terminology, we will introduce the area with the traditional and still more generally accepted "paranoid" terminology. There are no significant hallucinations in the paranoid disorders, and the symptoms are not primarily attributable to a schizophrenic, affective, or organic mental disorder or any combination of the three. Unlike paranoid schizophrenia, there is not much fragmentation of thoughts in the delusions. Also, there is seldom as severe an impairment in daily functioning as there is in paranoid schizophrenia. Paranoid schizophrenics typically have more than one delusional system, but it is not uncommon in the paranoid disorder that there is only a single focus in the delusions (Oltmanns and Maher, 1988).

The paranoid disorders can be oriented on a continuum based on the degree of integration in the delusions, with paranoid schizophrenia being the most fragmented and delusional (paranoid) disorder the least. The paranoid personality disorder can be seen as an extension of this continuum in that there is no true delusional system at all (Turkat, 1985). Though it is no longer formally included in the DSM, I will also discuss the relatively rare disorder of shared paranoid disorder, traditionally known as *folie à deux* and now incorporated into the concept of induced psychotic disorder.

The paranoid disorders seldom show marked disruption in occupational functioning or intellectual activities, but they do show disruption in marital and interpersonal functioning (Haynes, 1986). These are relatively rare disorders, and since these individuals are usually coerced into treatment, they are not always cooperative in a diagnostic situation. For that reason, the reader should consult the section on malingering (Chapter 12). Since anger is often a factor in the personality makeup and occasionally is so extreme that there is danger to others, the reader should consult the section of this book on aggression potential (Chapter 13).

□ MMPI

While one would expect scale 6 to be elevated in this disorder, this is not always the case. Paranoids with good defenses may not want to reveal their delusions and thus may score rather low on scale 6, in some instances being inordinately low, even relative to normal scores (Heilbrun et al., 1985). It must also be remembered when making a diagnostic judgment that blacks tend to score higher on scale 6 throughout the range of normal and paranoid patterns (Dahlstrom et al., 1986). Overall, paranoids are likely to skip a number of the questions and often express irritation at being forced to make true-false decisions.

Unlike persons with other psychiatric disorders, paranoids will show a high K score and a relatively low F score and, consistent with that, a lower score on scale 4 than would be expected. The more disturbed the individual is (the more toward the paranoid schizophrenic end of the continuum), the more likely the "paranoid trough" will occur, that is, high scores on scales 6 and 8 and a relatively lower score on scale 7. Since denial and projection are common features of the paranoid disorders, reasonably high scores on scale 3 can be expected. As noted in paranoid schizophrenia, if a profile has T well below 70, and L (in absolute numbers) greater than or equal to 7, paranoid mentation is probable, and elevations on 3 and 4 increase the probability of acting-out (Fjordback, 1985).

□ 16 PF

It was originally thought that paranoids would score high on the L scale, but this is not always so, which again reflects the situation where the client is guarded in revealing the content of his or her concerns. Hence, the diagnostician should score for faking-bad (Winder et al., 1975; Krug, 1980) in order to check for the extremity of this response pattern. On the paranoia end of the continuum, as opposed to the paranoid schizophrenic end, scores on B, N, and Q_3 are likely to be higher, while I is lower.

☐   TREATMENT OPTIONS

The concerns of the paranoid about intrusiveness make this set of disorders most difficult to treat, and the possibility of an underlying depression has to be kept in mind (Zigler and Glick, 1988). The therapist can crash through the defenses via such techniques as direct analysis, chemotherapy, or even psychosurgery. The consequently disrupted psychological functions then have to reintegrate—not always an easy task. In addition, the iatrogenic effect of coercively intruding on an individual who already has a low threshold for perceiving intrusiveness presents real difficulties in the later development of trust (Haynes, 1986).

To the degree the paranoid individual is more integrated in functioning, intrusive techniques can be avoided and the therapist can focus on developing trust. In that manner, paranoids may gain recourse to another individual, a pattern often absent in them. Therapists must attempt to maintain their integrity and honesty while empathizing with the paranoid's delusional beliefs. The critical feat is to gain the trust of an individual who is pervasively untrusting and to accept, and yet not participate in, the paranoid's delusional system.

■   # Delusional (Paranoid) Disorder (297.10)

Delusional (Paranoid) Disorder (DPD) is rarely observed in clinical practice, for several reasons. First, DPD apparently does not exist as commonly as many other disorders. Second, the higher level of personality integration allows DPDs to avoid seeing a clinician, even when their world is being disrupted. Since they are inclined to isolate themselves under stress, it is very hard to even coerce them into treatment.

It has occasionally been asserted that DPD is not a distinct diagnostic category, like schizophrenia or affective disorder. However, Kembler (1980) reviews research in this area and concludes that, indeed, DPD is separate from either schizophrenia or affective disorder and deserves to be designated as such.

☐   DSM-III-R

DPD is marked by a structured, chronic, and nonbizarre delusional system. If auditory or visual hallucinations are present, they are not prominent. This delusional system focuses on few issues (usually just one), and after the acceptance of the first premise, the logic is reasonable and orderly and consequent behavior is not obviously odd or bizarre. To apply a diagnosis of DPD, the clinician must find that (1) the person has not met the criteria for either schizophrenia or organic disorder, (2) any mood disorder has been brief relative to the delusional behavior, and (3) there is evidence of nonbizarre delusions (those that reflect real life: being cheated on by a spouse, being followed, etc.). DPD is subdivided, based on the type of delusion, into the following types: grandiose, erotomanic, jealous, persecutory, somatic, and unspecified.

☐   MMPI

There are fewer data in the literature on the MMPI responses of DPDs than there are for most other psychopathology groupings. On occasion, a DPD will show a spike on scale 6, with most of the other scales relatively low. This is not common, however, as the defenses usually do not allow that kind of disclosure. A moderate elevation on scale 6 along with an elevation on scale 4 is more common, reflecting the paranoid delusions and the hostility and social alienation that typically accompany them. At the same time, this suspiciousness and anger can result in a complaining attitude if the client has been forced into a diagnostic situation, and hence a higher K scale relative to other psychopathology groups, with a concomitant lower F scale, can be expected. In addition, scale 9 is usually moderately elevated.

☐   16 PF

Just as with the DPD, paranoid individuals may skip many items, and the clinician should examine this closely if someone else is doing the scoring. Scale L may be elevated, though DPDs are often well enough defended so that this is not the case. Q_3 is likely to be particularly high, and scales N and Q_1 are likely to be low. These scores all reflect the guardedness and the integration around the delusional system that mark a DPD. They are likely to be lower on scale A than their behavior would suggest, which reflects the inner guardedness not always directly manifest in their initial interpersonal contacts.

DPDs are likely to be relatively low on Q_4, indicating the denial of anxiety, and low on Q_1, again indicating a conservative and guarded approach toward the world. Scores are relatively high on B because DPD is a coping mechanism more common in brighter individuals. The chronic and unshakable aspects of the delusions are reflected in higher scores on scales G and E. Scale G points to the persistently moralistic nature of DPDs' belief systems, and scale E points to the need for dominance that is embedded in DPDs' coping strategies. The DPD is likely to be relatively low on M, as reflective inner fantasy is antithetical to the use of projection and denial (Heilbrun et al., 1985).

☐   OTHER TEST-RESPONSE PATTERNS

On the WAIS, DPDs are likely to attain high arithmetic and picture completion scores, reflecting their hyperalertness toward the environment. They also do well on similarities and comprehension, in large part because they take a meticulous approach to these tests and are thus likely to gain two-point answers. Their propensity toward abstraction also helps them in the similarities test.

During the tests, they are likely to be argumentative, critical, and condescending about both the purpose of the test and the actual questions used. They may even object to the examiner's writing down responses or ask to examine what has been written. On the Rorschach, they are likely to attain very high F and F+ percentages, reflecting their constriction, as well as many Dd and space responses. Unless they feel comfortable, they are likely to reject cards that the clinician is reasonably sure they could handle intellectually, and, in general, the record provided is sparse. Although they characteristically have few M and color responses, the more grandiose DPDs do show M responses. Phillips and Smith (1953) suggest that any "eye" or "ear" responses, as well as any looking at the back of the cards, are indicative of a paranoid orientation. There is a concern for the symmetry in the cards, and, as in other tests, there is criticism of the test itself, particularly if the ambiguity of the Rorschach stimuli becomes threatening (Beck, 1951).

Most common on the MCMI is an elevated P score—at least 75 and very possibly greater than 85—because this personality type is likely to develop acute paranoid disorders; PP may be raised, depending on the extent to which the paranoid defenses allow disclosure. Except for the occurrence of delusions, paranoids are generally cognitively intact, so scores less than 75 on SS should occur. Elevations on scale 6 commonly occur, indicating an aggressive component of paranoia and possible acting-out. Elevations on 5 are rather common, as paranoid features are present in the narcissist; variable scores on 7 occur, depending upon the degree of obsessive-compulsive features. Patrick (1988) found the MCMI to be more effective than the MMPI in assessing paranoid disorders.

☐   TREATMENT OPTIONS

DPDs will typically undergo treatment only when coerced by possible legal sanctions or the threat of the loss of a relationship (Haynes, 1986). They are inclined to be condescending and only make a pretense of interest, at least at first.

Since DPD is marked by a well-integrated system of personality functioning, albeit based on bizarre premises (Oltmanns and Maher, 1988), intrusive techniques are likely to backfire and further alienate the client from the treatment process. It is hoped that consistent contact in psychotherapy will lead to a development of some minimal trust in the relationship. This trust gives DPDs a much needed feedback resource, a person with whom they might test out the adequacy of their delusional system.

The therapist must accept and empathize with the DPD and yet not lose integrity as a therapist by participating in the delusional system. For example, the therapist may note correlates between his or her own life and the client's, which gives the client a potential new frame of reference as well as a new model for coping with vulnerability and fear. Humor, notably absent in many DPDs, can be modeled, as can other cognitive coping systems.

As they move away from their delusional systems, a variety of cognitive retraining procedures (Meichenbaum, 1985) can be brought into play. The clinician might also consider group therapy, though the transition from individual to group therapy is particularly tricky for the DPD. If it can be accomplished, an even greater potential for consensual feedback, so lacking for most DPDs, is then available.

■ Shared Paranoid and Induced Psychotic Disorders (197.30)

The Shared Paranoid Disorder has traditionally been called *folie à deux* ("the madness of two"). As noted earlier, this category is no longer included in the DSM per se. However, since it is a traditionally recognized pattern and still occurs, it is included here. This form of double insanity involves one person who is originally paranoid in some form and a receiver who passively incorporates the paranoid beliefs into his or her own system. The receiver is in an intimate relationship with the dominant individual and has a history of being psychologically dependent on the controlling person. When they break away from the relationship, the paranoid belief system dissipates.

The diagnosis of Induced Psychotic Disorder (297.30) applies specifically to the secondary individual, the receiver, and it requires that the delusion be similar to that of the sender. Since the paranoid ideation of the receiver is likely to dissipate if the relationship is broken (Oltmanns and Maher, 1988), the paranoid elements are not the dominant focus of the personality. The need for affiliative dependency is a primary factor, usually in conjunction with passive-aggressive hostility that is expressed through the channel of the shared paranoid belief system.

☐   MMPI

The receiver is typically very defensive about the paranoid beliefs and in one sense wishes to manifest them to gain the approval of the dominant other. Thus, a raised score on scale 6 is likely. Several questions on L tap a willingness to trust others, so the receiver's dependency keeps the L scale from being extremely high.

Interestingly, depression is common here, as are psychopathic components; hence, scales 2 and 4 are likely to be raised. Males who are receivers are higher on scale 5 than other paranoids, whereas females are lower on scale 5. Scale 7 is also likely to be moderately raised, as is scale 8.

☐ 16 PF

Since these individuals are fairly open about their paranoid beliefs, they score high on L, and the submissiveness is reflected in lower E and H scores. They are also, for the same reason, relatively higher on I and N. They are not likely to show as high a Q_3 score as other paranoid individuals, as their personality integration derives from the other person rather than from their own personality. They are also not likely to be as bright as other paranoids; hence, B should be lower.

☐ OTHER TEST-RESPONSE PATTERNS

On the MCMI, the features of the paranoid profile are present. While elevated 5 and 6 are likely in the dominating member of the pair, elevations on 3 and 4 would be the most prominent patterns in the dependent member of the pair.

☐ TREATMENT OPTIONS

The sender, the dominant individual in the shared paranoid disorder, often manifests classical paranoia and is thus now diagnosed as having a delusional (paranoid) disorder; the reader is referred to the previous section for the modes of treating this pattern. The first issue for the shared paranoid system is to separate the parties, either by hospitalization or by some other means. At this point, the paranoid elements of the receiver are likely to dissipate since they are heavily based on the dependent relationship with the dominant personality. Cognitive retraining procedures and assertive therapy for the dependency are especially appropriate. A group therapy experience can give the person the much needed personality support and at the same time provide access for modeling new and more appropriate belief systems.

CHAPTER 4

Mood (Affective) Disorders

In DSM-III-R, the focus is on two major subcategories: bipolar disorders and depressive disorders. It is important to note that DSM-III-R does not provide for a diagnosis where mania alone (without some evidence of depression) is found. The authors of DSM-III-R believe that such a pattern occurs very rarely, if at all. Thus, the diagnosis of whether there is a manic episode is useful to determine whether the affective disorder is a bipolar syndrome or depression alone.

Within the depressive disorder subcategory of the mood disorders, the formal DSM-III-R terms are "major depression" and "dysthymia." Likewise, the same differentiation is used for the bipolar disorders, substituting the terms "bipolar" and "cyclothymia" to designate the severe and the chronic behavior-problem patterns, respectively. The DSM-III-R also now provides for an optional diagnosis of late luteal phase dysphoric disorder.

■ Treatment Options

Treatment of the mood disorders depends on which affect is predominately manifested, mania or depression. When it is mania, the primary treatment of choice has been lithium therapy (Mander, 1986; NIMH Staff, 1977). If this is not successful, others have used some of the antipsychotic medications, which can at least suppress the behavior. ECT has also been used, but this is only reasonable as a last resort. When the quality of the manic episode shifts toward irritability and suspiciousness, appropriate techniques for the paranoid disorders, noted earlier, can be considered.

A wide variety of treatments have been useful for depression, although depression remains a pervasive problem for our society (Rutter, 1988; Roy, 1987). Classical treatment wisdom advises the use of chemotherapy and/or ECT. The problems with chemotherapy are the significant side effects, the further disruption of any sense the depressives might have that they can control their destiny, the fact that they do not work in all cases (although they do in the majority of them), the delay in action of often up to two weeks, and the fact that drugs only work to improve the activity spectrum and not the interpersonal dimension (Lyons et al., 1985).

ECT has been recommended where immediate disruption of the depression response is required, especially when suicide is a possibility. ECT is appropriate for the severe psychotic depressions, though the treater must consider the cost-benefit issues of short- and long-term organic dysfunction as a result of the ECT and the possible exaggeration of learned helplessness through the use of such a coercive treatment (many theories of depression emphasize learned helplessness as a generic factor).

Several studies, including that of Weeks et al. (1980), report no detrimental long-term effects from ECT. However, such studies usually contain methodological approaches that do not deal with the actual issues involved. In the Weeks et al. study, for example, the number of ECTs received by clients was low compared to the number administered in traditional psychiatric practice, and there was no random assignment of clients to the ECT and non-ECT group. Others (Breggin, 1979; Smith and Meyer, 1987) detail substantial data to indicate that ECT results in impaired judgment and insight, shallow emotional reactions, confusion, and global disruption of intellectual functioning, these effects being permanent and resulting from the electrical insult to the brain. And most researchers note that there is still very little informed consent obtained from patients for the use of ECT.

Existential therapies are useful where the central quality of the depression is apathy rather than psychomotor retardation. Also, the cognitive behavior therapies have been specifically helpful throughout the range of depressive disorders. The reader is referred to the individual sections in this syndrome grouping for further elaboration.

■ Manic Episode

Mania has been described since ancient times. Hippocrates accurately noted many of the symptoms but attributed manic behavior to an excess of yellow bile. While depression is a common affective disorder, mania is not: It accounts for only about 4 percent of psychiatric hospital admissions. Its incidence, however, appears to be increasing in the United States. A possible explanation for this increase is that there is now a reasonably effective and straightforward cure for mania, while in the past it was considered very difficult to treat (Mander, 1986), so clinicians may now be more amenable to putting borderline cases into a category that now has a better prognosis.

Throughout the literature, three cardinal features of the manic phase have been described: (1) hyperactive motor behavior, (2) labile euphoria and/or irritability, and (3) flight of ideas.

Four important behavioral variables are useful in making a differential diagnosis between severe manic episodes, schizoaffective disorder, and a more emotionally labile form of schizophrenia. First, while all three categories are distractible, schizoaffectives and schizophrenics are primarily distracted by internal thoughts and ruminations, whereas manics are distracted by the external stimuli that often go unnoticed by others. Secondly, schizoaffectives and schizophrenics during an active phase tend to avoid any true relationships with others, whereas the manic is usually profoundly open to contact with other people (Mester, 1986; NIMH Staff, 1977). Third, another useful distinction between mania and schizophrenia involves language organization. Though both manics and schizophrenics may exhibit thought disorder, the incoherence in manic speech is due to shifts from one coherent discourse structure to another, while the ability of schizophrenics to construct any discourse structure is different (Hoffman et al., 1986). Fourth, while the thought problems of schizophrenics are marked by disorganization, confusion, and peculiar words or phrases, the thought problems of mania are marked by odd combinations denoted by playfulness, flippancy, and humor (Solovay et al., 1987). Additionally, supersensitivity to light (noted, for example, by a marked reduction in plasma melatonin levels upon exposure to light at night) has been found to be a marker for manic reactions (Lewy et al., 1988).

Positron-emission tomography (PET) is a radiological technique that determines patterns of glucose metabolism in the brain. These patterns can be abnormal for both manics and schizophrenics and yet still differ from each other. Schizophrenics, especially schizophrenics of low competence, show decreased glucose metabolism in the frontal cortex; manics in the midst of an attack show increased glucose activity in the right temporal region. There are some drawbacks to this diagnostic technique. First, there is little evidence that PET can make that differentiation with any consistency when the behavior patterns are somewhat similar. PET is also expensive and requires the introduction of a catheter into a blood vessel, a small but clear risk. In addition, a radioactive substance is introduced to the brain, and the long-term risks of such a procedure are not yet known.

☐   DSM-III-R

To warrant a diagnosis of manic episode, the DSM-III-R requires the existence of one or more clear-cut periods of predominantly euphoric and/or irritable mood (not due to an organic cause); in addition, the person must show a distinct period of abnormality, with episodes usually lasting from several days to a few months. There must also be evidence that contraindicates schizophrenic symptoms—for example, no delusions or hallucinations for as long as two weeks in the absence of prominent mood symptoms – and at least three of the following symptoms must be present (four symptoms, if the mood is irritable rather than euphoric): hyperactivity, increased or pressed speech, flight of ideas, inflated self-esteem, less need for sleep, excessive distractibility, excessive involvement in pleasurable activities with ultimately negative payoff, and psychomotor agitation or increased goal-directed activities. These criteria constitute a hypomanic syndrome. With the addition of marked impairment of functioning in the social or occupational arena or the need for hospitalization because of dangerousness, it is a manic syndrome.

It must again be noted that the DSM-III-R does not provide for a diagnosis of mania in the absence of depression. Thus, the diagnosis of manic episode is a primary diagnostic question in the eventual decision as to whether a bipolar diagnosis or a diagnosis of depression alone is warranted. The primary diagnosis of manic episode may be further delineated by qualifiers, e.g., "in partial or full remission" or "with psychotic features," the latter requiring the presence of delusions or hallucinations, which may be either mood-congruent or incongruent.

MMPI

A high 9 scale, along with elevated scores on 6 and 8 and usually 4, are predominant in the severe manic episode. A very low 2 scale may indicate the manic component of a cyclothymic process. Winters et al. (1981) found the 9-6 code discriminated manics from schizophrenics effectively. Scales 3 and 0 are usually elevated in manics, and scale 2 is low, except in the depressive phase of bipolar disorders (Silver et al., 1981). The 6 scale is particularly related to the irritability factor. Those individuals who are not irritable but are primarily euphoric usually do not score high on the 6 scale or even on the 4 scale. Very irritable manics will occasionally have their highest elevations on scales 3 and 4, with lesser elevations on scales 6, 8, and 9. To the degree that there is an attempt to control tension and anxiety, scale 7 is higher. Severity is related to the F scale: The higher it is, the more likely the individual will manifest a psychotic level of disorder. In moderate-level manics, the F scale may be lower with the K scale raised, reflecting a denial of psychopathology.

16 PF

Manics score high on scales F and H and low on N. This results from their high activity levels, combined with a lack of insight about the reactions they engender in others. They also tend to be high on scales A and E.

To the degree they are euphoric, manics are a bit higher on A relative to E, and lower on L, whereas they tend to be the opposite to the degree they are irritable. Their high level of tense and driven behavior is reflected in a low Q_3 scale, with a tendency to be moderately low on C and Q_2, while moderately high on O.

OTHER TEST-RESPONSE PATTERNS

The frenetic behavior patterns of the manic should result in higher WAIS-R scores when speed per se is an issue, such as in digit symbol. However, the lack of allowance for feedback through checking of one's own performance results in lower scores on block design, picture arrangement, and object assembly. They may often come quite close to the required response, but in their impatience offer an incomplete solution as the finished solution. If their manic behavior includes continuous talking, they may do well on subtests such as comprehension, vocabulary, and similarities, in which persistence can result in extra points. However, at the same time, if the mania takes the form of impatience, they would likely also score low on these tests. Throughout both the WAIS-R and the Rorschach, they are likely to manifest a desire to move on to a new item or task.

The frenetic behavior should result in a number of poor W responses on the Rorschach, with simultaneous notice of details that others often ignore. Response latencies are typically very short, and there are usually a number of M responses (Wagner and Wagner, 1981). Shafer (1954) asserts that a high number of confabulation responses and/or shading responses, in combination with a high percentage of C, CF, Dd, S, and W responses, are indicative of mania, a result generally confirmed by Wagner and Heise (1981).

The emotional lability and ambivalence indicated by high scores on 8 and C on the MCMI suggest the predisposition of these persons toward development of manic episodes. During the period of mania, an N of 85 or higher should occur. Impulsive behavior during these periods may cause increase in the likelihood of drug abuse, evidenced by a T score of 74–85. The flight of ideas and sometimes confused state of the manic may produce some elevation on SS, but when it is 75 or higher, a diagnosis of schizoaffective disorder may be warranted.

TREATMENT OPTIONS

The single most recommended treatment for mania is lithium therapy; it is reported to reverse the manic factor in approximately 75 percent of the cases treated (Mander, 1986; NIMH Staff, 1977). However, further research demonstrates that combining psychotherapy with lithium therapy is superior to the use of lithium alone (Mester, 1986).

Lithium salts were originally used, but lithium carbonate is now used because it is less toxic, is chemically convenient, and contains a high percentage of lithium relative to weight. Since lithium is rapidly absorbed by the kidneys, it has to be taken in divided doses to prevent any cyclical physiological response from overwhelming the client. As a result of the need for consistently administered divided doses, education of the patient is critical. Doses must be taken on a schedule, so when a patient indicates a lack of intelligence and/or discipline, mechanisms for their controlled administration are necessary.

Since manics may have elaborated some negative behavioral habits in addition to the apparent physiological disorder, behavioral training is advised in addition to the lithium. It is helpful to teach the client to consider plans thoroughly before beginning to actuate them, to follow through with them once the decision is made, and to stay with interpersonal commitments.

■ Major Depressive Episode

As with the manic disorders, depressive disorders are divided between major depression and dysthymia (or depressive neurosis), based again on chronicity and severity. It is estimated in DSM-III-R that approximately 3 percent of males and 6 percent of females have had a depressive episode sufficiently severe to require hospitalization. An important aspect of the explanation for the twofold incidence of depression in females compared to that in males is the accentuation of behavior prescribed by traditional sex role expectations (Meyer and Salmon, 1988).

Several factors predict depression in women: low self-esteem, a preoccupation with failure, a sense of helplessness, a pessimistic attitude toward the world, and narcissistic vulnerability (Roy, 1987; Altman and Wittenborn, 1980). Cofer and Wittenborn (1980) specifically found, in addition to the factors just mentioned, that a critical mother and a dependency-fostering father were also important in the genesis of depression in females.

□ DSM-III-R

If there is a single major depressive episode, the formal DSM-III-R diagnosis is Major Depression, Single Episode (296.2x), whereas the occurrence of more than one is diagnosed Major Depression, Recurrent (296.3x). Both require an absence of any manic episodes.

The diagnosis of major depressive episode requires evidence of dysphoric mood or loss of interest or pleasure in most of one's usual activities for at least two weeks. This reaction cannot be the result of a schizophrenic or organic disorder or simple bereavement such as follows the loss of a loved one. At least five of the following consistently present depressive symptoms are required for the diagnosis: (1) sleep disturbance, (2) agitated or retarded psychomotor ability, (3) weight gain or loss of appetite, (4) loss of interest in usual activities, (5) fatigue or loss of energy, (6) guilt or sense of worthlessness, (7) slowed or disrupted thinking, (8) suicide or death ideation, or (9) depressed mood nearly every day (or irritability for adolescents).

A major depressive episode is delineated by most of the same qualifiers as the manic episode, e.g., "in partial remission" is between "in full remission" and "mild." The psychotic designation requires evidence of either hallucinations or delusions. The disorder can also be sublabeled as to mood-congruent or mood-incongruent psychotic features. Again, severity per se is not enough to warrant a psychotic diagnosis. There is also the possibility of a subdiagnosis of melancholic type, or a seasonal pattern. Spitzer (1988) suggests that the latter may eventually emerge as a separate diagnostic category: seasonal affective disorder.

□   MMPI

Scale 2 is, of course, consistently elevated in chronic depressive disorders. The 2-7/7-2 combination is commonly noted across the depressive spectrum (Lachar, 1974). A concomitant high scale 4 suggests possible passive-aggressive accompaniments to the depression (Anderson and Bauer, 1985), and it has been noted by several observers that a high scale 4 in depressives correlates best with both hostility and depressive thoughts rather than with psychomotor retardation. The 3-2 and the 2-8 profiles are also indicative of possible depression (Lachar, 1974; Silver et al., 1981). As the 8 score rises, the latter profile is more likely to be schizoaffective, and such persons are likely to be agitated and have a specific suicide plan. Johnson et al. (1980) found the 2-8-7 combination to be characteristic of severe depression. Overall, Winters et al. (1981) found codes 2-7-8, 2-8, and 4-8-2 to discriminate a group of depressives from schizophrenics effectively.

In all of these situations, as scores rise on both F and 8 and scores on scale 9 become lower, the depression is proportionately more severe, there is retarded motor behavior, and the depression is prone to move into the psychotic range. Scale 9 is also an indication of avoidance patterns and correlates with the depression. In some cases, a high 9 signals a frenetic counterphobic response to depression, and the 1-9 code is often a masked depression. The clinician occasionally sees a 2-0 profile, which suggests a chronic depression. Also, the profile of a high 1 and relatively low 2 scale, along with verbalizations of depression, suggests a situationally generated depression, possibly even an extended bereavement.

□   16 PF

In the marked and moderate range of the depressive episode, individuals are likely to score relatively high on scales I, L, M, O, and Q_4, particularly where there is still a degree of agitation in the depressive response. They also score high on Q_2. As the disorder moves toward a psychotic dimension, scores are higher on L, M, and O and lower on C, H, and Q_3. They revert to average on Q_2 and are now lower on A. Because of their apathy toward the environment, they also score low on B.

☐   OTHER TEST-RESPONSE PATTERNS

There are several good rating scales—e.g., the Beck, Zung, and Hamilton scales—designed specifically to assess depression, each with its own strengths and weaknesses (Lambert et al., 1986).

On the WAIS-R, the classic sign of depression has been an overall performance-scale score significantly less than the verbal-scale score, as well as generally brief responses (Swiercinsky, 1985). Depressed clients are likely to fail on WAIS-R items that they should typically be able to answer, simply because they give up on them. Within the performance-scale scores, picture completion is usually the highest. Within the verbal-scale scores, digit span is expected to be the lowest (Keiser and Lowy, 1980), with arithmetic also being very low, and vocabulary rather high. "I don't know" responses and general lack of persistence are common.

Depressive inpatients, in common with other inpatients, are likely to score high on MCMI scales 1, 2, 3, and 8 (McCann and Suess, 1988). Both CC and D of 85 or higher should occur on the MCMI in most major depressive eipsodes, especially where there are psychotic features. The uncomfortable depressed state may be represented by some elevation on A. The intense moods and dysregulated activation of the borderline will predispose him or her to react with a depressive episode. The emptiness and dysphoria experienced by the avoidant can often escalate to a major depressive episode. Therefore, elevations between 74 and 85 are likely on scales C and 2. Overall, the MCMI does not appear to be as effective in assessing depression as does the MMPI (Patrick, 1988).

On the Rorschach, long reaction times to the cards and the rejection of several cards are probable. Furthermore, the number of responses is usually less than twenty. The individual is often highly self-critical while responding to the Rorschach. A low percentage of good W or original responses and high F percent and a high percentage of popular responses are common (Swiercinsky, 1985). FY or MY responses are seen as indicative of depression (Phillips and Smith, 1953), and something like a YF response would in particular suggest depression. There are typically few C and CF responses, a low number of M responses, and a low number of W or Wt responses (Wagner and Heise, 1981). Dysphoric content is common, and cloud and vista responses occasionally occur. Within the Exner system, Mason et al. (1985) found that depressives scored significantly lower than normals on Rorschach scoring criteria M,

Xt%, Pop and significantly higher on DQv, Col-Shd, Sum V, Sum SP.SC. They also scored lower than normals but higher than schizophrenics on (FQw) − (fQ−), Xt%, Pop.

Figures on the Bender-Gestalt are likely to be boxed, to show a confused order, and to be drawn overly large (Rossini and Kaspar, 1987). Stories on the Thematic Apperception Test are short and stereotyped and are often only descriptions of the cards rather than an actual story. It is difficult to carry on an inquiry in either the TAT or the Rorschach since the person may give only monosyllabic portrayals of each card. Themes of guilt, lack of success, expiation through suffering are common (Rutter, 1988). Bellak (1986) points out that cards 12BG, 14, 3BM, and 3BF may bring out the depressed feelings of a subject. Card 9GF can also bring out depressed feelings, even suicidal tendencies, as when a story involves circumstances in which the girl below in the picture is made into someone who panics and runs into the sea.

Severe endogenous depression, which is primarily denoted by motor retardation, depressed mood, lack of reactivity, depressive delusions, and self-reproach (Andreasen et al., 1986), shows some promise of being reliably diagnosed by the overnight Dexamethasone Suppression Test (DST) (Dam et al., 1985).

TREATMENT OPTIONS

Since the major depressive episode often involves a severe level of depression, possibly including psychotic components, more intrusive techniques are likely to be used (Simons et al., 1986). However, the techniques discussed in the next subsection (Dysthymia) are useful as well.

ECT has often been used for severe depression; it is probably one of the few syndromes for which there is good evidence of ECT's effectiveness (Valenstein, 1986). However, that effectiveness must be balanced against the high psychological and physical costs of the technique. Similarly psychosurgery has been used in which a lesion is placed in areas that control emotional response, such as the limbic system.

Since ancient times, humans have used drugs to alleviate depression, notably alcohol and other self-medications. Though new medications, such as gepirone, are constantly being developed, the two traditional major subcategories of antidepressants used in recent times are the tricyclics and the monoamine oxidase (MAO) inhibitors (see Appendix B). Both drug classes require substantial trial-and-error adjustment on dosages (titration), and both require from several days to several weeks before any positive effects occur. Since the MAO inhibitors have more significant side effects, the tricyclics have been favored in recent years. They are most effective with severe depressions that have a significant endogenous component, but the rate of effectiveness is seldom better than 70 percent (Andreasen et al., 1986; Fabry, 1980). When the tricyclics are administered to someone who actually has a bipolar disorder in a depressive phase, there is a very real danger of stimulating a manic episode. Some depressives have responded well to high doses (3,000 mg.) at bedtime of L-tryptophan, a naturally occurring amino acid. A dose of nicotinic acid needs to be taken at the same time to protect the liver from destroying all of the L-tryptophan. Also, in a study in which imipramine and lithium were used, Prien and Klupfer (1986) found that drug therapy should be maintained for at least 16–20 weeks following a cessation of significant depressive symptoms. Additionally, even mild symptoms during the period indicated that the depression had not run its course and that continued drug therapy was essential to contribute to the absence of relapse in the treatment group.

When there is a strong seasonal variation in the depression (it occurs significantly more often in winter), sessions of bright, incandescent light can be effective (Yerevian et al., 1986); it is equally important to avoid or remedy disruptions of the individual's circadian rhythms. Also, there is some evidence that a certain small subgroup of major depressives may have a disturbance in rapid eye movement (REM) sleep patterns. This specific pattern is marked by an abnormal temporal distribution of REM sleep. This inadequate capacity to sustain REM sleep tends to worsen with age in all individuals and may explain why sleep problems are much more common as we age. Vogel and his colleagues (1980) treated this subgroup of depressives by depriving them of REM sleep for short periods of time and found that this significantly decreased their depression. It is interesting that depressed patients who are responsive to this technique were unresponsive to the tricyclic antidepressives, though in a comparison among studies, REM sleep deprivation and drug treatments were equally effective. However, it takes about three weeks for the REM sleep deprivation technique to bring about improvement. When specific brain dysfunction has caused depression, the disease is more likely to be found in the left frontal region (Reitan and Wolfson, 1986).

Any of the intrusive techniques have a number of risks, which, of course, can be balanced by gains in controlling the depression and in preventing any suicide behaviors. Yet it is most important that they be implemented in an overall treatment that includes a variety of techniques designed to control the depression psychologically and to upgrade the skills needed to prevent future depression (Simons et al., 1986).

■ Dysthymia (Depressive Neurosis) (300.40)

Many of the symptoms characteristic of the depressive episodes are noted here. However, although they are not as severe or as common, they are of greater duration. A duration of two years is required for the diagnosis (except for children and adolescents, where the requirement is one year and where also irritability can substitute for depression), and periods of dysphoria cannot be separated by periods of normal mood of more than two months. Dysphoria and apathy are commonly noted, though neither severe impairment in social or vocational functioning nor significant suicidal preoccupation is consistently present. Along with the above characteristics, the DSM-III-R requires that at least two depressive symptoms occur, such as sleep disturbance, poor appetite or overeating, low self-esteem, low energy or fatigue, problems in concentration or decision-making, or feelings of hopelessness.

☐   MMPI

Since this personality profile does not show the anxiety, agitation, and possible psychotic components of major depression, a lower overall profile is expected. For example, scale 9 is not as likely to be low nor is scale 0 likely to be as high as in the depressive episode. Yet, scales F, 2, and 7 are high. If scale 4 is raised, there is reason to look for a passive-aggressive use of the depression (Anderson and Bauer, 1985; Silver et al., 1981; Fowler, 1981). If somatization is a major factor, scale 1 should be high.

☐   16 PF

Similarly, the 16 PF profile is not as extreme for dysthymia as in the depressive eposode, though the general outline is the same and is similar to the pattern for the more neurotic aspects of the depressive episode. With that stipulation, scale C is not as likely to be low nor is Q_4 likely to be quite as high.

☐   OTHER TEST-RESPONSE PATTERNS

In contrast to the profile of the major depressive episode, the highest elevation on the MCMI is likely to occur on D, with the more severe symptomatology of CC less prominent. To the degree anxiety is present, there is an elevated A. Borderline and negativistic personalities can be susceptible to developing this disorder, so elevations on scales 8 and C are indicated. Very low scores on 7 are expected, in that the restrained affectivity and conscientious self-image of the conforming personality are not compatible with the depressive affective features of the dysthymic disorder.

Several short scales (approximately twenty questions) have been specifically designed to measure depression and can be helpful in screening procedures and measuring outcome (Lambert et al., 1986). Three of the most commonly used have been the Zung Self-Rating Depression Scale, the Hamilton Rating Scales, and the Beck Depression Inventory. All three have been found to have adequate validity, though Lambert's data seems to favor the Zung. Others have commented, however, that the Zung scale is too age-specific for certain groups, since normals under nineteen years of age or over sixty-five unfortunately tend to score in the depressive range.

Performance on other tests will be similar to that of the depressive episode, though again the clinician should temper the interpretation of these patterns with the awareness that this is less severe than major depression, with the symptoms more integrated into the ongoing personality.

☐   TREATMENT OPTIONS

Monitoring is a worthwhile first step in any treatment of depression (Rutter, 1988). Simple self-monitoring of both mood and activity produces decreases in depressed mood, as well as some increase in self-reported participation in chosen activities. With regard to their future perspective, depressives should understand that occasional upsurges of anxiety and depression will occur throughout their life and that these should not be construed as indications of a return to pathology. This is an important admonition for all groups with psychopathology. In many cases, as these persons move toward a cure, they develop hope that they will never encounter any experiences similar to their past disorder. Hence, when these naturally emerge in at least a minor form, there is a tendency to drop their coping patterns. Adopting a cognitive set to counteract this phenomenon is most important.

Chemotherapy is often used with dysthymia, but it is not as appropriate as it is for the more severe depressive episode (Simons et al., 1986). Since learned helplessness is often a factor in dysthymia, chemotherapy, ECT, or similar treatments can easily exacerbate this component by pointing out in a direct way that patients cannot play a major role in redirecting their life situation. As a result, a package derived from the following psychological treatment methods is recommended.

The clinician can employ contingency management techniques, as they aid the client especially in developing a new self-percept less confounded by helplessness and apathy. It is initially advisable for the therapist to avoid reinforcing any of the client's depressive verbalizations. The clinician can use audiotapes of the sessions to indicate to clients how thoroughly they are inclined toward these verbalizations. This approach can be augmented by a contractual agreement with the client to avoid such verbalizations and instead to increase the number of positive verbalizations (Meichenbaum, 1985). Such behaviors can be consolidated by using the Premack Principle and, in addition, by training the family and friends of the client to reinforce positive behaviors and verbalizations (Kolevzon and Green, 1985).

Imagery techniques are also helpful. For example, Lazarus (1971) recommends a variation of systematic desensitization that he terms "time projection with routine reinforcement." Clients are first hypnotized, deep relaxation is induced, and then they are asked to imagine that they are in the future and are engaged in what had been previously pleasant activities. The client is then asked to return to the present while still maintaining these positive feelings and images from the future. By continually shifting back and forth, this time-projection strategy aids the depressed person to develop more-consistent present images of pleasurable activities; Lazarus indicates that this then generalizes into behavior.

Probably the most important psychological treatment methods of depression are the cognitive-behavioral techniques, derived originally from Beck (1976). Through discussion and consciousness-raising techniques, clients are taught to view their thoughts more objectively (to distance themselves from these maladaptive thoughts). Such common depressive thoughts as "I am totally worthless" are suggested as hypotheses rather than facts, a phenomenon rather than a reality. In addition, the client is taught to "decenter." Through feedback, possibly in a group, depressives learn that they are not the focal point of all events, such as a disparaging glance on the street. Implicit in all this is the need for clients to learn to validate any self-made conclusions more objectively, a behavior notably absent in depressives. The belief systems that a person lives by are then examined, since impossible standards are commonly promoted within the self-system. This is not unlike the approaches of George Kelly's (1955) personal construct theory or Albert Ellis's Rational-Emotive Therapy (Ellis and Dryden, 1987).

Another useful cognitive-behavioral treatment for dysthymia is covert negative reinforcement, since depressed individuals often find it difficult to envision positive behaviors at all and therefore are not particularly responsive to covert positive reinforcement techniques. In covert negative reinforcement with depression, a highly aversive image is developed and is then terminated by the imagination of the performance of the desired behaviors. It is critical that the switchover of images take place as quickly as possible.

Finally, a number of life-style modification techniques can be used (Cattell, 1986). Assertiveness training is appropriate (Wickrameseka, 1988) so that the person does not introject anger and frustration. Inducing the individual to take more frequent and more strenuous exercise can help in many cases (Tomparowski and Ellis, 1986), and if the depression has a seasonal component, sessions of bright, incandescent light can be helpful (Yerevian et al., 1986). Within the context of group therapy, the person can contract for a series of graded tasks, all of which are increasingly pleasurable and thus likely to change the overall negative set these individuals carry. Such experiences appear especially therapeutic to the degree that they also increase the client's sense of mastery over events in the world.

■   Bipolar Disorder

The diagnosis of Bipolar Disorder, Manic (296.4x) requires that the individual has in the past shown a depressive episode and is now manifesting or has recently manifested a manic episode (the reader is referred to the criteria in the sections on depressive episode and manic episode).

The converse is required for the diagnosis of Bipolar Disorder, Depressed (296.5x). The diagnosis of Bipolar Disorder, Mixed (296.6x) requires that major depressive and manic episode symptomatology occur in rapid alternation or in combination and that the depressive symptoms that do occur are prominent, lasting for at least a full day. Bipolar Disorder, Mixed replaces the traditional term "manic-depressive psychosis," as it is usually understood.

The MMPI, 16 PF, and other test data patterns are generally similar to what is expected in single episodes. The reader is referred to the appropriate sections for the behavior pattern manifest at the time. However, it should be noted that depressives tend to be lower on scales K, 2, 6, 7, and 8 than do bipolars (Donnelly et al., 1976). Clients with bipolar affective disorder show larger average cortical-evoked potentials than do normals, who in turn are higher than schizophrenics, with this particularly so at high stimulus intensities. It has also been found that the shift from mania to depression is physiologically marked by increases of blood levels of phosphorous and calcium. A similar phenomenon has been observed when certain withdrawn depressives move toward more agitated behavior.

□   TREATMENT OPTIONS

The treatment of the bipolar is directed in large measure toward the dominant affective mode at the time. Lithium therapy is used to alleviate severe mania and has occasionally been effective with the depressive component as well, though the standard chemotherapy for the depressive component is that noted in the previous section on the depressive episode. It should again be noted that administration of the tricyclic antidepressants to an individual with bipolar disorder who is in a depressive phase may induce a manic episode. As the person moves toward a better level of functioning, the psychological treatment techniques noted in the sections on manic episode and dysthymic disorder become the primary mode.

■   Cyclothymia (301.13)

Cyclothymia is the DSM-III-R term for the traditional term "cyclothymic personality." As with dysthymia, this diagnosis requires a disorder duration of two years (though not symptom-free for more than two months); and one year for children and adolescents, as well as alternating numerous hypomanic episodes and depressions or loss of pleasure, that were not major depressions. The reader is referred to previous sections for those diagnoses as well as the concomitant patterns expected on the MMPI, 16 PF, MCMI, and other tests. This disorder has traditionally been thought to be very rare, but recent evidence suggests that it is at least moderately common.

□   TREATMENT OPTIONS

In most instances, the manic phase of cyclothymia is not severe enough to warrant significant intervention. Rather, it is more like a relief stage and, at worst, requires the psychological techniques noted in treatment of the manic episode. The depressive components are appropriately treated by the techniques detailed in the section on dysthymia. The clinician should be careful to watch for the possible emergence of a classic bipolar disorder, and if the client shows any increasing pathology, lithium might be considered. Some clinicians have found the use of a diary helpful with cyclothymia. As clients keep a diary, they become more attuned to those factors in their world that are likely to set off the pattern.

Atypical Mood Disorders

The DSM-III-R has provided categories labeled Bipolar Disorder NOS (296.70) and Depressive Disorders NOS (311.00). These are simply residual categories in which there is clear evidence of a general pattern, though it does not exactly fit the specific diagnostic requirements of any mood disorder or the adjustment disorder with depressed mood.

Schizoaffective Disorder (295.70)

This disorder was traditionally (i.e., in DSM-II) included as a subgroup under schizophrenia. However, it is now listed as a separate disorder, probably because of the evidence that it has several characteristics different from those disorders that remain under the "schizophrenic" rubric. Schizoaffective disorder is more likely than schizophrenia to have an acute onset, and it has a better prognosis for avoidance of a long hospitalization and recovery to a premorbid level of functioning. In addition, it has been noticed that blood relatives of persons with the schizoaffective disorder do not have a significantly higher proportion of the same disorder than do normals, a finding different from that of schizophrenia.

☐   DSM-III-R

The essential feature of this disorder is a combination of schizophrenic and affective symptoms. The affective component (either significant depression, mania, or an alternating mixture of the two) occurs before or concomitant with the onset of the schizophrenic symptomatology. Evidence for both clear schizophrenic and affective symptomatology must be present, but there is no requirement of a duration of six months to diagnose this disorder. At some point, there is at least a two-week episode of delusions or hallucinations, but without prominent mood symptoms. This is essentially a residual category, as the clinician should have ruled out the major depressive disorders, schizophrenia, and the schizophreniform disorder.

☐   MMPI

Because of the confluence of two pathological trends, the profiles in schizoaffective disorders are likely to appear quite disturbed. Johnson et al. (1980) find that a spike 8, with high scores on scales 2 and 7, is characteristic of the schizoaffective disorder, particularly when depression predominates. Another common pattern for the depressive schizoaffective is the 8-2 profile (Kelley and King, 1979a). It is probable that these individuals have considered suicide and even have a specific suicide plan. The possibility of acting out this plan is often related to the 9 scale. As the score moves up, it indicates an increase in the amount of available energy and makes actualization of the plan more likely.

If the affective component is more in the manic direction, a common profile is an 8-9/9-8, with a higher score on scale 4 as compared to the schizoaffective, depressed type. In both types, scale 7 is elevated, as is the F scale (though both are more elevated in the depressed type).

☐   16 PF

The 16 PF resembles the overall schizophrenic profile, but with the following qualifications. In the manic type of schizoaffective disorder, a higher A, F, and H and a lower N and Q_4 are more probable than in schizophrenia or schizoaffective, depressed type. Conversely, the schizoaffective, depressed type is inclined to show the reverse profile, having a fairly low F score, as well as lower scores on A, B (reflecting less attention to the task), E, H, and M. They also manifest a lower C and a higher O score, indicating more-blatant distress and emotional upset.

On the other tests, the typical patterns obtained by the schizophrenic are likely, with the added content and style factors specific to either the manic or depressed syndrome.

☐   OTHER TEST-RESPONSE PATTERNS

The characteristics of the schizophrenic and affective disorders will appear in varying combinations on the MCMI as well. Typically, one would expect the profile of the affective disorder that is present along with elevation above 74 on S and a higher elevation on SS. Since avoidant characteristics often occur, there may be a moderately high score on 2.

☐   TREATMENT OPTIONS

As with the bipolar disorder, the treatment in large part depends on the affective flavor of the disorder. Since it is usually depression, the reader is referred to the sections on the depressive episode and the dysthymic disorder. In those rarer cases that have a manic component, the reader is referred to the section on the manic episode. The section on the schizophrenic disorders is also relevant here.

Late Luteal Phase Dysphoric Disorder (LLPDD)

The concept of a specific syndrome related to negative mood changes premenstrually was first introduced by Frank in 1931 (Dawood, 1985). Since then, many studies have been conducted on premenstrual syndrome (LLPDD), but there is still much that is not known about the disorder. As with many syndromes, failure to agree on a definition has led various investigators to utilize different criteria, creating inconsistencies among research findings.

Traditionally termed "premenstrual syndrome," the DSM-III-R uses the term "late luteal phase dysphoric disorder" to avoid what many perceive as prejudicial implications that have encrusted on the traditional term. As noted in the Introduction to this book, this category is not an official DSM-III-R diagnosis, but it is included in the DSM-III-R as an optional diagnosis.

The DSM-III-R offers a rather complex diagnostic requirement in order to make a diagnosis of LLPDD, as opposed to the more general concept of premenstrual syndrome. At least five of the following ten symptoms must occur, with at least one of the symptoms being number 1, 2, 3, or 4: (1) persistent and significant anger or irritability, (2) marked affective lability, (3) marked tension or anxiety, (4) marked self-deprecation, depression, or feelings of hopelessness, (5) lessened interest in usual activities, (6) significant fatigue or loss of energy, (7) insomnia or hypersomnia, (8) subjectively experienced problems in concentrating, (9) marked change in appetite, such as specific food cravings or overeating, and (10) other physical symptoms, such as sensations of bloating, swollen or tender breasts, headaches, joint pains, or weight gain.

Just as importantly, these symptoms must occur during the last week of the luteal phase and be remitted within a few days after onset of the follicular phase (in nonmenstruating females, determination of these phases may require measurement of circulating reproductive hormones). Also, the LLPDD cannot be simply an exacerbation of another disorder, such as major depression (though it can be superimposed on it), and the symptoms must be confirmed by prospective daily self-ratings during at least two symptom cycles.

Some LLPDD women have been found to have personality characteristics of instability, suspicion, guilt-proneness, apprehension, tension, and self-conflict. Women with LLPDD commonly show problems in coping successfully with environmental stress or the added stress from internal changes. On the average, LLPDD sufferers were found to have significantly lower self-esteem; more negative attitudes about their bodies, their genitals, sexual intercourse, and menstruation; and the feeling of less control over the events of their lives (Price et al., 1986; Clare, 1985).

The incidence of LLPDD has been reported to range from 2 to 90 percent (Dawood, 1985). The widespread media attention given to LLPDD over the last few years has certainly made this disorder into a household word and influenced the way women perceive their symptoms. Different definitions of LLPDD by researchers can also account for the wide variability of sufferers. A critical reassessment of the literature suggests that the incidence of LLPDD may be closer to 2–5 percent (Dawood, 1985)—reflecting the extent to which women are seriously debilitated by the disorder.

In the past, clinicians used questionnaires that focus on premenstrual symptoms to diagnose patients with LLPDD. However, these questionnaires are often unreliable because they depend on retrospective reporting of symptoms. Patients tend to remember the symptoms that occur near menstruation but ignore those symptoms during the intermenstruum (Rubinow and Roy-Byrne, 1984).

Rubinow et al. (1984) have developed a 100mm visual analogue scale to assess LLPDD. Women rate their mood symptoms, or any other symptoms, over time. The rating scale is easy to use and readily translatable into a graph that permits evaluation of the severity and the degree of fluctuation of symptoms in relation to menstruation. LLPD is defined in this way as at least a 30 percent increase in mean negative mood rating during the week before menstruation over that of the week after cessation of menstruation (Dejong et al., 1985).

The specific cause of LLPDD is still unknown, although numerous hypotheses have been generated. The most popular explanation focuses on hormones. The first theory involves an estrogen excess and progesterone deficiency. Emotional symptoms have been related to decreasing levels of progesterone and to estrogen levels that are at their highest when premenstrual symptoms are at their worst (Clare, 1985). Prolactin is another hormone thought to be related to LLPDD symptoms. Prolactin causes water, sodium, and potassium retention and is increased during the premenstrual phase of the cycle.

Other theories include vitamin B_6 and A deficiency, hypoglycemia, high prostaglandin concentrations, and excessive exposure to or abrupt withdrawal of endogenous opiate peptides (Dawood, 1985). So, it appears that LLPDD is a complex disorder comprised of several overlapping syndromes. It is likely that there is more than one specific cause in any individual case.

MMPI

Stout and Steege (1985) administered the Minnesota Multiphasic Personality Inventory to women suffering from LLPDD during their non-premenstrual phase and found that almost all of them had normal profiles. The most common feature of the profiles was a low scale 5, which reflects a strong endorsement of the traditional feminine role. This is in striking contrast to the overall characteristics of that sample. Most of the women had completed college and were working outside the home. This may suggest that this group of women is particularly stressed by role conflicts related to career goals and stereotypical female values. Along with a low scale 5, a good percentage of the women had two-point codes of either 3-4 or 3-6, reflecting strong tendencies to overcontrol or repress angry feelings. Surprisingly enough, in light of all the physical symptoms experienced during the premenstrual phase, only 3 percent of the profiles met the criteria for conversion V on scales 1, 2, and 3.

As women move into their premenstrual phase and their LLPDD symptoms become extreme, one would expect a rise in scales 1, 2, and 3, reflecting the physical changes, and symptoms: edema, weight gain, breast tenderness, headache, and depression. Scales 7 and 8 would also likely increase mildly as symptoms of anxiety, irritability, depression, and dissatisfaction increase. Scores on scale 9 should be in the moderately low range, reflecting the lethargy experienced by some women.

MCMI

On the Millon Clinical Multiaxial Inventory, women with LLPDD may show basic personality patterns of a high scale 8 with a possible increase on scale 3. This would reflect emotional lability, hypersensitivity to criticism, and a lower frustration tolerance. LLPDD women should show an average response level to the pathological personality disorders scales C, P, and S.

On the clinical symptom scales, scale A would tend to be a bit high, reflecting feelings of restlessness, tension, and physical discomfort. Scale H would be elevated to the extent that the woman is affected by physical symptoms. Scales N and CC are likely to be mildly elevated. This may seem contradictory, but it reflects the extent to which the client experiences unstable moods, distractability, impulsiveness, and irritability, as well as depressed mood and lack of hope for the future.

□   16 PF

For the woman with LLPDD, the 16 PF profile would generally resemble a normal profile, but it might destabilize somewhat as the woman approached the premenstrual days of her cycle.

Q_4 and I are likely to be high, reflecting the frustrations and overall sensitivity and stress. A low score on C, combined with a high Q_1 and low Q_3 may indicate the extent to which the woman is suppressing anger. Scale F is likely to be lower, as well as scale H, consistent with her tendency to focus on the inner aspects of the self, more often with negative perceptions and a feeling that she is being threatened.

□   OTHER TEST-RESPONSE PATTERNS

If LLPDD women took the Rorschach during the premenstrual cycle, one would expect a higher CF + C response, emphasized by several pure C responses. There would be an elevation of An + Xy responses, a high F+%, and possibly the presence of a V response. D scores would be around the −1 or −2 range (Exner, 1986). A person with this type of profile is one who is fairly intelligent but who is unable to respond as well cognitively as usual because the affective experience is so intense.

On the TAT, women with LLPDD are likely to tell stories with themes of an overall depressed mood and self-deprecation, without reference to the future. They may show affective lability, overreacting affectively to the stimulus picture. The overreacting may take the form of explanations, criticisms, affectively charged descriptions, arbitrary shaping of the story, and emotional eruptions, even to the point of crying. They may also show blocking on a picture as a result of the interference of affects or of being able to describe only the mood or affective tone of the picture. There may be plots emphasizing sudden physical accidents and emotional trauma, such as the loss of husband, mother, sweetheart, job, or house by fire.

□   TREATMENT OPTIONS

There are almost as many treatments as there are proposed etiologies for LLPDD. Since the 1950s, progesterone has been used extensively on the basis that premenstrual-syndrome patients have either progesterone insufficiency or a high estrogen-to-progesterone level premenstrually. Although results of well-controlled double-blind studies show that progesterone and drugs like spironolactone are not generally more effective than a placebo, all were better than no therapy at all (Dawood, 1985; Rubinow and Roy-Byrne, 1984). Other common treatments include diuretics, oral contraceptives, and vitamins A and B_6, again with varying though not marked success.

LLPDD has biological, behavioral, and psychological components, and in that vein, Price et al. (1986) propose an effective multidimensional biopsychosocial approach. The first step is to record daily symptoms of mood and physical well-being in order to chart out a monthly pattern. This helps the clinician assess the problem, as well as educating the client as to what to expect during different times of the month. By the use of a 100mm visual analogue scale devised by Rubinow et al. (1984) the therapist can better assess whether the woman has LLPDD. If she has definite mood swings but they are unrelated to her menstrual cycle, another treatment would be appropriate.

Next, the client is asked to regulate the intake of certain foods and beverages. Reduction in caffeine and nicotine can help reduce premenstrual anxiety and irritability. Women with LLPDD should avoid alcohol because it can facilitate depression and feelings of hopelessness. They can cut down on their salt intake to help reduce the physical symptoms of edema, weight gain, and breast tenderness, but they should not cut down their water intake (continuing to drink at least six glasses of water a day). Naturally-diuretic foods, such as cucumbers, asparagus, and watermelon, can help here. Also, women with LLPDD should be encouraged to eat small, frequent meals, rich in protein and complex carbohydrates, in order to decrease symptoms of anxiety, irritability, and lethargy. This helps to keep blood glucose levels stable, which in turn stabilizes estrogen-linked increases in insulin production.

Another step is to engage in a daily aerobic (though not overly vigorous) exercise program. Exercise cuts down the amount of body fat, which in turn reduces the amount of estrogen the body produces. It has consistently been found that women who are physically active tend to suffer less from LLPDD (Price et al., 1986). Efforts should be made to decreasse stress, especially premenstrually, because stress exacerbates the symptoms of LLPDD. A stress reduction program may include yoga, meditation, or relaxation exercises.

Finally, if these measures fail to alleviate the symptoms of LLPDD, medications may need to be prescribed, often amplified by standard treatments for depression (Rutter, 1988). The choice of medication should be determined by the prominent symptoms. In this regard, clinicians group LLPDD clients into four categories, characterized by a different cluster of symptoms and thus by different therapies.

First there are women whose main symptoms are anxiety, irritability, and mood swings. They respond best to magnesium and B_6 supplements and sometimes progesterone suppositories. Other women with LLPDD experience depression, insomnia, and mental confusion and are best treated with progesterone suppositories and, in some cases, an antidepressant drug like Elavil.

A third category includes women who primarily report bloating, swelling, weight gain, headaches, and breast soreness. They may be helped by the drugs bromocriptine or spironolactone or by supplements of B_6 or vitamin E. The fourth group of women is characterized by increased appetite and cravings for sweets. They respond well to the hypoglycemic diet and a B-complex supplement.

CHAPTER 5

Anxiety Disorders

This grouping of disorders is a subgroup of the disorders traditionally termed "neurosis," and indeed, this subgroup of disorders is subtitled the Anxiety and Phobic Neuroses in DSM-III-R. The anxiety disorders in DSM-III-R do not encompass such traditionally included categories as conversion reactions or dissociative reactions, which are now dealt with in separate sections. The DSM-III-R category of anxiety disorders is meant to include only those in which anxiety is still present or at least operative. Some clinicians would argue that this is not necessarily so for the obsessive-compulsive disorder or the post-traumatic stress disorder, but they are included here nevertheless.

■ MMPI

The classic general signs for neurosis on the MMPI are elevations on scales 1, 2, 3, and 7. In fact, scales 1, 2, and 3 are often referred to as the "neurotic triad." The neurotic disorders, of which the anxiety disorders are a traditional subclassification, have an MMPI that slopes from left to right, whereas the psychoses are expected to slope from right to left. The character disorders tend to peak more in the middle, though the word "tend" is emphasized.

The F scale is high in the neurotic profile. If it is very high and scales K and L are 50 T or less, the clinician should look for (1) a blatant cry for help that could point to a variety of disorders, (2) faking-bad, or (3) in a hospitalized psychiatric population, the diagnosis of confused psychotic (Gynther et al., 1973b). As a result of the relative openness about anxiety, anxiety disorder profiles show some elevation on most of the scales, with the exception of 5, 6, and 9.

■   ## 16 PF

The general profile for the anxiety disorders has higher scores on I, L, M, O, and Q_4, with a moderately high score on Q_2. In addition, one would expect scores to be lower on C, E, F, G, H, and Q_3.

Karson and O'Dell (1976, p. 83) list the individual scales in their order of importance in contributing to the second-order anxiety scale derived from the 16 PF. They list these as Q_4, O, C, L, and Q_3. If very high, Q_4 can additionally be interpreted as a cry for help, as it shows an r of .75 with scale 7 of the MMPI. Q_3 is an index of emotional lability, that is, a reflection of the ability to bind up anxiety. Scales I and M pick up an ongoing vulnerability or sensitivity to stress.

The anxiety disorders, especially in males (Krug, 1980), are relatively higher on scale M than are those who suffer psychosomatic disorders. It is hypothesized that in neurotics with anxiety, the greater inclination to fantasy makes them more prone to anxiety reactions, whereas psychosomatics have a more practical and concrete cognitive process, so they are more likely to use denial (Silverman, 1976) and less prone to use fantasy behavior to cope with distress.

■   ## Other Test-Response Patterns

On the MCMI, the single most prominent indicator, in most cases, of the presence of an anxiety disorder is the highest elevation on A. Because features of somatic disorders and depression are often involved, scales D and H frequently lie in the 75-or-higher range of scores. Personality types indicated by elevated scales on 2, 8, C, and S are subject to anxiety experiences that may develop into anxiety disorders. Scale 7 is negatively correlated with the overt experience of anxiety. To the extent to which alcohol is used to cope with chronic anxiety, high scores on B occur.

Impaired concentration from high anxiety would likely result in lower scores on arithmetic and digit span on the WAIS-R. In addition, as a result of anxiety and its accompanying inefficiency, lowered performance scores in general could be expected. In particular, awkwardness and a lack of orderly checking could lead to mistakes on object assembly and block design that one would not otherwise be expected to make. This anxiety may also result in surprising errors in the early part of the information subscale.

A classic sign on the Rorschach of high anxiety and the inability to cope with it is extreme (both ways) reaction time to the cards. Color shock, or the inability to integrate and respond appropriately to the color cards, is also commonly noted as a sign of anxiety or neurosis (Exner, 1986; Beck, 1951). The novelist Joseph Heller (*Something Happened,* p. 435) described the phenomenon of color shock well:

Some look like Van Dykes, and these I'm tempted to tug. Others have sideburns and shock me a moment like card number eight on the Rorschach test again. I was struck speechless when that damned color shock card appeared. I was stupefied.

Poorly integrated W responses, a form level below the acceptable range of 65–80 percent, and vague responses—such as clouds, smoke, maps, etc.—are also a common result of the high anxiety. Shafer (1954) states that several C or P responses, a moderately low F percentage, and oral-threat-content responses (such as wolves) are indicative of potential for anxiety moving into panic. Shading, tiny figures, and fine and/or broken lines are traditionally thought to connote anxiety in figure drawings (Oster and Gould, 1987).

■ Treatment Options

A wide variety of techniques are used in the treatment of the anxiety disorders (Emmelkamp, 1988; Hoehn-Saric and McLeod, 1988; Holcomb, 1986). One option is the development and maintenance of a relaxation response as an antidote. Other possible options are systematic desensitization, implosive therapy techniques, chemotherapy, and covert conditioning techniques. They aid in the avoidance of anxiety-generating situations and facilitate the ultimately critical variable in the treatment of the anxiety disorders: helping clients to confront the sources of their fear (Boudewyns and Shipley, 1983). To the degree that the client is highly labile and physiologically reactive, the anxiety-lessening techniques, such as relaxation training, are useful; if that is not as strong a factor, an emphasis on skills training may be more productive (Cattell, 1986). Stress inoculation training is also effective and has been proven superior to chemotherapy (Holcomb, 1986). Treatment requirements for the obsessive-compulsive disorder differ markedly from those of the generalized anxiety disorder or even the phobias. The reader is referred to the specific sections for treatment suggestions.

■ Agoraphobia

The phobic disorders in general are patterns in which chronic avoidance behavior is combined with an irrational fear of a particular object or situation. Many people experience similar nondisabling phobias of one sort or another. For example, many people avoid extreme heights or strongly fear touching snakes. Since either of these fears can easily be controlled by environmental avoidance patterns, they are not usually disabling. A classic phobia is disproportionate, disturbing, and disabling and is marked by responses to a discrete stimulus. People with phobias may assert that their avoidance is reasonable because of the overpowering anxiety they feel, but they do not usually claim that this is rationally justified (Emmelkamp, 1988).

Agoraphobia is a more complex phobia. The essential marker is a severe fear of being left alone in unfamiliar circumstances or of being in the midst of people with no help available. Typically, the development of agoraphobia is preceded by a stage of panic attacks, and that diagnosis is technically Panic Attacks with Agoraphobia (300.21), while the converse is Agoraphobia without panic attacks (300.22).

Agoraphobics develop a strong sense of helplessness and anticipate that panic will set in at any time, leaving them without any means of control or defense. Their ultimate fear seems to be that they will be left alone, with the possibility that panic will occur and overwhelm them. As Ellis and Dryden (1987) note, such individuals have a very low threshold for discomfort anxiety.

Even though agoraphobia was an important concept in DSM-III-R, it had not even been listed in DSM-I and II. It could be hypothesized that the rapid rise in the occurrence of this disorder reflects the increasing interpersonal alienation and heightened requirements for competence in vocational and social functioning that mark our society (Kleinknecht, 1986). In addition, such factors as the rising divorce rate and alleged breakdown of the family unit, along with our increased urbanization and the high level of social and geographic mobility, make it easier than ever to experience being alone in facing change and stress.

Such pressures often first coalesce in adolescence, though they may have been preceded by attacks of separation anxiety and occurrences of school phobia in childhood (Hoehn-Saric and McLeod, 1988). Social or vocational role changes make one particularly vulnerable to this disorder. Hence, women in a traditional housewife role who are going through menopause at the same time their children are leaving home are likely to be vulnerable to this pattern. Agoraphobics are prone to become housebound and attempt to break up their anxiety through manipulative behaviors toward significant others. Since these defenses are seldom effective, such individuals may with time become bothersome to those around them and consequent depression will then complicate the agoraphobia. Alcohol and other drugs may be used to dilute the anxiety, leading to an overlay pattern of addiction. Approximately 5 percent of the population has at some time suffered from agoraphobia; the disorder is common in both psychiatric and cardiac practices.

□   DSM-III-R

The two specific DSM-III-R diagnoses are Agoraphobia without History of Panic Attack (300.22) and Panic Disorder with Agoraphobia (300.21). Agoraphobia is specifically defined as the avoidance of any situation, particularly being alone, where people fear they could not be helped or get in touch with help in the event of sudden incapacitation. These fears pervade their world, and as a result, they avoid being alone in open spaces or avoid public places where help is possibly not available if there is an emergency. As a result, their normal behavior patterns and experiences are disrupted.

☐   MMPI

Agoraphobics, whether or not they experience panic attacks, should score relatively close to the modal pattern for anxiety disorders presented in the previous subsection. Even when the diagnosis "with panic attacks" is warranted, it is not likely that the person would be experiencing the panic at the time of testing. It would, however, suggest that the individual is not adept at binding up anxiety, so there will be some scores on the MMPI and 16 PF that will differ. The 2-7/7-2 profile with scales 1 and 3 close to average is a likely one here, reflecting the high level of anxiety, the rather vague targets for the anxiety, and the absence in most cases of accompanying extensive somatic concerns or conversion reactions. Scales 4 and 9 would also be expected to be relatively low, and scale 8 would depend partially on how well the anxiety is integrated. The 0 scale is likely to be raised, even above the other neurotic disorders. The uncommon 7-0/0-7 profile, which reflects anxiety and inadequacy, might well suggest an agoraphobic orientation.

☐   16 PF

Mlatt and Vale (1986) found that female agoraphobics who have families score significantly higher on the relaxed-tense dimension (Q_4) on the 16 PF, while male agoraphobics who are married with children score significantly higher on the dimension of tension (Q_4), warmth (A) and suspiciousness (L) and significantly lower on emotional instability (C). Generally, scales such as O and Q_4 will be high and somewhat dependent on whether or not there are panic attacks, with the latter suggesting higher scores. Slightly higher scores on scales I and L might also occur, reflecting the isolation of the individual who has developed agoraphobia. Similarly, scale A would probably be low in this disorder, though it is not commonly as low in the anxiety disorders.

☐   OTHER TEST-RESPONSE PATTERNS

The typical indicators of anxiety on the MCMI – great elevation on A and possibly on H and D – are expected here. With respect to precipitating personality styles, however, dependent types (scale 3) are more vulnerable to agoraphobic attacks.

☐   TREATMENT OPTIONS

Chambless (1985) points out that agoraphobia is particularly difficult to treat, with only about 20 percent of cases receiving significant, lasting relief. Chambless states that the agoraphobic very much needs to feel accepted, and the initial fostering of dependency is encouraged here more than with most other types of clients. As clients are eventually weaned from dependency, assertiveness training is useful to help them deal with their personality dependency and general lack of self-sufficient behaviors. The repressed feelings, often directed toward significant others, can be elicited by having the client write a diary with a focus on those feelings, and then catharsis techniques can be more systematically employed (Telch et al., 1985).

The tricyclic antidepressants, which appear to block the reuptake of serotonin and norepinephrine by the presynaptic neurons and thus to increse their concentration at the synaptic cleft, can help eliminate the panic aspects of agoraphobia with panic attacks, but they do little for the agoraphobia. Down-regulators of 5-HTZ receptors, such as busiprone, have proven helpful here, as has alprazolam (Ballenger et al., 1988).

The panic experience, so common in agoraphobia, is probably most effectively dealt with by implosive therapy, or flooding (Boudewyns and Shipley, 1983). Implosive therapy can be presented either in imagination or in vivo, depending on the particular case, and it is more successful if the implosion is carried out when anxiety is not muted by tranquilizing drugs. The stimuli can be presented either live or via audiotape, though therapist presence facilitates the effects in the latter condition (Sherry and Levine, 1980). The client's ability to develop vivid imagery is a positive factor.

Even clients who are able to approach and handle the feared object after implosive therapy may still retain a basic fear sensation. This feeling typically dissipates with time, though it can initially be disconcerting to the client and even to the therapist. As the fears of the agoraphobic become more specific, usually as the panic recedes, techniques such as relaxation training, systematic desensitization (SDT), and other behavioral control methods offer the highest chance of a successful intervention (Foa and Kozak, 1986; Telch et al., 1985). In certain situations, the use of a neighborhood self-help group can reduce agoraphobia, and the training of the spouse to be a "coach" and supportive companion is also effective.

■   Overanxious Disorder (313.00)

If the person is under eighteen and is manifesting anxiety similar to agoraphobia, the appropriate diagnosis could be either Overanxious Disorder (313.00) or Separation Anxiety Disorder (309.21). These two disorders are typically seen in childhood or early adolescence rather than in late adolescence. They predict later disorders, such as agoraphobia, the phobic disorders in general, the generalized anxiety disorder, or other similar patterns.

The diagnosis of overanxious disorder requires symptomatology of excessive worry or anxiety for at least six months and evidence of at least four of the following: (1) unrealistic worry about the future or past or about ability in such areas as academic subjects, athletics, and social interactions, (2) tension and inability to relax, (3) proclivity toward self-consciousness and embarrassment, (4) an excessive need for reassurance, or (5) somatic complaints without a physical basis.

Diagnosis and treatment for adolescents who show this disorder are similar to those advised for the anxiety disorders in general, the panic disorder, and the identity disorder, and the reader is referred to those sections.

■ Separation Anxiety Disorder (309.21)

The correlation of separation anxiety and school phobia is high and in some cases may precipitate referral for treatment (Bloom-Feshbach and Bloom-Feshbach, 1987). While refusal or reluctance to go to school often accompanies separation anxiety, the use of the term "school phobia" to describe these children is frequently misapplied. Whereas simple phobias refer to anxiety responses associated with specific stimuli, such as school, and typically involve otherwise stable personalities, disorders such as separation anxiety and agoraphobia generally suggest more deep-seated personality disorders and are characterized by an overlay of symptoms that may include generalized anxiety, depression, and somatic complaints. For the child experiencing separation anxiety, it is usually not the stimulus of school from which she or he retreats that is of clinical significance, but the attachment to parents or others that is sought. Thus, "school phobia" is a misnomer when applied to children experiencing separation anxiety associated with refusal or reluctance to attend school, and the term "school refusal" is generally more appropriate. Separation anxiety disorder commonly develops after a loss (the death of a relative or pet), after a change in the child's environment, or after a change in school or neighborhood.

A diagnosis of separation anxiety disorder requires evidence of disturbance for only two weeks, onset before age eighteen, and significant anxiety regarding separation from attachment figures, as evidenced by at least three of the following symptoms: (1) worry that major attachment figure, such as a parent, will be harmed or will not return, (2) worries about being separated from attachment figures, such as being lost or kidnapped, (3) nightmares about separation, (4) resultant school phobia, (5) resultant reluctance or refusal to sleep, (6) apparent resultant physical symptomatology at points of potential separation, (7) temper tantrums or evidence of psychological distress upon potential separation, (8) recurrent signs or complaints of excessive distress when separated from home or attachment figures, or (9) reluctance to stay alone or at home without the major attachment figure.

School refusal is often hard to sort out from a normal response (Bloom-Feshbach and Bloom-Feshbach, 1987). Most school children's worst fear upon entering kindergarten or the first grade is leaving home and their mother. The first symptoms may include waking up in the morning with somatic complaints such as headache, stomach pain, vague "aches," or nausea, though without any fever. So, after recurrences of these alleged illnesses, most parents become concerned. As school refusal worsens, actual symptoms may occur, including sleep disorders, disrupted peer relationships, low school achievement, and distinct school avoidance. Poor attendance in school naturally disrupts peer relationships and school achievement. A fear of being teased by other children and disapproval from the teacher for the child's ongoing absenteeism can cause the child to further refuse school. Such fears may also be expressed in nightmares and fantasies, resulting in requests for someone to sleep with him or her at night. School refusal is often preceded by episodes of separation anxiety (Gittelman, 1986).

□   TREATMENT OPTIONS

Cases of school refusal and separation anxiety provide an opportunity for treatment from a variety of theoretical perspectives, largely due to the range of clinical symptoms that arise and the nature of etiological factors. From a behavioral perspective, treatments involving contingency management programs and systematic desensitization have been found to be successful in reducing symptoms of anxiety and improving school attendance (Phares, 1988; Dangel and Polster, 1986). In SDT, the emphasis is placed on developing a relaxation response in association with a feared stimulus—school, separation from mother, riding a school bus, etc.—in an attempt to reduce and eventually eliminate fear responses, while at the same time assessing the system of overt and covert reinforcements that is maintaining the target behaviors. In a contingency management program, reinforcers are used to reward school approach behaviors rather than school avoidance behaviors, and school refusal results in such punishments as time out, loss of privileges, or extra household chores.

From a psychodynamic or developmental perspective, symptoms of separation anxiety may be seen as mechanisms of defense that function to reduce the anxiety generated from intrapsychic conflict (Bloom-Feshbach and Bloom-Feshbach, 1987). Unconscious conflicts are worked through using the therapeutic relationship as a mechanism of change, perhaps involving such techniques as psychodynamic play therapy, fantasy storytelling, and art therapy to express unconscious material indirectly.

Using a family systems model, the structure of family relationships might be emphasized, with a goal of treatment being to restructure family boundaries and communication patterns. Attempts are made to strengthen the boundary between parent and child and to more clearly establish family roles.

■ Social Phobia (300.23)

Social phobics are marked by anxiety about possible scrutiny of their behavior by others, usually accompanied by clear anticipatory anxiety of panic and/or acting in a manner that will be considered shameful by others (Hoehn-Saric and McLeod, 1988). As a result of the anticipatory anxiety, social phobics make strenuous efforts to avoid such situations. Social phobias are centered on such behaviors as eating or riding in public, using public lavatories, or blushing.

The most common social phobia, however, is one in which the person is acutely fearful of public speaking. This often leads to a classic vicious cycle (Kleinknecht, 1986). First, such persons experience anxiety about a public performance. If they then attempt to proceed in spite of the anxiety, the upset often detracts from the adequacy of the performance, possibly even causing them to twitch or shake visibly. Their prophecy that they will perform poorly and be embarrassed is then fulfilled, and future anticipatory anxiety is facilitated.

This disorder in severe form is relatively rare; it usually begins to evolve in late childhood or early adolescence, although spontaneous eruptions in adult life are not that uncommon (Mattick and Peters, 1988). The disorder is rarely incapacitating, though it may stunt an individual's professional and economic advancement, particularly if the person's position requires making public presentations. Social withdrawal is not characteristic of this pattern, and if this is present in a substantial fashion, the diagnosis is not appropriate.

☐   DSM-III-R

Social phobics show consistent avoidance of specific social situations in which they could be scrutinized and/or possibly be embarrassed. Accompanying fear is disruptive and irrational, there is marked anticipatory anxiety, there is often avoidant behavior, and at some point there is an exposure to the feared situation, which in turn generates immediate distress. However, they have insight into the inappropriateness of their behaviors, and the pattern in not accompanied by severe psychopathology in other areas.

☐   MMPI

Since these individuals are not markedly disturbed in any area other than their social phobia, their MMPI profiles are relatively normal. The F scale is at least mildly elevated, which reflects their concern about obtaining help. They are higher on the O scale, reflecting their problems in social functioning, though this elevation is not consistently high. They are a bit lower in the 9 scale, indicating their lowered interest in interacting with the environment, and scales 3 and 2 may be somewhat elevated.

☐   16 PF

Again, there is an absence of the more extreme scores that are found in the anxiety disorders, even including the obsessive-compulsive personality. Yet, scores on scales E and H are usually low, and scores on I and Q_4 are reasonably high. Scores on scales C and L should be more toward the average than they are in the more blatantly disturbed anxiety neurotics.

☐   OTHER TEST-RESPONSE PATTERNS

In social phobia, the related symptoms indicated by elevation on D and H are less likely to occur on the MCMI than in other anxiety disorders. The elevation of A may vacillate depending on the imminence of a situation in which they may be scrutinized. Social phobias are deeply ingrained in the style of the avoidant so that some elevation on 2 is probable; however, an extremely withdrawn avoidant would not receive a diagnosis of social phobia.

☐   TREATMENT OPTIONS

The standard treatments for phobias—systematic desensitization and implosive therapy—are helpful with the social phobic, especially when combined with cognitive restructuring and guided imagery (Mattick and Peters, 1988). Analogously, the clinician can train clients to overcome their fear in a graded-task approach, wherein they gradually develop their public presentation and social skills in front of increasingly larger groups (Cappe and Alden, 1986). Role playing that develops specific skills, such as rescuing a mistake made in front of an audience (a technique refined and made famous by Johnny Carson) is helpful in giving such clients a sense of control that allows them to go on if the anticipated and feared mistake does occur.

Propranolol, as well as the standard minor tranquilizers, can at times be helpful with that anxious mood that often accompanies the social and simple phobias, though it does not cure the phobia, particularly for the subgroup of phobics who are found to have a hyperresponsive betaadrenergic system. Propranolol, however, is contraindicated when there is indication of a tendency toward asthma or congestive heart failure.

■ Simple Phobia (300.29)

The simple phobias are those that most people commonly associate with the term: fear of bugs, snakes, or any other discrete objects or situations not included in social phobia or agoraphobia. The simple phobias are usually relatively chronic disorders, typically arising in childhood, and tend to occur more frequently among (or are more commonly reported by) women (Emmelkamp, 1988).

As noted earlier, most individuals have at least one mild, nondisabling phobia of one sort or another. A fear of heights or snakes is very common, though usually it can be easily controlled, whereas a classic phobia is a disturbing, disproportionate, and disabling response to a discrete stimulus.

□ DSM-III-R

The DSM-III-R criteria for simple phobia are similar to those for the other phobias except that the targets are simple and specific. The person shows avoidance behavior, which is distressing to the individual or interferes with functioning. At some point, exposure to the feared stimulus generates an immediate anxiety response. This behavior must be in response to an irrationally feared situation or object. If there is an element of active danger in this situation or object, such as in fear of heights, the reaction must be disproportionate. It is also required that phobics recognize the irrational aspect of their anxiety.

Fear of dirt or contaminated objects may at first appear to be a simple phobia. However, such a fear is more often a sign of the complex anxieties and conflicts that suggest an obsessive-compulsive disorder.

□ MMPI

Simple phobics are more logical and rational in their thought processes, as well as less emotionally labile, than are people with more-complex phobias, such as agoraphobia. As a result, their MMPI profiles usually are not particularly remarkable. Both F and K may be at least mildly elevated, the F elevation reflecting the expression of concern and the K simultaneously reflecting an attempt to keep the disturbance compartmentalized as to type of phobia. Minor elevations on scales 2, 3, and 7 can be expected, reflecting the mild to moderate anxiety combined with the symptomatic depression that can be expected by the time they seek help. This also reflects the tendency toward denial and a lack of insight that is occasionally characteristic of such persons. If their controls appear to be breaking down and they are becoming concerned that panic will set in as a result of an expansion of the phobia, an elevation of scale 8 occurs, and possibly on scale 6, too.

☐   OTHER TEST-RESPONSE PATTERNS

On the MCMI, the degree of elevation on A, D, and H may depend on the depth of the confrontation with the feared stimulus. Those whose prominent personality features are represented by scales 2, 8, C or S may be more likely to develop phobias in that they may connect their anxieties to many aspects of life, increasing the chance that a formerly innocuous situation will become phobic.

☐   16 PF

As with the MMPI, it would be extremely difficult to differentiate a simple phobic based on the 16 PF profile, since such phobias are so common and so close to normal functioning. However, following the theory that the individual has attempted to provide a focus for vague anxieties with the phobia, I would hypothesize at least some elevation on the Q_3. Yet the fact that it has not been entirely successful should lead to a mild elevation on O and Q_4. The H scale has been hypothesized as a measure of autonomic overreactivity, or what might be more broadly termed "emotional lability," and as a result, a lower score on H would be expected.

☐   TREATMENT OPTIONS

The classic treatment for simple phobia is systematic desensitization, and it is effective throughout the range of phobias usually seen by clinicians (Emmelkamp, 1988). The clinician can actuate this approach either in imagination or in vivo.

The therapist can vary the desensitization procedure by including a modeling phase. In this approach, the therapist first models the desirable behavioral pattern and then physically guides the person through the performance of the desired behavior (e.g., actually helping the person pick up the feared object). This can be combined with verbal support as one goes through the procedure, as well as with covert conditioning techniques.

For those clients who are not responsive to SDT or implosive therapy, the technique of aversion relief, pioneered by L. Solyom, is often effective. Simple phobics who have obsessive or hysteric trends benefit more from this procedure. An application of aversion relief would be to ask the client to tape record organized narratives of past and potential phobic experiences in the first person, present tense. The tape is then played back to the client through earphones, and lapses of silence, approximately twenty seconds in duration, interrupt the narrative at the appropriate juncture and are followed by electric shock. The tape then resumes immediately after the cessation of the electric shock (see Solyom, in Goldstein and Stein, 1976).

As noted in the prior section on social phobia, propranolol can reduce some of the accompanying anxious mood, though it does not cure the phobia. Propranolol is contraindicated when there is any evidence of asthma or congestive heart failure.

■ Panic Disorder

The panic disorder is primarily denoted by recurrent anxiety attacks and nervousness that the individual recognizes as panic. The person experiences anticipatory anxiety, an initial period of often intense apprehension, and the thrust of anxiety that is accompanied by autonomic symptoms and discharge. On occasion, these attacks may last for a period of hours, though attacks are typically for a period of minutes during which the person literally experiences terror (Hoehn-Saric and McLeod, 1988).

The disorder is recurrent and episodic, though in a few cases it may become chronic. The panic attacks are clearly separate incidents, and the anxiety experience is not a response to a phobic stimulus or to any event that is very dangerous in reality. Also, unlike the avoidance patterns noted in the phobias, panic disorder focuses more on the experience of terror and the temporary physiological discharge symptoms, such as cold sweats or hyperventilation. The terror experiences are not unlike "free-floating anxiety," an experience of anxiety with the inability to specify any source or reason for the anxiety. The panic disorder is a good example of Albert Ellis and Dryden's (1987) contention that "discomfort anxiety," the fear of being overwhelmed by the experience of anxiety, is central to the phobic and anxiety disorders.

□ DSM-III-R

The DSM-III-R offers the specific diagnoses of Panic Disorder with Agoraphobia (300.21) or without Agoraphobia (300.01). To diagnose a panic disorder, the DSM-III-R requires that there be either one or more attacks with a month of persistent fear of another attack or at least four panic attacks within a month and that these not be in response to a naturally anxiety-arousing stimulus, heavy physical exertion, a phobic stimulus, or a situation in which the person was the focus of other's attention. It also requires the presence of at least four of the following symptoms during most of the attacks: dyspnea, palpitations, chest discomfort, choking or smothering sensations, dizziness, feelings of unreality, paresthesia, hot or cold flashes, sweating, faintness, trembling, nausea or abdominal distress, or fears of going crazy, losing control, or dying. During the attack, at least four of these symptoms develop suddenly and increase in intensity within ten minutes of the appearance of the first symptom.

To cope with these panic attacks, some individuals respond to this anticipatory fear of helplessness by becoming increasingly reluctant to leave the comfort and familiarity of home. If this fear increases, the diagnosis will likely change to agoraphobia with a panic attack. With this disorder, it is important to rule out physical disorders such as hypoglycemia, hyperthyroidism, withdrawal from certain drugs, or any other disorders that could engender such psychopathology.

□   MMPI

A common MMPI pattern for the anxiety neurosis—particularly where the emphasis is on anxiety, such as in the panic disorder and the generalized anxiety disorder—is a 2-8 code, with high scores on 7, 3, 1, and 4, in that order (Johnson et al., 1980). As such individuals move toward chronicity, they show profiles similar to agoraphobics (see the preceding section). One fairly rare MMPI profile, the 3-9/9-3 pattern, has been characterized as typical of free-floating anxiety. As such, it would predict this disorder, as well as a disorder to be discussed later: generalized anxiety disorder.

The 1-3-7 profile has been characterized as showing high anxiety, passive dependency, and proneness to develop psychophysiological disturbance. Hence, it is possible for this profile to show up in a panic disorder. Scale 7 is likely to be consistently elevated in this profile, as well as scales 1 and 3, whether or not here is a primary elevation on other scales. In some individuals, an accompanying high scale 2 reflects a feeling of loss of control and a sense of hopelessness. As these feelings increase, 2-3/3-2 or 1-3/3-1 profiles are likely.

□   16 PF

The 16 PF profile of the panic disorder is similar to the standard profile for the anxiety disorders: high scores on I, L, M, O, and Q_4; a moderately high Q_2; and low scores on C, F, E, G, H, and Q_3. Since the Q_4 score is the measure par excellence of anxiety, it should be particularly elevated here, and in that regard Q_4 shows a consistently high correlation with scale 7 on the MMPI. Other differences from the standard anxiety disorder profile are: Scale L is not quite as high, Q_2 may be moderately low rather than moderately high, and scale G is not as low.

☐   OTHER TEST-RESPONSE PATTERNS

High scores on A and D are expected on the MCMI. The autonomic arousal that occurs may produce substantial elevation on H. If the individual becomes increasingly withdrawn and begins to confine himself to avoid the possibility of panic, he may become more dependent, producing increasing elevation on 3.

☐   TREATMENT OPTIONS

Since the hallmark of the panic disorder is episodic anxiety reaction accompanied by a high level of psychological tension, the development of a controlled relaxation response has first priority. Progressive relaxation, autogenic training, or any other form of systematized relaxation training is helpful. Also, inhalation therapy using carbon dioxide can be very effective in some cases (Wolpe, 1987). These approaches can be amplified by encouraging the client to take up ancillary interests, such as meditation or yoga. In the initial treatment stage, it may be helpful to give the client a small prescription of tranquilizing medication to be used as needed. This helps avoid problematic side effects, only moderately intrudes on the person's sense of being able to handle it alone, and gives the person a sense that control is immediate and available (Foa and Kozak, 1986). If more long-term medication is needed, alprazolam has been effective here (Ballenger et al., 1988).

Treatment can be amplified by having clients work on the relaxation training in a group setting. Not only does this give them the awareness that others share this problem, but it also easily sets up a discussion of problems in a quasi–group-therapy setting. Later, they are more amenable to entering actual group therapy and thus may come into greater touch with the sources of their anxiety. As they do so, techniques more appropriate for the phobias, noted in prior subsections, can be brought into play so that they can confront and stay with the feared stimuli, a critical variable in obtaining a significant cure (Wickramasekera, 1988).

■   ## Generalized Anxiety Disorder (300.02)

Though the next consecutive listing in the DSM-III-R is the Obsessive Compulsive Disorder (300.30), the Generalized Anxiety Disorder (300.02) will be discussed first because it is functionally a chronic and less cyclical version of the panic disorder. Again, as in the panic disorder, there is autonomic disturbance, although this is now evident in more chronic manifestations. Some free-floating anxiety may be present in the generalized anxiety disorder, but the essential feature is chronic autonomic hyperactivity (Hoehn-Saric and McLeod, 1988). Thus it is similar to the general physiological-stress syndrome originally described by Hans Selye (1956).

Because it is a chronic disorder, persons have more apprehensive rumination and muscular tension than would be expected in a panic disorder. Emerging patterns of hypervigilance and self-checking will crystallize into the variety of patterns that are subsumed under the diagnosis of obsessive compulsive disorder, which will be described next.

☐   DSM-III-R

The DSM-III-R requires evidence of persistent and generalized anxiety and worry about two or more life circumstances, as manifested in at least six symptoms out of a possible eighteen within the following three categories: (1) motor tension (high fatigue, muscular aches, twitches, or easy-startle responses), (2) autonomic hyperactivity (dry mouth, gastrointestinal distress, heart racing or pounding, or sweating disturbance), and (3) vigilance and scanning (hyperalertness, irritability, or related sleep difficulties). The DSM-III-R also requires that this anxiety occur more days than not during a six-month period and that it not be caused by an organic factor or be a part of a mood or psychotic disorder.

☐   MMPI

The profile of this disorder parallels the general profile for the anxiety disorders. Similar to the panic disorder, the profile will show high 2, 3, and 7 scores. The chronic autonomic hyperactivity is reflected in a relatively high 9 score, and if the person is beginning to fear loss of control about these behaviors, a rise on scale 8 is likely. A high F scale is also expected.

☐   16 PF

As with the MMPI, the profile should resemble the modal anxiety disorder profile, with the extremes accentuated, as in the panic disorder. O and Q_4 should be very high, and H should be low.

☐   OTHER TEST-RESPONSE PATTERNS

The impairment and tension resulting from high anxiety should lower the digit span and arithmetic scores within the WAIS-R verbal scale scores. In general, the performance scores should be lower than the verbal scores, particularly object assembly. The rest of the notations in this section about overall anxiety disorders are also applicable.

High scores on A are expected on the MCMI, along with H representing the considerable physiological symptoms that occur. For the most part, the scores here should be similar to those of anxiety disorders. Elevation on scale 2 indicates the individual's feared cognitive failure, low self-esteem, and helplessness. Scale 8 would also be high, stemming from the impatient, irritable factors usually present in the anxious individual. Among the pathological-personality scales, elevated S may occur if the individual is withdrawing from other people and social situations because they cannot handle the ensuing pressure. The interrupted sleep patterns, moodiness, and anxious worry typified by the borderline predisposes to this disorder. Combinations of elevations on A, D, and H may be expected, depending on the individual pattern of disturbance.

□   TREATMENT OPTIONS

The focus in the generalized anxiety disorder is on chronic states of autonomic arousal, accompanied by apprehension. Biofeedback is particularly helpful in the treatment of autonomic tension, and the clinician is advised to use a variety of modalities sequentially, such as electromyography (EMG), EEG, or the various measures of skin change (Schwartz, 1987). Concomitantly, teaching the client a controlled relaxation response is helpful (see prior section on panic disorder). Some form of meditation training may be useful, as is inhalation therapy using carbon dioxide (Wolpe, 1987).

It may be necessary to administer tranquilizing medication as needed in the initial stages, then to move quickly toward treatments that emphasize the client's increasing ability to control the response. As a client begins to gain more control over the anxiety, a treatment technique such as client-centered therapy, as originally advocated by Carl Rogers, may become the primary treatment mode. The focus on empathy and warmth, combined with the initial low demand for specific discussion material, proves helpful here.

■ Obsessive-Compulsive Disorder (300.30)

Although the obsessive-compulsive disorder is listed as one of the anxiety disorders in the DSM-III-R, the direct experience of the anxiety is not as evident as in the other anxiety disorders (Kozak et al., 1988). Obsessive-compulsive patterns are seen by the person performing them as irrational and ego-alien, yet there are usually no panic experiences or sudden upsurges of anxiety on encountering the anxiety-arousing stimuli or mental images. At least initially, the person attempts to resist the obsession or compulsion.

The obsessive-compulsive disorder is an excellent transition category to the somatoform disorders. These disorders were traditionally included in the term "neurosis," but anxiety is often not apparent in them, just as it is also not so obvious in the obsessive-compulsive disorder. The ego-alien quality is what discriminates the obsessive-compulsive disorder from the obsessive-compulsive personality disorder (Kozak et al., 1988). In the personality disorder, the compulsions are ego-syntonic (that is, they are not viewed by the person as in conflict with the essential qualities of the personality).

The usual age of onset for the obsessive-compulsive disorder is late adolescence or early adulthood. By the age of twenty-five, more than half of the treated obsessive-compulsives have already shown clear symptoms (Reed, 1985). This syndrome occurs proportionately more often in middle- and upper-class individuals. This should not be surprising, especially in a society that so highly values achievement, since those with compulsive patterns are often quite efficient and productive. Obsessive-compulsives are brighter on the average than individuals with the other anxiety disorders—obsessions are intellectual coping strategies for anxiety (Kozak et al., 1988).

The obsessive-compulsive disorder has traditionally been thought to be relatively rare, at least as compared to the other anxiety disorders, at a rate of around 3 percent of all "neurotics" and a rate of a bit less than 1 percent of the general population (De Silva, 1987). This could be a function of the embarrassment that many of these individuals experience, which would result in a lower reported incidence (Kozak et al., 1988). Many who might be willing to report phobic anxiety would be more distressed to disclose that they think and act in ways they cannot control.

The most common obsessions seen by clinicians are repetitive thoughts of contamination or of violence, doubts about religion and one's duties, and self-doubts. The most common compulsions include checking behaviors, repetitive acts, and handwashing. The obsessive-compulsive disorder does not include compulsions to perform behaviors that are inherently pleasurable, such as alcohol indulgence or overeating. A person may not be able to control these latter behavior patterns, but they are not ego-alien. While they do not want the detrimental effects of their behavior (e.g., alcoholism or overweight), they do not experience inherent discomfort about eating or drinking behaviors.

☐   DSM-III-R

The DSM-III-R requires evidence of obsessions (recurrent and persistent ego-alien impulses and ideas) and/or compulsions (repetitive behaviors viewed not as a product of one's own initiative, accompanied by a sense of subjective compulsion and a desire to withstand the compulsion). In addition, the person must be distressed and recognize the irrationality of the behaviors, which need to occupy at least an hour of the day or significantly disrupt one's life. Also the clinician must rule out such syndromes as schizophrenia, organic mental disorder, or a major depressive disorder, since all of these may be accompanied by obsessions or compulsions. The obsessive-compulsive disorder is often chronic and accompanied by some disruption in personal functioning.

☐　　　　MMPI

The two common profile combinations related to the obsessive-compulsive disorder are the 7-8/8-7 and 2-7/7-2 (Lachar, 1974). If a person obtains an 8-7 profile, the clinician is more likely to encounter a combination of deteriorating personality function and depression, whereas a 7-8 profile indicates some continuing struggle and in that sense is more benign. In the 2-7/7-2 profile, depression about one's functioning is a major component, and the person may have begun to show signs of social withdrawal.

It has been noted that the 2-7-8 high-point combination is a common profile in patients but rare in normals. It reflects people who are self-analytic and inclined toward catastrophic expectations and a sense of hopelessness. They require goal-directed therapy combined with emphasis on reinforcement for any achievements, with a concomitant de-emphasis of their tendency toward introspection and extensive self-analysis.

The spike 7 profile is rare but suggests an obsessive-compulsive diagnosis. Such individuals show a high number of phobias and obsessions and are close to breaking down and deteriorating into a psychotic condition. It should be noted that the scores on the 7 scale predict obsessiveness more than the compulsive aspects of the disorder.

☐　　　　16 PF

The modal 16 PF profile obtained by persons with an obsessive-compulsive disorder (IPAT Staff, 1963) shows high scores on I, O, and Q_4 and moderately high scores on L and M. They obtain a moderately low score on C and low scores on E, F, H, and Q_3. A comparison with the modal profile for the anxiety disorder shows that obsessive-compulsives are only moderately low on C and only moderately high on L and M, whereas persons with the anxiety disorders are high on C, L, and M. Also, persons with anxiety disorders show a low score on G and a moderately high score on Q_2, whereas obsessive-compulsives perform in the average range on these variables. This is surprising; I would expect the obsessive-compulsive to score high on Q_2, relative to anxiety neurotics. Also, I would expect obsessive-compulsives to score high on scale B because they tend to be brighter than most individuals with a diagnosis of psychopathology. Clinicians should be aware of the possibility that the IPAT sample did not tape these variables. It also is probable that obsessive-compulsives—particularly if they are still gaining a sense of control from the patterns and thus are not yet deteriorating—should score higher on Q_3 than those with most other disorders, with the possible exception of the paranoid disorders. Furthermore, one should consider the possibility that the G score will be higher than average in obsessive-compulsives.

☐   OTHER TEST-RESPONSE PATTERNS

On the MCMI, extreme elevations of D and H are more prominent than A. Indeed, overt expression of anxiety may not be present at all, where obsessive-compulsives are very likely to express dismay regarding the ego-alien quality of their disorder and to express their anxiety through somatic channels. Those personality syndromes typically associated with anxiety, C, S, 2, and 8 are not as likely to be present in the obsessive-compulsive disorder. Rather, the controlled, conforming type is more likely to react to anxiety in an obsessive-compulsive way, very likely indicated by an elevated 7.

On the WAIS-R, there is an overall higher IQ than in other disorders, reflecting the obsessive-compulsive's average to above-average intelligence (Kozak et al., 1988). Those who are primarily obsessive score higher on the overall IQ score and also have a higher verbal- than performance-IQ score. Self-deprecation and questioning of one's performance, along with rather detailed verbalizations, are common. A meticulous approach to the block design and object assembly subtests is probable, occasionally leading to a loss of speed-bonus points but seldom resulting in inaccurate responses. Obsessive-compulsives usually do very well on vocabulary, similarities, and comprehension because of their meticulousness. At the same time, however, their inability to change "set" can sometimes penalize them on similarities. They also do well on both arithmetic and digit span (Rapaport et al., 1968). The intellectualization characteristic of the obsessive-compulsive disorder can result in a decrease in picture arrangement performance. A rather precise approach can again be expected on the Bender Gestalt figures. The figures may be placed in a linear path, and a counting of the dots in appropriate cards is common.

On the Rorschach, expressions of doubt are expected, along with pedantic and esoteric verbalizations. Additionally, one expects a high number of responses overall, a high number of W and/or Dd, a high F+ percent, edge details, and the likelihood of space responses. There are generally few color responses, and if color responses of poor form occur, they are thought to indicate decompensation (Shafer, 1954).

Obsessive-compulsives like to criticize the blots as well as their own responses and may express concern about the symmetry of the cards. Some surprising combinations or imagined responses (e.g., "two earthworms coming out of a rabbit's eyes" on card X) may occur. Similarly, pedantic wording ambivalence over themes, and an emphasis on details rather than story content are common on the TAT, especially if the individual is orientated toward paranoia as well. Idealistic stories and esoteric, though nonemotional, fantasies may occur.

There are several questionnaires and inventories that have been specifically devised to further elucidate the obsessive-compulsive patterns, e.g., the Leyton Obsessional Inventory and the Maudsley

Obsessional-Compulsive Inventory. An excellent review of these devices is found in De Silva (1987).

Most experts recommend a combination of treatments for the obsessive-compulsive disorder (Kozak et al., 1988; Reed, 1985). A clear and consistent program of response prevention (e.g., taking all soap and towels away from a handwasher combined with constant exposure to the eliciting stimuli to promote extinction provided in the context of a firmly and consistently demanding, though supportive, therapy relationship is the core of an effective treatment program for the compulsive aspects of the disorder (De Silva, 1987; Lazarus, 1987).

A dramatic example of this regimen is provided by Lazarus (1987):

We had him under 24-hour surveillance. He was not to do the circles. We even put mittens on his hands. Second, in terms of the germ phobia and the flooding, we got him to handle all of the dirty laundry in the hospital and he was not allowed to wash his hands for a week. He had to eat his food everyday without even washing his hands once. I was terrified that, with my luck, he would come down with the flu or a cold, and that would be the end of the therapy. Luck does play a great part. However, he was fine and of course he was flooded with anxiety. As for the obesity, we got everybody who was fat to sit on him, to roll him, to touch him; this was the flooding technique. Some people said to me, I hope you get a good EKG before you start these things. But the point is that sometimes these heroic methods are essential or else you are not going to get anywhere with these kinds of encrusted problems. However, if this is all you do, if breaking the web of obsessive compulsive rituals is all you do, my prediction is that relapse will be pretty rapid. But having broken through with response prevention and participant modeling and flooding, in my approach you proceed to work on the other residual problems; sensation, imagery, cognition, and personal and biological malfunctions have to be looked at as well. That is the multimodal concept. (p. 262)

The anxiety discomfort component can be handled by SDT techniques and in vivo exposure supplemented by self-instructional training. This approach is effective to the degree that the individual becomes more adequate in focusing on the sources of anxiety. It is also very helpful to first reduce any depressive components before administering any full-blown treatment directed at the obsessive aspects. Thought-stopping or paradoxical-intention techniques can also work to eliminate the ritualistic behaviors. Although thought stopping is especially efficient in dealing with the obsessive component, paradoxical intention (discussed in the subsection on the compulsive-personality disorder) is most efficient in controlling the compulsive aspects (Seltzer, 1986). As progress occurs on these fronts, standard group therapy and/or psychotherapy can be used, as these help obsessive-compulsives get in touch with their high level of repression and suppression and at the same time help them become willing to self-disclose more easily. Of the possible adjunct chemotherapies, chlorimipramine has been the most effective.

The standard thought-stopping procedure for the obsessions asks clients to let the obsessions flow as in free association. Clients are then told that on a cue (e.g., a raised hand by the therapist), they should shout "Stop!" Generalization is introduced by having clients practice this at home and to vary randomly the amount of time before vocalizing.

Thought stopping can be amplified by having clients visualize a pleasant scene immediately after saying "stop," thus furthering the relaxation and the control of the interruption sequence. In addition, moderately painful though harmless shocks can be administered by the therapist as the word "stop" is stated; this significantly reinforces the effect. The clinician can add biofeedback training to increase the percentage of alpha brain rhythms, since they are antagonistic to problem solving or ruminative thought sequences (Schwartz, 1987). However, remember that obsessives are so perfectionistic, particularly early in therapy, that they fight the process, which hinders progress and results in their viewing themselves as failing.

In those cases that do not show some reasonably immediate response to psychological techniques, a regimen of chemotherapy, usually an antidepressant, has been found to facilitate progress. Psychosurgery has had some traditional acceptance as a treatment for severe obsessive-compulsive patterns, though this has not received any consistent research support (De Silva, 1987). Ironic anecdotal support comes from the report about a young Canadian (*The New York Times*, 2/25/88) whose severe phobia of germs and obsession with washing his hands disappeared after a .22-caliber slug lodged in his frontal lobe during an unsuccessful suicide attempt. The left frontal lobe is the usual target for psychosurgery for obsessive-compulsive patterns.

■ ## Post-Traumatic Stress Disorder and Adjustment Disorder

The essence of the post-traumatic stress disorder (PTSD) is a delayed distress response pattern to an atypical and severe traumatic event, an event such that most people would have very negative and disturbed responses. Such clients generally reexperience the stressor in intrusive thoughts and dreams, and depression and anxiety are common (Hendlin and Haas, 1988). Delayed disturbances in combat veterans—as from the Vietnam conflict, which was a spur to the conceptualization of this disorder (Kelly, 1985)—are often appropriately diagnosed here.

If the stressor is more within the normal range, with little in the way of a vivid reexperience of the trauma, the appropriate diagnosis is the traditional one of adjustment disorder. The diagnosis is appropriately qualified by the following terms:

with depressed mood

with anxious mood

with mixed emotional features

with disturbance of conduct

mixed disturbance of emotions and conduct

with work or academic inhibition

with withdrawal

☐   DSM-III-R

To apply the diagnosis of post-traumatic stress disorder, there must be evidence of a substantial stressor that would seriously disturb most people, such as being raped or being in an airplane crash. Reexperiencing of the stressful event is indicated by at least one of the following: (1) direct evidence of persistent reexperiencing of the event, as in recurrent related dreams, *déjà vu* about the event, or persistent memories of the event, (2) persistent avoidance of the event or general numbness of response, as in lessened affect, lowered interest in at least one usual interest or activity, or detachment from others, etc., and (3) persistent indications of increased arousal, in two of the following behaviors that are existent, but not present, before the stress: sleep disruption, hyperalertness, guilt over survival, memory or attention disruption, or exaggerated startle responses.

The post-traumatic stress disorder is sublabeled "delayed" if onset of symptoms is at least six months after the stressor.

☐   DIAGNOSTIC CONSIDERATIONS

These disorders closely resemble the patterns seen in individuals with a panic disorder. The only major difference is that the person with a post-traumatic stress disorder or adjustment disorder may show fewer evident signs of disruption in overall personality functioning (Figley, 1988).

For example, MMPI scales 8 and F will probably be a bit lower. Interestingly, F scores were significantly lower among persons suffering from PTSD than those who were *faking* suffering from PTSD (Fairbank et al., 1985). The 7-2 code type is particularly likely, as it incorporates the emotional distancing and the distress that are characteristic of this disorder. Graham (1987) suggests that a 1-9/9-1 code is indicative of this disorder. Burke and Mayer (1985) found that PTSD patients in a VA hospital showed an 8-2-7 profile, as opposed to an 8-2-6 profile shown by random psychiatric VA patients, with the PTSD patients being noticeably lower in F, 6, 9, and the Goldberg Index. On the 16 PF, scales C, G, and Q_3 should not be as low as in the panic disorder. Scores on O and Q_4 are especially likely to be high. Clues to methods of crying come especially from selected TAT plates, e.g., cards 4, 6BM, 7BM, and 8GF (Swiercinsky, 1985). Otherwise, the diagnostic comments on panic disorders, the generalized anxiety disorder, and the anxiety disorders generally apply. In addition to the indicators of the panic disorder, 2, 6, and 8 may become more elevated on the MCMI as the disorder becomes more chronic, reflecting the lessened affect and detachment that occur.

☐   ## TREATMENT OPTIONS

Based on a comparison of psychodynamic, behavioral, and biochemical treatments for PTSD, it appears that direct therapeutic exposure to the trauma has emerged as the single most important factor in treatment, e.g., via systematic desensitization or flooding or even focused group discussion (Fairbank and Nicolson, 1987). Also, in treating post-traumatic stress disorders and adjustment disorders, the clinician is advised to keep in mind the principles of crisis intervention—immediacy, proximity, and expectancy—that were developed in World War II to decrease the consequent problems of the severe distress of combat. Immediacy emphasizes early awareness and detection by others close to the person, treatment as quickly as possible, and an emphasis on returning clients to their typical life situation as quickly as possible. Proximity emphasizes the need to treat clients in their own world—not distancing them from their upset by hospitalization. Lastly, the clinician must communicate a clear expectancy that although fear and anxiety are normal processes here, they do not excuse clients from functioning adequately; the sick role is not reinforced, and there is an emphasis on experiences that demonstrate that they are regaining control of their world (Hendlin and Haas, 1988).

These principles can be specifically amplified by the treatment techniques used for the panic disorder and the generalized anxiety disorder (the reader is referred to those sections). As the fears begin to focus more on specific concerns, SDT or implosive therapy is appropriate. Mild tranquilizers to be used as needed can also be a helpful adjunct treatment. Sessions with family and/or friends that help clients implement the principles of crisis intervention in his or her immediate world also facilitate a return to adequate functioning (Figley, 1988).

■   ## Anxiety Disorder NOS (300.00)

This category is a catch-all applied to apparent anxiety disorders that do not exactly fit the above categories. For example, where all the criteria for the generalized anxiety disorder are met, but the anxious mood has not lasted for up to six months, an anxiety disorder NOS diagnosis would be appropriate. Any other such mixtures of symptomatology where anxiety and its control are still the primary features can be placed in this category.

CHAPTER 6

Somatoform Disorders

Persons with somatoform disorders, like those with the factitious disorder, manifest complaints and symptoms of apparent physical illness for which there are no demonstrable organic findings to support a physical diagnosis. However, the symptoms of the somatoform disorders are not under voluntary control, as are those of the factitious disorders. Thus, the diagnosis of somatoform disorder is made when there is good reason to believe that the person has little or no control over the production of symptoms. Disorder and/or dominance problems in the nondominant hemisphere of the brain should be ruled out, because symptoms occur statistically more often on the left side. While factitious disorders are more common in men, somatoform disorders occur more frequently in women (Kellner, 1986).

There are five major subcategories of the somatoform disorders: somatization disorder, conversion disorder, somatoform pain disorder, body dysmorphic disorder, and hypochondriasis. There is also a catch-all category, somatoform disorder NOS, in which individuals are placed if they fit the general criteria for somatoform disorder but not the specific criteria of the other five major categories.

The somatization disorder is chronic with multiple symptoms and complaints, usually presented in a vague fashion. The conversion disorder usually focuses on one or two specific symptoms suggestive of a physical disorder, which on closer examination reflect primarily a psychological issue, either as a reflection of symbolic conflict or from the attainment of secondary gain. Somatoform pain disorder is functionally a conversion disorder that refers specifically to psychologically induced pain states. Hypochondriasis is the consistent overresponse to and concern about normal and/or insigificant bodily changes, in spite of expert reassurance that there is no reason for concern. Body dysmorphic disorder (dysmorphophobia) refers to rumination and preoccupation with some imagined defect in what is actually a normal-appearing person; in one sense, it is a variation of hypochondriasis.

■ Treatment Options

Even though conscious deception is not a factor with somatoform disorders, reality therapy (Glasser, 1980) can be appropriate, particularly to the degree the person becomes aware of the unrealness of the physical symptoms. The therapist can facilitate that awareness through such methods as consciousness raising, hypnosis, amytal interviews, or other methods of getting in touch with the repressed facets of the personality. In this regard, though biofeedback may not be directly appropriate since there is no strictly physical damage, it can be helpful in modifying some of the symptomatology. Also, it may give the person some insight that the disorder is not primarily physiological (Schwartz, 1987).

■ Somatization Disorder (300.81)

The chronic though cyclic multiple somatic complaints that mark this subcategory of the somatoform disorders are not primarily due to any physical illness. Yet they may be mixed with other symptoms derived from an actual disease, so arriving at this diagnosis is initially difficult. It is not uncommon for this disorder to be an exaggeration of symptoms associated with a previously cured physical disease (Landis and Meyer, 1988).

The diagnosis of somatization disorder is difficult because a self-report of symptoms combined with apparent prior history is convincing to most physicians. Family physicians or general practitioners are more often than not the target of these complaints and are not inclined to see the somatization disorder as real. Physicians often believe such people are only malingering or that, at the very least, there is a degree of faking involved. Hence, they are inclined to put them in the too commonly used category of "crank" and attempt in various ways to avoid spending any time with them.

Since it is the supportive atmosphere of the physician's manner and/or the hospital structure that is at least one of the needs of persons with a somatization disorder (and to a degree the conversion disorders), such evident rejections begin to lay bare the underlying inadequacy of these persons to cope effectively with their world (Kellner, 1986). Depression then becomes an emergent and eventually paramount symptom, and the person may develop methods (e.g., alcohol) to deal with the depression. Alternately, the person with a somatization disorder may develop a new symptom picture and generate new systems of hospitals and physicians to work through. Restrictions of time and money, however, often bring the person full circle.

Symptoms are often presented in a vague though exaggerated fashion. Incidentally, this dramatic component was the linkage between the traditional diagnostic terms "hysterical neurosis" and "hysterical personality." Fortunately, the DSM-III-R terminology does away with some of the confusion inherent in these labels. Hysterical personalities are now referred to as having a histrionic personality disorder. Hysteria is typically subsumed under one of the somatoform disorders, usually as a conversion disorder that is still sublabeled the hysterical neurosis, conversion type.

One disorder occasionally misinterpreted as a somatization disorder, hypochondriasis, a conversion disorder, or even depression is myasthenia gravis, an immune-mediated polyclonal antibody disorder of receptors in the postsynaptic membrane. Referral to a neurologist for further consideration is advisable when the client shows the following symptoms: (1) significant somatic weakness, occasionally resulting in collapse after use of any particular muscle group, (2) visual disturbances, including the dropping of one or both eyelids (more likely to occur in the evening), and (3) difficulty in speaking and swallowing (Sneddon, 1980).

☐ DSM-III-R

The DSM-III-R requires evidence of a vague though dramatic and complicated medical history, focused on a belief that one is sickly, with evidence that the physical symptoms began before the age of thirty. A person's own report of personal physical history is considered enough to substantiate the diagnosis. In addition, there must be evidence of at least thirteen reported symptoms out of the thirty-five symptoms listed in DSM-III-R under the following six subgroups: gastrointestinal, cardiopulmonary, pain conversion, female reproductive system, or psychosexual.

Confirmation that the symptom has physically occurred is not required, but there should be indications of symptoms severe enough to require the individual to seek medical help or to alter the life situation in some way in response to the belief that it occurred.

Depression may accompany this pattern, but it is not diagnosed unless it is severe enough to warrant the diagnosis of depressive episode. In a schizophrenic with somatic delusions, the schizophrenic diagnosis takes precedence. The somatization disorder is thought to be diagnosed rarely in males, but approximately 1 percent of females are alleged to have this disorder at some point in their lives.

Systems of health care based on the group practice model make restriction and detection of this disorder easier, since this model facilitates higher levels of interspecialist communication. Also, these practices are more likely to include psychological services and be more sophisticated in implementation than an individual physician. Inclusion of psychological services actually reduces the cost of health care in most physical disorders, mainly by a reduction of repeated visits and unnecessary surgery (Olbrisch, 1977).

☐   MMPI

Scales 1, 2, and 3, and to a lesser degree 7, are elevated in most of the somatization patterns (Dahlstrom et al., 1986). Combinations of 1, 2, and 8 accompany the more bizarre somatic complaints. As has been noted, some depression naturally accompanies this syndrome and is reflected in the moderate elevation on scale 2. If scale 2 is high, it is possible that the person is beginning to feel that he or she is losing control. Scale 1 is elevated in most of these profiles, and the 1-2/2-1 profile is best thought of as somatization disorder with underlying depression. In this instance, one might also consider alcohol abuse as a compounding variable.

Elevations on scale 7 point to the degree of passivity and complaining that can be expected. The 1-7/7-1 client expresses chronic tension-related complaints and demands physical care and responsiveness from physicians, but is resistant to following orders and is difficult to change. A 3-8/8-3 profile has also been associated with this disorder, though the chronic worry, dependency, and schizoid tendencies of these individuals should warrant consideration of a psychotic diagnosis.

The 1-4/4-1 profile reflects a high level of physical complaints, as well as excessive narcissism and egocentricity. If 6 is elevated, anger or rage in the face of rejection by the physician is to be expected. The 3-6/6-3 profile is similar—there is anger as well as rigidity and lack of cooperation. This anger is more often directed toward family members; clients are not quite as manipulative toward physicians.

When actual physical disorder is an accumulation of chronic psychological stress and accompanied by an equally high level of psychological repression, the 3-7/7-3 profile is common. A circumscribed physical disorder to which the person has responded with a reactive depression is more likely to produce a spike scale 2 profile.

The 3-9/9-3 profile is on the border between actual physical disorder and somatization disorder. A common complaint is acute upset accompanied by chest pain and anxiety. These individuals in particular respond well to superficial assurance and to continuing therapist contact.

A small subgroup of clients with a somatization disorder show virtually psychotic profiles. They are remarkably elevated on scale 4, sometimes above the 100 T level, and are also high on scales 6, 8, 2, 3, and 1, in that order. In fact, all scales except 0 and 5 may be well above the 70 T level (Propkop et al., 1980).

☐   16 PF

Characteristics of the 16 PF commonly noted throughout all somatoform disorders, but particularly in the somatization disorder, are at least moderately high scores on I, N, and Q_4, moderately low scores on H and Q_1, and a low score on S. Karson (1959) suggests that individuals who are lower on A and M are also inclined toward this disorder. The B and M scores reflect the client's degree of sophistication and in that sense correlate with different somatization patterns. The less sophisticated symbolic conversion patterns, which were seen more commonly in Freud's era, are more typical of naive and less educated individuals.

Men who have high E and I scores have conflicts between the need to be sensitive in interpersonal relationships and yet to dominate relationships. Ambivalence about assertion and aggression is common and may surface in a somatization pattern. It has been hypothesized that women will encounter the same conflict as they move away from traditional female roles.

Clinicians have noted that persons with a somatization disorder also tend to be more average on C and Q_4 than do those with the anxiety disorders. They vary markedly on scales I and Q_3, depending on the degree of depression. Though a pattern with a combination of a low E and a high Q_1 score is relatively rare, it predisposes that person to the somatization disorders.

☐   OTHER TEST-RESPONSE PATTERNS

Performance scale scores on the WAIS-R are usually higher than verbal scale scores. In particular, the performance subtests that depend on motor coordination and speed are relatively high, with an occasionally surprising exception in object assembly. Within the verbal scale scores, lower information and digit span scores are expected, relative to higher comprehension scores. In females, where the somatization disorder incorporates histrionic components, the arithmetic score is low.

The typically salient feature of the MCMI profile here is an elevation of 85 or higher on H. Somatically channeled anxieties are often the source of somatization disorders, and this is indicated by considerable elevation on A. Somatization also occurs as a result of motoric dysfunction present in psychotic depression, so an elevation of 75 or higher on CC may occur. Personality types most prone to developing somatization disorders are the avoidant, the negativistic, the schizoid, and the cycloid, so elevations of 75 or higher may be predictive of the development of this disorder as a coping mechanism or during periods of stress.

Persons with a somatization disorder typically do not provide a high number of responses on the Rorschach and occasionally "fail" to give a response, and the percentage of W or complex M responses is usually low. They are more likely to give simple, popular responses, using only the easily discerned details. A high number of M responses is rare, and when they are provided, they often have a more static quality than do normal M responses. Responses involving color as a determinant are uncommon. Responses focusing on bony-anatomy content and occasionally pure C responses, such as "blood," do occur (Wagner and Wagner, 1981).

The comments in the section on somatoform disorders are also applicable to the somatization disorders. The symptomatology here is more similar to actual physiological disorder than it is in several of the other somatoform disorders. Hence, biofeedback can be useful in turning around some of the surface physiological symptomatology and at the same time can give clients concrete feedback that may convince them, along with supportive therapy, to look at psychological vulnerability as the source of their disorder. Most persons with this disorder are defensive about it, and as a result, the comments about the paranoid disorders are applicable. At some point, a shift into an existential orientation may be necessary to confront clients fully with their escape mechanisms.

■　　　　**Conversion Disorder (300.11)**

The conversion disorder is similar in many respects to the somatization disorder. The difference is that in the conversion disorder there is a specific symptom or a related set of symptoms used for the attainment of some secondary gain or to express a psychological conflict. Conversion symptoms are not under voluntary control. Somatoform pain disorder, discussed in the next section of this chapter, can be considered a subcategory of conversion disorder where the specific symptom is simply pain (Srinivasan et al., 1986).

With some of the psychosexual dysfunctions (discussed later), it may be difficult to decide whether the problem directly expresses a psychological issue and is thus technically a conversion disorder or whether it is a physiololgical response to anxiety. In actuality, it may be a mixture of both (Lo Piccolo and Stock, 1986). For this reason, as well as for convenience, these cases are included among the psychosexual disorders. Some clinicians might also consider anorexia nervosa to be a conversion disorder; yet most consider the syndrome different enough to warrant separate discussions, but there are parallels.

A conversion disorder is still referred to as a "hysterical neurosis, conversion type," and an individual with one is said to manifest *la belle indifference,* an attitude in which there is little concern about the apparent serious implications of the disorder. Persons with a conversion disorder appear to be aware at some level that their complaints do not predict the further dire consequences that others might infer from them. Although indifferent to their presenting symptoms, emotional lability in response to other stimuli is commonly noted (Kellner, 1986).

The attitude of *la belle indifference* is not found in all conversion disorders: Some people develop their symptoms under extreme stress and manifest that stress quite directly. Even in *these* individuals, however, anxiety seems to dissipate over the duration of the disorder in favor of a focus on physical symptoms.

A dependent or histrionic personality predisposes individuals to the development of conversion symptoms. Another important predisposing factor is a history of actual physical disorder during which excessive caretaking behaviors or other secondary gains occurred.

□ DSM-III-R

The DSM-III-R requires evidence of a disturbance that implies a physical disorder, with symptoms that are not under voluntary control and in which psychological factors are seen as a primary cause. This is supported by evidence of a temporal relationship and is usually accompanied by avoidance or secondary-gain patterns. It cannot be explained by a known physical disorder or a culturally sanctioned response pattern. It is not limited to pain or sexual problems.

□ MMPI

Most of the comments made about diagnostic observations on somatization disorders are relevant here. It has been traditional to expect that in most cases of conversion disorder there is a classic conversion V, wherein scales 1 and 3 are both high and 2 is relatively low. This is especially indicative of a conversion reaction in which the individual takes a naive and Pollyannaish attitude and manifests *la belle indifference*. However, Johnson et al. (1980) found that the 2-1-7 pattern, with a high score on 3, is more common in this disorder. If scale 3 is very high, scale 4 is low, and scale 1 is around 60–70 T histrionic characteristics are emphasized. In persons where *la belle indifference* is lacking, a higher scale 4 is likely.

Another profile seen occasionally in conversion disorders is the 3-9/9-3. These people experience conversion reactions in acute form, accompanied by at least moderately high anxiety levels. Over time, they are likely to show more histrionic characteristics, and the 9 scale should be somewhat lower.

□ 16 PF

The observations on the 16 PF relevant to somatization disorders are applicable here as well. However, if there is *la belle indifference,* N and Q_3 are higher and there is a relatively lower score on L. A high F score is also probable. Since these individuals are usually not as sophisticated as others in the overall group of somatoform disorders, a lower B scale is noted. Also, the concrete quality of their thinking predicts a lower M score.

□ OTHER TEST-RESPONSE PATTERNS

Although the overall group of conversion disorders is similar to the somatization disorders, those with *la belle indifference* in particular show higher scores on digit symbol and digit span on the WAIS-R. In addition, they seldom show bright-normal or superior intelligence and do poorly on tests that measure more subtle intellectual discriminations, such as comprehension, similarities, and picture arrangement. Emotional distancing from the Rorschach cards—through such comments as "they are weird" or "they are ugly"—is common. They are prone to deny depressive or aggressive feelings in the content of the Rorschach and the TAT.

Because physical symptoms in conversion disorder are usually specific, elevated H is not highly likely on the MCMI. The submissive personality (scale 3) and the gregarious personality (scale 4) are most likely to develop conversion disorders as a way to achieve secondary gain. The submissive personality is especially likely to exhibit *la belle indifference*. High scores indicating the presence of these personality patterns may be predictive of the development of conversion disorders. The ambivalence and psychological conflicts of those with elevated scores on scale 8 may be predisposed toward developing this disorder.

☐   TREATMENT OPTIONS

Since the time of Freud, hypnosis is a means of directly suggesting a cure or as a means of exploring unconscious conflicts has been effective in the treatment of conversion disorders (Edmonston, 1986). Also, it is worthwhile to include a variety of placebo techniques with a client with conversion disorder, particularly one who focuses on the dramatic.

Hendrix et al. (1978) successfully used behavioral techniques to cure the conversion disorder symptom of a clenched fist. In general, aversion relief and variations of the time-out technique (removing the person from the situation and not responding to his or her disturbed behaviors) can be useful here. In the cognitive behavioral technique of covert extension, the conversion disorder client would be asked to imagine the general conversion pattern while at the same time imagining that the reinforcing events that usually occur with this behavior in the real world do not occur in imagination. The effectiveness of the technique depends on already having attained some awareness as to the source of the conversion disorder. Thus, it is best used as a subsequent procedure to such techniques as hypnosis, psychotherapy, or free association, which are used to first explore these unconscious ties.

■   Somatoform Pain Disorder (307.80)

Somatoform pain disorder is a conversion disorder that specifically involves pain not due to a physical cause. Yet, as with the other somatoform disorders, a history of physical disorder involving the actual symptom is common (Keefe and Gil, 1987). The emergence of a somatoform pain disorder is facilitated by developmental-stage transitions and by specific stressful events. Somatoform pain disorder differs from the other conversion disorders in that the commonly associated histrionic features of sexual ambivalence, *la belle indifference,* and dependency are not usually observed.

As with the other conversion disorders, somatoform pain disorder may reflect a psychological conflict and/or exert a controling influence on the person's interactions with other people, resulting in some secondary gain and/or allowance for avoidance. The pain seldom follows known anatomical or neurological patterns, and extensive diagnostic work reveals no evidence of organic pathology. In the more sophisticated patient, it may mimic well-known diseases, such as angina or arthritis.

Benedikt and Kolb (1986) found in a study of those presenting themselves at a chronic pain center of a VA hospital that a large subgroup had undiagnosed post-traumatic stress disorder. It was postulated that—since the pain was usually focused in areas of injury related to the disorder, such as shrapnel wounds—the reexperiencing of the events had precipitated in this form. Many in this subgroup had been previously treated for the chronic pain with medications, surgery, or electrical stimulation—it seems the psychological nature of their pain had been unrealized. The finding that chronic pain may be associated with post-traumatic stress syndrome should alert the clinician to alternative treatment strategies.

☐ DSM-III-R

The DSM-III-R requires evidence of nonorganic severe pain in which psychological factors are seen as a primary cause, as shown by an absence of support for any organic pathology, or excessive response to actual organic pathology. There is often a maintenance of the pain by reinforcement of avoidance pattern or by secondary gain. The symptoms are of at least six months duration and are not under voluntary control.

☐ MMPI

Though somatoform pain disorder can be considered a conversion disorder, the classic conversion V is not always found (Love and Peck, 1987; Strassberg et al., 1981; Fordyce, 1979). Since depression is evident in many cases, the 2 scale may be elevated. Elevations (in order of degree) in the 1-2-3 scales are common (Love and Peck, 1987). Interestingly enough, clients with a single pain complaint tend to score higher on these scales than do clients with multiple pain complaints (Strassberg et al., 1981). Clients who are using their illness to obtain compensation are more likely to score higher on scale 4 and, to a lesser degree, scale 9, and other cues for malingering should be considered.

As symptoms become more chronic and patients are rejected more often by diagnosticians and treaters, a rise in scale 7 is probable. When pain is focused in the extremities or is manifested in headaches or back problems (a pattern in which repression and denial are common), a 1-3/3-1 profile is likely.

One group of patients with multiple pain complaints shows high scores on 1, 3, 7, and 8, in that order. This group is characterized by somatic preoccupation, obsessive thinking, isolation, and denial of psychological problems. Another subgroup is denoted by high scores on scale K and scale 1 and a low score on scale 6. This group is particularly inclined to deny their psychological difficulties, almost in a naive fashion, and is interpersonally insensitive (Propkop et al., 1980).

Clients with actual chronic pain do not often show much elevation immediately after the injury. However, if they are tested several months after it occurs, elevations on scales 1 and 3 are likely. Also, an elevated conversion V along with an elevated scale 4 predict poor recovery from pain or from surgery in general (Love and Peck, 1987).

Patients with chronic pain also are likely to become increasingly depressed, so an elevation on 2 is even more common. Many patients with chronic pain become addicted to toxic levels of pain-killing drugs and as a result begin to show cognitive slippage and other indications of brain damage. A 2-9, with an 8 that is high and greater than 7, or other indicators of disinhibition, such as a high 4, accompanied by indications of distress are potential indicators of this addiction and toxicity (Fordyce, 1979).

Certain patients with chronic pain appear to reflect a one-trial learning process associated with the originating trauma. As a result, they emit indications of phobiclike behavior on the MMPI. They are often suggestible and thus manifest high K and L scores, with a high scale 3 and a relatively high scale 1, often accompanied by a 7 scale that is elevated at least 10 points over scale 8 (Fordyce, 1979).

☐   16 PF

The comments regarding conversion disorders are appropriate here, except those that focus on the symptom of *la belle indifference,* since this is not typical for the somatoform pain disorder.

☐   OTHER DIAGNOSTIC CONSIDERATIONS

Extreme elevation on H on the MCMI is not likely here, though some specific patterns of pain may be indicated by elevations between 75 and 85. Some elevation on A and D are also likely. Those with elevations of 75 or higher on 2 may utilize psychogenic pain as a way to avoid interpersonal interactions, while the psychological conflict and ambivalence of the 8 and C patterns predispose them to the development of psychogenic pain. The personality patterns indicated by elevated scores on 2 and 8 are more likely to be present here, in contrast to conversion disorder, where the most likely patterns are indicated by elevations on 3 and 4.

Beyond the standard means (psychological tests, hypnosis, "truth serums") for differentiating a conversion disorder from an organic condition, there are other methods specifically helpful in discriminating psychogenic from organic pain (or from malingering; see Chapter 12). Cortical evoked potentials have shown promise as a diagnostic instrument in this area, as well as in many other diagnostic situations. Also, certain EEG patterns appear more consistently in organic than in psychogenic pain, and assessment of blood plasma cortisol can be a helpful discriminator. Unfortunately, most people with somatoform disorders, particularly conversion disorders, are seldom seen by a psychologist or psychiatrist, and such specific and more sophisticated assessments are never made.

□   TREATMENT OPTIONS

The major goal in a pain management approach is to work to help patients through social-skills training, assertiveness training, vocational rehabilitation, and the like to a more independent, active lifestyle (Love and Peck, 1987). Also, since somatoform pain disorder is a specific form of the conversion disorder, the comments in that section are appropriate. As noted, hypnosis is appropriate in conversion disorders. David Cheek (1965) has pioneered in the use of hypnosis to find the subconscious causes for chronic psychogenic pain. While his clients are under hypnosis, Cheek asks them to gradually release this symptom, often having them point to a date on the calendar designating when they might be willing to give up the symptom. He then makes an appointment for that day and gradually ties the insights under hypnosis into conscious awareness. With chronic pain, the musculature has often conformed over time to a bodily posture that continues the pain. Hence, even psychogenic pain may have an overlay of real pain. Biofeedback to release this tense muscle posture can be helpful. Other clinicians would argue that techniques derived from chiropractic, such as Rolfing, are useful here as well.

Secondary gain is particularly important in the conversion disorders. Therefore, the clinician should look at family and marital situations for possible reinforcement patterns, as well as for possible sites for intervention.

■   **Hypochondriasis (300.70)**

Hypochondriacs unreasonably interpret normal or relatively unimportant bodily and physical changes as indicative of serious physical disorder. They are constantly alert to an upsurge of new symptomatology, and since the body is constantly in physiological flux, they are bound to find signs that they can interpret as suggestive of disorder.

In one sense, hypochondriacs do not fear being sick; they are certain they already are. Hypochondriasis is a relatively common pattern from adolescence to old age. It is seen most frequently in the age range thirty to forty for men and forty to fifty for women (Meister, 1980). Meister also believes that there are many "closet hypochondriacs," those who do not constantly go to physicians, yet are heavily involved in health fads, checking of body behaviors, and discussion of their concerns with close friends (who may relish this quasi-therapist role). These closet hypochondriacs would not earn a formal DSM-III-R diagnosis because they do not fit some of the specific requirements, such as seeking out medical reassurance and going through physical examinations. Nonetheless, they manifest the disorder.

A number of common factors have been observed in the development of hypochondriasis (Kellner, 1986; Meister, 1980):

1. For most hypochondriacs, there has been a background marked by substantial experience in an atmosphere of illness. This could include identification with a significant other who was hypochondriacal or early exposure to a family member who was an invalid.
2. Hypochondriacs often have had a strong dependency relationship with a family member who could express love and affection in a normal or intense fashion during periods when the hypochondriac had been ill, yet was distant or nonexpressive at other times.
3. Hypochondriacs often channel their psychological conflicts and their needs for existential reassurance into this pattern. As a result, the hypochondriac pattern of behavior may mask a mid-life crisis or some other challenge that is not being met effectively.
4. A certain subgroup of hypochondriacs are postulated as having a predispositional sensitivity to pain and body sensations. This could be stimulated by prior physical disorder in systems in which the hypochondriacal pattern is now manifest.

All of these factors are facilitated by reinforcement of the hypochondriasis in the client's world, and avoidance of tasks or demands because of being sick is often noted here.

□   DSM-III-R

There is not so great a focus on actual physical symptoms in hypochondriasis as in the somatization disorder. Rather, such people interpret physical sensations and natural changes in their body as indicative of significant physical disorder—though not at a delusional level and not in the midst of a panic attack—in spite of expert assurance that there is little danger. The duration of disorder is at least six months, and some area of social or vocational functioning is often disrupted. Persons with a cardiac neurosis or cancer phobia may be placed in this category.

□   DIAGNOSTIC CONSIDERATIONS

Hypochondriacs function similarly to individuals with the somatization disorder, except that hypochondriasis is more focused and intellectualized. As a result, the MMPI profile will be somewhat tempered, being lower on scales 7 and 8 in particular. Scale 1 is at least moderately elevated, and a common code type here is the 3-1/1-3 profile, as is the 1-2/2-1 when there is evident distress. Since there is at least a moderate amount of defensiveness associated with this disorder, the scales K and 6 and 7 are usually moderately high. If the person is relatively naive in response to personal conflicts, the L scale is also somewhat elevated. Hypochondriacs who are inclined to discuss their problems with others should score lower on scale 0, indicating the extroverted aspect of their pattern.

As with the MMPI, the 16 PF is tempered from the profile usually noted with the somatization disorder. Specifically, C is usually not as low nor is Q_4 as high. However, E, I, and Q_3 are usually higher, reflecting the even more controlled psychological world of hypochondriacs in comparison to that of persons with a somatization disorder.

Preoccupation with matters of health will serve to moderately elevate H on the MCMI, so that scores of 75 or higher might be expected. A and D scores of 75 or higher are likely because hypochondriacal symptoms often occur in response to underlying anxiety and/or depression relevant to external situations. Those personality patterns that are likely to develop hypochondriacal disorders are those presenting a great deal of anxiety and compulsive behavior. Prominent patterns indicated by elevated 7, 8, and C are particularly likely.

Due to the mild obsessive component usually found in this disorder (Kozak et al., 1988), hypochondriacs overelaborate their responses on the WAIS-R and thus tend to do better on comprehension, similarities, and vocabulary. These are people who cope with words; as a result, the verbal scale is often higher than the performance scale. Blatt et al., (1970) found that a low score on object assembly was predictive of high bodily concern, including hypochondriacal patterns.

The same mild obsessive factor should result in longer latencies to the Rorschach cards, as well as a number of the other response patterns manifest in the obsessive-compulsive disorder. Anatomical responses to the cards are expected, and there is some indication that this anatomy content increases as they proceed through the cards. CF is usually greater than FC, and there is a relatively low production of M responses.

Direct reassurance on medical symptoms is usually not a curative factor, though it is often important that some reassurance be given so that the therapy can then focus on consideration of psychological concerns. The development of trust is critical in this disorder; in that regard, the reader is referred to the discussion of trust development in the section on the paranoid disorders.

Another approach can be helpful with specific hypochondriacs: Therapists can suddenly state that they feel a hypochondriac client is "dead right" about his or her concerns. The shock from this unexpected agreement, with the apparent verification of their dreaded suspicions, can often elicit the underlying psychological concerns. This technique must be carried out with care, as it can backfire and solidify the hypochondriacal concerns.

Family therapy is often helpful with certain hypochondriacs. Many of them have evolved a response system in which significant others consistently reinforce their pattern; with the supervision of the therapist, this pattern can be broken. Family members can be taught to give the person psychological reassurance and caring responses, while at the same time ignoring or otherwise avoiding the reinforcement of the concerns about physical disorder.

Such a technique takes into account the importance of underlying existential issues in the treatment of subcategories of hypochondriasis, such as cancer phobia and cardiac neurosis. Several clients appear to use specific concerns in these areas as a distraction from more anxiety-arousing issues, such as a basic realization of mortality or facing the potential to fail. Existential confrontation (Budman and Gurman, 1988), in a context of supportive psychotherapy, allows the hypochondriacal concerns to cease so that clients may confront these deeper problems. Similarly, many of the techniques specific to the obsessive-compulsive disorder are applicable here.

Physicians who take the overall disorder as a serious problem and who do not write these patients off as "crocks" can go a long way toward breaking the hypochondriacal pattern. Once such patients begin to trust the physician, they can open up more about their total problems and then, under the umbrella of trust, possibly accept referral for psychological treatment.

■   ## Body Dysmorphic Disorder (300.70)

Body dysmorphic disorder (BDD) has been traditionally referred to as dysmorphophobia. BDD is characterized by a preoccupation with some imagined imperfection in physical appearance or an exaggerated reaction to some minor defect (not exclusively occurring during transsexualism or anorexia nervosa). It is not held so firmly as to be delusional in nature. Victims may, if pressed, admit to the possibility that their concern is excessive, but they persist in the concern and in behaviors related to that concern (Kellner, 1986). For example, they may make repeated visits to plastic surgeons or dermatologists in order to have their concern confirmed and to get some relief from the imagined defect. Unfortunately, there are a number of cases of such individuals undergoing extensive plastic surgery at the hands of careless or unscrupulous surgeons.

As is no doubt evident from the above, BDD is a variation of hypochondriasis. Hence, the comments on diagnostic indicators and therapeutic considerations for hypochondriasis apply to BDD as well, though there is usually a greater degree of narcissism and a general concern with controlling interpersonal relationships in BDD. Thus on the MMPI, BDDs tend to be higher on scales 4 and 0 and lower on scales 1 and 3 than classic hypochondriacs. Also, the BDDs tend to score higher on A on the 16 PF and generally show more of the indicators of narcissism on the Millon.

Undifferentiated Somatoform Disorder (300.70) and Somatoform Disorder NOS (300.70)

These catch-all categories include any pattern that generally fits the requirements for somatoform disorder but does not fit the specifics of the individual patterns just covered. In actual practice, many individuals do not fit a specific somatoform disorder—not fulfilling the requirement of evidence in four or five symptom groups—and hence are included here. In general, the "undifferentiated" label is used when the pattern persists for more than six months, "somatoform disorder NOS" if it is less than six months.

CHAPTER 7

Dissociative and Sleep Disorders

The dissociative disorders, traditionally referred to as the hysterical neuroses, dissociative type, are characterized by a sudden disruption or alteration of the normally integrated functions of consciousness. This disturbance is almost always temporary, though it may wax and wane, particularly in amnesia and fugue.

The various subcategories are: psychogenic amnesia, an acute disturbance of memory function; psychogenic fugue, a sudden disruption of one's sense of identity, usually accompanied by travel away from home; multiple personality, the domination of the person's consciousness by two or more separate personalities; and depersonalization disorder, a disturbance in the experience of the self in which the sense of reality is temporarily distorted.

There is also a category referred to as dissociative disorder NOS, simply a residual category. The patterns most commonly included in this diagnosis are those of persons who experience a sense of unrealness that is not accompanied by depersonalization and who also show some trancelike states.

It can be argued that the depersonalization disorder, also referred to as the depersonalization neurosis, is not appropriately included in this general category, as there is no substantial memory disturbance. Yet there is a significant disturbance, albeit temporary, of the sense of reality, and thus the identity is certainly affected.

■ Diagnostic Considerations

With the exception of the depersonalization disorder, the dissociative disorders occur rarely. As a result, there is not much significant literature on discrimination of these states by psychological tests. This is not as unfortunate as it might seem. In the dissociative disorders, the symptoms are usually reasonably clear indicators of the particular subcategory, even though other disorders have to be screened out.

For example, many of these disorders have to be initially differentiated from schizophrenia. However, people with a dissociative disorder do not show the confusion and deteriorated functioning in most personality areas that are indicative of schizophrenia. These disorders may also need to be distinguished from those in which the behavior mimics an organic condition, such as a tumor or epilepsy (Kopelmon, 1987). Indeed, when the clinician is confronted with the symptomatology noted here, a medical consultation is usually warranted.

■ ## Psychogenic Amnesia (300.12)

This is an instance when the commonly understood use of the term "amnesia" almost directly reflects the diagnostic implications. Psychogenic amnesia is a temporary loss of ability to recall personal information. It can be information about a specific topic or memories of the immediate or distant past. Although media portrayals lead people to believe that the memory for *all* past events is lost in amnesia, this is rare (Schachter, 1986). Recovery of memory is usually rapid, whereas the recovery is gradual in organic conditions, if it takes place at all. The alcohol amnestic disorder differs from psychogenic amnesia. In the former, the person is able to recall information for only a few minutes after it is obtained, since that ability to transfer information from short-term into long-term memory has been lost. This condition is also observed in some individuals who have had significant ECT treatments.

☐   DSM-III-R

The DSM-III-R requires evidence of sudden memory failure for important personal information that has been previously stored in memory. The memory failure is too significant to be explained by ordinary forgetfulness, and it is not explained by alcohol-related "blackouts," by other organic conditions, or by such disorders as catatonia and stupor or multiple personality. It also needs to be discriminated from malingering, but such discrimination is often quite difficult (Wiggins and Brandt, 1988; Schachter, 1986). The findings of faking scales on psychological tests are helpful here, as are interviews with the use of amytal or hypnosis.

This disorder is typically observed in adult and adolescent females who are undergoing significant stress and in young males experiencing the distress of wartime. A subjectively intolerable life experience, such as an unexpected loss, is a common catalyst for amnesia, as well as for the following related category, psychogenic fugue.

There are four common subgroupings of psychogenic amnesia. The first and most common type, localized, refers to the loss of memory for events during a circumscribed period of time (following a severe stressor, such as an accident). Selective amnesia is a loss of memory for only certain types of events during the circumscribed period of time. Generalized amnesia, a failure to recall all events in one's life, and continuous amnesia, a loss of memory from one time to another, are both rare.

☐ MMPI

A high 3-4/4-3 pattern on the MMPI, particularly the 3-4 profile, means fertile ground for the development of dissociative experiences. This pattern is marked by immaturity and significant difficulty in coping directly and maturely with disturbances in one's psychological world. It implies the use of denial, either psychologically (as in amnesia) or physically and psychologically (as in the fugue state). While scale 4 usually means sociopathy, it is also a measure of lack of social poise, naiveté, and immaturity and so may be high here.

Scale 1 is occasionally raised in this profile, as is scale 8, depending on whether the person is gravitating toward somatic concerns as an expression of disorder or into a general loss of integrated decision making. The F scale is low compared to other groups of pathology. If anger and hostility are being denied and avoided, an elevation on scales K and L is likely. The naiveté of the amnestic is especially reflected in a higher L score than would usually be obtained in an individual of similar social and intellectual level.

☐ 16 PF

A modal profile for this type of disorder has not been determined. However, most clinicians agree that low scores on H and N are to be expected. Suppressed anxiety should result in at least a moderate elevation on Q_4, and the increasing loss of integration of self-concept should predict a lower Q_3 score. Higher scores on O and I, reflecting oversensitivity and apprehension, can be expected, particularly in the young-adult and adolescent females who are manifesting this pattern. The suggestibility and sense of inadequacy often found in such individuals also reflect the contrast between their rigid problem-solving skills and their desire to place trust in an authority figure.

☐ TREATMENT OPTIONS

Hypnotic techniques to gain access to subconscious material have been a traditional treatment for amnesia (Crabtree, 1985), and they are generally effective (Edmonston, 1986). Psychotherapy, with an emphasis on interpretation of possible conflicts before adequate realization of them, is also useful, particularly if a supportive atmosphere both in and out of the therapy hour can be generated (Teyber, 1988). This gives clients the sense of safety and potential for reintegration that they so desperately look for. Since this disorder is so often a response to a significant stressor, the techniques discussed in the treatment of the posttraumatic stress disorder are also applicable here.

■ Psychogenic Fugue (300.13)

Psychogenic fugue is a specific form of amnesia in which people are unable to recall the essentials of their previous personality. In addition, they are likely to wander away from their home environment and assume an entirely new identity. Although they are seldom able to recall the behaviors that they carried out while in the fugue state, the recovery is usually complete.

The syndrome often occurs as a reaction to a severe psychosocial stressor, such as the unexpected breakup of a marriage or loss of a job without warning. It is facilitated by previous heavy alcohol or drug use, which points to the dissociative quality inherent in states of consciousness engendered by drug abuse.

Somnambulism, traditionally considered a dissociative reaction, is now listed in DSM-III-R as a sleep disorder. This is reasonable since it is usually not associated with any significant pathology. When it is clearly not associated with organic disorder, as is true in most cases, it is best considered a simple learned behavior that was not suppressed in the early stages of development (Kopelmon, 1987).

☐   DSM-III-R

To diagnose psychogenic fugue, the DSM-III-R requires evidence that the individual suddenly assumed at least some elements of a wholly or partially new identity, left the normal home or workplace, and could not recall his previous life. This is not due to organic conditions or multiple personality.

This relatively rare disorder bears some similarity to the multiple personality, since the new identity is often in sharp contrast to the previous one. As previously noted, the pattern usually occurs in response to a significant loss of some sort and is catalyzed in some individuals by the shock of a natural disaster or a war.

☐   TESTING CONSIDERATIONS

These individuals are seldom tested while they are in the midst of the fugue state. As they are brought back into their natural environment, the recovery of memory begins to occur. When they are tested, they show patterns similar to psychogenic amnesia.

☐   TREATMENT OPTIONS

Since psychogenic fugue is analogous to psychogenic amnesia, the techniques described for the treatment of the post-traumatic stress disorder are also applicable; a subjectively disturbing stressor is almost always a critical catalyst here. As a follow-up, it would be useful to deal with the subjective reasons for the severity of this trauma through humanistic and existential techniques, for example, through gestalt therapy, since its emphasis is on reintegration of the person's wholeness. Hypnosis is also used for this purpose, but care has to be taken because what appears to be a reintegration of true memories may in actuality be virtually new memories.

Janov's primal therapy (1980) is a technique that could be useful as one part of the treatment for the dissociative disorders, partiularly with psychogenic fugue, as such clients have abruptly denied underlying conflicts and feelings. However, this is a good example of how a specific technique has unfortunately been elevated, at least by some disciples, into the status of a school of psychotherapy.

■   ## Multiple Personality (300.14)

The multiple personality receives a great deal of attention in the media (Crabtree, 1988), in part because it is often confused with schizophrenia. From this attention, it could be concluded that it is a common disorder. However, Winer (1978) notes that there have been only about 200 reasonably well documented cases. The multiple personality should be considered extremely rare, and many clinicians never see a true multiple personality in their entire career.

Multiple personalities come into treatment because they note some peculiarities in their world: forgetting of certain interactions with people, general confusion, and loss of memories. A different personality is then discovered through psychotherapy, which is often supplemented by hypnosis. In some cases, personalities continue to be produced, first by the indirect suggestion of the therapist's interest and reinforcement, then by the reinforcement of the therapist's reinvigorated concern for the person's problems (Spanos et al., 1985).

Amnesia is a pathognomonic sign of a future multiple personality, a history of child abuse is a common precursor, and stress is an important precipitating factor in the genesis of this disorder. Stressors in a person's psychological world often trigger the sudden transitions in personality noted here (Clum, 1989).

☐   DSM-III-R

According to DSM-III-R, the multiple personality is a person who is consecutively dominated by at least two separate and distinct personalities that determine separate behavior patterns, and at least two of these personalities alternately take full control of the person's behavior. The personalities are complex and reasonably well integrated, often starkly contrasting, and the transition from one to another is sudden. The disorder is most commonly observed in young-adult and adolescent females. The later personalities are usually a crystallization into a personality of opposite facets from the original one.

☐   TESTING CONSIDERATIONS

Since the personalities of a multiple personality will vary markedly (Crabtree, 1985), depending on what facets of that individual they are expressing, no particular patterns could be expected, though a 3-8/8-3 MMPI pattern is commonly noted in dissociative reactions. A high L scale is also occasionally noted. Fowler (1981) suggests that a 1-3/3-1 code type is also probable here. Histrionic and dependent personality components are often found in the separate personalities, and there is a greater likelihood of an acting-out of aggressive and sexual impulses. The sections on the histrionic and the dependent personality disorders deal with this. The confusion and peculiarities initially presented by the multiple personality may be present as an elevated S or SS on the MCMI. However, because of the nature of the disorder, no single prediction can be made; profiles should vary as personalities do.

Osgood et al. (1976) demonstrated an ingenious application of the semantic differential to the assessment of the contrasting features of a multiple personality. Clinicians who happen to see this rare disorder could apply this method to monitor changes in the individual as he or she goes through various personalities and then begins to integrate again into a single personality. Also, in a few cases, EEG indicators of amplitude (attention) and latency have discriminated various personalities over time. Chapter 12 is useful here since some people are inclined to feign this disorder for the sake of media attention.

☐   TREATMENT OPTIONS

The classic treatment for the multiple personality has been hypnosis, which is used to get in touch with the dissociated subpersonalities (Kluft, 1987). In the few cases that have been available to clinicians for study, this has generally been reasonably successful, though the cost in time has been high. Also, it is arguable that since hypnosis itself may involve a dissociative experience, it may iatrogenically increase the tendency to produce multiple personalities, particularly in the short run.

One could argue that transactional analysis (Berne, 1964) would also further the dissociative process, since it so clearly emphasizes separate ego states. However, it could be useful in getting the person in touch with the message that all of us play different roles and when these roles become crystallized, the potential for dissociative experience is heightened. This would at least place this experience closer to a normal experience and thus foster reintegration. Psychoanalysis has been used effectively with the multiple personality (Osgood et al., 1976), though the therapist may have to deal with the unique problem of multiple transferences.

■ Depersonalization Disorder (300.60)

As noted earlier, the depersonalization disorder is dissimilar to other dissociative reactions, since consciousness is never truly segmented and significant memory loss is not a factor in the depersonalization disorder. Because there is no better place for depersonaslization disorder in the DSM-III-R and because it includes dissociation from the usual sense of reality, it is listed here.

In the depersonalization disorder, individuals experience a sense of separation from normal consciousness and may report feeling as if they are a separate observer of the self. The typical reality of the usual world seems as if it has been altered. This is an experience that many people have on occasion—the issue is whether it is a consistent pattern. (It is interesting to note that if one follows certain modern gurus, such as Krishnamurti, the ability to constantly perceive one's functioning as a separate observer is the mark of progress toward enlightenment.)

Since depersonalization is experienced by many people at times, the definition of disorder is appropriate on the basis of either frequency or a feeling of lack of control. Many people are not really bothered by such experiences, whereas others feel as if they are going crazy. In the latter situation, the sense of depersonalization can be conditioned to anticipatory anxiety, leading to a vicious cycle: reinforcing the belief that they might indeed be going crazy (Spanos et al., 1985).

Since this disorder focuses on an experience of a changing identity, it is not surprising that it occurs most frequently during adolescence. There is little impairment from the experience itself, but when it is accentuated by a conditioned anxiety response, it becomes troublesome. In that sense, it is similar to the conditioned anxiety response that many argue is the cause of the flashbacks during certain drug experiences. Abuse of alcohol or drugs facilitates the development of this disorder.

☐ DSM-III-R

Referred to as the depersonalization neurosis, the present category retains some of the DSM-II characteristics. There is usually more anxiety here than in the other dissociative disorders, though the dissociative aspect is the essential feature.

DSM-III-R requires substantive indication of an episode of depersonalization potent enough to cause significant distress, though reality testing remains intact, and there must be a persistent experience of either being outside of and/or detached from one's body, or feeling as if one were an automaton or in a dream. The possibilities of minor organic dysfunction, anxiety disorders, or even a developing depressive episode must be ruled out.

☐   MMPI

This disorder was included in the DSM-II as the depersonalization neurosis, and the modal profile still reflects this. Elevations on scales 3, 7, and F are likely, as these tap both the anxiety and hysteric components. The anxiety and identity confusion also lead to an elevated 8 scale, and since identity is threatened, changes in scale 5 away from stereotypical sexual-role scores are expected. Since these individuals are usually young, active in their response to their distress, but inclined to denial accompanied by somatic concerns, elevations on scales 1 and 9 may also occur. The various possible scale 4 elevations reflect the degrees of hostility and anger and the lack of social sophistication that vary within individuals with this disorder. In rare cases, a spike 0 profile may be noted early in its development (Kelley and King, 1979c).

☐   16 PF

Instability and loss of a sense of reality are reflected in moderately low C and Q_3 scores. O and M are likely to be high, while the low score on N reflects naiveté and a relative lack of sophistication. Individuals who manifest a depersonalization disorder are usually of higher intelligence, so scale B should be average or above.

☐   TREATMENT OPTIONS

Since in some respects the depersonalization disorder is as much an identity development disorder as it is a dissociative experience, any techniques useful for getting in touch with the less integrated aspects of the personality might be useful here. This could range from Rogers' (1951) client-centered therapy through gestalt therapy, supplemented by an emphasis on the problems of self-labeling, as detailed by Meichenbaum (1985). In this approach, clients are trained to label experiences viewed as alien as actually an integral part of their personality, to be dealt with in a confrontational and honest manner.

Psychodrama could also be useful here. In this vein, Yablonsky (1976, p. 4) states, "In psychodrama a person is encountering his conflicts and psychic pain in a setting that will more closely approximate his real life situation than in most other therapeutic approaches. A young man in conflict with a parent talks directly to a person as an auxiliary ego playing his parent. His fantasy (or reality) of his hostility or love can be acted out on the spot."

The acting-out of such fantasies about one's own reality, or the experiencing of that reality, can ultimately lead to a positive, integrative experience.

Sleep Disorders

The humorist and movie star W. C. Fields once quipped that "the best way to get a good night's sleep is to go to bed." Unfortunately, it's not that simple for many people. In fact, sleep disorder plagues everyone at one time or another. While estimates range widely, it's reasonable to assume that up to 15 percent of all adults will suffer a period of chronic insomnia at some point in their lives (Gackenbach, 1985; Van Pat, 1984).

There is a wide variety of sleep disorders, even though such disorders were not clearly recognized in the DSM until DSM-III-R, which included sleepwalking and sleep terror disorder (referred to as parasomnias) and sleep-wake schedule disorder, primary hypersomnia, primary insomnia, and insomnia disorder (referred to as dyssomnias).

An alternative and very well respected diagnostic classification system for sleep disorders is that of the Association of Sleep Disorder Centers (ASDC), published in their booklet "Diagnostic Classifications of Sleep and Arousal Disorders." It includes, for example, the sub-categories for insomnia by etiology:

1. *Psychophysiological.* Insomnia is based on chronic tension and anxiety. It is unrelated to medical disease or psychiatric problems.

2. Insomnia due to *psychiatric disturbance* is the most commonly diagnosed insomnia. Insomnia is a symptom of psychopathology.

3. The use of *drugs and alcohol* can often lead to insomnia. Hypnotics described for insomnia may pose a special problem. The individual gains a high tolerance for the drug and takes more, resulting in an eventual rebound problem.

4. Some insomnias are caused by *sleep-induced respiratory impairment.*

5. Insomnia associated with *sleep-related mycoclamus and "restless legs"* is characterized by periodic episodes of repetitive leg muscle jerks.

6. Insomnia may be associated with other *medical, toxic, and environmental conditions.*

7. *Childhood onset* of insomnia is characterized by a history of complaints well before puberty.

8. Insomnia *associated with other conditions* includes such things as repeated awakenings and intrusion of alpha waves into REM sleep.

9. Insomnia due to no abnormality includes those insomniacs who do not have psychopathology or medical problems. They experience difficulty sleeping only during conventional sleeping hours.

☐   DIAGNOSTIC CONSIDERATIONS

The first diagnostic recommendation is that any apparently serious sleep disorder should be evaluated at a sleep disorder center; a thorough evaluation should include physiological monitoring of at least a couple of nights of sleep.

As regards standard psychological tests, Keles (1983) found that insomniacs show a significant level of pathology on the MMPI. The highest three-scale code was 2-7-3. Fifty-six percent of the insomniacs tended to have a pathological elevation on scale 2, while 42 percent had a pathological elevation on scale 7 and 38 percent a pathological elevation on scale 3. The 2-7-3 code reflects the chronic anxiety, difficulty expressing feelings, denial, and feelings of depression common to the insomniac. Interestingly, Keles found that 30 percent of his subjects had pathological elevation on scale 8, which reflects self-image problems and difficulty integrating emotions. Scale 1 was significantly elevated in 20 percent of his subjects. Keles also found significant differences between age groups in their MMPI scores. The most common three-scale code in those younger than thirty was 2-7-8; in ages thirty to forty-nine, 2-7-3 was the most common.

On the 16 PF, it is hypothesized that the insomniacs would have high scores on scales I, L, O, and Q_4, while scores on scales E, F, and H would be low and C relatively low. A high Q_4 would tap the high anxiety level that is common to most insomniacs. A high score on O would reflect the insecure and oversensitive nature of the insomniac. Introspection, rumination, and inability to deal with conflict would be reflected by a high scale I and at least a mildly elevated M.

On the eight basic personality pattern scales of the MCMI, an elevated scale 2 and moderately elevated 8 may be expected. A high scale 2 (avoidant) would tap two common personality characteristics of the insomniacs: mild cognitive intrusions and perceptual hyperactivity. Since many insomniacs have problems expressing their emotions, this may be reflected on scale 8 (conforming). On the pathological personality disorders (scales C, P, and S), little elevations are expected.

☐   TREATMENT OPTIONS

Many insomniacs have significant anxiety, depression, and/or obessive-compulsive features that contribute to the insomnia, as well as to other aspects of functioning. If these exist, the reader is referred to those chapters for relevant treatment recommendations.

Chemotherapy is commonly used for insomnia, sometimes with a very specific focus, e.g., oxycodone for restless-leg syndrome. However, chemotherapy directed toward the sleep disorder as a whole must be administered with caution. It can be especially useful in breaking the insomnia cycle, but if prescribed for any length of time loses its effectiveness, brings on the risk of drug dependence and/or addiction, and can generate a rebound effect of even greater insomnia.

Various behavioral techniques have been found to be effective (Higginbotham et al., 1988), but the most efficient techniques are probably relaxation training and biofeedback, especially where the emphasis is on muscle tension release. Ancillary techniques include (1) initiating a regular program of vigorous exercise, (2) avoiding large or late meals, (3) avoiding long or late naps during the day, (4) cutting down on caffeine or heavy smoking or alcohol use, and (5) relearning a more appropriate bedtime routine by (a) going to bed only when feeling tired, (b) awakening at the same time each morning, (c) avoiding all nonsleep-related activities (within reason) in the bedroom, and (d) leaving the bedroom in ten minutes if sleep has not occurred, i.e., as the philosopher Friedrich Nietzsche said in *Thus Spake Zarathustra,* "It is no small art to sleep: to achieve it one must stay awake."

CHAPTER 8

The Sexual Disorders

This category in the DSM-III-R is used for those disorders in which a psychological variable is a significant factor in a sexual disturbance or disorder. If the disorder is caused by a physical factor, such as impotence from arteriosclerosis, it would be coded as an organic mental disorder.

In DSM-III-R, there are two divisions: the gender identity disorders and the sexual disorders. The sexual disorders are then subdivided into the paraphilias (the DSM-III-R term for the traditional "sexual deviations" and the sexual dysfunctions. There is also a residual category: paraphilia NOS. Gender identity disorder is differentiated from transsexualism only in that there is no persisting preoccupation with changing (via medication or surgery) into the sexual characteristics of the opposite sex. Thus, the following discussion will focus on transsexualism with the understanding that most of this discussion applies equally well to the gender identity disorder. Although the DSM-III-R does not directly provide for a diagnosis of sexual compulsion, it is a factor in many of the following diagnoses, and there is evidence that it may even be a recognizable pattern occasionally found apart from these other diagnoses (Masters et al., 1988; Coleman, 1987).

■ Transsexualism (302.50)

The DSM-III-R category of gender identity disorders is hardly a category, as it comprises only Transsexualism (302.50; usually considered the major subcategory) the parallel category for children called Gender Identity Disorder of Childhood (302.60), Gender Identity Disorders of Adolescence or Adulthood, Nontranssexual Type (GIDAANT) (302.85), and a residual category called Gender Identity Disorder NOS (302.85).

Transsexuals are persons who strongly identify with the opposite sex, as manifested in cross-dressing and a persistent desire for a physical change to the opposite sex. This strong desire to change gender and the feeling of having an underlying opposite-sex identity are what primarily differentiate the transsexual from the transvestite (Blanchard et al., 1985). Transsexualism is a chronic disorder, and it is almost always preceded by gender identity problems in childhood. A disturbed parent-child relationship, particularly the absence of a model of the same sex, predisposes a child to this disorder. Also, any other characteristics, either physical or psychological, that cause identification of a child by others as one of the opposite sex (such as long hair and soft features in males) also facilitate transsexualism.

The first sex-change operation occurred in Europe in 1930. Most changes are made from male to female, in large part because there is a greater initial demand for this type of change, but also, just as importantly, because the surgery for the reverse procedure, female to male, is much more difficult and has a higher likelihood of failure. Money and Wiedeking (1980) argue that this tendency is because maleness genetically is "femaleness repressed" (an extra Y chromosome that modified the basic genetic structure), and thus males become more vulnerable to gender confusion.

Clinicians have an important role not only in diagnosing transsexualism in standard clinical settings, but also in the psychological screening of such persons as appropriate for sex-change surgery. It is controversial whether this surgery is necessary. However, because such surgery is likely to continue, it is most important that people be thoroughly screened. Most reputable surgeons who deal with these problems mandate a team assessment by a psychologist, psychiatrist, and an endocrinologist. The early success rate of this surgery, about 90 percent in male or female sex reassignments (Pauly, 1968), undoubtedly reflects the thorough psychological screening techniques that have been done. As this procedure now becomes even more commonplace, screening will probably become more lax and individuals who are inappropriate candidates will have an increasing chance of being operated on. For example, certain schizophrenics have a delusional belief that they are of the opposite sex, and some disturbed homosexuals and transvestites who cannot deal with the demands of their perceived role conflicts may unconsciously view a sex change as an escape from these conflicts. The clinician involved in such procedures should especially consider indicators for schizophrenia, paranoia, transvestism, and homosexuality when dealing with potential transsexual candidates (Money, 1987).

☐   DSM-III-R

There should be evidence of continuous (at least two years) and pervasive feelings that one is the wrong sex, with a consequent desire to change genital structure to the other sex and then to live in the life-style of the opposite sex. There should be no evidence of directly related genetic abnormality, such as hermaphroditism. To warrant a diagnosis of transsexualism, individuals should first be screened for such conditions as schizophrenia, as well as for a primary or ancillary diagnosis of transvestism.

The disorder is subcoded "heterosexual," "homosexual," or "asexual," with the label determined solely by the dominant sexual preference in the history of the individual.

☐   MMPI
_____

Tsushima and Wedding (1979), in a study that looked at the MMPI profiles of transsexuals, found them to be surprisingly within normal limits. Of course, scale 5 is high in males due to nonidentification with the traditional male role, along with the conflicts about sexual identity. While presurgical males-to-females were found by Fleming et al. (1981) to be high on 5, 6, and 8, presurgical females were high on 5 and relatively high on 6, 7, and 8. Postsurgical females (those who had been male) were high on 5 and relatively high on 6 and K. Postsurgical males were high on 5 and relatively high on 6. Fleming et al. note that the tendency to peak on 5 and 6 is consistent with the early research literature about MMPI profiles of transsexuals.

On occasion, scale 1 and, to a lesser degree, 3 may be slightly elevated, reflecting preoccupation with body structure. In accordance with the preceding, scale F may be elevated. On the other hand, if transsexuals perceive the need to present themselves as healthy to pass the screening, scale K would be quite high and signs of pathology would be suppressed. If they are anxious and ambivalent about the identity issue, scales 4 and 8 may be slightly elevated; and if this has generated depression, scale 2 is raised.

☐   16 PF
_____

As with the MMPI, the pattern is generally within reasonable normal limits. However, the mode of sexual adjustment results in slightly higher I scores and slightly lower E, H, and N scores in most males, with the converse being true in most females. Scale B should reflect the average or above-average intelligence in most transsexuals, and since they endorse attitudes that differ from the average, they are likely to be higher on M and Q_1 and moderately low on G.

☐   OTHER TEST-RESPONSE PATTERNS
_____

On the Rorschach test, transsexuals (compared to normals) displayed significantly more intense levels of aggression, a lower level of object relations, poorer reality testing, and impaired boundary definition, being in this way similar to a borderline personality.

On the MCMI, the distress and confusion about gender identity may cause elevation on A and D to 75 or higher, and very likely on C as well. Although no clear-cut pathological indicators are typically present, some generalizations may be possible. Males who seek to be females may be more likely to have personality types that are more commonly characteristic of females, so the prominent scale indicator may be 3 or 4. Conversely, females wishing to be males may have personality characteristics traditionally thought of as male, so scale 6 may be prominent.

☐   TREATMENT OPTIONS

A classic option for the transsexual has been surgery to change the genitalia to that of the opposite sex. There is good evidence (Pauly, 1968) that in certain individuals this is an effective procedure, although psychotherapy for the social adjustment to the new sex is also an important adjunct. Also, covert modeling to retrain more appropriate sex-typed mannerisms and behaviors has proven helpful for all clients (May et al., 1981). In general, the surgical success is higher when the change is from male to female. In large part, this reflects the much more complex surgery required when the change is from female to male, as well as the accompanying higher probability of problematic side effects and outright failure.

In some cases, surgery is an unnecessary intervention, as psychotherapy and the passage of time can deal effectively with these identity concerns. This is particularly true when therapy is combined with aversive sexual-reorientation training and other techniques of psychosocial conditioning (Abel et al., 1986; Money, 1987). The clinician might also take note that the well-known attorney Melvin Belli (1979) argues persuasively that therapists can come under tort liability for taking a person through transsexual surgery, and it can possibly be considered under "criminal mayhem" statutes if there is any lack of clarity about the person's consent or ability to consent. Belli argues that adequate consent is problematic in most cases because the "compulsive" quality of the need to change sex is contradictory to the law's requirement that consent be "an affirmative act of an unconstrained and undeceived will" (p. 498). However, could not this concept of being compelled into treatment be applied to almost any disorder?

■   **Paraphilias**

"Paraphilia" is the DSM-III-R term for the sexual deviations, and both terms will be used interchangeably. The authors of the DSM-III-R assert, not totally convincingly, that the term "paraphilia" is superior to "sexual deviation" or "variation" because in paraphilia it is correctly indicated that the deviation (para) is in that to which the individual is attracted (philia).

Paraphilias consist of sexually arousing fantasy behavior associated with nonhuman sexual targets or nonconsenting humans and/or sexual activity with humans that involves either simulated or actual pain or humiliation or nonconsenting partners. As with most of the DSM-III-R categories, the paraphilias are classified as (1) mild–marked distress but no acting-out, (2) moderate–occasional acting-out, and (3) severe–repeated acting-out.

The essential disorder is in the lack of capacity for mature and participating affectionate sexual behavior with adult partners. Traditionally, these disorders have been far more common in males, but this discrepancy has decreased in recent years. Occasionally engaging in such fantasy or behavior does not usually qualify one as a paraphiliac. Exclusivity, persistency (even compulsivity), and pervasiveness are the hallmarks of the disorder (Coleman, 1987).

The specific paraphilia categories included in DSM-III-R are: (1) Fetishism, (2) Transvestic Fetishism, (3) Frotteurism, (4) Pedophilia, (5) Exhibitionism, (6) Voyeurism, (7) Sexual Masochism, and (8) Sexual Sadism. There is also a residual category, Paraphilia NOS (302.90), that could be used often when making a diagnosis, since the range of potential sexual deviations is restricted only by the limits of the imagination. The variations included in the DSM-III-R are those that have traditionally been labeled as deviant and/or that have involved a legal issue. Thus "variation" is an even more appropriate term than "deviance," since "variation" more clearly implies this wide range of potential behaviors and the fact that many of these patterns may in certain circumstances be acceptable and adaptive and that the "deviance" of the disorder is often only in the eye of the beholder.

DIAGNOSTIC CONSIDERATIONS

In general, the paraphilias, unless they are confounded by the presence of other psychopathology, do not present modal abnormal patterns on either the MMPI or the 16 PF, though convicted sex offenders tend to obtain 4-5/5-4 or 4-8/8-4 profiles (Erickson et al., 1987). Since they are obtained in a clinical setting, some pathology is suggested, or else society, through a legal or social agent (e.g., a marital therapist) is concerned about the pattern. Certain scales may then be markedly elevated.

Measuring sexual responses to suggested imagery or to actual pictures of various stimuli is helpful in specifying the focus of the sexually deviant fantasies that are a key to behavior. Direct measures of penile tumescence (via changes in a rubber tube encircling the penis, as in a pneumograph) are the most precise, though in some cases thermography has distinct advantages of ease of access and less embarrassment (Earls and Prouix, 1986).

Since the paraphilias range from disorders that involve passivity (sexual masochism) to those that involve coercive aggression and legal sanctions (pedophilia), treatments will differ as well. In general, behavioral (and often, more specifically, aversive) conditioning techniques have been useful, e.g., using electric shock or inhalation of valeric acid, much as they are throughout the habit disorders (Higginbotham et al., 1988). Since fears of heterosexuality are often involved, psychotherapy is a useful adjunct; and if fears become specifically focused and take on a phobic quality, systematic desensitization and the implosive therapies can be used. Cognitive behavioral approaches, such as covert sensitization, as well as the existential therapies, are useful adjuncts to deal with the issues of sociolegal guilt and lack of responsibility.

■   Fetishism (302.81)

The DSM-III-R defines fetishism as a condition wherein for a period of at least six months nonliving objects generate intense sexual fantasies, urges, and arousal, and the person has acted on these or is markedly distressed by them. Though the traditional use of this term included an attraction to isolated though still-attached body parts, this does not fit with the DSM-III-R definition. If the fetish is simply an article of clothing used in cross-dressing, the diagnosis could be transvestic fetishism. Also, if the arousal value is inherent in the object, such as a vibrator, the diagnosis of fetishism would be inappropriate.

Sexual stimulation from fetishes is typically obtained by tasting, fondling, kissing, or smelling the objects. Bras, panties, and shoes are the most common objects. The objects may be used while masturbating alone or, in some cases, as a necessary preliminary to intercourse. A degree of fetishism is associated with any sexual experience. Normal foreplay includes attention to sexually arousing objects or parts of the body, with consequent sexual arousal and progression toward coitus. In fetishism, however, the fetish takes primacy as a necessary means for developing arousal and allows avoidance of intimacy (Levin and Stava, 1987).

A confounding variable in fetishism, as well as in a number of other paraphilias, is the potential legal issue. Acts of breaking and entering are occasionally committed by the fetishist who is seeking a supply of women's used bras or panties. New articles of clothing are seldom arousing, in part because they are not identified with any individual person and also because they do not have the odors that are often arousing to the fetishist. In many cases, the illegal behavior itself increases the excitation and consequently increases the sexual arousal.

Although fetishism tends to crystallize as a behavior pattern in adolescence, it often has precursors in childhood. It is chronic, and most fetishists are men.

☐   DSM-III-R

To diagnose a person as a fetishist, it is required that the fetish, a nonliving object, be a preferred mode of arousal while the client is alone or is a necessary factor when used with a partner. It may occur in either actual behavior or fantasy. Transvestism or objects that are inherently sexually stimulating as the only evidence of fetishistic behavior would not warrant this diasgnosis.

☐   MMPI

Fetishists seldom show a markedly elevated MMPI profile. If the fetishism reflects some insecurity with the male sex role or some disguised homoerotic trends, an elevation on scale 5 is expected (Graham, 1977). In fetishists who indulge alone, a fear of the opposite sex may exist, which would elevate scales 4 and 7 to a degree. When the fetishism is embedded in heterosexual relationships, such elevations are less probable. When there is a legal problem involving fetishism, the reader should consult the section on malingering.

☐   16 PF

The fetishist who indulges while alone is more likely to be low on factor A. Those who accept their fetishistic behavior should have a reasonably high Q_1, whereas if they do not accept it, Q_1 may be at an average level or even lower. These clients are also likely to be relatively low on scale G and moderately high on M. If distressed by their pattern, high scores on O and Q_4 are likely. If they are being legally or socially coerced because of their behavior, such defensive patterns as malingering may be expected, with a higher score on L.

☐   TREATMENT OPTIONS

The aversive conditioning therapies are especially appropriate with fetishism, since specific behavior patterns are the central focus. Mild electric shock, inhalation of valeric acid and nausea-inducing drugs have been successfully used in aversive conditioning procedures in which the object of the fetish, or fantasy of it, is paired with the aversive stimulus. In general, mild electric shock is preferable to such nausea-producing drugs as apomorphine because the contiguity between the avoidance stimulus and the deviant response is more easily controlled when shock is used. The aversion therapy procedures of both fear conditioning and aversion relief have also been used. Once the person has decreased the arousal value contingent on the fetishistic object, training in more normal sexual patterns is possible (LoPiccolo and Stock, 1986; Meyer and Freeman, 1977).

■   Transvestic Fetishism (302.30)

Transvestism, or transvestic fetishism (the DSM-III-R term), is the dressing in clothes of the opposite sex for a period of at least six months, accompanied by intense sexual urges and fantasies that result in acting-out and/or distress. It also includes any other voluntary manifestations of those behaviors traditionally thought of as specific to the opposite sex. DSM-III-R limits this concept even more by asserting that it is only diagnosed in males, a perversely chauvinistic position for which there is no clear supportive rationale.

Beyond simple cross-dressing, the behavior must be sexually arousing. In most transvestites, the cross-dressing behavior was initiated in childhood and in some was significantly reinforced by parents, sometimes by "petticoat punishment," the humiliation of a boy by dressing him in a girl's clothes. It typically becomes paired with masturbation and eventuates in the classic transvestite pattern.

Transvestic fetishism (TF) is considered to be a rare disorder; an even smaller subgroup eventually goes from TF to transsexualism, where the diagnosis of transsexualism takes precedence. TF is obviously related to fetishism. Just as in fetishism, an inanimate object is the stimulating variable, and there is often little or no dependence on human relationships for sexual gratification. When the transvestite has a partner, there may be masochistic fantasies that progress into behavior (Malamuth, 1986). This then adds a secondary diagnosis of sexual masochism.

□   DIAGNOSTIC CONSIDERATIONS

Transvestites do not show particularly pathological MMPI or 16 PF profiles. The clinician can expect a high scale 5 whether this is a male or female transvestite (though DSM-III-R limits this disorder to males dressing as females). There is also a moderate rise in scale 3, which indicates some histrionic components, and possibly mild elevations in scales 4 and 6, reflecting concern about being discovered in a secret lifestyle and hostility toward standard social mores.

On the 16 PF, moderately elevated L and Q_1 scales and moderately low scores on G and Q_3 occur. A higher score on N is also probable; and if anxiety is a reason for this clinical situation, elevation on Q_4 in particular, and possibly on O, could be expected.

Anxiety and depression may occur if dressing is inhibited, producing significant elevations on A and/or D on the MCMI. As in other psychosexual disorders, 1 and/or 2 may occur as the most prevalent personality syndrome. C is also likely to be high. Additionally, the indifference to social expectations may also be reflected by elevation on 5.

☐   TREATMENT OPTIONS

Since TF is easily considered a subcategory of fetishism, the procedures noted in that section are equally applicable here. In addition to using aversive procedures, the therapist could use thought-stopping to control the initial impulse to cross-dress. Since TF may have certain compulsive features, the reader is referred to the section on the obsessive-compulsive disorder. Both the aversion therapy and the thought-stopping can be amplified by the use of a portable, self-administered shock unit. The person can wear this unit discreetly under clothing, and when the impulse arises, a shock can be administered in conjunction with the aversion or thought-stopping procedure.

   Covert sensitization (Cautela and Wall, 1980) is particularly helpful in the habit disorders and can easily be dovetailed with the aversive conditioning procedures in the therapist's office. In the covert sensitization procedure, some highly aversive contingency is imagined immediately on the occurrence of the fantasy of the undesired behavior. In this case, it is the transvestite pattern. As a result, the undesired impulse toward TF is weakened.

■   Pedophilia (302.20)

Pedophilia literally—and ironically—means "love of children," and a pedophiliac is one who consistently seeks out sexual experiences with children.

   Pedophilia is extremely rare in females and, although it is not a particularly common behavior in *any* demographic group, it has traditionally been viewed as a disorder of middle-aged males—"dirty old men." Recent research (Abel et al., 1986; Levin and Stava, 1987) has shown, however, that while the offender is almost always male, the molestation typically started by age fifteen; most early victims are known to the pedophile; boys are more likely to be victims than girls; girls are more likely to be victims of "hands-off" crimes like exhibitionism; most pedophiles over time commit a wide range of crimes, including exhibitionism, voyeurism, and rape; and pedophiles who molest boys do it a great deal (an average of over two hundred incidents), whereas female-oriented pedophiles average approximately twenty-five incidents and rapists of adults five to ten incidents. Not surprisingly, few sex offenders will admit to such numbers unless given complete anonymity.

   There are significant differences between those pedophiliac men who are exclusively inclined toward sexual experiences with male children and those who primarily seek out females. Heterosexual pedophiles are more likely to be married and prefer a younger target—females aged eight to ten—as opposed to the homosexual pedophile's preference for boys aged twelve to fourteen. Homosexual pedophiles show a poor prognosis for change, are less likely to know their victim, and are more interested in proceeding to orgasm rather than focusing on the touching and looking behavior often preferred by heterosexual pedophiles. Many heterosexual male pedophiles have problems with potency and are likely to prefer ejaculation achieved through voyeuristic-exhibitionistic masturbation. When they do attempt intercourse with a child, they are more likely to generate trauma and pain and in that way raise their chances of being reported and eventually apprehended (Finkelhor, 1985).

Pedophiles, whether homosexual or heterosexual, often feel inadequate about their sexuality, and the contact and/or comparison with the sexually immature target may alleviate this anxiety and allow a nonthreatening release for sexual tension.

Alcohol abuse is a common catalyst for this behavior, as are marital problems among married pedophiles. Another catalyst (which does not detract in any way from the pedophile's responsibility for the act) is victim behavior. Finkelhor (1985) points to interesting data showing that an unusually high percentage of sexually victimized children had lived without their mothers for a significant length of time prior to the age of sixteen. It is possible that they may have missed a subtle training in behaviors conducive to fending off this type of sexual coercion. Evidence shows that when the pedophiliac is mentally retarded or schizophrenic, the victim sometimes initiated the contact (Virkunen, 1975).

A subcategory of pedophilia is incest. While incest occurs in any potential family structure relationship, father-daughter incest is by far the most common target of societal concern. Three psychological subpatterns occur in this specific form of incest (Finkelhor, 1985; Smith and Meyer, 1987). The first pattern is the inadequate and psychosexually immature father who is functionally a pedophile and who often has sexual contact with his daughters, sons, and other children. Such individuals show a combination of pedophiliac and psychopathic diagnostic indications. The second is a true "primary psychopath." This person relates to virtually all people as objects, is promiscuous in all directions, and shows little remorse over any behavior patterns.

Family-generated incest is the third pattern, and it is usually marked by a passive and inadequate father and an emotionally disturbed mother. Persons engaging in this type of incest show characteristics of the pedophile plus aspects of the passive-aggressive and dependent personality disorders.

☐   DSM-III-R

To warrant a diagnosis of pedophilia, the person must over a six-month period experience strong urges and fantasies for sexual contact with a prepubescent child (thirteen or younger), resulting in marked distress or acting-out. The DSM-III-R arbitrarily defines the required difference between the ages of the persons as five years, with the perpetrator being at least sixteen years old. The diagnosis should be further specified as to whether it is (1) same sex, opposite sex, or same *and* opposite sex, (2) limited to incest, and (3) exclusive or nonexclusive.

☐ MMPI

As might be expected from society's repugnance for this type of behavior, pedophiliacs are far more defensive than persons with most other paraphilias. As a result, elevated K and L scales are common, and elevations on 4 and 8 are most common in the clinical scales (Hall et al., 1986). Denial, along with an avoidance of intrapsychic concern, is reflected in an elevated 3 scale.

Erickson et al. (1987) found that offenders against children were more likely to obtain 4-2/2-4 profiles, whereas offenders against adult women tended to obtain 4-9/9-4 profiles. While the most common MMPI profile in child molesters is a 2-4/4-2, the particularly inadequate pedophile who has significant difficulties in dealing interpersonally with the opposite sex often presents a 1-8/8-1 profile. Likewise, incestuous pedophiles score higher on 0 than nonincestuous pedophiles, who in turn are higher than normals (Levin and Stava, 1987). Those who show a consistent immaturity throughout many of their behavior patterns and who have problems in controlling impulse behavior may show a 3-8/8-3 code. Where the pedophiliac behavior is a classic counterphobic mechanism to deny feelings of inadequacy about masculinity, the 4-8/8-4, with a surprisingly low scale 5 score (considering the person's general behavior patterns), is obtained. Where the person is more aware of the disturbance in sexual identity, an elevation on scale 5 is seen.

☐ 16 PF

On the 16 PF, the emotional disturbance, impulsivity, and deviant mores are reflected in low scores on A, C, G, and Q_3. Anxiety and insecurity, possibly induced by the potential for being apprehended, elevate scores on O and Q_4. The deviant fantasy and the isolation from society because of the repulsiveness of the acts result in high scores on L and M. Homosexual pedophiles are moderately high on E and H and moderately low on I; the reverse is true for heterosexual pedophiles. Scores on scale B vary markedly, though they are usually moderately low.

☐ OTHER TESTS

In human-figure drawings, Johnson and Johnson (1986) found pedophiles, when compared to normals, to show poorer overall quality in the drawings, poorer gender differentiation, the female figure often larger than the male figure, and a number of male figures with blank or missing eyes.

Except for possible elevation on B, the clinical-symptom syndromes do not usually show much disturbance on the MCMI. The interpersonal indifference and behavioral apathy indicated by elevated 1 are less likely here than elevated scores on 2, 5, and 6. Although high scores on 2 indicate a detached style, pedophiles may seek less threatening children as a source of sexual satisfaction to deal with their interpersonal inadequacy. A and D are likely to be high if the behavior is ego dystonic; and 6 may be high if the person has become embroiled in legal troubles.

☐   TREATMENT OPTIONS

Because of the disgust with which most people respond to this disorder, it is not surprising that the typical treatment approaches are somewhat coercive. Pedophiles rarely bring themselves into treatment and are typically coerced by sociolegal pressure (Abel et al., 1986). Castration is still a favored response in some cultures, and in our society, chemocastration is still considered to be a reasonable option. Antiandrogens such as cyproterone acetate (in Europe) or medroxyprogesterone acetate (in the United States) suppress the sexual libidos of male pedophiles; these drugs have also been used with rapists and exhibitionists (Abel et al., 1986). They function by reducing serum testosterone levels to a level at which sexual arousal is diminished or absent, and they have moderate success when combined with psychotherapy. The aversion therapies have also been used with moderate success.

Covert sensitization has been successfully used to treat pedophilia. Aversive mental images are immediately associated with images and impulses for initiating and continuing pedophiliac behaviors. Forgione (1976) presented an interesting variation on this approach. He filmed pedophiliacs while they reenacted their pedophiliac behaviors in response to a childlike manikin; simply watching the playback proved aversive and reduced the pedophiliac behavior. The clinician could vary this procedure by making slides from the tape and pairing electric shock with them to further the aversive response.

Since inadequacy in social interactions is a major factor in most pedophiles, assertiveness training, particularly directed toward adults of the opposite sex, is helpful here. It can be complemented by general social retraining toward an ability to attain mature heterosexual partners.

■ Exhibitionism (302.40)

The term "exhibitionism" was first introduced into psychopathology by Lasegue in 1877, though the act itself was described as early as 4 B.C. (Cox, 1980). It is the act of exposing the genitals to a stranger in order to obtain sexual arousal. Certain rare individuals do expose themselves without ever having been aroused, but they usually turn out to be psychotic, senile, or at least moderately mentally retarded.

The DSMs traditionally argued that the condition was found only in males, but this proviso is dropped in DSM-III-R. There are few reports to police of females who exhibit themselves, but to assert that the behavior *never* occurs in females is unsubstantiated (Grob, 1985). Along with voyeurism, exhibitionism has had the highest recidivism rate of all the sexual disorders (Cox, 1980).

☐   DSM-III-R

The DSM-III-R requires, for at least six months, recurrent sexual urges and sexually arousing fantasies involving the exposure of one's genitals to an unsuspecting stranger. The person has either acted on these urges or is markedly distressed by them.

☐   DIAGNOSTIC CONSIDERATIONS

From the legal perspective, exhibitionism is probably the most commonly reported paraphilia, but the cost to victims and society is lower than that of some of the other disorders, such as pedophilia. It is estimated to account for about one third of all sexual offenses reported to authorities, and only a small percentage of exposure acts are ever reported to the police (Cox, 1980; Hendrix and Meyer, 1976). Indications are that there is a bimodal distribution of the mean age of onset of first exposure, with peaks in the age ranges eleven to fifteen and twenty-one to twenty-five. The mean age of first arrest is approximately twenty-five. Exhibitionists seldom gravitate toward more serious sexual offenses (Cox, 1980).

The high overall recidivism rate is partially explained by a markedly increasing recidivism rate for those who are convicted more than once. Even though there is a conviction rate of only 10 percent for first offenders, the rate is almost 60 percent for those with more than one previous sexual offense and 70 percent for those with previous sexual and nonsexual offenses. If intervention can keep the exhibitionist from exposing himself for at least eighteen months after treatment, there is a low likelihood of future exposures (Cox, 1980).

There is a high incidence of disrupted father-son relationships in the background of exhibitionists—indeed, this is true to a degree for most of the paraphilias (Levin and Stava, 1987). Exhibitionists show poor interpersonal relationships during adolescence, and masturbation is always of unusual importance to them as a sexual outlet, even when other partners are available.

Of the personality types that eventuate in exhibitionism (Smith and Meyer, 1987), the "characterological type," a small group, is the only one that shows any significant danger to the victim. They have profiles similar to rapists, with the same elements of anger and hostility. The shock response of the victim is a major reinforcement, and there is little guilt or remorse.

A second subtype is the "unaware group," where the act is an outgrowth of extreme alcohol intoxication, organic brain disorder, or severe mental retardation. A third type is the "inadequate group." These individuals are similar to those with the avoidant personality disorder, though they have a few more obsessional features and more anger. The reader is referred to the section on the avoidant personality disorder, with the notation that scales 4 and 6 on the MMPI, as well as the correlated scales on the 16 PF, should be a bit more elevated here.

The fourth group, the "impulsive-compulsive type," is obsessional, tense, anxious, and both sexually compelled and confused (Coleman, 1987). Their behavior is an impulsive response to intrapsychic conflict and distress. It is this last group, the largest group of exhibitionists, that we will focus on in the following discussion of diagnostic parameters.

☐   MMPI

A summary of MMPI data collected on exhibitionists shows them to be moderately nonconforming individuals who have a history of mild violations of social norms, but with no extensive allied psychopathology (Cox, 1980). The standard elevations throughout most studies are on scales 4, 5, and 8 though these are often below 70 T. The elevations on scales 4 and 8 reflect the mild antisocial nature of the behavior, the lack of impulse control, and a degree of hostility toward the general environment. The elevation on 5 reflects sexual confusion, but there are "macho" exhibitionists who are low on 5. Exhibitionists are usually very low on scale 0 and moderately low onscales 1 and 9. To the degree scale 8 is elevated in relation to other scales, these persons are likely to be self-defeating and their exposure patterns more likely to be discovered. For example, the author is aware of numerous exhibitionists who have admitted exhibiting themselves over five hundred times without ever being apprehended. Similar cases have shown a low 8 scale, with a high 4 scale and moderately high 5 and K scales. Exhibitionists are generally lower than rapists on 4, 8, 6, 3, 2, and F, in order of magnitude (Levin and Stava, 1987).

☐   16 PF

Exhibitionists score moderately high on O and Q_4, though their scales may revert to average if they are not under some kind of legal scrutiny. Similar to obsessives, they are only moderately low on C and moderately high on L and M. To the degree they have been self-defeating in their exposure patterns, they are likely to show a low score on N and Q_3 and a high score on H. Other scales are usually not remarkable.

□   TREATMENT OPTIONS

Exhibitionism, like pedophilia, shows a high rate of recidivism. For that reason, some therapists eventually resort to chemocastration through the use of such antiandrogen drugs as medroxyprogesterone acetate. However, the major treatment for exhibitionism is some form of aversion therapy (Cox, 1980). Some retraining in social skills and orgasmic reconditioning also are usually necessary (Davey and Cullen, 1988). Covert sensitization can be used, amplified by adding noxious odors and shocks at the time the exhibitionist is presenting the aversive images to himself.

Hendrix and Meyer (1976) demonstrated that exhibitionism can be controlled through a multifaceted treatment approach that includes no aversive techniques. They used progressive relaxation to lower a client's tension-anger pattern and cassette tapes and autogenic training to further the relaxation response. Psychotherapy uncovered the suppressed anger and fear of interacting with females, and assertiveness training was used to control these situations. This was combined with increased self-verbalizations designed to heighten self-esteem and confidence. At that point, standard sexual counseling helped in the attainment of adequate heterosexual relationships. Also included was systematic desensitization, which was used to dissipate a phobic fear of being rebuffed by females. In addition, Dr. Hendrix accompanied the exhibitionist to in vivo situations, such as the campus snack shop (being introduced as his friend, if necessary). Dr. Hendrix monitored the situation and then later counseled the client on his socialization patterns.

Wickramasekera (1976) proposed a unique treatment. He required the patient to undress and dress several times before a mixed-sex audience of therapists who had the subject explore associated affect, bodily sensations, and fantasy during exposure. The patient was asked such questions as "What do you think we see (feel/think) as we look at you right now?" in an objective, noncritical yet unempathic manner. During the second part of the session, the patient was again required to undress and dress several times (at his therapist's direction) and was asked questions to facilitate comparison of present feelings with antecedents, moods prior to and during exposure, and consequent moods and events. Videotaping (to be reviewed later by patient and therapist) and having the patient observe himself in a mirror are also part of this procedure. The treatment induces a high degree of anxiety in patients for whom it is appropriate (those who are nonpsychotic, nonpsychopathic, and somewhat anxious), which appears critical to the success of the treatment.

In persons who do not experience the required level of anxiety, it could be increased by bringing into the audience either victims or people close to the exhibitionist (wife, mother, daughter) or even by chemically increasing anxiety, e.g., by injections of sodium lactate prior to the sessions (Liebowitz et al., 1985).

Wickramasekera offers several explanations for the treatment's effectiveness: (1) it involves extinction of the exhibitionist's private fantasies, since the female or mixed-sex audience does not react with shock or fear, (2) punishment by the connection of aversive visceral consequences (profuse sweating, headache, rapid heartbeat) to other internal cues or self-disclosure, and (3) cognitive dissonance, which predicts maximum attitude and behavior change with voluntary participation, minimal reward, and maximal effort (all of which are involved in the treatment).

No matter what technique is used or how effective it appears to be, periodic "booster" sessions are worthwhile because of the high level of recidivism.

■ Voyeurism (302.82)

Voyeurs continually search for situations in which they may view individuals or groups of individuals in the nude or in some form of sexual activity in order to obtain sexual arousal. Like pedophiles and exhibitionists, voyeurs show a high recidivism rate (Levin and Stava, 1987). Virtually all cases of voyeurism reported to the authorities are males, though there is no evidence that this behavior never occurs in females. Our society is organized to respond differently to exhibitionistic and voyeuristic behavior by females.

Approximately one third of voyeurs are married. Even though the age of the voyeur at the time of the first voyeuristic act is the middle to late twenties, there has usually been a significant history of sexual and other offenses throughout adolescence. As with exhibitionists, there is a large history of broken homes and marital distress. Voyeurs seldom maintained close relationships with sisters or other girls when they were young.

Most voyeurs are not markedly disturbed, and the simple act of obtaining arousal from looking is of course a normal part of many sexual experiences. Triolism, or the sharing of a sexual partner while one observes, is a major reinforcement in group sex experiences and is not classified as voyeurism.

Only a small proportion of voyeurs pose a danger to their victims. They are psychopathic in personality and show the following specific behavior patterns: They are most likely to enter a building in order to carry out their voyeuristic behaviors, and in some way, they draw attention to themselves while they are in the act (Smith, 1976).

☐   DSM-III-R

To make the DSM-III-R diagnosis of voyeurism, the clinician must establish that the behavior occurs over a six-month period; the person experiences strong urges and fantasies to observe an unsuspecting person disrobe, be in the nude, or engage in a sexual act; and acts-out or is distressed by these urges. The DSMs traditionally limited the diagnosis to males, but this has been dropped in DSM-III-R.

☐   DIAGNOSTIC CONSIDERATIONS

Like the exhibitionist, the voyeur does not show extensive psychopathology on psychological tests and has similar personality test patterns. Lachar (1974) suggests that the prototypical pattern for a voyeur shows elevated scores on 3, 4, and 5, with the elevation on 3 or 4 being the highest, and with a T score seldom being above 70. On the average, the score on scale 9 tends to be lower for the voyeur than for the exhibitionist. That very small subgroup of voyeurs who pose a danger to others has diagnostic patterns parallel to those of primary psychopaths, although they show more elevation on scale 5.

On the 16 PF, voyeurs are relatively close to the pattern of exhibitionists, but voyeurs average a bit higher on scales L and Q_3. This reflects their more circumspect pattern of pathology, which is usually accompanied by a feeling that they would like to retain control of events in their world. Those with the detached personality characteristics indicated by elevations on 1 and/or 2 on the MCMI may be more predisposed to engage in this behavior.

☐   TREATMENT OPTIONS

All of the techniques noted for the treatment of exhibitionists are equally appropriate to the treatment of the voyeur. In particular, the aversion therapies have often been used. However, the treatment of one voyeur by a colleague of the author brought home the point that it is critical to be accurate regarding which stimuli are to be eliminated by the shock. This client had been administered shock upon presentation of the hypothesized arousal stimuli: a clear view of the nude bodies of a couple through a window. This treatment was ineffective until the shock was eventually paired with slides of open windows as they would appear from a distance of about thirty feet. This unique scene had become the initial discriminative stimulus for the arousal pattern, and the voyeurism decreased markedly when these slides were paired with shock in an aversive therapy procedure.

■   ## Frotteurism (302.89)

Frotteurism is generally defined as the act of rubbing up against the body of a stranger, usually the stranger's buttocks, in order to achieve sexual arousal or even organism, if feasible. The act is usually carried out in a crowded public place, like a subway, swimming pool, or dance floor. In the traditional literature, frotteurism was often not distinguished from fetishism or partialism, though there are fundamental differences. The fetishist becomes aroused by and attached to a particular nonliving object that symbolizes the desired love object; and unlike frotteurs who make attempts at heterosexual life and fail, the fetishist rarely attempts. Partialism is differentiated from frotteurism in that the partialist is attracted to and can only achieve arousal from a specific part of the body, whereas the arousal for frotteurs is generated in a more generalized manner and is not tied to a specific body part.

Not unlike many voyeurs and exhibitionists, the frotteur usually has evolved a series of cover-up plans to avoid the embarrassment of being caught and publicly humiliated. The violation of the taboo of sexual behavior in a public place is arousing, but the humiliation one could experience if caught is aversive enough to generate these cover-up behaviors.

□   ## DSM-III-R

In order to apply this diagnosis, the DSM-III-R requires that over a period of at least six months the person has experienced recurrent intense urges and fantasies of rubbing against or touching a nonconsenting person (but the touching, not the coercive nature of the act, provides the primary arousal) and that the person is significantly distressed by these urges or has acted upon them.

□   ## DIAGNOSTIC CONSIDERATIONS

Freund et al., (1983) note that the great majority of frotteurs also show other deviant behaviors, e.g., voyeurism and exhibitionism, rather than a pattern marked by frotteurism alone. Hence, many of the diagnostic responses and therapeutic considerations noted for voyeurism and exhibitionism also apply here. Like exhibitionists, elevations on MMPI scales 4, 5, and 8 can be expected, though frotteurs could be expected to be higher on scales 9 and 0.

On the 16 PF, O and Q_4 are likely to be elevated to the degree the frotteur labels his (virtually all frotteurs studied have been male) behavior as ego-alien. Scales A, G, H, and Q_3 are likely to be moderately depressed—especially G and Q_3, because they indicate a disregard for social norms and a lack of control over impulsive behavior. On the MCMI, scales 1 and 8 should be moderately elevated, 2 moderately to significantly elevated, and scales 4 and 7 likely lower, the latter reflecting the usual introverted personality style and the impulsive behavior pattern, respectively. With frotteurs who have sought therapy, scales A and D on the MCMI are often elevated.

On the Rorschach, one would expect a number of texture responses denoting a passively expressed need for affection, a higher incidence of shading and achromatic responses, a higher E-B ratio reflecting any introverted personality characteristics, and a high number of flexion-movement responses (toward the center) (Exner, 1986).

TREATMENT OPTIONS

The techniques applicable to voyeurs, exhibitionists, and fetishists are all applicable here, depending upon which components are paramount in the individual case. Shame aversion therapy (Wicksramasekera, 1988, 1976) would be especially useful here. For example, the frotteur would be required to perform his frotteurism on a woman in front of an audience of several women who were particularly selected for similarity in appearance to the type of woman the frotteur normally seeks out. During the act, the frotteur would be required to conduct a dialogue with himself discussing what he is thinking, describing physical sensations, predicting how the observers and the victim are perceiving him, and what their opinions of him may be. The observers and victim could be instructed to show no emotion and to stare at the frotteur for the duration or to spontaneously generate aversive emotions, such as laughter. As with exhibitionists, periodic "booster" sessions will likely be required to maintain any therapeutic effect, and social-skills training will be necessary in most cases.

Sexual Masochism (302.83)

Sexual masochism has traditionally been considered as a need to engage in fantasy or actual behavior in which the experience of having pain inflicted on oneself is necessary to gain sexual arousal. The DSM-III-R emphasizes that this be *actual* behavior rather than simply fantasy.

The term "masochism" was coined in 1896 by Kraft-Ebbing and was taken from the works of Leopold von Sacher-Masoch (1836–1895), whose novels focused on the theme of men being dominated by women. Sacher-Masoch actually primarily obtained excitement from the fantasy that his wife might be unfaithful to him and flaunt the fact to him.

Sexual masochism predominately occurs in males and has its beginnings in childhood experience where the infliction of pain in some way becomes tied to sexual arousal (Malamuth, 1986). Crystallized behavior patterns are usually evident by late adolescence. In some cases, there is an increased need for pain over a period of time. In extreme cases, a bizarre form of sexual masochism referred to as "terminal sex" occurs. A male (typically) hangs himself by the neck with a noose while masturbating, in order to increase sexual pleasure. Releasing the noose just before the loss of consciousness theoretically increases the pleasure. This practice has increased in recent years and occurs most commonly among fourteen- to twenty-five-year-olds. Miscalculation is thought to cause as many as two hundred deaths in the United States every year.

☐   DSM-III-R

A diagnosis of sexual masochism is applied if over a six-month period the person experiences an act (not simulated) of being humiliated, beaten, bound, or otherwise made to suffer and is distressed or acts-out.

☐   DIAGNOSTIC CONSIDERATIONS

Masochists seldom come to the attention of legal authorities, or even therapists, unless they have been a victim of extreme sadism that requires medical treatment, and this is uncommon. In many respects, they have the personality characteristics of the dependent personality disorder, except with a greater emphasis on a disordered sexual identification and a higher level of intrapsychic distress. Hence, higher elevations on scales 5 and 7 occur. Scores on scales 6 and 9 are substantially lower than would occur in sadism, which reflects the masochist's passivity and apathy, as well as the subtle defensive quality that may be hidden from others.

Again, the 16 PF profiles should be similar to those of a person with the dependent personality disorder, with some specific exceptions. I would hypothesize that scale N should be significantly higher, as should scores on Q_1 and, to a lesser degree, Q_2. L is not usually as low as one might expect, since the submissiveness and adaptation to another is balanced by a subtle paranoid element, usually resulting in scores that are not extreme on this variable. A lower G score also reflects the unconventionality of this behavior, and in those individuals with guilt and a punitive conscience, a high O score is obtained. Scale B is relatively low. An elevated 3 on the MCMI, represented by dependent submissiveness, is likely. The self-condemnatory and dependency aspects of the borderline (scale C) may predispose toward masochistic behavior. Again, some components of the avoidant personality may be present, indicated by elevation on 2. The masochist may well give Rorschach responses that clearly indicate a submissive control behavior pattern, such as being "yoked" or "chained." Small or passive animal responses may also be noted.

☐   TREATMENT OPTIONS

Sexual masochism, to the degree that it is motivated by a need for sexual arousal, can be treated with the aversion therapies (see the section on exhibitionism). In most cases, this deviant arousal pattern involves interpersonal inadequacy, and both compulsion and pathological dependency pervades the relationship (Coleman, 1987). In that regard, the reader is referred to the next chapter on treatment options for the obsessive-compulsive and dependent personality disorders.

The therapist can help the masochist focus on the quality of the relationship by a neoanalytic technique used by Kirman (1980) in which he has the client write letters to the significant other. This helps to focus the feelings and bring to consciousness the many aspects of the relationship that often remain out of awareness. One might also use the "empty chair" technique made famous by Fritz Perls. Rather than writing out his feelings, the client addresses the fantasized other in the empty chair in an oral dialogue; this is aided by its being done in a group. In either case, these feelings are used as a stimulus for new behavior patterns.

Covert extension can also be employed. Here, the client is asked to imagine the masochistic behavior pattern and then immediately imagine that the reinforcement that is expected to follow does not occur. Assertiveness training or psychotherapy with an Adlerian focus (since Adlerian therapy so directly focuses on inferiority issues) could complement and aid the development of a repertoire of more-positive behaviors.

■ Sexual Sadism (302.84)

Sexual sadism is a condition wherein a person obtains sexual excitement from inflicting pain, injury, or humiliation on another. It differs from the sadistic personality disorder, described in Chapter 9, which is an optional category in the DSM-III-R. The term "sadism" is taken from the writings of the Marquis de Sade, whose works focused on sexual pleasure gained from inflicting pain and even death on others.

Most sadists show evidence of this pattern by early adolescence. The condition is chronic and is seen far more frequently in males than females. Sadism overlaps the concept of rape (Malamuth, 1986), though not all rapists are sadists, and vice versa. However, the reader is referred to the section on rape because there are parallel diagnostic considerations.

☐   DSM-III-R

A DSM-III-R diagnosis of sexual sadism is appropriate if over a period of six months occur recurrent intense sexual fantasies and urges toward acts (real, not simulated) in which another person is hurt (physically or psychologically) or humiliated and the person is distressed by or acts on these urges.

☐   MMPI

Unlike the sexual masochist, the sadist shows significantly disturbed patterns on the MMPI, with one or more scores above 70 T. This usually indicates a lack of impulse control, specifically on scales 4 and 8 (Hall et al., 1986); scale 9 is also usually elevated. The high score on 8 shows the unusual attitudes and thought patterns as well as the hostility and aggression inherent in this disorder.

Most male sadists present a macho image, with stereotypical male behaviors. Physical prowess and aggressive thrill-seeking behaviors are often evident. This can result in a low score on scale 5, except that the confused sexual identification may counterbalance this, particularly if the person is oriented toward homosexual sadism. Females involved in sadistic behaviors tend to score high on scale 5.

☐   16 PF

Sadists are likely to show high scores on scales E and H, emphasizing the dominant and aggressive components. In addition, their distance from standard moral systems results in a low score on G and high scores on M and Q_1. Scores for L and Q_3 are also likely to be moderately high. A is usually low, reflecting the lack of any true interest in interpersonal relationships.

☐   OTHER TEST-RESPONSE PATTERNS

A score of 85 or higher on the MCMI scale 6 is common here, with elevation on 5 likely. Some paranoid qualities may be present, causing relative elevation on P. The impulsivity present in these persons may cause some elevation on N, while traits represented by elevated A, D, and H are not present. In addition to Rorschach content responses that directly portray a sadistic element, such as hammers, explosions, and needles, figures that symbolize controlling authority, such as eagles, are occasionally noted. Mutilation content is also thought to be indicative of sadistic fantasy and possible sadistic behavior (Schafer, 1954).

☐   TREATMENT OPTIONS

Since sexual sadism more often focuses on deviant sexual arousal than does sexual masochism, the aversive therapy techniques are appropriate (see the section on exhibitionism). This approach could be aided by some of the cognitive approaches, such as covert sensitization. The person should also somehow be made aware of the psychological effect on the "victim," and "couple" therapy with the victim could be instituted. Other techniques for teaching more appropriate interpersonal behaviors, such as those noted in the section on exhibitionism, would also be helpful because sadism is often a reaction to inadequacy and/or modeling from early training where physical abuse was common.

■   # Zoophilia

Though this disorder was included in DSM-III, it has since been dropped as a formal diagnostic category, probably because of the rarity of its occurrence. The essential variable in zoophilia is the use of animals as the means of producing sexual arousal. This label is most appropriate when such behavior or fantasy is consistently preferred even though there are other outlets reasonably available. Zoophilia, which occurs primarily in males, is very rare. It may occasionally be a sign of schizophrenia.

The traditional term, "bestiality," referred primarily to having sexual intercourse with animals, whereas "zoophilia" refers to *any* type of sexual contact with animals. The preferred animal is usually one with which the person had contact during childhood, such as a pet or farm animal. Zoophilia is a moderately common theme in pornography and usually involves a female having a sexual experience with a pony or a dog. This theme is common because the usual consumer of pornography is male, and this appears to be an exciting theme for males. In actuality, the data of Kinsey et al. (1948, 1953) suggest that such patterns are extremely rare in females and only a bit more common in males, at least where the pattern has clinical significance.

DIAGNOSTIC CONSIDERATIONS

In the typical person who shows clinical zoophilia, the major features are significant depression, problems in interpersonal skills, and anxiety. Hence, I would expect elevations on scales 2, 7, and 0, respectively. Also, the disordered sexual life could cause at least a mild elevation on scale 5.

In the 16 PF, the shame, anxiety, lack of interpersonal skills, and social isolation mean to this author that there should be high O and Q_4 scores and relatively low A, C, and F scores. Scale B is low in these individuals, and similarly, N is expected to be low and Q_2 moderately low. One may, again, expect 1 and/or 2 as a prominent feature of the MCMI profile, though the behavioral apathy of the asocial type may make a prominent score on 1 less likely here. Any depression and anxiety will be indicated by elevations of at least 75 on scales A and D.

TREATMENT OPTIONS

There are few reports in the literature concerning the treatment of zoophilia. Aversive conditioning procedures would be helpful regarding any fetishistic components. Since immaturity and inability to make adequate heterosexual contacts are often a factor, social retraining and the techniques of rational-emotive therapy (Ellis and Dryden, 1987) might also be applied.

Male Psychosexual Dysfunction

There are three major subcategories of male psychosexual dysfunction. First, Hypoactive Sexual Desire (302.71) refers to a condition, psychologically generated, where a person consistently experiences few fantasies about or little interest in proceeding into a sexual act. This occurs rarely as a separate disorder, and organic dysfunction should always be ruled out. It is often a reflection of disorder in a marital relationship rather than evidence of significant individual pathology. A more extreme variation is the Sexual Aversion Disorder (302.79). It refers to extreme aversion to and avoidance of virtually all genital sexual contact with a partner.

The third category is Premature Ejaculation (302.75). This disorder is an inability to exert voluntary control over ejaculation accompanied by persistent or recurrent ejaculation with minimal stimulation and before the person wishes it; it occurs in the absence of other significant pathology and is not an organic condition. It is difficult to define exactly what an absence of voluntary control means, and the DSM-III-R does not directly deal with this. Masters and Johnson define premature ejaculation as a clinical problem if the orgasm occurs involuntarily more than half the time before the partner's orgasm. Males may also now be diagnosed as suffering from Dyspareunia (302.76).

Premature ejaculation can be further subdivided into primary premature ejaculation (related to inexperience in the sexual area): a chronic, high state of arousal, possibly accompanied by fear of dealing with intimacy. As might be expected, it is most often a disorder of the young, and it does not correlate with any significant pathology. In secondary premature ejaculation, it's common that a disturbance in the relationship with a partner results in conflict expressed through premature ejaculation. The trouble is in the relationship, though individual personality factors of the partners may contribute (Masters et al., 1988).

Other major DSM-III-R categories in this area are Male Erectile Disorder (302.72) and Inhibited Male Orgasm (302.74), which refer to a disruption (at different points) of attempts to attain orgasm. The major organic factors to be ruled out are spinal-cord disorders, nondominant-hemisphere parietal-lobe dysfunction, significant circulatory problems (often found in severe diabetics, though not that uncommon in otherwise normals), and consistent alcohol or drug use (Luria et al., 1986).

The research literature refers to male erectile disorder as "erectile dysfunction," and most people simply term it "impotence." The latter term is undesirable for several reasons, primarily because it connotes general personality inadequacy and weakness of character. It is interesting to note that weakness in the male and coldness in the female, as connoted by the terms "impotence" and "frigidity," respectively, are opposites of the characteristics most commonly prescribed for sexual roles in our society: power and competence for males and sensitivity and warmth for females. Most erectile dysfunction is partial; that is, a man can attain erection but either cannot reach orgasm or does not maintain the erection for very long. Total erectile dysfunction over a significant period of time is relatively rare and suggests a biological cause.

□   DIAGNOSTIC CONSIDERATIONS

The following cues are suggestive of erectile dysfunction in which organic factors play a major part:

Gradual onset

Sequentially deteriorating erections

Normal libido

Can initiate but not maintain erection

Loss of nocturnal and masturbatory erection

while the following are generally indicative of psychogenic erectile dysfunction:

Episodic

Sudden onset

Acute; brought on by life stresses

Normal morning and nocturnal erections

Loss of libido

Most researchers agree that persons with psychosexual dysfunction do not show markedly deviant profiles on standard psychological tests. There are some trends and differences, depending on whether the dysfunction is psychologically or biologically generated. Beutler et al. (1975) report a 90 percent success rate in using the MMPI to differentiate psychogenic versus biogenic erectile dysfunction, by two rules: (1) In psychogenic erectile dysfunction, scale 5 is typically above 60 T, whereas it is typically below 60 T if it is biogenic. (2) There is no consistency in the scores that are above 70, but those scales that are, are usually the ones that reflect the sexual role problems (i.e., scale 5, a histrionic denial of problems, as in scale 3, or in depression on scale 2). Munjack et al. (1981) also noted relatively high scores on 8.

Another effective factor in clearly differentiating psychologically generated dysfunction from biogenic cases is the occurrence of nocturnal penile tumescence (NPT), or erections that occur during sleep. Just as most females show clitoral arousal while sleeping, most (though not all) sexually normal males experience a number of NPTs every night during sleep. Those individuals with biogenic erectile dysfunction tend to have few if any NPTs while sleeping, whereas those whose dysfunction is psychogenic show a number of NPTs. The one problem with this diagnostic cue is having someone stay awake all night to watch. The solution is to put a postage-stamp-size piece of paper around the penis during sleep–if it is regularly broken, NPTs are occurring. Measurements need to be taken for more than one night, ideally with a device that measures strength and persistence of erection in addition to simple occurrence (Lo Piccolo and Stock, 1986).

On the 16 PF, persons with erectile dysfunction are likely to show higher than average scores on Q_4 and O, reflecting their anxiety and insecurity. Their scores on E and Q_3 will vary depending on whether they have coped with the dysfunction by resorting to even more stereotyped masculine behaviors (resulting in high E and Q_3 scores) or they have become more submissive in relationships and see themselves as unable to control their world (low scores). If they experience guilt over failing in their relationship, scores on O are likely to be raised. A high level of performance anxiety is likely to correlate with at least an average or moderately elevated M score. They show more reproductive anatomy responses on the Rorschach, as well as more emphasis on pelvic anatomy and more use of the internal white space.

Though no particular personality syndrome is commonly associated with male psychosexual dysfunction, a scale 4 score of 85 or higher on the MCMI may predispose one toward this disorder. To the extent that performance anxiety, guilt, and depression are present, elevations of 75 or higher on A and D should occur. Scale 3 may also be elevated. High scores on B and/or T should alert the clinician that the dysfunction may be caused by organic factors.

TREATMENT OPTIONS

A number of physical, chemical, and psychological techniques have been developed to treat erectile and orgasmic dysfunctions (Lo Piccolo and Stock, 1986; Masters et al., 1988). Penile artery bypass surgery can be used where a specific circulatory problem is the issue. Certain prosthetic devices can be used for organically based cases and occasionally for severe psychogenic cases as well. The Smith-Carion penile prosthesis is a silicone sponge that is surgically implanted in the corpora cavernosa, the parts of the penis that engorge with blood in an erection. The consequent permanent erection can be an embarrassment, and it interferes with urological diagnostic procedures. An alternative is a hydraulic system. For example, erection is attained when a rubber bulb implanted in the abdomen or scrotum is pressed. It has the disadvantages of any implanted mechanical device and is also expensive.

It's noteworthy that the idea of a prosthesis is not necessarily a product of our modern, high-tech culture, as is documented in this true anecdote reported by R. O'Hanlon in his book *Into the Heart of Borneo* (1984).

"But Leon, when do you have it done? When do you have the hole bored through your dick?"

"When you twenty-five. When you no good any more. When you too old. When your wife she feds up with you. Then you go down to the river very early in the mornings and you sit in it until your spear is smalls. The tattoo man he comes and pushes a nail through your spear, round and round. And then you put a pin there, a pin from the outboard motor. Sometimes you get a big spots, very painfuls, a boil. And then you die."

"Jesus!"

"My best friend—you must be very careful. You must go down to the river and sit in it once a month until your spear so cold you can't feel it; and then you loosen the pin and push it in and out; or it will stick in your spear and you never move it and it makes a pebble with your water and you die."

"But Leon," I said, holding my knees together and holding my shock with my right hand, "do you have one?"

"I far too young!" said Leon, much annoyed; and then, grinning his broad Iban grin as a thought discharged itself: "But you need one Redmon! And Jams—he so old and serious, he need two!" (pp. 82–83)

Testosterone derivatives have been helpful in some cases, but a hormone deficiency is seldom the critical issue. Injections into the penis, at the time sex is desired, of a vasodilator such as papaverine, along with the alpha blocker phentolamine, is effective in providing erections in 75–80 percent of cases; those who don't respond are usually the very old and those very ill with circulatory problems. Aside from the requirement of self-injection, other drawbacks are the high cost and, in some cases, accumulated scarring.

However, the safest and generally most effective treatments are the psychological techniques developed by Masters and Johnson (1970), in which "sensate focusing" is used to help the client stop spectatoring (becoming too distanced from the act). This is particularly effective if it is carried out with a stable partner from the client's natural world. Again, sensate focusing is not a totally modern development. Sir John Hunter, a physician practicing around 1750 would advise his clients to go home and lie in bed "a fortnight and caress and fondle." His only reported difficulty was that "no one ever completed the treatment" (Lo Piccolo, 1985). Sensate focusing can be aided by systematic desensitization for specific phobias that might hinder erection, such as vaginal odor. In many cases, problems in the interpersonal situation are major contributors to the erectile and orgasmic dysfunction, so marital (or couple) therapy, including an emphasis on improving communication skills in the distressed couple, is necessary to eliminate these precursors to the dysfunction sequence (Bornstein and Bornstein, 1986).

The other major problem in males, premature ejaculation, is usually treated by the "squeeze technique." The couple is admonished to engage in sensate focusing without attempting intercourse. As ejaculation appears imminent, the partner squeezes hard just below the rim of the head the penis, interrupting the cycle of pre-ejaculatory muscle spasms, and then the couple continues in the sensate focusing until control is gained (Masters et al., 1988). In many cases of premature ejaculation, a very high sexual drive level is operating, so counseling about increased frequency of masturbation can help alleviate it.

Treatment for inhibited sexuality components (whether with males or females) is difficult, first and foremost, because a low desire for sex predicts a low desire for sex therapy. Also, a low sex drive, in an otherwise healthy adult, is a paradoxical disorder in that we are "hard-wired" rather than programmed for sex and a low interest in sexuality runs so counter to our cultural values. In addition to couples therapy and sensate focusing, therapy here usually needs to focus on helping the person become more aware of both general affect and body states and also to include some sexual-drive induction techniques. The latter could include training the person to use sexual fantasies (have them written out, but make it clear you only want to know that the task was carried out, that you're not going to cause embarrassment by checking the content). Very likely, this will need to be amplified by the use of erotica and instruction in masturbatory techniques and the control of masturbatory fantasy.

■ Female Psychosexual Dysfunction

Some of the same issues, as well as most of the diagnostic considerations, noted about male psychosexual dysfunction apply equally well to the problems of female psychosexual dysfunction. The categories entitled Hypoactive Sexual Desire (302.71) and Sexual Aversion Disorder (302.79) mean exactly the same for women as they do for men, though obviously there is no category similar to premature ejaculation. Other female categories include Dyspareunia (302.76) and Vaginismus (306.51). Dyspareunia refers to significant pain during intercourse. It is most common in females, but can be diagnosed in males as well. Vaginismus refers to the correlated muscular spasm that prevents intercourse, or at least makes it extremely painful. There is no significant personality pathology correlated with these patterns, though scales reflecting depression and immediate anxiety are likely to be raised, just as they are in premature ejaculation and in erectile dysfunction.

The category of Inhibited Female Orgasm (302.73) is also similar to that for males. Female Sexual Arousal Disorder (302.72) specifically refers to the woman's inability to attain or maintain the swelling and lubrication responses of sexual excitement for a long enough period of time to allow the completion of sexual intercourse—even though the person engages in sexual activity of sufficient preparation and duration—accompanied by a persistent lack of a subjective sense of sexual excitement.

□   DIAGNOSTIC CONSIDERATIONS

It is generally agreed that female sexual dysfunctions are less likely to reflect allied pathology, either generic or situational, than male sexual problems (Masters et al., 1988). In part, this is because the female can perform adequately in spite of inhibited responses in different phases or activities of sexual arousal.

The 2-3/3-2 MMPI code is often found in these cases, though the elevations are not usually above 70 T. This reflects an overcontrolled individual, one who is denying responsibility for problems and yet is experiencing depression from them. An anxious and introverted woman with psychosexual dysfunction is more likely to have a 1-2/2-1 profile, again without the scales being markedly elevated.

To the degree that anxiety and guilt are a result of the psychosexual problems, a high I and Q_4 are likely on the 16 PF. The other scales do not vary in any consistent manner. In that small subgroup of females with psychosexual dysfunction who have been traditionally labeled as hostile and castrating, high scores on E, L, Q_1, and, to a moderate degree, on H and Q_3 are found.

Scale 4 on the MCMI is likely to be high. The superficial flirtatiousness and seductiveness of the histrionic may be a predisposing factor toward psychosexual dysfunction. As psychosexual problems serve a psychological function, scale N will be elevated. As with male psychosexual dysfunction, elevations on A and D may indicate anxiety, depression, and guilt concerning dysfunction.

Scales of the MCMI that correlate most highly with coexisting conditions are as follows: elevations on scales A, H, D, 8, and C. Elevations of A, H, or D indicate conditions especially likely to foster or coexist with sexual dysfunction. Those with personality patterns represented by scales 8 and C may be more likely to experience inhibited sexual desire.

☐   TREATMENT OPTIONS

Just as with the male, the techniques of Masters and Johnson (1970) are particularly effective and can be similarly aided by systematic desensitization of specific fears and phobias. Masturbatory training is emphasized more in the treatment of female dysfunction than in male dysfunction (Masters et al., 1988). The woman is advised to masturbate regularly (and the use of a vibrator is often helpful here) with fantasies of intercourse, with the male gradually taking his place in the masturbatory experience and then literally in the vagina while masturbation still takes place to facilitate orgasm.

Some nonorgasmic women, or those who are weakly orgasmic, have improved their ability to experience orgasm through exercise of the pubococcygeal muscle. To perform these exercises, referred to as the Kegal exercises, the woman contracts the pubococcygeal muscle as though she were trying to keep from urinating. This is performed in sets of ten, several times a day. Various companies market electronic devices that act to stimulate the muscles of this area through electrotherapy. These devices are purported to tone and condition, involuntarily and quickly, the pelvic muscles and thus to facilitate orgasm, though it is clear they are not effective with all women (Chambless et al., 1984).

The other major female psychosexual dysfunctions, vaginismus and dyspareunia, are usually the result of involuntary spasms of the vaginal musculature. Vaginismus has been most effectively treated by the insertion of graduated catheters into the vagina. The first one used may be as thin as a pen, and only when it can be tolerated comfortably for a period of time is one of somewhat larger dimension inserted. Eventually, a catheter the size of an erect penis is used. The technique is most efficient when the partner participates in the insertion of the catheters. It is also advised (Masters and Johnson, 1970) that the partner witness a pelvic examination, since this helps to dispel any irrational fears that may have developed. Possibly more important, it reassures the partner that the physical responses are not specific to his overtures for intercourse. Cox and Meyer (1978), as well as others, have found that various forms of relaxation training and general sexual counseling have also been helpful with dyspareunia. (Though psychological factors can be causal, the primary causes are painful childbirthing, abrasion by pubic hair, and inadequate lubrication for intercourse.)

CHAPTER 9

The Personality Disorders

The personality disorders are chronic, pervasive, and inflexible patterns of perceiving and responding to the environment that are sufficiently maladaptive to cause disruption in functioning and environmentally generated subjective distress. In DSM-III-R, the personality disorders are listed on axis II. Even if a prominent personality pattern does not warrant a formal diagnosis of personality disorder, it can still be listed on axis II, but without the relevant code number that formally designates it as a disorder.

Most individuals in need of a personality disorder diagnosis do not originally see much reason for changing themselves (Morey et al., 1988). This realization only comes when they move into situations that require higher levels of intimacy or more flexible behavioral adaptations. The fact that they cannot meet these requirements results in coercion from the environment, or at least feedback that they cannot ignore, resulting in referral for therapy.

The clinician needs to decide whether the personality disorder pattern is an outgrowth of another disorder, such as a major depressive disorder. For that reason, the clinician needs to assess carefully the issues of chronicity and pervasiveness of behavior. The DSM-III-R does not list a specific time or duration necessary to warrant a personality disorder diagnosis, except when a personality disorder is diagnosed in children. In that instance, duration of at least one year is required, and even then, the DSM-III-R still forbids the application of the term "antisocial personality disorder" before the age of eighteen.

The DSM-III-R personality disorders have traditionally been grouped into three clusters in the DSMs. The first includes the paranoid, schizoid, and schizotypal personality disorders, as these are denoted by peculiar or eccentric behavior. The second cluster focuses on dramatic and emotionally labile behavior: It includes the histrionic, narcissistic, antisocial, and borderline personality disorders. The last cluster, which emphasizes chronic fearfulness and/or avoidance behaviors, includes the avoidant, dependent, obsessive-compulsive, and passive-aggressive personality disorders. There is of course a catch-all category termed Personality Disorder NOS (301.90), used for individuals who do not fit any of the criteria for a specific category, yet clearly fall within the overall patterns of the personality disorders.

Morey (1988) studied the application of DSM-III and DSM-III-R diagnostic criteria to the same patients. The highest agreement between these two systems was found with the borderline personality disorder category, with the antisocial and histrionic categories also showing a high level. The lowest level of agreement was with the schizoid (more diagnosed by DSM-III-R criteria), and low rates of agreement were also found with the paranoid and narcissistic categories.

■   ## Treatment Options

By definition, individuals with the personality disorders are not likely to seek therapy out of a perception of intrapsychic deficit or conflict. Their presence in therapy has usually been stimulated by some social or legal coercion (Morey et al., 1988). For the clinician in private practice, this is most likely in the form of distress generated among the client's intimate others. As a result, some form of marital therapy or family therapy is often required. In addition, some modification of long-standing habit patterns is also necessary, and for that, the assertive therapies, aversion therapies, and milieu-control therapies are often necessary.

A variety of family therapy options are available (Kolevzon and Green, 1985). The most frequent approach, in which the nuclear-family members are seen by one or two therapists during the sessions, is termed "conjoint family therapy." It is the type most often used with the personality disorders, as it provides the duration and intensified focus that are important here. Multiple-impact therapy has a therapist team see family members both individually and in most of the possible combinations of relationships in the family. The emphasis is on an intensive therapeutic period lasting for days rather than weeks. It is particularly helpful where the family is reacting to stress or catastrophe.

The last type, kin network therapy, brings close friends, neighbors, and more distant family members into the therapy attempt. It is particularly useful in the schizophrenic disorders or allied disorders where the person has deteriorated socially. It could also be useful in personality disorders, such as the schizoid, avoidant, and dependent personality disorders. Of course, any of these techniques can be worked into a multiple-family group treatment model. In addition to its lower cost, it increases the breadth of feedback and possibly the breadth of impact.

■   Paranoid Personality Disorder (301.00)

The paranoid personality disorder can be thought of as anchoring the other end of the continuum of paranoid disorders from the most disturbed and fragmented pattern, paranoid schizophrenia (Oltmanns and Maher, 1988). However, since there is neither thought disorder nor even a well-formed minor delusional system in the paranoid personality disorder, it is not listed under the paranoid disorders and is not a psychotic condition. Like the other personality disorders, it is a chronic, pervasive, and inflexible pattern of behavior that typically has been in evolution since childhood and is already recognizable in adolescence (Barkley, 1987). Modeling of parental or other significant others is possibly even more important in this disorder than in the psychotic paranoid conditions.

Paranoid personalities manifest hyperalertness toward the environment and have a chronic mistrust of most people. As a result, their information base is continuously distorted and their affect is constricted. Consequently, they find it difficult to adapt adequately to new situations or relationships, which is paradoxical because of their hyperalertness to their environment. As Turkat (1985) has pointed out, they will frequently be correct in assuming that other people are against them. Yet the paranoia is usually a disabling overreaction to a low initial level of scrutiny by others.

Unless these individuals have almost absolute trust in another person, they cannot develop intimacy and are continually seeking various ways to be self-sufficient. They avoid the emotional complexities of working out a meaningful relationship and tend to be litigious. For example, they may write negative letters to public figures or bring lawsuits on minimal grounds. It is rare for them to come into therapy without significant coercion from others. The disorder is more common in men.

□   DSM-III-R

The DSM-III-R's desire for an operational definition for paranoid personality disorders results in clumsy criteria. The DSM-III-R requires evidence of chronic, pervasive, and unreasonable mistrust of others, beginning by early adulthood as indicated by at least four of the following behaviors: (1) expects harm or exploitation, (2) reads hidden threatening or demeaning messages where unwarranted, (3) is unforgiving and bears grudges, (4) fears confiding in others, thinking the information will be used against him or her, (5) is easily slighted or angered, (6) questions sexual fidelity of partner without warrant, (7) questions loyalty of others without warrant. Finally, the occurrence must not be exclusively during the course of schizophrenia or a delusional disorder.

☐   MMPI

As with the paranoid disorders, it might be expected that the paranoid personality will be high on scale 6. However, this is not always the case, as such individuals are hyperalert about being perceived as paranoid and may guard against this. Hence, there is a wide range of scores for the paranoid personality disorders on scale 6, though on the average it is well above the mean. Blacks score higher on scale 6 throughout the range of both normal and paranoid patterns.

The paranoid personality will occasionally use some kind of random or devious answering scheme with the MMPI, so the reader is referred to the section on malingering. They are easily irritated at the forced-choice format, especially since they are only allowed a binary decision. They also become irritated at the significant self-disclosure required in many of the MMPI items.

The scales that tend to be highest in the paranoid personality disorders are scales 3, 6, 1, and K. This reflects the use of denial and projection, the inclination to focus on physiological concerns when in treatment, and the need to present a facade of adequacy. Since the clinician is not likely to see paranoid personality disorders unless persons have somehow been coerced into treatment (as in marital therapy), there may also be a mild elevation on scale 8, reflecting immediate distress and the dawning awareness that the personality system is maladaptive. A moderately elevated scale 4 is also expected, though it is typically not as high as in many other disorders.

☐   16 PF

Just as on the MMPI scale 6, a person with the paranoid personality disorder does not always score as high as might be expected on the L scale. This is another disorder where it is particularly worthwhile to score for faking-bad on the 16 PF (Winder et al., 1975; Krug, 1981) to assess the extremity of the response patterns.

The suspiciousness, guardedness, and lack of a disintegrating delusional system suggest that Q_3 will be high and scales Q_1 and N will be low. Q_4 can be expected to be low, though if persons are seen for testing in a mental health situation, that score is raised.

The moralistic nature of the paranoid personality attitude system (Turkat, 1985) predicts a higher G score. The need for dominance combined with a fear of vulnerability suggests high E, low I, high N, and high H scores. Scale A is likely to be lower than might be expected from overt behavior, reflecting an inner reluctance to be self-disclosing and to exchange intimacy. These people are usually higher on scale B than are most other psychopathology groups.

☐   OTHER TEST-RESPONSE PATTERNS

The most typical feature of the MCMI profile is an elevation on scale P. Because paranoid personalities often sense themselves incapable of judging safe from unsafe, experiences of apprehension may be present and reflected in an elevated A scale. Paranoid-personality styles are more likely to occur with the antisocial personality (elevations on 6 and P), the narcissistic personality (elevations on 5 and P), and the passive-aggressive personality (elevations on 8 and P).

The paranoid personality responds to the WAIS-R with the same argumentativeness and even condescension that are consistently seen in the other tests. (Allison et al., 1988). Their meticulous approach results in many details, which aids their score in such tests as comprehension and similarities. At the same time, their rigidity, suspiciousness, and peculiar information systems can detract slightly from the comprehension score, so the highest score in the profile is on similarities. These factors can result in good scores on both arithmetic and picture completion, as well as some peculiar picture arrangement sequences. If they become too meticulous and detailed, they do poorly on digit symbol.

On the Rorschach, they are prone to resent the ambiguous stimuli and hence respond with condescending criticism, occasional rejection, flipping of the cards, and a focus on detail responses. F% and F+% are high, and there are relatively few M responses (particularly in light of their intellectual level) and few color responses. The more grandiose they are, the more likely they are to have W responses. Animal and popular responses are common, and the record is generally constricted.

☐   TREATMENT OPTIONS

The reader is referred to the earlier section on the paranoid disorders, since most of the comments there relate to this disorder as well. As with other disorders in which there is a paranoid issue, it is essential to gain the trust of the client through empathy, but not through participation in the disorder patterns. It is especially necessary to empathize with and articulate the consequences of the client's behavior, such as the sense of being isolated and not understood or the interpersonal rejection that appears unfair to the client (Turkat, 1985). If there is any positive change because of these approaches, catharsis techniques may be helpful to get at the conflicts that are causing the avoidance patterns. Then the therapist can begin to build-in more appropriate socialization patterns.

■   ## Schizoid Personality Disorder (301.20)

The essential feature of this disorder is impairment in the ability to form adequate social relationships. As a result, schizoid personalities are shy and socially withdrawn or, as Joan Didion states in *The White Album* (p. 121), "only marginally engaged in the dailiness of life." They have difficulty expressing hostility and have withdrawn from most social contacts. But, unlike that of agoraphobia, the behavior is ego-syntonic.

If, in addition to inadequate interpersonal skills, the person shows peculiarities and difficulties in communication, the appropriate diagnosis is the next disorder to be considered: the schizotypal personality disorder. Schizotypals are more likely to have a family history of schizophrenia. Thus, that category predicts more consistently the eventual emergence of a schizophrenic disorder than does the schizoid personality disorder (Widiger et al., 1986).

The temperament of schizoids is such that they gravitate into jobs that require solitude, such as work as a night watchman (Rutter, 1987). As they age or become vocationally dysfunctional, they are likely to move into a skid row, particularly if they are males. Even though they excessively fantasize and also communicate in peculiar ways, they show no loss of contact with reality.

□ DSM-III-R

According to the DSM-III-R, though schizoids have few if any friends, they show no communication disturbance. The disorder—which is marked by social-relationship deficiencies, introverted behavior, and constricted affect—causes vocational or social disruption. It is noted specifically in a pervasive pattern of indifference to emotions and social relationships as indicated by at least four of the following: (1) typically chooses solitary activities, (2) does not appear to or claim to have strong emotions, (3) neither enjoys nor desires close friendships, (4) shows little interest in sexual experience with another, (5) is indifferent to criticism or praise, (6) has no close friends or confidants (other than first-degree relatives), or (7) shows constricted affect. Before the age of eighteen, the appropriate diagnosis would be Schizoid Disorder of Childhood or Adolescence, which would be coded on axis I. If the person is under the age of eighteen and only avoids relationships with strangers, not with family or close friends, the diagnosis of Avoidant Disorder of Childhood or Adolescence (313.21) would be appropriate.

□ MMPI

When the schizoid is reasonably well integrated and is not disturbed by pressures from the environment to change, a predominantly normal MMPI profile is attained. As Lachar (1974) points out, a high score on the 0 scale is obtained, but the other scores are not usually consistently elevated. If schizoids become more disturbed by the environment and begin to question the appropriateness of their functioning, a raised scale

2 occurs. As upset increases, a rise on scales F and 8 is likely, with a lesser rise on scale 9.

The 1-8 profile has been labeled as that of a nomadic individual in whom there is little clear evidence of emotional lability. Attempts at interpersonal interaction are sporadic, and significant problems occur in dealing with persons of the opposite sex.

☐   16 PF

The social isolation of schizoids is evident in low scores on scales A, E, F, and H. They are high on Q_2 and, to a lesser degree, on Q_3. To the degree that they fit the characteristics of the classic schizoid personality, they are lower on M, O, and I and higher on C, whereas these scores move in the opposite direction as the criteria fit the schizotypal personality disorder more closely.

☐   OTHER TEST-RESPONSE PATTERNS

The most salient indicator in the MCMI profile is elevation on scale 1. Low scores on scales 4, 5, and N are likely. To the degree this pattern is closer to the schizotypal, elevations should be higher on 2, 7, and 8 (Edell, 1987). Depersonalization can occur, which may cause elevation on S. When decompensation occurs or during periods of great stress, elevation on SS may occur, though SS is more typically in the low range of scores.

The schizoid personality, as is true of most of the character disorders, shows somewhat higher WAIS-R performance scale scores than verbal scale scores. The interpersonal problems of both the schizoid and the schizotypal affect the verbal scales more directly. Within the verbal subtests, higher arithmetic and digit span are characteristic of this and other groups that tend toward an interpersonal-detachment syndrome (Keiser and Lowy, 1980). Within the performance subtests, lower picture arrangement and picture completion scores occur. Golden (1979) states that such individuals demonstrate a constricted use of space on the Bender-Gestalt test.

Both the schizoid and the schizotypal, particularly the former, provide a constricted response record on the Rorschach, as well as some rejections. A high percentage of animal content responses and few color-based responses are expected. Occasionally, there is a vague response that cannot be pinned down, or even an occasional oddly supported FC response. Exner (1978, 1986) asserts that similar individuals are likely to have a higher Experience Potential than Experience Actual and that their M production is usually high relative to the overall quality of the protocol. They are also likely to show slow reaction times to many of the cards. A constricted response record along with a blandness of theme and character portrayal is a common performance on the TAT.

☐   TREATMENT OPTIONS

Like the person with an avoidant personality disorder (discussed later in this chapter), the schizoid has inadequate interpersonal relations. But unlike one with an avoidant personality disorder, the schizoid does not care, so therapy is quite difficult. In fact, these clients are not likely even to enter into therapy because such a relationship is the magnification of what is usually avoided. If for some reason they do become involved in therapy, the therapist must help them develop trust in that relationship and yet not overwhelm them with initial confrontations.

Thus, the therapy process is analogous to gaining the trust of the paranoid personality. If that trust *is* obtained, the source of avoidance can possibly be located and dealt with via systematic desensitization, client-centered therapy, or some other means to dissipate withdrawal patterns.

Covert extension may even be useful here. Schizoids would be asked to imagine their distancing patterns vividly and then immediately complete the image by envisioning that the usually occurring reinforcing events do not occur. Since in many ways the schizoid is trying to develop a completely new response pattern, covert modeling may also be used. In this, the client repetitively imagines the desired behavior, probably an interpersonal pattern, and reinforces it by imagined positive outcomes.

■   ## Schizotypal Personality Disorder (301.22)

The reader is referred to the previous category, the schizoid personality disorder, since many of the features of that disorder are found here. The essential difference is that in addition to the disturbances in social functioning, the schizotypal personality manifests peculiarities in the communication process (Rosenbaum et al., 1988). Schizotypal individuals are much more likely than the schizoid to show dysphoria and anxiety, and because of the odd thinking patterns, they are more likely to have developed eccentric belief systems and become involved in fringe religious groups. The schizotypal personality is also more likely to be emotionally labile, overtly suspicious, and hostile of others than is the schizoid (Rosenbaum et al., 1988; Widiger et al., 1986). Many schizotypal individuals also meet the criteria for the borderline personality disorder, to be discussed in a subsequent section. In that case, both diagnoses should be given.

☐   DSM-III-R

A diagnosis of schizotypal personality disorder can be supported by establishing at least four of the following: (1) evidence of magical thinking or odd beliefs, (2) ideas of reference, (3) high social anxiety, (4) presence of occasional illusions (rather than delusions) or odd perceptual experiences, (5) peculiar communications (metaphorical, vague, digressive), (6) inappropriate or constricted affect, (7) suspiciousness, (8) no close friends or confidants (other than first-degree relatives), or (9) odd or eccentric behavior or appearance.

It is not rare to find some evidence of schizophrenia in family members. If blatant schizophrenic symptoms begin to occur, the schizophrenic diagnosis takes precedence and the schizotypal label is not used.

MMPI

Edell (1987) finds the 2-7-8 code to be especially likely to be manifest in the schizotypal personality disorder. As with the schizoid, scale 0 is typically raised. Because of the more pervasive disorder reflected in communication problems and labile emotionality, scales F and 4 are also relatively high, in addition to 2, 7, and 8. If depression is not a major factor, 2 and 7 will be lower. If the person is more inclined to be nomadic and to have flat affect and somatization in addition to the communication problems, a pattern with a moderately elevated F and higher scores (in order) on 8, 1, 2, and 3 can be expected.

16 PF

To the degree the schizotypal shows aspects similar to the schizoid, the profile will resemble that discussed in the prior subsection. However, as is more likely, emotional lability, confusion, and suspiciousness are present, so scores on B, C, and Q_3 would be lower, and scores on Q_4, E, A, and L will be somewhat higher. Also, the score on O is typically higher than in the classic schizoid personality disorder.

OTHER TEST-RESPONSE PATTERNS

As is evident, there are some similarities to the test patterns of schizoids. However, in many respects the schizotypals are closer to the schizophrenic and the borderline personality disorder, particularly in their performance on such tests as the WAIS-R and Rorschach (Swiercinsky, 1985). The patterns noted previously for the acute or less disturbed schizophrenic are applicable here.

TREATMENT OPTIONS

The comments noted in the subsection on the schizoid apply to a degree to the schizotypal personality disorder. The section on schizophrenic disorders is also useful because the schizotypal individual is seen as predictive of later schizophrenic functioning. Hence, the therapist's attention must be directed not only toward the interpersonal withdrawal processes, but also to the emergent disturbances in affect and thinking that are common. Family therapy may be useful in preventing the emergence of a full-blown schizophrenic disorder. These individuals have great difficulty in group therapy because they are quickly perceived as "weird" and may be scapegoated or even directly attacked by the group.

Histrionic Personality Disorder (301.50)

The histrionic personality disorder is commonly encountered in clinical practice (Kernberg, 1984; Gardner, 1965). The disorder is marked by dramatic and intense behavior, problematic interpersonal relationships that others perceive as superficial and shallow, and problematic sexual adjustment. These persons seek attention and are overreactive, with the response being expressed more dramatically and intensely than is appropriate—hence, the term "histrionic." This category has traditionally been labeled the "hysterical personality." However, as noted earlier, "hysteric" wrongly suggests a disorder that parallels the causes and symptoms of what has been previously labeled "hysterical neurosis."

Histrionic personalities may elicit new relationships with relative ease, as they appear to be empathic and socially able. However, they turn out to be temperamentally and emotionally insensitive and have little depth of insight into their own responsibilities in a relationship (Rutter, 1987). They quickly avoid blame for any difficulties of interpersonal relationship and, in that sense, show a degree of the projection that is characteristic of paranoid disorders. Even though they may be flirtatious and seductive sexually, there is little mature response or true sensuality. If one accepts the apparent sexual overture in the behavior, the histrionic individual may act as if insulted or even attacked.

There has been a continuing controversy as to whether this disorder occurs with any frequency in males. This is not surprising, since the meaning of the Greek root term "*hystera*" is "uterus." Ancient explanations for this disorder blamed an unfruitful womb, which became distraught and wandered about the body. Hippocrates thought marriage would cure hysteria by anchoring the womb. Even Freud suggested marriage as a cure. Since conflict over expressing sexual needs may be a factor, such medicine might even work at times. But just as often, this medicine brings on "iatrogenic" problems that are worse than the "disease."

It is clear that this disorder is found in males, but because the symptoms are a caricature of the traditional role expectations for women, it is more common in women (Millon, 1981). The DSM-III-R suggests that it is uncommon in males and that when it does occur, it is likely to be associated with homosexuality, an assertion that is best regarded as a theoretical speculation. There is evidence that the same developmental patterns in females that eventuate in histrionic behavior lead to more antisocial behavior patterns in males, and this would fit with the role expectation theory.

☐   ## DSM-III-R

In general, histrionic personalities show attention seeking and overly emotional and dramatic behaviors and are seen by others as shallow and insincere. DSM-III-R requires dramatic and intensely manifested behavior, beginning by early adulthood, as evidenced by at least four of the following: (1) constantly seeks or demands reassurance, (2) is inappropriately sexually seductive, (3) is overly concerned with physical attractiveness, (4) expresses emotion with inappropriate exaggeration, (5) is uncomfortable at not being the center of attention, (6) has rapidly shifting and shallow emotions, (7) is self-centered and has no tolerance for frustration, or (8) has a style of speech that is excessively impressionistic and lacking in detail.

☐   ## MMPI

The 2-3/3-2 profile is the one most commonly encountered in the histrionic personality disorder. When the histrionic personality is seen in the clinical situation, there are usually distress and upset, possibly accompanied by manipulative suicide gestures. Thus, an elevation on scale 2 of greater than 70 T can be expected. When distress is not so marked, the expected elevation on scale 3 takes precedence. The rare 3-9/9-3 profile is also indicative of histrionic functioning (Kelley and King, 1979c), as is the more common 3-4/4-3 and 4-9/9-4 patterns (Graham, 1987).

Scales 4, 7, and 8 are also likely to be moderately elevated. Scale 4 reflects the histrionic's tendency toward egocentricity, overdramatization, and shallow interpersonal relationships. The underlying self-doubt and anxiety raise the 7 score, and the tendency toward impulsive emotionality and self-dramatization elevates scale 8.

Scales L, F, and K usually fall within normal limits. If the individual has begun a defense by focusing on somatic complaints, scale 1 may be elevated. Scale 5 is likely to be elevated in males, reflecting the association of hysteria with traditional feminine role behaviors. It is usually quite low in females. Scale 0 is not usually markedly elevated; *any* elevation, however, is surprising because these people make a first impression on the unsophisticated that they are highly sociable. If controls are breaking down and the histrionic feels that he or she is losing control, a higher score on scale 9 is expected, though it is usually within normal limits.

□   OTHER TEST-RESPONSE PATTERNS

Elevation on scale 4 would be expected on the MCMI. Because histrionics are often seeking attention and validation from others, scales 1 and 2 should be relatively low. The somatization factor may be used as an attention-getting device, in which case one would expect an elevation on scale H. Other scales that may be periodically elevated because they serve as methods for dramatic attention-getting devices include N and S. Anxiety may be experienced when needs for dependence are not being met, resulting in elevated A, though typically the histrionic's style is quite ego-syntonic.

A classic sign of the histrionic on the WAIS-R is that the verbal score is typically less than the performance score. Within the verbal scales, the information subscale is usually low, as is the arithmetic subscale (particularly in females). Histrionic females are prone to make complaints about the arithmetic test or to make comments like "I've never been able to do math at all." Digit span is expected to be moderately high, and comprehension is often the highest subscale. The histrionic is occasionally inclined to moralize in response to some of the items, particularly in the comprehension subtest.

Within the performance subtests, those that tap speed and visual-motor coordination (such as digit symbol) are high, as is picture completion. Block design is sometimes surprisingly low compared to the other tests of similar skill requirements.

On the Rorschach, histrionics often provide a surprisingly low number of responses, considering their apparent intensity and involvement; there is a low W%; and there is an emphasis on easy, obvious details. They may portray some of the cards as scary or ugly. They may see monstrous or frightening animals and give responses involving sexual innuendo. At the same time, they deny dysphoric content in the cards. There are a relatively low number of W and M responses, relative to intelligence. There are blocked responses to color or shading, and one could expect a reasonably high number of M responses. Occasionally, the histrionic will make "blood" responses to the color cards.

TAT stories often contain dependency and control themes, and they may even become personalized and generate some affective display. Blocking occasionally occurs to "sexual" or "aggressive" pictures, and some cards may be called "ugly," "sickening," or the like.

□   TREATMENT OPTIONS

Histrionics being prone to dramatic and exaggerated patterns, they are most responsive, at least initially, to a dramatic therapy approach. Hypnosis, some of the consciousness-raising techniques, and even dramatic placebos can be useful here. Low-key or nonintense therapy approaches may be seen as invalid by such clients simply because of the lack of intensity.

Once there is some engagement in the therapy process, a shift has to be made to an approach that deals with the disturbed interpersonal relationships and avoidance of responsibility (Teyber, 1988). Group therapy can eventually be helpful because it provides the consensual data so important to convince histrionics of their disorder. However, unless there has been some trust and dependency generated in the group and/or with the therapist, the group will quickly perceive the histrionic as shallow and deceptive. Denial and flight from therapy will be quick, and the critically necessary confrontation with the fear and anxiety that have been kept out of consciousness is avoided.

Narcissistic Personality Disorder (301.81)

This category, new in the DSM-III, centers on individuals who are to a degree products of our modern social-value systems. They are "flattery-operated"; more specifically, they manifest an unrealistic sense of self-importance, exhibitionistic attention seeking, inability to take criticism, interpersonal manipulation, and a lack of empathy, resulting in substantial problems in interpersonal relationships.

No doubt, such people have always existed, but it appears that this pattern has become more common recently. It is not a surprising development when there are advertisements about "The Arrogance of Excellence" and self-help seminars unequivocally urging people to live out the axiom "I'm number one" (with little evidence that there is much room for a number two or three close behind). As the cultural historian Christopher Lasch (1978) so lucidly describes, a narcissistic personality is a logical development from such societal values.

The pattern is usually evident in adolescence, and the disorder is chronic. As with other personality disorders, narcissistic personalities only come to the attention of a clinician when coerced by circumstances (Kernberg, 1984). The prognosis for major change is moderate at best. Narcissistic personalities are similar to antisocial personalities, except that they are not so aggressive or hostile and their value systems are more asocial and hedonic than antisocial (Meissner, 1981).

DSM-III-R

According to DSM-III-R, the essential diagnostic features of the narcissistic personality disorder—which is a pervasive pattern of grandiosity, hypersensitivity, and lack of empathy, beginning in early adulthood—must include five of the following: (1) grandiose self-evaluation with related fantasies, (2) consistent need for attention, (3) emotional lability after criticism or defeat, (4) little ability to empathize, (5) an assumption that they will receive special treatment from others without any need for reciprocal behavior—entitlement, (6) exploitative interpersonal behaviors, (7) belief that his/her problems are unique,

(8) preoccupation with fantasies of unlimited success and power, beauty, brilliance, or love, or (9) preoccupation with feelings of envy.

Such people naturally have a rather fragile personality integration and may on occasion manifest brief psychotic episodes. As a character in Peter de Vries's novel *Consenting Adults* (1980, p. 183) so aptly puts it, "I have this crush on myself—but the feeling is not returned." They also may show characteristics of the histrionic and/or antisocial personality disorder, and if so, an additional diagnosis can be used.

☐   MMPI

Lachar (1974) finds that individuals who can develop only superficial relationships score low on scale 0. Since the narcissistic personality disorder is so interpersonally exploitative, an elevation on scale 4 is also expected. They often fit a stereotypical sexual role, so males are low on scale 5 (though certain male homosexuals manifest a high level of narcissism, and scale 5 would then be high) (Graham, 1987).

If their patterns are ineffective in coping with the environment, they show situation-generated depression, so a rise on scales 2 and 9 can be expected. If instead, they become suspicious and irritable, a rise on scale 6 occurs. If they begin to descend emotionally into a brief psychotic disorder, scale 8 should reflect this.

☐   16 PF

Their inflated sense of worth and extroverted assertiveness are expressed in high scores on A, E, and H, while the asocial value system and exploitativeness are evident in low scores on G and Q_3. They also score moderately high on Q_1. They are variable on scales C, O, and L, depending on the degree of personality integration and whether or not they are moving toward a brief psychotic episode, suspiciousness, or depression.

☐   OTHER TEST-RESPONSE PATTERNS

The most prominent indicator on the MCMI is elevation on scale 5. Scale 4 may also be elevated. Because these persons do not like to admit personal weaknesses or admit psychic distress, elevation on scales A, D, and S are rare, though when they do occur, they may be used as rationalizations for being unable to live up to their inflated self-image. During periods of stress, elevations on P and PP may occur.

Throughout the testing situation, narcissistic personalities are prone to avoid tasks that demand introspection and/or persistent problem solving, particularly if they can use wit or charm to distract the clinician (Meissner, 1981). If the charm does not work effectively, they occasionally feign inadequacy, to avoid a task. They are also likely to produce some pedantic, almost condescending responses. They occasionally will assert that they only guessed when they sense that they have missed an arithmetic solution, even when the evidence shows that they did not guess.

As a result of these tendencies, they do more poorly on WAIS-R tasks that demand persistence and detailed responses, such as object assembly, arithmetic, vocabulary, comprehension, and block design. The picture arrangement subtest occasionally elicits personalized comments that reflect the narcissism. Overall, they do a bit better on the performance scales than on the verbal scales.

On the Rorschach, such personalities are inclined to give "to me" responses. If they feel the clinician is positively attending to them, they provide more responses than do histrionic individuals, yet seldom in accurate detail, particularly in the M and W responses. As a result, these responses show poor quality. In a related fashion, the F+% is not high. If they are at all distressed, they produce constricted records that focus on popular and animal responses.

They have a higher number of C responses than individuals with the obsessive-compulsive disorder, and those that occur in the obsessive record are better integrated into the overall response pattern. The narcissistic personality seldom responds directly to shading, but often makes texture responses that are apparently suggested by form or outline. If the narcissism is channeled into direct body expression, responses such as "people exercising" may be noted. Responses that have an ornate or flashy quality are found. Responses focusing on fancy food or clothing, particularly exotic forms of clothing, or gem or perfume responses are also thought to be indicative of the narcissistic personality disorder (Shafer, 1954). Also, an emphasis on both CF and pure C responses is indicative of narcissism.

TAT stories are often void of meaningful content, and the narcissist may detract from the essence of the story by a cute ending or a related joke. Cards that demand a response to potentially anxiety-inducing fantasy, such as 13 MF, may result in either a superficially avoidant story or one with blatantly lewd or shocking content, again reflecting an avoidance of the essential features of the cards (Bellak, 1986).

TREATMENT OPTIONS

The narcissistic personality may be even more difficult to engage in therapy than is the antisocial personality, in large part because the therapist seldom has as much coercive control. Almost the only time narcissistic personalities enter therapy is when they fear the loss of a dependency role, as in a marital situation. Psychoanalytic therapy appears well suited to confront the pathology of narcissism (Meissner, 1981), and transactional analysis within marital therapy (Berne, 1964) may be of help because it can give both spouse and client a way of more positively conceptualizing the narcissism, that is, as the "child" in the personality. Groups can be initially "seduced" by the narcissist, but with time they are viewed as exploitative and self-centered, often resulting in anger and rejection from the group.

To the extent the pattern can be more easily accepted, feedback should be followed by some modeling of new behaviors, either in role playing with the therapist, in a multiple marital-group setting, or in imagination. Role playing and *quid pro quo* behavioral contracting are useful adjuncts in attempting to change these behaviors, though they require helping the narcissistic personality to articulate needs, a difficult step.

■ Antisocial Personality Disorder (301.70)

The essential characteristic of the antisocial personality disorder is the chronic manifestation of antisocial behavior patterns in amoral and impulsive persons. They are usually unable to delay gratification or to deal effectively with authority, and they show narcissism in interpersonal relationships. The pattern is apparent by the age of fifteen (usually earlier) and continues into adult life with consistency across a wide performance spectrum, including school, vocational, and interpersonal behaviors (Barkley, 1987; Hare, 1986).

Although the DSM-III-R discusses only the overall category of antisocial personality, there is good evidence that it can be further subdivided into categories of primary psychopath and secondary psychopath (Lykken, 1957; Zuckerman et al., 1980; Quay, 1987). The primary psychopath is distinguished by the following characteristics: (1) they have a very low level of anxiety and little avoidance learning, (2) they are significantly refractory to standard social control procedures, (3) they are high in stimulation-seeking behaviors, particularly the "disinhibition" factor that refers to extroverted, hedonistic pleasure seeking. The reader is referred to a detailed discussion of personality, diagnostic, and treatment considerations dealing with this subdivision in Meyer (1980). It is advisable to delineate the consequent ramifications of the differences in a primary and secondary psychopath in a clinical report, since such discriminations are glossed over by the use of the overall term "antisocial personality disorder."

☐   DSM-III-R

The DSM-III-R term "antisocial personality disorder" has evolved through a variety of terms and now supersedes the terms "psychopathic" and "sociopathic," at least in formal diagnostic labeling. Pritchard's (1835) term "moral insanity" is considered by many to be the first clear forerunner to the present "antisocial personality disorder" label. "Psychopath" first emerged in the label "psychopathic inferiority," introduced by Koch late in the nineteenth century (Cleckley, 1964).

Terms incorporating "psychopath" were common until the DSM-I, published in 1952, used "sociopathic personality." The DSM-II, in 1968, introduced the term "antisocial personality," which is used in the DSM-III-R.

In spite of this evolution (or possibly because of it), there have been significant data indicating that this diagnostic grouping is a meaningful concept to clinicians (Hare, 1986). In an early study on the diagnostic reliability of the standard categories, Spitzer et al. (1967) found the highest level of agreement (r = .88) when clinicians assigned persons to the "antisocial personality" category. It is interesting that the lowest index of agreement (r = .42) was found with psychoneurotic reactions. Since Spitzer is the chief architect of DSM-III and DSM-III-R, it is not surprising that the term "neurotic" has been so ambivalently treated in both.

To apply the diagnosis of antisocial personality disorder, the DSM-III-R requires that the individual be eighteen years old. There should also be evidence that the behavior has been relatively persistent. Incidentally, if the individual is younger than eighteen, the appropriate diagnosis is conduct disorder (Quay, 1987).

Onset before the age of fifteen is supported by evidence of three or more types of acting-out behavior. At least four of the following must have occurred since the age of fifteen: (1) problematic occupational performance, (2) repetitive, easily elicited fighting, (3) repetitive avoidance of financial responsibility, (4) failure to plan ahead, as indicated by transient traveling without a goal or a lack of a fixed address for a month or more, (5) recklessness, (6) failure to accept social norms, (7) no regard for the truth, as indicated in repetitive deception of others, (8) indication of inability to function as a responsible parent, (9) inability to sustain a monogamous relationship for a year, or (10) lack of remorse.

☐   MMPI
_____

Since scale 4 is typically high in this group, it may be worthwhile to examine the contribution to scale 4 of various subcomponents, as reflected in several of the Wiggins scales (Colligan and Offord, 1988). For example, those high on 4 where the contribution comes from the family problems (FAM) scale are likely to be less pathological than those whose 4 scale is primarily elevated by scores from the authority conflict (AUT) scale, and especially the manifest-hostility (HOS) scale.

The 4-9/9-4 profile has been considered the classic profile of the antisocial personality. As Megargee and Bohn (1979) show, distinct bimodality indicates an amoral psychopath who fits most of the classic descriptors of the antisocial personality, yet is not particularly hostile. The following section details the MMPI subclassification system on the criminal personality as researched by Megargee and Bohn (1979) and researched and reviewed by Gearing (1979).

When the profile contains a definite spike 4 profile with only a secondary moderate elevation on scale 2, it is more likely to be a primary psychopath who in addition is easily provoked to violence. The primary psychopath who is prone to violent behavior commonly scores high on scales 8, 6, and 4. Such individuals appear to be especially dangerous if they have a high scale 9 score in addition to high scores on scales 8, 6, and 4. Within a psychopathic population, the level of scale 6 is an indicator of whether hostility is overt or suppressed.

The bimodal 4-9/9-4 profile, noted earlier, is more indicative of secondary psychopathy, as is another common code, the 2-4/4-2 profile with moderate elevations on the other scales. In the 4-9/9-4 group, to the degree that 9 is greater than 4, one is likely to observe a higher level of tension and more somatic concerns. The rare spike 9 profile (when not under treatment because of a spouse's complaint of marital difficulties) is indicative of a primary psychopath who has also abused drugs heavily.

A high F scale is more characteristic of the secondary psychopath and/or the younger psychopath than the primary psychopath and/or the older psychopath (Gallucci, 1987). When one obtains a 4-8/8-4 profile and most other scales are low, a hostile, cold, and punitive psychopath who borders on schizophrenia should be considered (Lachar, 1974). The expression of aggression in the psychopath appears to be inhibited to the degree that scales 2 and 3 (and 5 for males) are high. Aggression is much more likely, as noted earlier, when scales 6, 8, and 9 are high. When psychopathic individuals are seen in a hospital setting rather than as outpatients, they are more likely to score higher on scales F, 1, 2, 3, and 7, reflecting their greater situational distress.

□   16 PF

The modal 16 PF profile for primary psychopaths finds high scores on scales 0, L, and M, with average high scores on Q_4 and A. They obtain low scores on Q_3 and G, with moderately low scores on C and B and a moderately high score on A. They generally score high on E, though this fluctuates rather wildly and some primary psychopaths may obtain very low scores.

Golden (1979) also suggests that a high N score is typical of the psychopath, and this appears to be logical, since shrewdness and manipulation of others are characteristic of this pattern. Those psychopaths who are particularly high on the stimulation-seeking variable should score low on G and Q_3 and high on Q_2 and L. Within all subgroups of the antisocial personality disorder category, a high M score is thought to predict recidivism.

The modal profile for secondary psychopaths shows high scores on scales Q_4, O, and A, with low scores on C, Q_3, and H. They are also moderately low on G and Q_1 and tend to be average or below on N (in contrast to the primary psychopath), though again they also vary widely on N. On the average, they are not as low on scale B as the primary psychopath.

OTHER TEST-RESPONSE PATTERNS

The highest MCMI elevations are expected on 5 and 6. When the 5-6 code is highest, B, T, and PP also tend to be somewhat elevated, and P, S+P, and C+P are high as well. Because the antisocial personality is generally not highly distressed, marked elevations on, A, D, and H are not likely. Elevations on A may occur, however, especially just prior to acting-out. Because alcohol and drug abuse are common here, elevations on B and/or T are likely.

On the WAIS-R, antisocial personalities, especially those more inclined toward primary psychopathy, generally have a performance IQ higher than the verbal IQ, sometimes by 10 points or more. If they have had school-related problems, as is almost always the case, their low scores in the verbal subtests are on information, arithmetic, and vocabulary, reflecting their lack of adequate achievement in academic subjects. On the comprehensive subtest, the "marriage," "bad company," and "laws" items can bring out relevant content. Also, some explanations of the picture arrangement subtest elicit similar material. Picture completion and block design usually give two of the higher scores, and these persons usually do reasonably well on object assembly. Digit symbol and digit span are also often quite high (Keiser and Lowy, 1980).

In certain older individuals (with a mean age of forty-four), probably best viewed as secondary psychopaths, Heinrich and Amolsch (1978) found an unusual WAIS-R pattern consistently associated with persons who have a poor work and marital history, show drinking problems, are assaultive while drinking, and are inclined toward somatic concerns and situational depression. They show a verbal IQ greater than a performance IQ by 6–21 points; high vocabulary and comprehension scores; low digit symbol, block design, and object assembly scores; and an average picture completion score.

On the Rorschach, antisocial personalities usually present a casual though alert facade (Hare, 1986), which is in contrast to their at least moderately constricted and shallow protocol. If they are defensive, the record will be quite constricted, and they may reject cards that they can clearly handle cognitively. Otherwise, a low to average number of responses is provided. Vague percepts may be seen at first and then developed in a flashy and flamboyant manner, possibly accompanied by cute though hostile comments. There may be guarded rejections of cards, and there is usually a delayed response to the color cards. They do respond to color (particularly the primary psychopath), though often in a fairly primitive and impulsive manner, with pure C responses. While there are a low number of M and W responses, an absence of shading, and a low F+%, there are a high number of popular responses. There are a high number of animal responses, rather than human responses, and weapons are occasionally noted (Wagner and Wagner, 1981; Shafer, 1954).

The TAT stories are often somewhat juvenile in theme, and though the protagonist may be caught in a negative act, there is little mention of deserved punishment. If, on the other hand, they perceive the social demand of the situation as requiring some commentary on punishment, they will so comment, yet with a superficial shallowness (Karon, 1981).

☐   TREATMENT OPTIONS

The treatment problem with all the personality disorders—getting the client into therapy and meaningfully involved—is acute in the antisocial personality disorder. Most effective are controlled settings, with personnel who are firm and caring and sophisticated in controlling manipulations, in which the antisocial client resides for a significant period of time. Confrontive therapies can also be effective (Quay, 1987; Meyer, 1980), but they require some form of coercion, such as institutionalization, to keep the person in therapy. In such a setting, behavioral techniques, notably the aversion therapies, have been used to reduce some of the disordered habit patterns. Aside from institutional settings, the chief time a therapist is likely to see an antisocial personality disorder is in a disturbed family situation. Marital and family therapies that work on a *quid pro quo* rather than on a good-faith contracting approach are of most help.

Attention should also be paid to the stimulation-seeking nature of these clients (Quay, 1987; Zuckerman et al., 1980). This need can be interpreted to one with an antisocial personality disorder as similar to that of the alcoholic, in that the person needs somehow to fulfill this drive or be inclined to indulge in deviant patterns. The paradoxical effect of stimulant drugs (as with hyperactives) can be helpful with a small subgroup of the more manic psychopaths, but much care must be taken in management.

Therapists can work with psychopaths to develop means of gaining stimulation in less self-destructive ways. A consistent pattern of engagement in sports and other strenuous and/or exciting activities and jobs that provide for a high level of activity and stimulation are helpful.

■ Conduct Disorder

According to the DSM-III-R, the conduct disorder is the precursor to the antisocial personality, but unlike it, the disorder is broken down into three subcategories (group, solitary aggressive, and undifferentiated) and thus may actually predict some other disorders as well.

The conduct disorders are marked by a persistent pattern of behavior that violates major age-appropriate social norms and the rights of others. To earn the basic diagnosis of conduct disorder, at least three of the following factors—in descending order of discriminating power—should be in evidence: (1) more than one occasion of stealing without confrontation, (2) at least twice running away from home, (3) frequent lying, (4) an incident of deliberate fire setting, (5) frequent truancy, (6) breaking into a car, building, or house, (7) deliberate property destruction (other than fire starting), (8) physical cruelty to animals, (9) an incident of coercive sexual activity, (10) use of a weapon in more than one fight, (11) frequent initiation of physical fights, (12) theft while confronting the victim, or (13) physical cruelty to people.

If the predominate pattern is aggression toward others and it is initiated individually, the diagnosis is the Solitary Aggressive type (312.00); if most of the problem behaviors occur as a group activity with peers, the diagnosis is the Group type (312.20); otherwise, the diagnosis is Undifferentiated type (312.90).

The diagnosis of conduct disorder requires evidence of the pattern for at least six months. If the person is eighteen or older, there should be evidence that the criteria for the antisocial personality disorder have not been met. A full evaluation of the family is essential for adequate diagnosis of the conduct-disordered child (Barkley, 1987).

The breakdown of the conduct disorder categories in many ways reflects a refinement of the concept of the primary versus the secondary psychopath discussed previously. The Solitary Aggressive type (312.00) comes closest to the violent acting-out of the primary psychopath, and the Undifferentiated type (312.90) at least includes the secondary (or neurotic) psychopath who is engaged in passive acting-out behaviors. The group type is close to the classic concept of the "gang-oriented" juvenile delinquent (Binder, 1988). The categories are also reflected in some of the differences noted in Megargee's research on the criminal personality (Megargee and Bohn, 1979; see Chapter 10).

□			MMPI

Overall, scales 4, 8, and 9 have been "excitatory" in regard to acting-out in adolescence, whereas scales 0, 2, and 5 have been sent as "suppressor" scales. A moderately elevated 4-9 code, with most of the other scales not particularly high, is typical of the group-type conduct disorder, but it is also occasionally seen in the other types too. A combination of the 4-8-9 scales with generally elevated scales throughout would be more consistently found in the solitary-aggressive conduct disorder. Adolescents typically show higher F scales (Gallucci, 1987), and a caret-

FIGURE 9.1   Evolution of Aggressive Delinquency

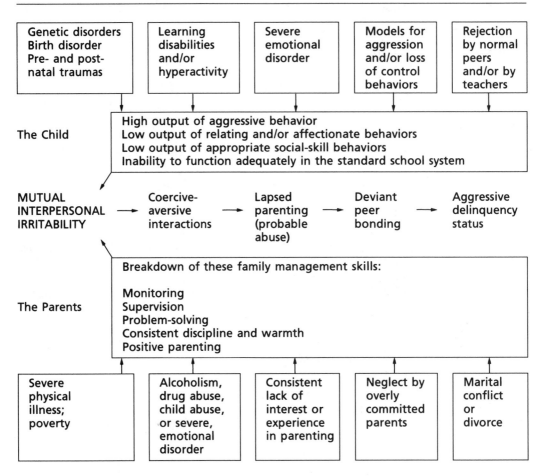

shaped profile on the validity scales (low L, high F, and low K) typifies the most severely emotionally disturbed subgroup of this disorder.

The 8-4 profile, with an elevation on 6 as well, is likely to be found in the solitary aggressive who also has a paranoid component, but the 8-4 profile without a high 6 would be more likely with an individual who is acting-out aggressively but is at least somewhat more socialized. The 2-4/4-2 profile, with a distinctive slope to the right and possibly a mild elevation on scale 6, is characteristic of those who are more likely to be undersocialized and nonaggressive–they are usually placed in the undifferentiated category. In general though, scales 0, 2, and 5, if high, predict lower rates of delinquency.

☐   16 PF

On the 16 PF, the group type should score somewhat higher than the solitary aggressive on scales A, B, G, and, to a moderate degree, N and

Q_3. They are likely to be lower on L and Q_1 and, to a moderate degree, on E. The aggressive continuum is reflected in several scores: likely higher on E, H, and L, lower on B, C, G, I, and M, and moderately lower on N and Q_3. Q_4 particularly reflects the anxiety experienced in the evaluation situation, as well as other environmental conditions. The more socialized the individual, the more situational anxiety and thus a higher score on Q_4.

OTHER TEST-RESPONSE PATTERNS

To the degree that the client is socialized and more likely to be the group type, WAIS-R and WISC-R scores will be more even between and within the verbal and performance tests, and the differences are more pronounced with the WISC-R than the WAIS-R (Grace and Sweeney, 1986). To the degree that the client is more aggressive and undersocialized, performance scores are likely to be higher than verbal scores. To the degree that avoidance of school is a factor, scores would be lower on information, arithmetic, and vocabulary than on other subtests. The ability to abstract has been hypothesized as important in curbing physical aggression; hence, aggressive individuals may be lower on similarities, all other variables being equal.

The solitary-aggressive individual is more likley to be resistant to the testing process itself and to show negativism throughout both this test and the Rorschach. To the degree the person is undersocialized, he or she should do somewhat less well on comprehension and picture arrangement than clients who are more aware and attuned to social norms. From a general perspective, individuals with conduct disorders who are more involved with passive or status offenses are more likely to have higher intelligence overall than those who are involved in more aggressive acting-out behaviors (Quay, 1987).

On the MCMI, the group type may experience more distress related to associated behaviors, producing more frequent elevations on A and D, where the solitary-aggressive type may show relatively higher elevations on 1, 2, 5, and 6. To the degree the person is undersocialized yet nonaggressive, elevations on 1, 2, 6, 8, S, B, and T and low scores on 4, 7, and N can be expected.

On the Rorschach, solitary-aggressive individuals are likely to reject cards, to avoid the task in a variety of ways, to give more personalized (PER) responses, and to show more direct manifestations of violent and bizarre content than are more socialized and/or less aggressive clients. Those tending to be undersocialized, solitary, and aggressive are also likely to show the following characteristics: lower F percentage, higher F-percentage, lower W percentage, lower M percentage, more pure C, CF greater than FC, more animal responses, higher white-space responses, more emphasis on D and popular responses in an overall protocol with a low number of responses (Quevillon et al., 1986).

On the TAT (Quevillon et al., 1986), conduct-disordered male youths typically make more mention of parents, give more-aggressive stories, and give responses that involve materialistic objects and a need for achievement. Aggressive youths in general give stories in which the hero was aggressive but received little punishment for his actions, as well as themes that include vivid and instructive stories about murder, burglaries, and hold-ups. These youths tend to ramble on without any clear themes and often have difficulty describing card 2. Stories that are superficial and have an absence of empathy or sympathy are common. Some youths give stories that are evasive, and they frequently mention that the stories are not autobiographical.

Quevillon et al. (1986) review the large number of scales specifically designed to assess conduct disorders.

☐ TREATMENT OPTIONS

Early intervention is critical, and indeed, children first arrested at a young age are more likely to commit a greater number of and more-serious crimes. If the individual is more solitary, undersocialized, and aggressive, there is a need for a highly controlled living system that includes all aspects of functioning. Token economy programs, combined with an emphasis on basic academic and vocational skills, will likely be necessary, along with a focus on the control of behavior (Barkely, 1987). The more subtle strategies designed for the primary psychopath and the paranoid may also be appropriate. In response to the group type, especially when nonaggressive, the requirement of a highly structured and supervised residential program is lessened (Binder, 1988). An emphasis on a group-living model comes to the fore, and in some cases, outpatient treatment with such approaches as reality therapy, support groups, and the more traditional psychotherapies can be useful (Brigham, 1988). A focus on parent training and classroom control using time-out procedures, contracting, and reinforcement structuring would also then be appropriate. Family therapy is usually necessary, and community-based interventions (e.g., setting up sports activities, scouting programs, and other positive group experiences) can also be effective (Mash and Terdal, 1988).

■ Borderline Personality Disorder (301.83)

This disorder was a confusing entity in the original DSM-III-R drafts, but now it seems to be more clearly defined (Widiger et al., 1986). At first glance, it may seem to overlap with the schizotypal personality disorder, as both imply an easy transition into a schizophrenic adjustment. However, individuals with borderline personality disorder are neither as withdrawn socially nor as bizarre in symptomatology as are schizophrenics. Though the DSM-III-R does not specifically mention it, this category seems to be a resurrection of an old term at one time much favored by clinicians: "emotionally unstable personality." Persons in the borderline personality disorder category show significant emotional instability, are impulsive and unpredictable in behavior, are irritable and anxious, often show "soft" neurological signs, and avoid being alone or experiencing the boredom to which they are prone (Gardner et al., 1987). There is some evidence that as these individuals improve, they show more predictable behavior patterns, yet this is combined with increasingly evident narcissism (Meissner, 1981).

An additional feature of this disorder is pseudologia phantastica. Snyder (1986) reports several case studies in which pathological lying is a cardinal feature. This lying may reflect an attempt to control or to enhance self-esteem. Some borderline individuals may be aware of their lying, while others may not be. In clinical cases where the individuals were confronted with their inaccuracies, they quickly dropped or changed the stories.

☐ DSM-III-R

To diagnose borderline personality disorder—a pervasive pattern of mood, self-image, and interpersonal instability, beginning by early adulthood—at least five of the following are required: (1) unpredictable impulsivity in two areas, such as sex or drug or alcohol use; (2) physically self-damaging behaviors; (3) uncontrolled, inappropriate anger responses; (4) unstable and intense interpersonal relationships; (5) unstable mood; (6) unstable identity; (7) persistent boredom experiences; or (8) avoidance of being or feeling alone or abandoned.

This disorder is thought to be relatively common, and it is the most consistently diagnosed personality disorder in a comparison across clients using DSM-III and DSM-III-R terminology (Morey, 1988). Yet, it may be a confusing diagnostic category for clinicians. This category would probably be more commonly used if the older term "emotionally unstable personality disorder," were reinstituted. A multiple diagnosis with schizotypal and histrionic components is not improbable (Widiger et al., 1986). If the person is under the age of eighteen, a diagnosis of identity disorder takes precedence.

☐ MMPI

In many respects, the syndrome of borderline personality disorder parallels that of schizophrenia, not with the distinct emphasis on delusions or hallucinations, but at the same time with a higher level of responsiveness toward other persons. Elevations on scales 2, 4 and 8 should be expected (Edell, 1987). While the F scale should be lower, scales O and K should be higher than in schizophrenia. Scale 6 should show elevation if problems in management of anger are involved, and the rare 2-6/6-2 type is likely to receive a diagnosis of borderline personality disorder or a similar one (Kelley and King, 1979c). If mood instability is involved and the person is in a manic phase, a rise in scale 9 and a drop on scale 2 are likely, with the opposite expected in the converse mood situation (Graham, 1987).

☐   16 PF

If these persons avoid being alone, even though there is instability in interpersonal relationships, A should be high and Q_2 should be low. Overall, scales C, H, and Q_3 should be low, with high scores on Q_4 and O. Mood at the time of the testing will determine the score on F, and the degree of suspiciousness will be reflected in the height of the L scale. On the average, moderately low scores on M and N can be expected, though these can fluctuate markedly.

The variable self-assertion and avoidance exhibited in borderline personality disorders emerge on scale E, although such individuals can be docile and passive in order to fulfill their dependency needs. At other times, they are aggressive, paranoid, and manipulative, particularly when they are rejected. Also, since their social instability and irritability disrupt their social functioning, probable rejection results in their occasionally appearing at the more assertive end of the E continuum.

☐   Other Test-Response Patterns

From an overall perspective, the inadequate insulation of intellectual abilities from the intrusion of emotion can be observed in the connotations of the borderline client's language. It often becomes colored by personal concerns, though it usually stays within the bounds of appropriateness. For example, an explosive borderline client, when asked to define "terminate," replied, "To murder or kill someone—say, for revenge" (Swiercinsky, 1985). While some of these impairments may suggest organic dysfunction, borderline clients do not usually show such features as perplexity, concreteness, perceptual failure, constriction, oversimplification, or psychomotor retardation.

The most likely elevation of the borderline's profile on the MCMI is elevation on scale C. These individuals are subject to most of the clinical-symptoms syndromes at some time or another, so periodic and variable elevations on A, H, N, and D are to be expected. Elevations on scale 8 may be present, in that the moodiness and behavioral unpredictability that characterize the passive-aggressive are often present in a more extreme form in the borderline. Those with high scores on 3, 4, and 7 and/or 8 are at risk with respect to this pattern in that these types are more prone to borderline functioning as they deteriorate.

On the performance subtests of the WAIS-R, in particular object assembly and block design, the increasing difficulty of the tasks often elicits haphazard trial-and-error efforts that are laced with noticeable displays of frustration and impatience. Their inclination to resort to arbitrary solutions is often evident in the arithmetic subtest, especially when these clients are requested to reveal the manner by which they came to the incorrect response. Requests as to how they arrived at their response on other subtests can often be similarly useful. On the Rorschach, illogical and fabulized combinations occur, though when actual contaminations occur, it more likely bodes a schizophrenic disorder (Swiercinsky, 1985).

□   TREATMENT OPTIONS

This category is truly a polyglot syndrome and will therefore require equally variable treatment responses. The impulsivity demonstrated in this disorder suggests that the reader should refer to comments regarding the antisocial personality disorder, as well as those regarding substance abuse or possibly one of the sexual deviations. The comments on the antisocial personality regarding stimulation seeking are also particularly relevant, since boredom is common in the borderline personality. Schizotypal and histrionic components are also typical and require the treatment responses noted in those catergories (Widiger et al., 1986). Since there is usually some disordered autonomic-emotional functioning, biofeedback and relaxation training may be appropriate. If there are a number of neurological soft signs, treatment will have to take probable CNS involvement (see Chapter 14) into account (Gardner et al., 1987). Group therapy can be helpful if the person will allow the development of trust in the group, but such clients are often unwilling to share the attention of the therapist and are so emotionally unpredictable that they are difficult to work with. They can exert such a high cost on the progress of the group that they make it unwise to include them.

■   Identity Disorder (313.82)

The identity disorder has occasionally been related to the borderline personality disorder, yet they are not highly similar (Widiger et al., 1986). To diagnose an identity disorder, the DMS-III-R requires evidence of disturbance for at least three months, impairment in social or occupational functioning, and uncertainty about identity in three of the following areas: career choice, sexual patterns, friendship choices and behavior, moral values, religious identification, peer group loyalties, and long-term goals. This disorder naturally occurs most commonly in late adolescence, when people are forced by society to make choices and face changes in these areas. Most people who face these choices experience some distress; a clinical diagnosis is indicated when this distress persists and is so severe that it results in significant disruption of coping with life challenges (Clum, 1989).

☐   DIAGNOSTIC CONSIDERATIONS

The depression and anxiety consistently found in this syndrome predict elevations on MMPI scales 2 and 7, and there is some elevation on scale 8, reflecting a sense of alienation and isolation from others with a consequent feeling of self-doubt. Scores on scale 5 are usually at either extreme, depending on which way the person's identification is swinging. People of higher intelligence and socioeconomic status tend to move to the upper extreme of scale 5, particularly males. Where this disorder has resulted in impulsive behaviors and/or feelings of alienation from others, elevations on scales 4 and 6 are probable. The F scale is typically elevated a bit in adolescents anyway, so it is particularly likely to be so here (Gallucci, 1987).

As a reflection of high anxiety, Q_4 is typically elevated on the 16 PF, and the concern about values is manifested in a high O and F, as well as a low Q_2. There is a degree of guilt, which differentiates this pattern from that of a psychopathic personality, and this is seen in the elevations on G and O.

High scores on scales A and/or D of the MCMI would be expected; anxiety may also be represented by high scores on H, N, B and T. The aliented quality experienced by these persons may be reflected in moderate elevation on 1 or 2.

Performance on the WAIS-R is similar to that of the depersonalization disorder and the anxiety and depressive disorders. The thrust of the person's identify disorder will determine the patterns here. The most probable marker of an identity disorder on the WAIS-R is the comparison of obtained IQ scores to academic or work achievements, as it is likely that the IQ score will be above the level of achievement.

The depression and anxiety usually evident in an identity disorder are reflected in the standard Rorschach patterns for this disorder. The responses are usually filled with figures that are more passive and inadequate than normal, and occasionally there is an allusion to young humans or animals, which suggests an attempt to hold on to an earlier period of a more integrated identity. If the identity disorder is focused on the sexual area, responses similar to those noted in ego-dystonic homosexuality can be expected.

☐   TREATMENT OPTIONS

Therapies that are effective here are similar to those usually applied to the depersonalization disorder and to some of the more neurotic disorders. In some of these clients, a low dose of antidepressants—e.g., 25–50 mg of imipramine or its equivalent—may be of signficant help.

The client-centered therapy of Carl Rogers is especially appropriate, since he initially developed this while working with young ministerial and graduate psychology students who were going through various identity conflicts.

If the client has moved too far in avoidance of choices, the reality therapy of William Glasser may be more appropriate. An existential perspective is important in whatever therapy takes place. Clients need to face the choices that they are avoiding and to envision and accept the consequences. An adolescent therapy or support group is often useful here because it gives such clients awareness that others are moving through the same choices and it provides feedback about new choices and initiatives (Brigham, 1988).

■   Avoidant Personality Disorder (301.82)

These individuals are shy and inhibited interpersonally, yet at the same time desire to have interpersonal relationships, which distinguishes them from those with the schizotypal or schizoid personality disorders. They also do not show the degree of irritability and emotional instability seen in the borderline personality disorder.

A major feature of this chronic disorder is an unwillingness to tolerate risks in deepening interpersonal relationships (Millon, 1981). These persons are extremely sensitive to rejection and seem to need a guarantee ahead of time that a relationship will work out. Naturally, such guarantees are seldom available in healthy relationships. Thus, the friends they manage to make often show a degree of instability or are quite passive.

In many ways, this disorder is close to the anxiety disorders, since there is a degree of anxiety and distress, and low self-esteem is common (Eysenck, 1985). However, the behaviors that produce the distress are relatively ego-syntonic. Their depression and anxiety are more related to the perceived rejection and criticism of others.

This common disorder is seem more often in women. Any disorder in childhood that focuses on shyness predisposes one to the avoidant personality disorder.

☐   DSM-III-R

To diagnose an avoidant personality disorder, the clinician must observe the following as consistent and chronic behaviors: a persistent pattern of timidity, social discomfort, and fear of rejection, beginning by early adulthood, and at least four of the following: (1) an unwillingness to be involved with people unless sure of acceptance, (2) no confidants or close friends (except first-degree relatives), (3) avoidance of occupational or social activities high in social contact, (4) reticence in social situations, (5) embarrassment easily shown by anxiety or blushing, (6) exaggeration of risks and strong need for routine, or (7) strong fear and sensitivity to criticism or rejection. If they are under age eighteen, the appropriate diagnosis would be Avoidant Disorder of Childhood or Adolescence (313.21).

☐   MMPI

A 2-7/7-2 profile is common, reflecting depression about assumed rejection and apprehension and self-doubt about the ability to deal with others. To the degree that this has resulted in social withdrawal, a high score on scale 0 is expected, as well as a moderate decrease on scale 9. Since this disorder often appears in females who are strongly identified with the traditional feminine role, a low score on scale 5 occurs. If the individual still has energy that is being channeled into anger, a 3-4 profile can be expected, with allied mild elevations on 2, 7, and 6. Indeed, a 6-7/7-6 profile is indicative of this disorder (Graham, 1987). If functioning is beginning to go to pieces as a result of the rejection and social withdrawal, an elevation on scale 8 occurs.

☐   16 PF

Low scores on scales E, C, and H are consistent with this syndrome, reflecting shyness, threat sensitivity, passivity, and emotional upset. High scores on Q_4 and O are evidence of the expected tension and insecurity, and a moderately high score on I reflects fear of rejection and sensitivity. Social clumsiness is balanced by a hyperalertness in social situations, hence particularly deviant scores on N are not too common. The self-perception by avoidant personalities that they should automatically be accepted interpersonally results in a higher than average A score. However, actual experience, of which they are somewhat aware, keeps this from being extremely high and may even temper it to average or below in some profiles. These people tend to be moderately low on Q_3 and M, though this is highly variable. The L score, usually low, will depend on whether they have begun to channel their rejection into anger and suspiciousness of others.

☐   OTHER TEST-RESPONSE PATTERNS

To the degree avoidant personalities feel accepted by the examiner, they do better on the verbal subscales of the WAIS-R than on the performance subscales. Since they are often females with strong traditional role identities, low scores on arithmetic are common. Dependency may be reflected in some of the content of the comprehension items, as well as in the picture arrangement subtest, which is low in introverted clients. Blocked or relatively inactive M responses on the Rorschach are common. A high number of popular responses occur, and content may focus on more-passive animals, such as rabbits and deer (occasionally being hurt or killed), or on passive interactions in the M responses.

The most prominent characteristic on the MCMI is an elevation of 85 or higher on scale 2, with depressed scores on scales 4 and 7. Generalized anxiety, a common symptom in this pattern, is evidenced by elevation on A. The ego-dystonic detached style of the avoidant personality causes elevation on D. Moderate elevations (75–85) may occur on scales 8 and C, in that characteristics of these disorders are likely to occur concurrently. The higher the elevation on S, the more decompensation has occurred.

☐   TREATMENT OPTIONS

Training in social skills is critical here (Cappe and Alden, 1986). Also, the need for assertiveness training is often as great in this disorder as it is in the dependent personality (see the following subsection for suggestions equally applicable here). In addition, since the avoidant personality is more concerned with the risk in relationships, existential and confrontive therapy approaches are useful adjuncts. Rational-emotive therapy (Ellis and Dryden, 1987) is especially useful because it was worked out on a population that had these kinds of concerns. Since the Adlerian therapies focus on issues of inferiority, there may be special applicability here. Also, since there is a neuroticlike component to this pattern (Eysenck, 1985), paradoxical-intention approaches may be useful. Avoidant personalities may elicit "protective responses" within a group therapy setting, but an unwillingness to self-disclose may eventually lead to rejection by the group.

Another helpful treatment for dependent and avoidant personality disorders is covert negative reinforcement; this technique is most useful when the client cannot easily envision the desired behavior and would not be highly responsive to covert positive reinforcement. In covert negative reinforcement, the client imagines a highly aversive event and then imagines this event is terminated by the performance of a new set of desired behaviors. It is critical that there be as little time lapse as possible during the switch-over in images.

■   ## Dependent Personality Disorder (301.60)

People with the dependent personality disorder have a pervasive need to cling to stronger personalities who are allowed to make a wide range of decisions for them. They are naive and show little initiative. There is some suspiciousness of possible rejection, but not to the degree found in the avoidant personality disorder.

In one way, dependent personality disorders can be seen as successful avoidant personality disorders. They have achieved a style that elicits the desired relationships, though at the cost of any consistent expression of their own personality. They show elements of agoraphobia, not crystallized, and they lack any real self-confidence (Morey et al., 1988).

Since this is an exaggeration of the traditional feminine role, it is not surprising that it is far more common in women (Kernberg, 1984). If the individual is not in a dependent relationship, anxiety and upset are common. Even if enmeshed in a dependent relationship, there is still residual anxiety over the possibility of being abandoned.

☐   DSM-III-R

To make a formal diagnosis of dependent personality disorder, five of the following should be noted with some regularity over a significant period of time: (1) unable to make everyday decisons alone, (2) allows others to make most decisions, (3) overly agreeable, (4) lacks initiative, (5) volunteers in order to gain approval, (6) uncomfortable or helpless when alone, (7) devastated by losses, (8) preoccupied with abandonment, or (9) easily hurt by criticism.

☐   MMPI

The 2-7/7-2 profile is characteristic of an individual who is experiencing anxiety and depression, who is passive-dependent and docile, and who presents a picture of severe dependency. A high 3 scale and a mildly elevated K scale are common. Naiveté and passivity are reflected in a surprisingly elevated L scale, but the F scale is usually in the average range.

The acceptance of the stereotypical feminine role shows up on a low scale 5, and the lack of resistance to coercion from authority is reflected in a low 4 scale. There is a subgroup of dependent personalities who are a bit more aggressive and manipulative, and they tend to show the 2-4/4-2 profile (Anderson and Bauer, 1985). Scale 9 is also low, reflecting passivity and lack of initiative. Scale 0 tends to be elevated, although this is variable, depending on emerging concern about their own behavior and their sense of comfort about the permanence of their dependency relationships. If anger is beginning to develop as a result of any consistent rejection of the dependency, some elevation on scale 6 occurs. Otherwise, this is rare.

In young men, an interesting and rather rare profile, the 1-9/9-1 type, with both T scores greater than 70, has been found to indicate passivity and dependency. However, there is a hostile component directed toward females that is associated with this profile, so the dependency relationship would probably be directed toward males. Thus, one would look to the 5 scale for elaboration on the issue of sexual identity and possible preference.

☐   16 PF

The dependent personality disorder should result in scores quite low on the classic 16 PF dependency factors: scales E, L, M, Q_1, and Q_2 (Karson and O'Dell, 1976, p. 90). In addition, the I score should be high in females. In males, moderately low scores on Q_4 may be noted and A is high.

There are probably low scores on Q_3 and N and a high score on O. Surprisingly, there is not a particularly low H score—it may even be above average.

It is also noteworthy that a low score on L is not consistently found in this disorder, which may reflect not only a high threshold for jealousy but also the unconscious anger alleged to be a result of the submergence of one's personality to another.

☐   OTHER TEST-RESPONSE PATTERNS

A high score on scale 3 of the MCMI would be expected, along with an elevation on A when any insecurity about having placed their welfare in the hands of others occurs. Dependents often adopt physical problems to further the pattern of requiring help and care, resulting in an elevation on H. An elevated D may appear during periods when the individual is not getting needed nurturance and security. Because elements of the avoidant and histrionic personality disorders are often present, elevations on scales 2 and 4 may occur.

On the WAIS-R, the performance scale score may be higher, although this is not as consistent as in some of the other personality disorders. Arithmetic and information seem to be consistently low, relative to other scores, reflecting a withdrawal from a problem-solving approach to the world. Within the performance subtests, lower scores on object assembly occur and odd responses indicating a need for support are occasionally found in picture completion.

A constricted use of space is a common feature in the drawing of the Bender-Gestalt figures.

The Rorschach record is highly reflective of the attitude of the examiner. If the dependent personalities feel accepted in the testing situation and believe that the examiner desires a high number of responses, they will produce an extensive record. Otherwise, a record with a less than average number of responses can be expected. As with the avoidant personality, passive animal and passive M responses are found, as well as a high number of popular responses. There is also a tendency toward use of color rather than form in determining responses, relative to other personality disorders, and there is a likelihood of perceiving small-detail responses.

☐   TREATMENT OPTIONS

Assertiveness training is a standard feature in the treatment of the dependent personality disorder. It may need to be preceded by methods that help clients gain a greater awareness and articulation of their dependency, via consensual feedback from a group, from catharsis, or from other consciousness-raising techniques (Higginbotham et al., 1988).

In the response acquisition stage of assertiveness training, modeling is carried out with audio- or videotaped demonstrations by same-status, -age, and -sex models. Covert modeling is particularly helpful where persons are trying to develop a whole new behavior style. Clients imagine another person performing the assertive behaviors that they wish to have in their repertoire. After response acquisition, there is response reproduction, in which behavior rehearsal, role playing, and even directed practice are useful. After this, response consolidation is effected through clear feedback, again possibly using audio- or videotape. Changes are crystallized into the ongoing personality through cognitive self-reinforcement and by requests and contracting for increasingly widening the range and targets of the assertive behavioral responses. Since this disorder often occurs in the context of family or marital difficulties, attention will have to be paid to the partner, who may view any change as threatening.

■ Obsessive-Compulsive Personality Disorder (301.40)

This disorder is occasionally confused with the obsessive-compulsive disorder, but there are significant differences between the two syndromes (De Silva, 1987). First, the obsessive-compulsive personality seldom becomes obsessed about issues. Second, the term "obesssive-compulsive" here refers to a life-style in which obsessive-compulsive features are pervasive and chronic; it does not refer to a specific behavior. Third, the obsessive-compulsive life-style is ego-syntonic, and for the most part, persons only come to treatment when coerced in some fashion.

Obsessive-compulsive personalities are preoccupied with rules and duties, are unable to express warmth and caring except in limited situations, are highly oriented toward a life-style marked by productivity and efficiency, are temperamentally and emotionally insensitive, and are generally distant from other individuals (Rutter, 1987). They can be described as workaholics without warmth. One associate of the author commented that this is the type of person who can obtain a complete physical exam from a proctologist.

It is true that a degree of compulsivity is effective, particularly in our society. It becomes a problem when it overwhelms the rest of the personality. Paradoxically, obsessive-compulsives are often indecisive and poor planners of their time, a result of their narrow focus and concern with precision, even when precision may be irrelevant. They are inclined to be excessively moralistic, litigious, and hyperalert to criticism and perceived slights from others (Kernberg, 1984).

☐   DSM-III-R

To diagnose an obsessive-compulsive personality disorder, the DSM-III-R requires a clear pattern of rigidity and perfectionism, as indicated by at least five of the following: (1) overemphasis on details, to the exclusion of an overall perspective (they see the trees rather than the forest, and not even all of the trees); (2) perfectionism that interferes with tasks; (3) constriction of affection and emotionality; (4) excessive devotion to vocation and productivity; (5) need for dominance in personal relationships; (6) indecisiveness; (7) hoarding behavior (even where there is no sentimental value); (8) lack of personal generosity where no personal gain accrues; (9) overconscientiousness or inflexibility in matters of ethics or morality.

☐   MMPI

Obsessive-compulsives attain a moderately high K scale and seldom have highly elevated MMPI profiles because they are not inclined toward self-disclosure. They often attain elevations on scales 3 and 1, the latter particularly so if physical complaints have become a focus for their distress. They find it more comfortable to see themselves as having a physical rather than a psychological disturbance. The 9 scale is also elevated; in large part, this elevation reflects how autocratic and dominant the individual is in personal relationships. Litigiousness and developing paranoid concerns are reflected on scale 6. A moderately high 7 score may occur if there is a querulous and complaining attitude, though scale 7 usually reflects obsessionalism rather than compulsive factors.

☐   16 PF

Obsessive-compulsives also present a reasonably normal profile here. It is recommended that if there is a suspicion of compulsivity, the protocol should be scored for faking-good. Since there is denial of anxiety, Q_4 is low, and the need for control of intrapsychic processes leads to a high Q_3. Isolation from other people results in a high Q_2 score, and the rigidity and possibly developing paranoia lead to a high L score. Scale A is also lowered for the same reasons. Scores are not particularly low on C or high on O. They tend to be high on E, the degree depending on the orientation toward dominance in interpersonal relationships. Scores are moderately high on G or N and moderately low on I and F. Since the coping system of obsessive-compulsives results in better academic performance and intellectual achievements, they attain one of the higher scale B scores.

☐   OTHER TEST-REPSONSE PATTERNS

On the MCMI, a high score on scale 7 is expected. Elevation on A is rare, as anxieties are usually controlled. Occasionally, anxieties are expressed as psychosomatic or physical complaints, represented by elevation on H. Characteristics of the dependent or paranoid personalities may be present, causing elevations on scales 3 or P, respectively.

As a result of an emphasis on achievement and productivity, persons with an obsessive-compulsive personality disorder score at least in the average range—usually above—on the WAIS-R. They will give overly precise and detailed answers, which helps on comprehension and similarities. But in tests based on speed, such as digit symbol, block design, object assembly, and picture arrangement, the same traits can lower the scores. Their interpersonal and problem-solving rigidity causes difficulties with the more complex puzzles in picture arrangement. Generally, they attain a higher verbal IQ than performance IQ.

On the Bender-Gestalt test, they are inclined to count the dots or small circles in the cards and also may orient all the figures in a precise arrangement.

On the Rorschach, there is an emphasis on Dd and D responses, with a high F+% and fewer W and color-based responses. Some responses are described in overly specific detail, and they make criticisms of the blots. Relative to those with the other personality disorders, they provide a high number of responses overall. TAT stories are often lengthy, with varied themes offered. Occasionally, the primary theme is lost in a focus on details.

☐   TREATMENT OPTIONS

Cautela and Wall (1980) suggest the use of covert-conditioning procedures to counteract the compulsivity; in particular, they recommend the use of the covert-sensitization technique. This technique involves the imagination of a highly aversive event or contingency immediately after developing the imagery of the undesired behavior—in this case, the compulsive pattern to be eliminated. The technique is effective not only for this pattern but for a number of the habit disorders.

In paradoxical intention, clients are simply instructed to do the very act they have been resisting (Seltzer, 1986). As this proceeds, clients are told, by a number of apparently absurd instructions, to vary the circumstances and quantity of the behavior produced. As this occurs over time, they develop a greater sense of control over the behavior and may then choose to give it up. Group therapy is a helpful follow-up because these clients are likely to regress into their cold and distancing compulsive behaviors if the changes are not thoroughly incorporated into their life-style for some length of time. However, the group can be impatient with the judgmental behaviors and condescension of this type of client.

■ ## Passive-Aggressive Personality Disorder (301.84)

The essential behavior pattern in the passive-aggressive personality disorder is indirectly expressed resistance to social and occupational performance expectations that results in chronic ineffectiveness. The core disorder is hostility that is not directly expressed, so "double messages" to others result (Morey et al., 1988). The underlying hostility affects significant others, yet the passive-aggressive denies, often as if insulted, any aggressive or hostile motivation. The actual behavior expressed may be either passive or aggressive, but physical aggression seldom occurs.

Most parents have had the experience of a child pushing them to the limit of their control and then backing off. Like that child, the passive-aggressive becomes acutely sensitive to such limits and is consistently able to go so far but no further (Barkley, 1987). When this pattern becomes an integral part of a social and vocational life-style, a passive-aggressive personality disorder exists. Although these patterns are commonly modeled and learned in childhood, such a family usually reaches a state of mutual détente. The pattern then causes severe problems when it is transferred into any new intimate, consistent contact relationship, such as marriage.

The passive-aggressive personality disorder takes the standards and the belief system of significant others and turns them around to immobilize the others effectively. The strategy (which is not thought to be a conscious behavior) is to present the "enemy" (often a person depended on) with a choice that forces one either to capitulate or to violate an individual belief system. That person is thus immobilized, with no adequate reason to justify retaliation.

☐ ### DSM-III-R

Since the authors of DSM-III-R were initially concerned about the rationale for continuing this diagnostic category, surprising in light of the consistent use it receives, they emphasize that it is only used when behavior does not first meet the criteria for other personality disorders. To warrant the diagnosis, there has to be evidence in social or vocational areas that there has been indirect resistance to performance demands resulting in chronic problems in these areas. At least five of the following behaviors are required to substantiate this resistance: (1) dawdling; (2) sulkiness, irritability, or argumentativeness when asked to do something he or she does not want to do; (3) procrastination; (4) purposeful inefficiency; (5) convenient forgetfulness; (6) unjustified protests that others are unreasonably demanding; (7) resentment of productive suggestions from others; (8) unreasonable criticism or scorn of authority figures; or (9) belief that he/she is doing a much better job than others think. If the client is under the age of eighteen, the appropriate diagnosis would usually be oppositional defiant disorder.

☐   MMPI

The 3-4/4-3 combination is commonly seen in the passive-aggressive personality disorder (Graham, 1987). Where scale 3 is greater than 4 and both scales are relatively high, the individual is oriented toward the passive mode. When scale 4 is higher than 3, accompanied by a moderate to high elevation on scale 6, the aggressive mode is predominate. If both scales 3 and 4 are high together, there is a tendency toward dissociative responses (Lachar, 1974).

Elevation on scale K is also probable since passive-aggressives will downplay their faults and show a lack of insight about intrapsychic dynamics. An avoidance of responsibility, possibly through somatic complaints, produces mild to moderate elevations on scales 1 and 7. Scale 9 is average to low in this pattern, except when hostility is a counterphobic defense against dependency, when the rare 3-9 profile may be given. Also, when a man is being seen as a result of his wife's complaint of marital problems, a spike 9 profile has been found to be indicative of passive-aggressive functioning (King and Kelley, 1977). Graham (1987) also notes that a 1-2/2-1 profile may be indicative of this disorder.

The passive-aggressive personality who is closest to actual loss of control of aggression shows a 4-6/6-4 profile, with high F and 8 scales, as well as a low scale 2 score. Persons with this profile have much cross-sex hostility. If the scores here are very high, consider an emerging paranoid schizophrenic adjustment.

☐   16 PF

The 16 PF profile of the passive-aggressive personality disorder is generally not remarkable. The E score fluctuates, depending on whether the passive (low E score) or aggressive mode is operative. The apparent dependency of many passive-aggressives would suggest a low Q_2 score. However, this is balanced by underlying hostility and resistance, which raises the score into the average range and occasionally to an above-average score. Passive-aggressives are usually moderately low on G, though not markedly low on C. The interpersonal manipulation inherent in this pattern results in a high N score and at least an average L score. The L and H scores are higher in the aggressive mode, with the I score being lower.

☐   OTHER TEST-RESPONSE PATTERNS

An MCMI scale 8 score of 85 or higher suggests a passive-aggressive personality disorder. During stressful periods, elevations on A and D are likely to occur. Psychosomatic complaints may occur, causing a raised H score. Moderate to high elevations on scales 4 and especially C are possible since these disorders occur relatively frequently in conjunction with 8.

Golden (1979) found passive-aggressive individuals to be high on the comprehension scale of the WAIS; but in general, the performance scale score is slightly higher than the verbal scale score. They do well on visual-motor tasks, such as digit symbol, block design, and object assembly. They also do well on digit span but are only average on arithmetic. Elaboration of responses on picture arrangement and comprehension may cue the passive-aggressive orientation.

On the Rorschach, a high percentage of FC and space responses are noted, as well as a relatively high number of texture and popular responses. Occasional odd combinations of aggresssive and passive content may occur, such as children and guns, or there may be rather arbitrary assignments of color or content to a space (Wagner and Wagner, 1981). Passive-aggressive personalities may produce responses that directly suggest their pattern of relating, such as people passively manipulating others or arguing or animals sneaking around.

Many authors have asserted that the use of white space suggests the negativistic tendencies that are characteristic of a passive-aggressive personality. An aggressive-content response, such as bombs, fire, scissors, or volcanoes, is more likely to be evident in the passive-aggressive personality who is inclinded to actually threaten aggression on occasion. Phillips and Smith (1953) assert that a rough-texture response is also characteristic of this pattern.

☐ TREATMENT OPTIONS

The critical task for the clinician treating a passive-aggressive personality disorder is to set up feedback situations so that the person can no longer effect their interpersonally controlling patterns and yet cannot deny their existence (Teyber, 1988). Some form of family or marital therapy is often indicated.

Also, any form of effective data presentation about personality patterns is helpful, especially if it can be stored for future use (Cattell, 1986). For that reason, audio- or videotapes of different sessions are useful in confronting passive-aggressives with their patterns. Consensual feedback from a group is also useful in overcoming avoidance mechanisms, though some passive-aggressives may be too sophisticated for some groups and, as a result, will absorb too much of the therapist's psychic energy. Since inadequacies are often at the core of this pattern, assertiveness training may be appropriate. If anger is the focus, it is still helpful, but it may need to be embellished with methods that focus on catharsis.

■ **Oppositional-Defiant Disorder (313.81)**

The oppositional-defiant disorder is commonly considered to be a precursor to the passive-aggressive disorder. Many of the same behaviors are noted, although there is a more direct expression of hostility and negativism in the oppositional-defiant disorder. The DMS-III-R requires that the pattern last for at least six months and that there be evidence of at least five of the following symptoms: (1) defies adult rules or requests, (2) argues with adults, (3) swears or uses obscene language, (4) deliberately irritates others, (5) projects blame on others, (6) has temper outbursts, (7) is easily irritable, (8) easily angers, or (9) is spiteful or vindictive. DMS-III-R also requires that there be no evidence that the behavior goes so far as to violate or aggress against the rights of another, such as is found in the conduct disorder. It is subcategorized into mild (a few symptoms), moderate, or severe. This behavior is typically carried out toward significant others, such as teachers and parents, and it may persist into various self-destructive social interactions. Such children and adolescents show a degree of conformity and usually resist any interpretation that they are oppositional, just as passive-aggressives do (Barkely, 1987).

☐   DIAGNOSTIC CONSIDERATIONS

In general, the diagnostic considerations here are analogous to those in a passive-aggressive personality. There are some differences, however, since aggression may be more overtly expressed, rebelliousness is more commonly a factor, and the client is younger. As a result, scales 4 and 6 on the MMPI are more likely to be high. On the 16 PF, scale E would typically be somewhat higher, reflecting stubborn aggressiveness, and G would be quite low, reflecting rebelliousness. Since the oppositional-defiant individual is likely to be more naive socially, N would be lower than in the passive-aggressive personality, and Q_1 and Q_2 would probably be a big higher. A more overt antiestablishment attitude is probable, so persons would be more resistant to taking the tests. An MCMI profile similar to that of the passive-aggressive is likely, with some elements of scale 6 present, as minor acting-out is more likely to be present here. On the the Rorschach, more pure C and fewer popular responses can be expected than in the passive-aggressive personality disorder. They express both avoidance and negativism on both the Rorschach and TAT (Quevillon et al., 1986).

☐   TREATMENT OPTIONS

Treatment is similar in many respects to that for the passive-aggressive personality disorder. Considerations expressed in the section on the paranoid disorders regarding the development of trust are also relevant here. Since the oppositional-defiant disorder is often evidence of a family disorder, family therapy should be considered.

■   ## Sadistic Personality Disorder

As noted in the Introduction, the term "sadistic personality disorder" does not officially appear in the DSM-III-R, though it is made available in an Appendix as an optional diagnosis for clinicians to add when they find it helpful. In any case, the concept has a long history (Kernberg, 1984). He terms the sadistic personality the "malignant narcissistic" and places it between the antisocial and the narcissistic personalities on this continuum. The personality might also be thought of as an antisocial pattern, though with better socialization and a more prominent quality of revenge.

To make this diagnosis, the DSM-III-R requires that a pervasive pattern of cruel, aggressive, and demeaning behavior, starting at least by early childhood, be established by the repeated occurrence of at least four of the following: (1) uses violence or cruelty to establish a dominance relationship, (2) demeans or humiliates people in the presence of others, (3) takes pleasure in physical or psychological suffering of other humans or animals, (4) has, with unusual harshness, disciplined someone under his or her control, (5) has lied with the goal of inflicting pain or harm, (6) uses intimidation, or even terror, to get others to do what he or she wants, (7) restricts the autonomy of someone with whom he or she has a close relationship, or (8) is fascinated by weapons, martial arts, injury, torture, or violence in general.

The dominant trend is a love of cruelty and an absence of remorse (Kernberg, 1984; Weinberg, 1984). Extreme cases are described in the literature including the torture and murder of innocent victims with knives, garroting, or flagellation. The motive for these actions is described as an irresistible urge, the fulfillment of which produces strong satisfaction for the sadist. The sadist is most often male and his behavior is described as being both coercive and yet seductive, frequently promising children amusement, candy, or gifts and attracting women by posing in some fashion, e.g., as a scout for a modeling agency.

There is a noteworthy distinction between sadism, which is a paraphilia and thus appears on axis I of a DSM-III-R diagnosis, and the sadistic personality disorder, which is an axis-II diagnosis. While sadistic sexual patterns are common in the sadistic personality disorder, it is not a necessary part of the pattern. In essense, the sadistic personality disorder is marked by a very assertive life-style based on power motives, commonly accompanied by gender dominance, the inflicting of pain for pleasure, and extreme aggression with or without sexual motivation. Yet, the sadistic behavior is well rationalized, and the individual may even present a very self-righteous air. Two childhood patterns of behavior are often noted (Kernberg, 1984; Weinberg, 1984; Magnusson, 1988). One is similar to that of the antisocial personality, that is, inordinate lying, gross disrespect for authority, impulsive anger, temper tantrums, and excessive truancy. The other involves a shy, introverted child who shows few or only subtle early signs of aggression, with sadism later used as a method for covering feelings of inferiority.

☐   MMPI

The primary elevation in the sadistic personality disorder is commonly on scale 4, reflecting the aggressive hostility, interpersonal exploitiveness, and lack of respect for social norms found in such individuals (Morey et al., 1988). Scale 6 should be at least moderately elevated, reflecting the paranoia mentioned earlier. Scale 3 may also be elevated due to the narcissistic elements of the disorder. Scale 9 is often above average, though not usually as high as in the antisocial personality. The 9-3 or 9-4 profile, which is found in the narcissistic and aggressively competitive person who inflates his or her self-esteem by the devaluation of others, would apply here. This pattern of sadistic behavior is occasionally found in athletes, who may receive significant reinforcement for such attitudes.

Scale K is commonly higher than F. Low scores should be expected on scales 2, 0, and 7 because these individuals are generally socially adept, if somewhat superficial, and because the sadistic behaviors and attitudes are typically ego-syntonic. In males, scale 5 is usually low, just as this scale is generally low in narcissistic and antisocial individuals. As noted earlier in this book, a punitive or interpersonally destructive person who goes about in the guise of a helpful role often shows elevations on 4 and 8 and could fit this pattern.

☐   16 PF

Sadistic personalities should score quite high on E, reflecting their aggressive dominance, on N because of their manipulativeness, and on H because of their usual interpersonal boldness (Golden, 1979). Scales A and F should also be moderately high, reflecting the extroversion and level of socialization that would be high, yet usually not so clearly pronounced as in the narcissistic individual. The lack of respect for social norms is usually reflected in a low score on G and a high score on Q_1. The lack of remorse and guilt and the inflated self-esteem of such individuals should show up in higher scores on C and Q_3 and lower scores on I, O, and Q_4. L should be at least moderately high, reflecting the lack of trust of the world in general.

☐   MCMI

On the MCMI, persons with sadistic personality disorder are most likely to score high on scale 6, antisocial (aggressive), and on scale 5, narcissistic, because of the similarities they share with these patterns. A high score on scale P, paranoid, is also likely. Drug and alcohol abuse are frequent complications of this pattern, so there should be elevations in scales B and T as well. Low scores should occur scales 3, dependent; 7, compulsive (conforming); A, anxiety; and D, dysthymia. These scales reflect anxiety and a low sense of self-efficacy and self-esteem, seldom the problem for a sadistic personality. Scale H, hypomania, is elevated in some sadistic individuals, though usually not to the extent that one would find with antisocial persons.

□   ## OTHER TEST-RESPONSE PATTERNS

Sadistic personalities usually give constricted and guarded responses to the Rorschach. Like antisocial and narcissistic individuals, F+% can be expected to be low, but not quite as low as the antisocial because of often greater sophistication and integration (though a distorted form) of the personality (Hare, 1986). The number of W responses is indicative of the grandiose rationalizations and sense of entitlement (Exner, 1986). M should be low, as it is the case with the antisocial personality. But when it *is* present, it is likely to be active and, quite frequently, aggressive. Animal and popular responses should be common as well, reflecting guardedness. An analysis of the content of responses may show some ostentatious and flamboyant responses, reflecting grandiosity.

Responses to the TAT are not likely to manifest much overtly aggressive content in more socialized and sophisticated subjects. Since many sadistic personalities rationalize their behavior, they are often quite frank about their violent proclivities. Many statements they make will be interpreted by others as jokes when they are actually quite earnest. Some of this ideation may appear in responses to the TAT. Sexually aggressive stories would not be surprising in many of the cards representing male-female interactions, and perhaps in other cards, depending on the sexual orientation of the sadist or the degree to which he reduces others to external objects (Kernberg, 1984). Intimidation through shocking stories would not be surprising in such persons. The sadist is likely to denigrate the task here, as well as in other projective tests. Answers are also likely to be short and constricted, reflecting the more suspicious orientation of some of these individuals, especially if they feel unable to gain a sense of control over the task.

Many of the comments regarding the Rorschach and the TAT apply as well to the production of drawings. The sadistic personality will either try to shock the clinician with an overtly grotesque drawing or will draw overly simple pictures to avoid disclosure of any intrapsychic contents. In either case, the sadistic personality is likely to approach the task with contempt. The human figure he identifies with is likely to be complete and to seem powerful and confident, reflecting the feelings of superiority. When he draws others, they are likely to be smaller and less detailed and to have a generally inferior aspect about them. Drawings of trees and houses are also likely to be large, powerful, and indicative of a well-defended self.

☐   TREATMENT OPTIONS

As with any disorder of personality, and especially with a sadistic personality disorder, the problem is to bring the client into therapy in the first place and then to get him to participate in a meaningful way (Quay, 1987). In addition, his behavior and threats of violence represent a significant danger to the clinician and others. Direct financial or other exploitation is to be expected. As one clinician facetiously (I think) commented, "This is the type of client you refer to a colleague you never liked."

Kernberg (1984) offers some helpful suggestions: Eliminate possibilities of harm to the client or therapist, establish honesty, confront the inability of the client to depend on the therapist, confront the client's desire to destroy the therapist because he or she represents an autonomous nurturing person and generates resentment. Any confrontations should be calculated to cause the sadistic personality to project dishonesty and attempts at sadistic control onto the therapist, a process Kernberg calls "paranoid regression in transference". Yet there is an emphasis on maintaining a consistent affirmation of reality. When the syndrome is accompanied by a paraphilia or a disorder of impulse control, behavior therapies could prove helpful. Risky and/or competitive sports or strenuous physical activity can be useful as socially acceptable outlets for the client's aggressive impulses (Zuckerman et al., 1980). Marital counseling is in order when the individual is involved in a long-term dominance-submission relationship. Overall, a strong emphasis on the concrete consequences of destructive behaviors is important, and though long-term therapy is almost always required, it is not often effective.

Self-Defeating Personality Disorder

Self-defeating behaviors can be defined as any behavior one employs to achieve a desired consequence or goal that paradoxically inhibits the attainment of that desired goal. Self-defeating behaviors can be observed in all persons to some degree (Magnusson, 1988). Such behaviors may be recognized by the person even though they are continued. In other cases, the individual may be unaware that her actions are self-defeating, similar to the "oppositional" child who may long for closeness with her parents but distances herself through hostile and rebellious behaviors. In all instances, self-defeating behaviors are dysfunctional and bring dissatisfaction and discomfort to the individual. These behaviors are paradoxical in that they are at one and the same time self-perpetuating and self-defeating—thus, the traditional term "neurotic paradox" (Kernberg, 1984). Indeed, the self-defeating personality disorder seems as much akin to some of the more "neurotic" diagnoses as it does to the personality disorder diagnoses. However, it is likely to be listed as a personality disorder, if and when it is officially included in a future DSM.

In order to diagnose a self-defeating personality disorder, the DSM-III-R requires a pervasive pattern of self-defeating behaviors, starting at least by early adulthood, manifested in a variety of contexts, and indicated by at least five of the following: (1) chooses situations and/or people, even when better options are evident and available, that lead to disappointment, failure, or mistreatment, (2) rejects or subverts the efforts of others to help him or her, (3) responds with guilt, depression, and/or pain-producing behavior (e.g., accident-proneness) to positive personal events, (4) incites rejecting or angry responses from others, then feels devastated, (5) rejects opportunities for pleasure or has difficulty acknowledging that he or she is enjoying him- or herself, (6) subverts or fails to accomplish tasks critical to personal objectives, (7) engages in excessive self-sacrifice that is unsolicited by the intended recipient, or (8) rejects or is uninterested in people who consistently treat him or her well. It is also required that these behaviors do not occur only when the person is depressed and do not occur exclusively in response to, or anticipation of, some form of abuse.

Unlike the other new, optional diagnoses offered by DSM-III-R—late luteal phase dysphoric disorder and sadistic personality disorder—the self-defeating personality disorder does not as neatly fit into either traditional or consensually agreed-upon parameters. Thus, it would be premature to assert, or even speculate about, the test results that might be expected (Morey et al., 1988). Treatment approaches will depend on whether the primary component in an individual case is closer to the characterological disorders or to the anxiety disorders.

CHAPTER 10

The Criminal Personality

Although the DSM-III-R discusses the category of antisocial personality, it does little to distinguish the great variety of individuals who are easily subsumed under the label "criminal personality" (Hare, 1986; Meyer and Salmon, 1988). There are a number of general characteristics of the criminal personality. The majority of offenses are caused by individuals aged twenty-one or younger, and approximately 80 percent of adult chronic offenders were chronic offenders before age eighteen. Overall, criminals are male by about a 5:1 ratio—up to 50:1 in the various categories of aggressive crime. With the rise in feminism, we are increasingly closer to parity in "white-collar crime," but the high ratio of males has persisted in aggressive crimes. Both poor sociocultural conditions and heredity are major factors. Other more specific factors are: low intelligence, especially verbal intelligence; mesomorphic body type; a history of hyperactivity; left-handedness; cold, harsh, and/or inconsistent parenting, psychopathy, and impulsivity.

By far the most exhaustive and elegant research on the psychological test discrimination of the criminal personality has been carried out by Edwin Megargee and his colleagues (Megargee and Bohn, 1979; Carbonell et al., 1984). Their typology, based on empirically derived and validated MMPI research, has been exhaustively studied by Megargee and his colleagues and students in a variety of settings, and it has received strong and independent verification from other researchers (Edinger, 1979; Gearing, 1979; Hawk, 1983; Kalichman, 1988).

Megargee established ten reasonably discrete subcategories of the criminal personality, using incarcerated prisoners. These ten typologies and their associated MMPI patterns are presented here; readers are strongly cautioned, however, to use Megargee's computer tapes if they are going to do any extensive diagnostic work in this area, as these tapes would provided a much more accurate assessment of those individuals who fall on the borderline of two or more patterns. Any reader who is regularly involved in diagnostic work with prisoners should be familiar with both Megargee and Bohn (1979) and Gearing (1979). The system is not generally applicable to short-form MMPIs. Even if one is not doing computer assessments, Megargee and Bohn provide more-extensive decision rules for the categories than are available here. Megargee will provide computer tapes for his system at cost or will score, profile, and classify MMPIs if a special answer sheet is used; he also encourages people to send him research information concerning his classification system. He can be reached at the Department of Psychology, Florida State University, Tallahassee, FL 32306.

Megargee's ten subtypes were given alphabetical names (e.g., Able, Baker) and in the early publication were listed in that order. In the later and more comprehensive publication (Megargee and Bohn, 1979), the subtypes were listed in order from the least pathological to the most pathological, and that system will be used here.

■ Megargee's Ten Criminal Subtypes*

□ ITEM

Individuals in the Item classification show little or no psychopathology, which is fortunate since this is the largest group of the ten, comprising 19 percent of his prison sample. They are generally nonaggressive, friendly, and extroverted and are likely to have been incarcerated for a victimless crime. They come from stable and warm family backgrounds and have had the fewest problems when growing up. They seem able to make committed and lasting friendships.

They present an essentially normal MMPI profile, with the major characteristic being an overall absence of elevations, though about 50 percent manifest one T score greater than 70. That high point is usually on the 5 or 9 scale. There is no consistent two-point code associated with this group; any elevation tends to be on scales 4, 5, or 9.

Though Items are inclined to pilfer things while on prison work assignment, they are at the same time rated as the most dependable workers by their supervisors. They show a low recidivism rate, and it would probably be just as useful to them, and certainly far less expensive, if they were to be immediately placed on probation.

* This material, adapted from *Classifying Criminal Offenders* (Sage Library of Social Research, *82*, 118–35, 177–233), by E. Megargee and M. Bohn, copyright 1979, is reprinted by permission of the publisher, Sage Publications (Beverly Hills).

☐   EASY

The Easy group, like the Item group, has relatively benign psychopathology. They comprise 7 percent of Megargee's sample. They are brighter and appear to have had more natural advantages than the other groups. Coincidentally, they are well characterized by their randomly assigned label: Not only has life been easy, but they have also taken it easy—they are classic underachievers. Interestingly enough, they have had a high number of siblings who were behavior problems, though all indications are that the parental situation was good for Easy inmates themselves.

On the average, they show a "benign profile" on the MMPI, with all scores under the 70 T mark. A 4-3 profile is most common, and scale 2 is often relatively elevated. This group is occasionally confused with subsequent groups Baker and George, although these groups are more likely to show a spike on 2 than is the Easy group.

Easys show little upset or discomfort at being in prison. They have the lowest recidivism rate of all groups, probably because they have the most in the way of natural assets on which to draw. Probation into academic and vocational training would appear to be a much more efficient option for this group than incarceration.

☐   BAKER

Bakers are a relatively small group, only 4 percent of the sample, and they are best labeled "neurotic delinquent." They are passive, anxious, and socially isolated individuals who are inclined to depend on alcohol to deal with everyday problems and upsets.

The most common MMPI profile obtained is the 4-2, and the second most common is the 4-9. On the average, Bakers are moderately high on scale 4, with a secondary elevation of scale 2 and an interesting and consistent spike on 6 (though this is not a high spike). They can be confused with Georges, but Georges show a higher elevation on the neurotic triad: scales 1, 2, and 3. Also, a mild elevation of 6 is more characteristic of Bakers than Georges.

Oddly, Bakers are surprisingly disruptive in the institution, although in a passive-aggressive fashion. The combination of supportive psychotherapy, vocational counseling, and an Alcoholics Anonymous program is the optimal treatment.

☐   ABLE

Ables are the second most common group in Megargee's population, comprising 17 percent of the overall group. Ables are sociopathic, opportunistic, self-assured, and immature. Rather than being hostile or antisocial, they are amoral and hedonistic.

The essential feature of the Able MMPI profile is bimodality, with distinctive peaks on scales 4 and 9. The 4-9/9-4 two-point combination covers 83 percent of this sample. They are unlike the Delta group, where scale 4 is much greater than scale 9. Ables typically show little or no elevation on scales other than 4 and 9.

Though Ables move into subcultural delinquency at an early age, all indications are that they had a good family background. This background may explain why they perform well in the prison, at least when supervised. A controlled community-living situation is thought to be the best disposition for this group.

☐   ## GEORGE

The George group, 7 percent of the sample, closely resembles the Able group, except that Georges are brighter and come from a more deviant family background. Georges "do their own time" and are characterized as quiet though not passive loners.

The 2-4/4-2 profile, with a distinctive slope to the right, is characteristic of this group. They are close to the Baker profile in some respects, but show higher elevations overall and a greater slope to the right in the profile. Also, there is no secondary spike on scale 6 in Georges. They can be confused with the Easy group, but the scale 3 score is less prominent in the profile of Georges.

☐   ## DELTA

Unlike previous groups, Deltas, who comprise 10 percent of the population, are a definitely pathological group. These bright psychopaths are sociable, yet they are easily provoked to violence. Reflecting the classic descriptors of the primary psychopath, Deltas are impulsive, unable to delay gratification, amoral, do not profit from experience, are prone to violence, and seldom experience guilt or anxiety.

Deltas are likely to show a spike on scale 4, with an occasional secondary spike on scale 2. They are relatively low on scales 6, 8, and 9, so on occasion they can be confused with the Able group, one that is very different behaviorally. The best method of discrimination is the distinct bimodality on scales 4 and 9 that marks the Able group.

☐   ## JUPITER

This rare group, 3 percent of the population, shows indication of making efforts toward a positive adjustment, but they are badly handicapped by very deprived family backgrounds. Unfortunately for this group, modeling is an enduring influence in teaching a person to deviate from the rules of society. As a result, Jupiters do not always make a good adjustment in spite of their apparent motivation.

The Jupiter MMPI profile is singularly marked by a climb to the right on the scales. Scale 8 is the most common peak scale, with scale 9 close behind, and then a high elevation of scale 7 further behind. This group is defined by exclusion. If an MMPI profile fits the concept of a climb to the right, and is excluded from other categories, it is labeled Jupiter.

Just the opposite of Easys, Jupiters do not have the good family background, skill preparation, or even the ability, but they do have the motivation. As a result, a heavy emphasis on developing basic academic skills, vocational training, and a supportive group experience at a half-way house are necessary ingredients for the rehabilitation of Jupiters.

□   FOXTROT

Foxtrots, 8 percent of the sample, have all the bad characteristics listed. They experienced poor family backgrounds, are poorly educated and not very intelligent, are antisocial, and are disturbed emotionally. They are evasive and easily provoke anger in others.

They are classically high on the 9, 4, and 8 scales. The elevation on the 8 scale is helpful in discriminating this group from the Ables, who appear more average on 8 and lower in general on the other scales.

Foxtrots do make friends with a few similarly deviant individuals, but by and large, they provoke hostility. They are readily aggressive toward the staff if there is much contact with them. Foxtrots can use help of any sort, but not surprisingly, they are quite unresponsive to any efforts to provide it. As a result, they have a very high recidivism rate.

□   CHARLIE

Charlies, comprising 9 percent of Megargee's population, are bitter and hostile antisocial personalities, with a definite paranoid element. In addition, they are usually intellectually, academically, and socially deficient. They are alienated and hostile loners who easily become violent.

Charlies show characteristic MMPI elevations on 8, 6, and 4. The 8-6 and 8-4 profiles are the most common. Charlies can be confused with Foxtrots, but they have a high 6 score relative to Foxtrots. Charlies may also be confused with the How group, although Hows tend to be high on scales 1, 2, and 3.

From the perspective of violence in the prison or in the community and the high probability of recidivism, Charlie is one of the most disturbed criminal subgroups. Treatments useful for paranoid individuals are especially applicable here.

□   HOW

The How group is large, comprising 13 percent of the sample. They are similar to Jupiters in that they are significantly handicapped by a deprived early environment, but Hows are much more psychologically disturbed and less willing to change than are Jupiters. They are highly anxious individuals who also show some depression. Part of this depression stems from their role as "reluctant loner," since they continually face rejection by others rather than withdraw from social contact.

Like the Item group, their MMPI profile is defined more by elevation than by specific subscale scores. Whereas Items are defined by low elevations across the scales, Hows show high elevations on most scales, especially elevations in a jagged pattern on scales 8, 2, 4, and 1. The profile is distinctive in its jagged elevation throughout the right and left sides of the profile. Scale 8 is the highest scale in more than 50 percent of the profiles obtained.

Like Foxtrots, Hows are prone to be aggressive toward staff if there is a high amount of interaction. Psychotherapy and chemotherapy, as well as any vocational and social-engineering program available, are needed in rehabilitating them. Unfortunately, rehabilitation is seldom successful, and the recidivism rate is high.

■   ## Summary

Megargee and Bohn (1979) have collected data from a number of researchers indicating that their system is relevant throughout most state and federal penal institutions. They also have supporting data to show that the system is applicable to women with almost the same accuracy and efficiency as it is for men, the sample from which it was derived. Race was considered throughout Megargee's research, so this does not seem to be a disqualifying factor in applying this MMPI system. There are expected minor age differences among the subgroups, and an offender's subgroup type may change with age. Overall, Charlies and Jupiters tend to be younger, and Easys tend to be older. The reader is also directed toward the discussion of the antisocial personality disorder, as well as the juvenile delinquent or conduct disorder (Binder, 1988), in Chapter 9.

CHAPTER 11

Disorders of Impulse Control

This section in DSM-III-R is primarily a catch-all grouping for those patterns that are not efficiently classified elsewhere. The essential features of a disorder of impulse control are a buildup of tension prior to the act, failure to resist the impulse, an experience of pleasure or release on carrying out the act, and consequent harm to others and/or oneself. Even though there may be some guilt after the act, it is essentially ego-syntonic, and there may be little in the way of conscious resistance to the impulse.

The subcategories in this section of DSM-III-R are pathological gambling, kleptomania, trichotillomania, pyromania, and intermittent explosive disorder. There is also a residual category: other-impulse disorder. Rape will be discussed in this section because it fits well here, even though it is not specifically mentioned as a category heading in DSM-III-R. Anorexia nervosa and bulimia nervosa will also be discussed here.

■ Overall Test-Response Patterns

On the MMPI, a lack of impulse control is generally reflected in elevations on scales 4, 6, 8, and 9. On the 16 PF, high scores are usually obtained on F and Q_1, whereas low scores on Q_3 and G are typical. Performance scale scores are higher than verbal scale scores on the WAIS-R. Within the verbal scale, arithmetic and information are usually two of the lower scores. Response times to the Rorschach are short, and the record may often have a lower than average number of responses. F and F+% are lower than normal, and there is a greater use of color than in most disorders.

Oas (1984) found that certain variables in drawing tasks, particularly the Draw-A-Person and Bender-Gestalt tests, predicted to a general trait of impulsivity. Oas studied samples of adolescents, but the experience of a number of clinicians suggests many of these variables apply equally well to adults. The variables that Oas found to discriminate impulsive from nonimpulsive individuals are as follows: (1) quick completion time, (2) obvious aggressive content, (3) poor overall quality, (4) discontinuity, (5) obvious omissions, and (6) lack of proportion. Nonimpulsivity is indicated by the (1) degree of overall detail, (2) amount of sketching, (3) eye emphasis, (4) mouth detail, (5) amount of shading, and (6) absence of omissions and discontinuities.

Pathological Gambling (312.31)

The characteristics of this category are a progressive and chronic preoccupation with the need to gamble and a consequent disruption in some area of the individual's world. Estimates of the number of gamblers in the middle 1970s in the United States varied between one and ten million. Since more states have moved toward legalized gambling, thus making it increasingly accessible to people, it is expected that the rate will continue to rise. Compulsive gamblers, like antisocial personalities, are stimulation-seeking, and both specifically show "disinhibition," or the inability to control impulses (Zuckerman et al., 1980). The initial streak of compulsive gambling is usually set off by a first big win.

Many compulsive gamblers report that they only feel alive when they are gambling and may refer to the rest of their life as boring. They are generally nonconformists and are narcissistic and aggressive (Walker, 1985). A number of compulsive gamblers work only to make enough money to gamble heavily when they get to a spot like Las Vegas. Others have a more normal outward appearance, especially those who gamble in more legitimate outlets like stock and commodities markets.

Most gamblers are extroverted and competitive individuals. They are brighter than average, yet surprisingly they often experiences learning difficulties as they grew up. Many had placed their first bet by the age of fifteen (Quay, 1987). Other factors that predispose to pathological gambling are an overemphasis in early family life on material symbols, with little value placed on financial planning and savings; an absent parent before the age of sixteen; and availability in the family of a gambler as a model.

DSM-III-R

To diagnose pathological gambling, the DSM-III-R requires that an individual show progressive preoccupation with gambling, which consequently disrupts their world in at least four of the following ways: (1) preoccupation with gambling or with obtaining money to gamble; (2) gambling larger and larger amounts; (3) a need to increase both size and frequency of bets; (4) restless need to gamble; (5) repeated loss of money and attempts to win it back; (6) repeated efforts to stop; (7) interference with important social obligations; (8) social or occupational sacrifice to gamble; or (9) gambling despite inability to pay debts.

MMPI

There are few data on the modal test patterns for this group, although the variables noted above correlate with the personality descriptors associated with the bimodal, moderately elevated 4-9 profile. When pathological gamblers are seen by a clinician, however, they have already begun to experience substantial distress and hence are likely to score higher on scale 2. The stimulation-seeking quality is reflected on scale 9, and the extroversion characteristic of this pattern is seen in a low scale 0. At the point of referral, they would also probably be agitated and distressed, which in combination with their impulsiveness should result in an elevation on scale 7. A moderate elevation on scale 3 can also be expected since the tendency to reject responsibility for changes and forces in their world is reflected here. F or K scale elevations will depend on the situation in which the gamblers are being tested. If for some reason they are defensive about gambling, the K scale would be elevated. On the other hand, there are situations in which being labeled "disturbed" would help them avoid some of the consequences of their behavior. As a result, a high F scale would occur, which in turn would also elevate a number of the other scales.

16 PF

On the 16 PF, the extroversion, stimulation-seeking, and lack of self-control that characterize this pattern are reflected in high A and H scores and a low Q_3 score. Q_1 and, to a slightly lesser degree, C and O will be dependent on the characteristics of the testing situation, that is, on whether the subjects have reasons to be defensive or open about the pathological gambling.

They are also likely to be higher on E in particular, as well as on B, F, N, and L. A lower score is obtained on I.

OTHER TEST-RESPONSE PATTERNS

The nonconforming, narcissistic, and aggressive components present in the personality of the pathological gambler are likely to be evidenced by MCMI elevations of 75 or higher on 5 and 6, with low scores on 7. Elevations on A and D are likely when the life-style of the pathological gambler begins to create significant problems within the family or with financial status. Alcohol abuse may coincide with this disorder, producing an elevated B.

☐   TREATMENT OPTIONS

Since the disorder in pathological gambling is very likely to surface first in family problems, family or couples therapy is often necessary (Vollberg and Steadman, 1988). In addition, the following phases of intervention, similar to those used in the treatment of other addictions, are useful here (Brown, 1985; Walker, 1985).

1. Elimination of immediate opportunity to gamble by way of inpatient hospitalization.
2. Immediate initiation of an educational process about pathological gambling and the insidious role it takes in every individual's life.
3. Individual and group psychotherapy to help the individual explore attitudes and beliefs that have supported his or her gambling behavior over a period of years.
4. Economic counseling for living within a set income.
5. Possibly preventive periodic inpatient hospitalization as a preventive measure once every six to eighteen months.
6. Regular attendance at Gambler's Anonymous.

Since stimulation-seeking is often a critical variable in the reinforcement pattern for pathological gambling, the comments regarding fulfilling the need for stimuation-seeking detailed in the section on the antisocial personality disorder are relevant here.

Kleptomania (312.32)

Most authorities agree that thievery in various forms has been on the rise in our society. For example, statistics annually compiled by the U.S. Department of Commerce suggest that about 140 million instances of shoplifting occur every year, and that almost 25 percent of business losses are accounted for in this fashion. They suggest that about one in every twelve shoppers is a shoplifter, although no more than one in thirty-five shoplifters is ever apprehended.

Certainly, many people steal simply because it seems so easy to get something free, for a lark, or to be one of their crowd. However, a small proportion of these individuals show actual kleptomania. They are distinguished from typical thieves in that kleptomaniacs seldom have any real need for an object and may even throw it away. They usually prefer to steal while alone, and there is a quality of "irresistible impulse" in their behavior.

Kleptomania often begins in childhood, primarily through stealing small items or sums of money from parents or friends. Stealing, as a means of being accepted into an adolescent peer group is another common feature in the background of kleptomaniacs (Quay, 1987). There is usually evidence of depressive features, reflecting an inability to control the behavior, as well as some problems in interpersonal relationships. For example, many older women who show a kleptomaniac pattern are widowed or emotionally neglected by their husbands; the behavior gives them a thrill, sometimes sexually tinged, though they often pay for it with remorse. In fact, many show a clear sense of relief when apprehended. Kleptomaniacs are usually not significantly disturbed psychologically in areas other than this lack of specific behavioral control. Yet, the condition is often chronic.

☐   DSM-III-R

The DSM-III-R offers the following diagnostic criteria for this pattern: an irresistible impulse accompanied by rising tension before the act; the actual stealing behavior accompanied by a sense of release or even pleasure, sexual arousal, or euphoria; no apparent need for the item or important monetary profit; and no need to commit the act to express anger or vengeance. There is usually a lack of planning and little involvement with others in the pattern.

☐   DIAGNOSTIC CONSIDERATIONS

Consistent with the comment that kleptomaniacs are not often significantly disturbed psychologically, their MMPI and 16 PF protocols are also usually unremarkable. If persons are being seen in the criminal justice system rather than the mental health system, they are likely to show a higher K score on the MMPI and, to the degree they are unsophisticated, a higher L score. If they are being seen in the mental health system or if they are viewing psychopathology as a means to avoid criminal sanctions, F will be higher. Scale 2 is moderately raised, reflecting the situationally generated depression, as well as the sense of inability to control their impulses. In that regard, scale 3 is also likely to be mildly raised. Scale 9 is average or low, and scale 0 is usually a bit elevated, reflecting their propensity for being alone with their conflicts.

Similarly, on the 16 PF they tend to show some elevation on scales Q_4 and O and are usually not high on scale A. Scale Q_3 will vary depending on whether it directly reflects their inability to control impulses, which would result in a low score, or they are counterphobically trying to control their impulses, which would raise Q_3.

☐   TREATMENT OPTIONS

Since schizoid behaviors and/or depression are common precursors to kleptomaniac behavior, treatment approaches for those patterns are often important here. For the specific behaviors of kleptomania, the aversive therapies are often used. Kellam (1969) employed a particularly ingenous aversive procedure to control shoplifting in a chronic kleptomaniac. Kellam required this person to simulate his entire shoplifting sequence, which was filmed. As the film was played back, the client was asked to participate with internal imagery in what was going on, and a painful shock was administered at crucial points. Such a technique could be amplified by having a person take a portable shock unit and self-administer shock whenever the impulse arose. If the shock unit is clumsy, the person could be instructed to hold his or her breath until discomfort ensues, since this acts as an aversive cue.

An alternative aversive technique is to have such clients go into a store and when the impulse becomes so severe that they feel they will not be able to resist, they are to take an expensive and fragile object and drop it on the floor. Embarrassment, the need for a coping response with store employees, and the need for restitution all act to create a very aversive moment.

Other clinicians have treated kleptomania by systematic desensitization, hypothesizing that the behavior will subside if one can decrease the tension in the sequence of anxiety arousal-completion-release. As anxiety then lessens, better coping behaviors for dealing with anxiety are developed. Cognitive-behavioral techniques and/or existential approaches that deal with the loss of interests and meaning evident in some kleptomanics, particularly older females, may also be necessary.

■ Pyromania (312.33)

As with thievery, deliberate fire-setting behavior appears to have increased substantially in modern society. Of course, most cases of arson are not really indicative of pyromania. It is now estimated that as much as 80 percent of business property fires are caused by arson. In these cases, the perpetrator is far more likley to be an antisocial personality who is doing it for hire—a "paid torch." Cases of arson in which there is no clear reward for the individual who started the fire could indicate pyromania, but mental retardation should be also be considered.

Pyromaniacs, like kleptomaniacs, experience a buildup of tension prior to the behavior and a release of tension after performing the fire-setting. The behavior is often first seen in childhood or adolescence, and it is seldom the only antisocial behavior displayed. Hyperactivity, problems in school, poor peer relationships, and stealing are commonly associated behaviors. It has been found that fire-setting in childhood, when combined with enuresis and/or cruelty to animals, is predictive of assaultive crimes in adulthood, though these crimes may not include fire-setting.

Pyromania is much more common in males than in females and is often found in an individual who has had trouble in making transitions through developmental stages. There are analogous data showing that peaks in the incidence rate in arson occur around the ages of seventeen, twenty-six, forty, and sixty in males. If there is a problem with alcohol, pyromaniacs show patterns of alcohol abuse rather than addiction, and they often show an inordinate interest in fire-fighting paraphernalia. Pyromaniacs may be indifferent to a fire's destruction or stimulated by it.

☐   DSM-III-R

As with kleptomania, the DSM-III-R requires evidence of at least one deliberate fire-setting, with a buildup of an irresistible impulse before the setting of the fire, continuing inability to resist the impulse, and a release of tension after setting the fire. There should also be an indication that neither profit nor some sociopolitical belief system is the basic motive for the fire-setting.

☐   DIAGNOSTIC CONSIDERATIONS

As with kleptomania, there is not much consensual clinical literature nor are there hard data to indicate the patterns one can expect here. However, on the average, pyromaniacs are more disturbed than kleptomaniacs. They are likely to score high on scales 4 and 8 of the MMPI, though not usually at a psychotic level. They will probably also score higher on scales 6 and 9, and to the degree the impulses are denied, scale 3 is elevated. The F and the 4 scores are elevated to the degree there is an antiauthority component. Moodiness, a sense of alienation from others, and inability to control impulses are also reflected in any elevations on scales 8, 0, and 6.

On the 16 PF, pyromaniacs show more evidence of disorder than kleptomaniacs. Pyromaniacs will likely be low on scales C, G, and Q_3 and higher on scales L and Q_4. There are also likely to show some elevation on scales E and H, reflecting their destructive and controlling orientation toward the environment. Analogously, this latter component as well as the distancing from others may raise scale Q_1 and lower scale A. Scale B on the average is low, reflecting the usual less-than-average intelligence.

Pyromaniacs may show labile and impulsive affect responses, as indicated by a number of uncontrolled reactions to the color cards of the Rorschach. In fact, it is suggested that when children with borderline psychosis provide "blood," "fire," or other similarly destructive associations to the Rorschach color areas, potential dangerousness in general, and possible fire-setting behavior in particular, should be suspected (Armentrout and Hauer, 1978). MCMI elevations of 75 or higher on scales 5 and especially 6 are probable. Hypomania (elevated N) is more likely to be present in this disorder, though—as with anxiety—it may vacillate, depending on whether testing is done before or after pyromanic activity occurs.

☐ TREATMENT OPTIONS

The significant disturbance, often characterological in nature, that usually accompanies pyromania suggests that a wide variety of treatment options may have to be considered, depending on the trend of the overall pathology (Kernberg, 1984). Since these individuals are often adolescents or young adults, family therapy is especially warranted; and since schizoid patterns are typical, the reader is referred to that section of this book. A low level of serotonin is occasionally noted, so chemotherapy may be of help.

Two specific behavioral techniques are appropriate for the fire-setting behaviors. Overcorrection requires the individual to make a new, positive response in the area of specific disorder. For example, public confession and a restitution of damages through working for the individual who is offended would be one application for pyromania. Negative practice has also been used, wherein the pyromaniac is required to perform a behavior *ad nauseam* until it takes on aversive qualities. For example, the client is required to strike thousands of matches in a row, over several sessions. These techniques would be embedded in an overall treatment program.

■ Trichotillomania (312.39)

The term "trichotillomania" was first introduced into the clinical literature in 1889 by Hallopean (Krishman et al., 1985). However, it was not until the DSM-III-R that it was designated as a DSM diagnostic category. Trichotillomania is defined as recurrent irresistible impulses to pull one's own hair. It is more common in females and usually first starts in childhood or early adolescence, though it also erupts occasionally in a mature adult.

This behavior can persist for many years, often recurs after spontaneous remission, and is marked by efforts at concealment. Bald spots (alopecia) often appear, in some cases leading to total baldness, so wigs are frequently used.

☐ DSM-III-R

To warrant a diagnosis of trichotillomania, the DSM-III-R requires that there be noticeable hair loss resulting from the recurrent inability to resist impulses to pull out one's hair. There is an increasing tension experienced before giving in to the impulse to pull out the hair, with a sense of relief experienced afterwards. The diagnosis is not made when this is a secondary response to a hallucination or delusion or to a preexisting skin disorder.

□   DIAGNOSTIC CONSIDERATIONS

Since the literature suggests that there is a connection between trichotillomania and obsessive-compulsive disorders, and in some cases is a mask for depression (Krishman et al., 1985), a 2-7/7-2 profile or a 7-8/8-7 profile with some elevation on 2 is to be expected. In those cases with a strong hypochondriacal element, scales 1 and 3 should be effected, and to the degree denial and secretiveness are involved, K and 6 should be elevated.

On the MCMI, the commonly reported dependency-family conflict (Krishman et al., 1985) should generate a high scale 3, with the compulsive components raising scale 7. In those clients that are closer to the borderline personality disorder, scale C should be high. On the 16 PF, scales C and Q_3 should be low. And the dependency issues should generate low scores on Q_2, L, and E. Similar parallels to obsessive-compulsive, depressive, and dependency-oriented profiles should be noted on the Rorschach and TAT.

□   TREATMENT OPTIONS

For child and adolescent trichotillomaniacs, a central focus for the therapist will be the dependency issue within a standard psychotherapy format (Brigham, 1988). Chemotherapy will be useful, not only to quell secondary itching and skin problems, but—in older children and adults—to deal with obsessive-compulsive and depressive components. Hypnosis and certain behavioral techniques (e.g., thought stopping and aversion therapy) have proven useful as well.

■   **Intermittent-Explosive Disorder (312.34)**

The distinguishing feature of the explosive disorder is a sudden eruption of aggressive impulses and the loss of control of these impulses in an individual who normally inhibits or does not experience them (Goldstein and Keller, 1987). Regret and guilt are common, and the behavior is disproportionate to any environmental stressors. Because occasionally both prodromal physiological or mood symptoms and consequent partial amnesia for the behavior are reported, the pattern was traditionally referred to as "epileptoid." A concomitant clear diagnosis of organic epilepsy is not common. However, in a number of these cases, there are some nonspecific EEG abnormalities or minor neurological signs. The presence of such signs is not so rare , even in a sample of apparently normal individuals, but clear evidence for a physiological contribution should be thoroughly considered (Gardner et al., 1987).

☐   DSM-III-R

The DSM-III-R diagnosis for intermittent-explosive disorder requires (1) several discrete episodes of loss of control, as in property destruction or assaultive acts, (2) that the aggressiveness is clearly out of proportion to any precipitating event, and (3) that there be no signs of generalized impulsiveness between the episodes or that the episodes do not occur in conjunction with a diagnosis of any psychotic disorder. The disorder appears most commonly in late adolescence or early adulthood.

☐   MMPI

As noted in the section on aggression potential, persons who are continually assaultive and without guilt tend to score high on scales F, 4, and 9, with secondary elevations on 8 or 6. However, though the continuity factor does not fit with the descriptors of the intermittent-explosive disorder, Fowler (1981) notes that high 4 and 6 scores can be expected here. The degree of guilt and rumination over this behavior is reflected in the elevation on scale 7.

The 4-3 profile, as described by Davis and Sines (1971), would be more likely to call for the explosive-disorder diagnosis. In this profile, there is a peak on 4, a secondary peak on 3, and little significant elevation elsewhere. This profile, mainly seen in males, is particularly characteristic of individuals who maintain a quiet ongoing adjustment but are likely to demonstrate occasional hostile-aggressive outbursts. Such behavior may or may not warrant the diagnosis of intermittent-explosive disorder, depending on the characteristics described above. Gearing (1979) indicates that this profile is applicable to females and occurs quite generally, though there is some evidence that it is less applicable to adolescents.

To the degree that both 4 and 3 are highly elevated, the likelihood of aggressive episodes increases. In general, when scale 3 is greater than 4, the potential for control and inhibition of the aggression is increased, whereas to the degree that 4 is greater than 3, control dissipates.

Lachar (1974) suggests that the rare 3-9 code is indicative of persons who are emotionally labile and show recurrent hostility and irritability. Since they naturally suppress the hostility in clinical assessment, they could be diagnosed as an explosive disorder. However, it is more likely that they are a passive-aggressive personality disorder, a histrionic personality disorder, or both.

There is a derived scale on the MMPI, termed the Over-Controlled Hostility Scale (Megargee et al., 1967), composed of 31 MMPI items. Though a few studies have not been positive, most have supported the validity of this scale in predicting persons who show outbursts of aggression. Hence, they could easily fit the DSM-III-R diagnosis of explosive personality. The scale has been an accurate predictor in incarcerated adult populations, but it has sometimes been weak in the normal population. Nevertheless, it is one of the most well-researched scales and is worthy of consideration.

☐   16 PF

Since these individuals generally show regret over their behavior and see it as ego-alien to a degree, a low score on G is not likely, as it would be in most cases of aggressive behavior. Also, C is not usually low nor are Q_4 and N high, as would be common in the psychopath. Q_3 is usually high, reflecting the attempts at control that are characteristic of this person, and Q_1 is usually moderately low. In spite of their passivity, they do not score markedly low on E or H; neither are they very high. Scores are average or lower on M and N, reflecting the general denial of the aggression and the lack of introspection about motives and conflicts.

☐   OTHER TEST-RESPONSE PATTERNS

There is some evidence that quiet but potentially explosive persons attain lower picture arrangement scores on the WAIS-R than do more extroverted and consistently aggressive types. Comprehension and similarities subtests are usually relatively lower here. Rorschach patterns are quite constricted, and there is less abstraction content. M responses are not that uncommon, and when they do occur, they tend to be more passive. Responses with content like "blood" or "explosions" or responses indicating inner tension and turmoil occur in a number of explosive disorders. Responses with a color component tend to have poorer form than otherwise expected. Minor neuropsychological signs on a variety of tests are often associated with this disorder, and it is a reasonable axiom that there is some impaired brain functioning, though seldom any gross brain damage.

☐   TREATMENT OPTIONS

It is critical in treating this disorder to get the clients in touch with their ongoing anger responses, usually suppressed, and at the same time to teach them more effective ways either to abort the anger or to deal with it productively (Teyber, 1988). Awareness techniques, such as those found in gestalt therapy, can put them in touch with the anger that is typically not evident in their usual functioning. Group therapy can provide the feedback essential to breaking down their defenses against seeing themselves as having chronic anger. The keeping of a diary or the writing of (undelivered) letters to significant others who may be a factor in generating the anger (Kirman, 1980) also aids clients to get in better touch with their anger.

Once this is accomplished, the therapist could attempt to use the development of a controlled relaxation response to abort the anger. Similarly, biofeedback training to develop an overall relaxation response could be useful to mute or abort the anger. Assertiveness training or analogous procedures could then be used to structure more-effective ways to cope with the ongoing frustration and anger. Lithium treatment has been found effective with that subgroup of persons with intermittent-explosive disorders who show evidence of a latent or cyclical manic component. Clients in this category also occasionally respond well to ethosuximide, and those with a CNS lesion causing the rage have been helped by propranolol (Yudofsky et al., 1981).)

■   ## Rape

Rape does not appear directly as a diagnostic entity in DSM-III-R, but it is a most important syndrome, is often an impulsive behavior, and shows certain diagnostic correlates. A discussion is in order here.

There are a number of classification systems for rape (Malamuth, 1986), one of the most influential being that of Cohen et al. (1969). The following reflects their concepts.

Aside from the rapes that occur as an incidental result of such disorders as severe organic brain dysfunction or schizophrenia and those that are an impulsive and ritualistic gesture (the plunder of war), there is reasonable agreement that there are three major rape patterns. The first occurs where aggression is the major component and sexual satisfaction is somewhat irrelevant in the motivational system. These rapists are hostile toward females and in general carry a high level of aggression potential. The upcoming section on aggression potential deals with the diagnostic considerations relevant to such persons.

The second type of rapist needs to administer pain to another person to obtain sexual satisfaction. The pain is requisite, so this type of rapist is classified under the psychosexual disorder of sexual sadism (see that section).

The third major category of rapists is that where the aggression is an avenue toward sexual contact and satisfaction, yet also in some ways to interpersonal contact, and most cases of date-rape fit here (Follingstad et al., in press). This is the individual whose diagnostic correlates are presented here. This sexually motivated rapist fits the results of Barbaree et al. (1979), who found that, in most cases, forced sex for them fails to inhibit arousal, though it does so in most normal individuals. Incidentally, Abel et al. (1986) found that some rapists (the aggression subtype) are especially aroused by stimuli that connote a woman who is aggressive or manipulative or by sexual images that include aggression.

☐   CHARACTERISTICS OF RAPE

Rape has traditionally been defined as the unlawful penetration of a female's vagina by a man's penis, reinforced by some form of coercion and without the consent of the victim. However, it is increasingly recognized that it is absurd to require penile penetration to define rape (Smith and Meyer, 1987). Homosexual rape occurs, as does rape of men by women (though very rarely). Statutes have been rewritten in states to reflect this.

Rape is a common crime and is said to account for approximately 5 percent of all crimes of violence. Each year, about one in every 2,000 women is a reported rape victim. However, it is estimated that only about 10 percent of victims of rape ever report it to the police. Also, only about two in twenty rapists are ever arrested, one in thirty prosecuted, and one in fifty convicted. More than 50 percent of reported rapes take place in the victims' homes, and in about 40 percent of the cases, the rapist is known to the victim. (Follingstad et al., in press; Abel et al., 1986).

☐   THE RAPIST

Most rapists are married, and a great percentage of married rapists have regular sexual relations with their wives. However, their sexual performance is often impaired during the rape. Like most other antisocial personalities and criminals, rapists are generally lower than average in intelligence.

Rada et al. (1976) and other researchers have found elevated levels of plasma testosterone in some samples of the most violent rapists. In general, however, there is not much correlation between rape and physiological measures. An impossible problem is obtaining such measures at the critical predictive point, the time just before the rape, as many of these physiological variables differ markedly for any one individual depending on when they are assessed. However, measurements of penile response to sexual imagery (Earls and Prouix, 1986) may be useful here, as well as in making at least some tentative preditions about future behavior when that is important in disposition.

☐   MMPI

It has been generally found that rapists are more disturbed across the board on such tests as the MMPI than are assaultists *per se* or exhibitionists (Levin and Stava, 1987). In many ways, rapists correlate with the dimensions of the antisocial personality (the reader is referred to that section). Common profiles in rapists are the 4-9, 8-4/4-8, and 4-3. The 4-9/9-4 is the most common (Erickson et al., 1987). The 8-4 is characteristic of rapists of adults. The 4-8 is more characteristic of rapists of children (Armentrout and Hauer, 1978).

Rapists may obtain a high K score, reflecting the fact that they are typically under scrutiny for a criminal offense (see the section on malingering). Scale 5 is usually low in these individuals, especially if there is a strong identification with the stereotypical male role, Scale 0 is mildly elevated if there is general ineptitude in interpersonal skills. This type of behavior, along with an inclination to deny responsibility for it, is seen in an elevation of scale 3. Scale 4 reflects hostility and aggression and the lack of standard moral controls on behavior.

Rader (1977) has suggested that the 4-3 profile characterizes the more repressed rapist, who is inclined toward significant violence. In this case, scale 6 is also likely to be elevated, though this depends on the degree of hostility allowed into awareness. Scales F and 8 are elevated to the degree the individual is losing control of impulses and is degenerating into more-fragmented pathology, though faking-bad must also be considered.

☐   16 PF

Rapists, if they are at all self-disclosing, score away from the average on a number of dimensions (Masters et al., 1988). The primarily sexually motivated rapist is more likely to score toward the average profile than is the aggression-motivated rapist. However, both types are likely to have a low score on C, reflecting their emotional instability; low scores on Q and G from their inability to control impulses and urges; and a high score on O from their insecurity. The sexual rapist who is more naive, suspicious, interpersonally open, and less aggressive is likely to score low on N, moderately low on H, and moderately high on Q_4 and I. Aggressively motivated rapists will score low on A and moderately low on I, but high on E, H, and Q_2. Both types are less than average on scale B.

☐   OTHER TEST-RESPONSE PATTERNS

The hostile affectivity and interpersonal vindictiveness typical of the rapist predict MCMI scores of 85 or higher on scale 6. To a lesser extent, the exploitiveness of the narcissist may predispose toward rape behavior, so an elevation of 75 or higher could occur on 5. Scale C is also high.

☐   TREATMENT OPTIONS

Castration has been a time-honored approach for dealing with the rapist, but it runs afoul of legal considerations and the beliefs of some liberals. Nonetheless, chemocastration, via drugs that lower the serum testosterone level, is still used (Abel et al., 1986). These drugs lower the likelihood of sexual arousal, but side effects are substantial and the drugs are not consistently effective. Newer suggestions for the legal disposition of the rapist even include some irony analogous to the above suggestions. Fersch (1980) states that in rape "the criminal act ought to be brought under assault and battery with a dangerous weapon. Then the attention could be focused on whether or not the accused possessed a dangerous weapon" (p. 14).

The aversive therapies have been commonly used here and have shown moderate success. More-effective ways of coping with anger are also necessary, possibly introduced by modeling or role-playing. Marital therapy may be specifically indicated (Bornstein and Bornstein, 1986), since for many rapists the initiation of the rape sequence immediately follows a marital battle.

■   Anorexia Nervosa (307.10) and Bulimia Nervosa (307.51)

Anorexia nervosa is not a classic impulse disorder wherein the impulse overcomes the individual. Rather, there is an overcontrol of the impulse to eat. There is also occasional accompanying binge-eating (bulimia), so it is included in the impulse disorder section.

The essential features of anorexia nervosa, according to DSM-III-R, are an intense concern about becoming overweight and a persistent feeling of being fat, even when weight loss has begun or has even been substantial. This is combined with a refusal to regain or continue body weight at 15 percent of the minimally appropriate level, considering age and height; evidence of a weight loss of at least 15 percent from the original weight; and, in females, absence of three consecutive menstrual cycles otherwise expected to occur.

This apparently voluntary self-starvation is seen primarily in middle and upper socioeconomic classes of women (Bruch et al., 1988; Agras, 1987). It typically occurs first during puberty as a young woman becomes more conscious of her self-image. Sexuality may be channeled into the eating area, as these women usually avoid sexual acting-out. After the "sin" of eating, they may resort to self-induced vomiting and laxatives to "cleanse" the body of food. Though anorexia nervosa is rare in males, when it does occur, there are systematic differences from female anorectics. Males are less likely to use laxatives, are often less conscientious about school, are less likely to have had large appetites premorbidly, are more likely to have had enjoyable sexual experiences, and are less likely to die from the condition.

Anorectics who also show episodes of bulimia (binge-eating), in general are more disturbed than anorectics who do not (Bruch et al., 1988; Bruch, 1978). Approximately one in every 250 females between the ages of twelve and eighteen develops this disorder, and follow-up studies estimate mortality rates at between 5 and 15 percent.

The parents of the anorectic are typically very controlling, though caring, individuals. As a result, the anorectic appears to use the disorder as a statement of independence from the family in the narrow area that she can control. The salient personality characteristics are excessive dependency and sensitivity, introversion, perfectionism, and a subtle but persistent selfishness and stubbornness (Mash and Terdal, 1988; Bruch et al., 1988; Bruch, 1978).

The converse pattern is bulimia nervosa, a chronic pattern of binge-eating. Bulimia (from the Greek words for ox and hunger) is known as the gorge-purge syndrome. The essential features, according to DSM-III-R, are recurrent binge-eating, a sense of lack of control, a minimum of two binge episodes a week for at least three months, and persistent overconcern about body shape and weight. It is associated with attempts to control weight by diets or vomiting and also by eating high-calorie foods in an inconspicuous manner.

Although anorectics are typically shy, they are passively controlling and stubborn. Those bulimorectics who are also anorectic are more likley to be extroverted perfectionists who attempt to control their peers in direct ways (Agras, 1987). Many bulimorectics weigh in at normal levels and some are obese, whereas anorectics are almost always cadaverously thin. Both groups come from families in which food is a focus, as in socialization or recognition. Anorectics will often cook exotic meals for others, although they may eat only a small portion themselves. Bulimo-rectics do not usually like to cook because they are afraid they will eat all the food before the guests show up.

☐   DIAGNOSTIC CONSIDERATIONS

Where the anorectic pattern is similar to other adolescent patterns that emphasize rebelliousness, distress, and family discord, a 2-4-8 pattern can be expected. In the more classic anorectic patterns, the combined dependency and perfectionism of the anorectic are likely to elevate scale 7 of the MMPI, while the general psychopathology should elevate scales 6 and 8 (Small et al., 1981). The subtle selfishness, self-centeredness, and stubborness should elevate scales 1 and 3 somewhat. The inter-personal avoidance and sensitivity would tend to elevate scale O. At the same time, all of the patterns are influenced by the denial of path-ology, so scales L and K tend to be elevated while F is depressed, though less so to the degree she is an adolescent rather than an adult (Gallucci, 1987). The anorectic who also shows episodes of bulimia is more likely to score higher on scales 2, 3, 4, 6, and 7 than the anorectic who does not also manifest bulimia, and scale 7 is most often elevated in bulimorectics (Kirkley and Janick, 1987).

Bulimorectics are more likely to be extroverted and should therefore show a low 0 scale, as well as a higher scale 8, reflecting the sense of loss of control. Since they are more overtly self-disclosing, all scales should be more highly elevated, on the average, particularly scales 2 and 4.

On the 16 PF, the anorectic tends to score low on scales A, F, H, and Q_1 and moderately low on M, while the bulimorectic tends to score high on these scales, particularly A, H, M and Q_1. The anorectic is higher on Q_3 and Q_2; the bulimorectic tends to be in the middle on these scales. The anorectic also scores quite high on G, whereas the bulimorectic scores toward the middle. Surprisingly, the anorectic is toward the middle on scales I and L, reflecting the subtle stubborness and selfishness that are not apparent in initial interactions. Both usually score quite high on scale B, reflecting their tendency to be in the upper range in intelligence and socioeconomic status. Both also tend to be reasonably high on O.

Personality patterns most likely to develop anorexia or bulimia nervosa include those patterns represented by MCMI elevations on scales 3, 7, 8, 1, E, and C. Passive-aggressive controlling tendencies are evidenced by elevations on 8, while high scores on 3 indicate shyness and dependency and high scores on 7 point to compulsivity and perfectionism. Elevated scores on 1 and E are more likely in the anorexic than in the bulimic.

Higher intelligence and socioeconomic status predict overall high scores on the WAIS, with verbal scores usually being a bit higher than performance scores. The perfectionism and compulsivity evident in anorectics, combined with their conservative and production orientation to school situations, usually result in elevations of information and vocabulary scores. Their stubborn perfectionism usually slows them down somewhat on the digit symbol, block design, and object assembly tests, yet they seldom make the errors of impulse that are more often noted in the bulimorectic.

There has been little in the way of research on Rorschach patterning in anorexia nervosa (Wagner and Wagner, 1978), though there are some detected commonalities. Reflecting the perfectionism and denial of pathology, the total number of responses is low, there is a low proportion of movement (M) to detail (D) responses, and response latencies are slow. The M:D ratio is out of balance, as there are a low number of movement responses, a pattern often noted in persons who are striving beyond their resources. There is a high F and F+%, though occasionally closely integrated color responses and subtle sexual and anatomical responses are included. Not surprisingly, responses that focus on food are common. Wagner and Wagner (1978) conclude that in most other respects they resemble the conversion disorder.

The bulimorectic is believed by this author to have a higher number of responses and a more adequate W:M ratio, although content that focuses on food is similarly present. There is much greater use of integrated color, though the F+% is lower, and overall there is less use of form.

The Bulimia Test (BULIT) (Smith and Thelan, 1984) is a thirty-two-item, self-report multiple-choice scale that has been found to be a reasonably valid and reliable predictor of bulimia in a nonclinical poulation.

☐   TREATMENT OPTIONS

In all cases, a complete physical is recommended, including thyroid and other glandular tests to rule out such primary physical causes as

Simmonds' disease. General goals include weight restoration, treatment of physical complications, and "a change in the relentless pursuit of thinness." Since anorexia nervosa often results in a very severe—even life-threatening—weight loss, hospitalization combined with forced and/or intravenous feeding may be necessary. Nutritional counseling may be helpful, though one has to be careful to avoid moving back into the anorectic's favorite battleground—food. Noradrenergic-blocking medications, such as chlorpromazine, are effective with those anorectics who have high anxiety, peripheral vasospasms, and little appetite. Those who seem to show early satiety, rather than little appetite, may respond to low dosages of dopamine blockers. At this stage, a behavior modification program to develop feeding behaviors may be helpful, though the critical issue is in deriving the reinforcements that can build up the feeding behavior (Agras, 1987).

A more psychodynamic approach has been found to be useful as a person moves into more-normal functioning (Bruch, 1978), with a focus on the ambivalence over dependency, the high need for perfectionism, and, as trust develops, the subtle selfishness and narcissism that emerge. Family therapy is also likely to be necessary since so much of this pattern is related to the interactions over dependency and control in the family.

The bulimorectic can respond to many of the same therapy techniques noted for the anorectic (Agras, 1987). Those with an electrolyte imbalance from intense vomiting will need medical intervention—say, for a depletion of potassium. In addition, adolescent group therapy and/or a support group may be helpful (Brigham, 1988). This provides both a sense of control and a source of feedback. The adolescent group can be useful for anorectics, too, but only after they have made substantial improvements through other techniques. The bulimorectic may also need counseling regarding diet facts and simple control of eating behaviors, counseling of the type used with the more common problems of obesity and persistent-eating disorders (Ruderman, 1986), such as the following:

1. There is a biological drive toward high-fat and very sweet foods, so control should be directed toward "what" as much as "when" and "how much."
2. Weight loss is not hard to attain; keeping it off is.
3. It is more difficult to lose weight during the second diet than the first.
4. Most diets are broken in the late afternoon.
5. If activity level remains the same and there is a cessation of smoking, there will be a weight gain.
6. Changing exercise amounts and patterns is usually more effective in generating weight loss than changing diet amounts and patterns.

CHAPTER 12

Malingering and the Factitious Disorders

■ **Malingering (V65.20)**

The issues of malingering and distorted response sets are often a part of any clinical evaluation, but they are especially important in considering the categories of factitious disorder, antisocial personality disorder, substance dependence, schizophrenia, and the dissociative disorders.

The focus of the DMS-III-R criteria for malingering is the voluntary presentation of physical or psychological symptoms. Malingering is understandable by the evident incentives and circumstances of the situation, rather than from the person's individual psychology.

Malingering is likely to occur in job screening, military and criminal-justice situations, or wherever a psychological or physical disability has a payoff (Landis and Meyer, 1989). It occurs more commonly in the early- to middle-adult years, is more common in males than in females, and often follows an actual injury or illness. Problematic employment history, lower socioeconomic status, or an associated antisocial personality disorder are also common predictors of this disorder. The reader is advised to consult the section of Chapter 6 on the psychogenic pain disorder regarding the issue of chronic (actual) pain versus malingering.

☐ OVERALL INDICATORS

Several overall patterns have been found to be characteristic of interview and test data from malingerers (Landis and Meyer, 1989; Rogers, 1986; 1988b; Ekman, 1985). These characteristic patterns depend to some degree upon the specific distorted response pattern that is being observed, i.e., whether it is the result of malingering, defensiveness, disinterest, etc.

Overall, malingerers more often report relatively rare symptoms, as well as a higher total number of symptoms, than do honest respondents.

Malingerers are also more likely to be willing to discuss their disorder, especially how the negative effects of their disorder impact on rather narrow areas of functioning. They are more likely to report a sudden onset of the disorder; to report a more sudden cessation of symptoms if that has some functional value; and to endorse the more evident, flamboyant, and disabling symptoms. They are more likely to give vague or approximate responses when confronted, to make inconsistent symptom reports, to take a longer time to complete a test or an interview response, to repeat questions, to use qualifiers and vague responses, to miss easy items and then score accurately on hard IQ items, and to endorse the obvious rather than the subtle symptoms usually associated with a disorder. Because of the latter, obvious-subtle item discriminations on the MMPI are quite helpful here.

☐　　　　　　　MMPI

It is appropriate to broaden the concept of malingering to any type of response that distorts the production of an accurate record; this is the context in which the following discussion is placed. On the MMPI, interest is naturally centered on the validity scales as predictors of distorted response sets. Nevertheless, it appears that a number of other measures may be useful here—in numerous instances, *more* valuable than a direct reading of the validity scales.

One effective method is to compare differences on those items originally designated by Weiner and Harmon (1946) as obvious and subtle. After ruling out random or inconsistent responses, it has been found that a difference of 20 points or more in the same direction on four or more subscales is indicative of malingering if obvious items are elevated, defensiveness if subtle items are elevated. Also, if a total difference of at least 160 is obtained, symptom-overreporting has almost certainly occurred. Hovanitz and Jordan-Brown (1986) found that when diagnostic or drug-outcome criteria were used, the exclusion of the subtle MMPI items resulted in a statistically significant loss of predictive ability. The obvious items, however, were found to be related to many diagnostic constructs within the scales. Similarly, an endorsement of 70 or more of Lachar and Wrobel's critical items indicates malingering, and an endorsement of less than 11 indicates defensiveness (Rodgers, 1986, 1988b; Greene, 1980). Gough's Dissimulation Scale (Ds), which was subsequently revised (Ds-r), has also been found to be effective here (Walters et al., 1988).

The standard validity scales do, however, provide much valuable information in this regard. (The reader is referred to the discussion in Chapter 2 of the correlates of these scales.) The traditional rule of thumb has been that if the F-K ratio is +11, such people are trying to fake-bad; that is, to present a distorted picture of themselves that emphasizes pathology. If the score is −12 or more, the emphasis is on trying to look good and deny pathology. However, it is generally agreed that these axioms only hold if F and K are relatively low. For example, psychotic and other severely distressed individuals—e.g., with a high level of anxiety—are likely to score in a T range of 65–80 on the F scale and so at first may appear to be malingering. It's also noteworthy that when there is evidence of a defensive profile—e.g., a high K—elevations in the T range above 65 are usually of high clinical significance (Butcher and Graham, 1988).

Gynther et al. (1973b) have shown that profiles with F scores that are in the T range above 95 are commonly associated with extremely disturbed individuals who manifest hallucinations, delusions, and general confusion. This is particularly so when one is dealing with an inpatient population. Also, individuals who have a T score of greater than 100 on the F scale have probably either responded to the MMPI in a random fashion or have answered virtually all the items "true." If all or the great majority of items are answered "false," the T scores are typically in the 80–99 range. With adolescents, Archer (1987) advises that a "fake-bad" response set should be considered whenever the raw score F value exceeds 25 or if nine or more of the standard scales (including 0) have a T- score greater than 69. In addition to the high F, the highest scales, in order, are typically 8, 6, 1, and 4. A "fake-good" profile tends to have all scores well within the normal range, most near 50, with mild elevations on 5, 6, and 9.

Malingering or other response distortion (or low comprehension or reading ability) may be reflected in an irrelevant (if not irreverant) and/or random response pattern (Fekken and Holden, 1987). Two good measures of what can be termed "person reliability" are the TR Index and the Carelessness Scale. The TR Index was first proposed over thirty years ago (Buechley and Ball, 1952), yet, despite its apparent usefulness, surprisingly little research has been carried out on it (Fekken and Holden, 1987).

The TR Index measures response consistency by a procedure that is relatively uncontaminated by degree of psychopathology. It is a count of identical responses to sixteen pairs of repeated items of the group version (Form R) of the MMPI. (Unfortunately, the option of using the TR index will be eliminated in the revised form of the MMPI.) While the restricted range of scores results in low internal consistency and moderate test-retest reliability, the TR Index can provide a useful piece in the puzzle. The more recently developed and somewhat more sophisticated Carelessness Scale employs twelve pairs of items judged to be opposite in their content.

Utilizing these scales, Rogers (1986, 1988a, 1988b) suggests these two rules as each providing a 95 percent accuracy rate in classifying a respondent's profile as random: (1) both F greater than 70 and TR greater than 4, or (2) both F greater than 70 and Carelessness score greater than 4. Also, if either the Carelessness scale score or the TR score is above 6, or if the sum of both scales is greater than 9, then the profile should be considered to be distorted by a high level of inconsistency.

A well-designed effort to consider most of the relevant response distortion indices together, using a principal-components factor analysis, was carried out by Fekken and Holden (1987). By inserting the appropriate scores in the following regression equation: Item Change = $137.10 + (-1.22 \times K) + (0.59 \times \text{Cannot Say}) + (-4.32 \times \text{TR Index}) + (0.86 \times F)$, the respondent's profile is rejected for lacking person reliability if the item change score is greater than 87.24, using two standard deviations from the mean as the chosen cutoff point. The mean (within rounding error) was 66.92, with a standard deviation of 10.12. It should be remembered that this was a nonpsychiatric population, and so different cutoffs — say, at the first or third standard deviation — may prove desirable with other populations or situations. Fekken and Holden noted that, "At an interpretive level, the single largest predictor of unstable item responses was a low score on the K scale. Additional independent variance was associated with a high Cannot Say score, a low TR Index, and a high F scale score. Faking-bad and over self-criticalness may be reflected both in low K and high F scores" (p. 130). They also note that the Cannot Say scale is highly related to clinical profile stability and to item change measures; thus, "such findings provide clear support for limiting the number of allowable missed responses" (p. 131).

The overall profile for a totally random response set is an L scale of approximately 60 T, an F scale of approximately 115, and K around 55, with an elevation on scale of 8 being close to 100 T for females and approximately 115 for males. It is noteworthy that randomly generated MMPIs look very much like malingered fake-bad MMPI protocols in many respects. Scale 6 is usually the lowest score. If there are all "true" responses, the F scale is practically off the top, the L scale is about 35, and the K scale is at 30 T. The profile peaks are on scale 8: 130 for males and almost 110 for females, with a secondary peak on scale 6 of 100 T for both. It is worthwhile for the clinician at least to scan quickly the response sheet before turning it over for scoring. In cases where careless or random responding has occurred, it is often immediately evident, and the problem can be dealt with at that time.

By altering true and false responses, one obtains a T score of about 55 on L, a T of 110 on F, and 65 on K, with a particularly strong peak on scale 8 (up to 120 T). Scores throughout the rest of the profile are high (Graham, 1977).

A common profile for a malingerer has an inverted V with an F scale at approximately 80; the rest of the profile is a sawtooth pattern, with scales 4, 6, and 8 at approximately 80 T, scale 2 slightly above 70 T, scale 7 slightly below 70 T, and the other scales in the normal range. A person who is deliberately faking-good usually obtains a V on the validity scales, with L sometimes as high as 70, F around a T score of 50, and K again close to 70 T. Most of the scales on this profile are at or below the 50 T scale line, and the highest scores are usually on scales 1, 5, and 4, with low scores on 6 and 0 (Fowler, 1981).

In general, when F and K are both high, look for deliberate faking.

But if L is high and F and K are within acceptable limits, consider the individual to be either naive or very unsophisticated (or both) and at the same time trying to look good. If K is high and L and F are within the normal range, a more sophisticated defensive system is probable and the profile can be considered as an indication of subclinical trends.

Another relatively common pattern that results from a form of malingering is the 1-3/3-1 pattern, with a high K scale and very low scores on 2, 7, and 8. Such an individual is quite defensive and unwilling to admit any faults. These people will not tolerate the patient role and have a poor prognosis.

☐   16 PF

There are scales for faking-good or faking-bad on the 16 PF, derived by Winder et al. (1975). The faking-good scale, which they refer to as a "motivational-distortion" scale, is calculated by taking the sum of the responses that the individual gives to the following specific responses: 7-c, 24-c, 61-c, 62-a, 81-a, 97-a, 111-a, 114-c, 123-c, 130-a, 133-c, 149-c, 173-a, 174-c, and 184-a.

The faking-bad scale is calculated in the same manner, by totaling how many of the specific marker questions that an individual scores on the raw-data sheet. The responses that are used to calculate this score are 14-a, 38-a, 42-c, 51-b, 52-c, 55-c, 68-c, 80-a, 89-c, 117-a, 119-a, 123-a, 143-a, 176-c, and 182-c.

Winder et al. assert that a cutoff score of 6 is useful for determining both faking-good and -bad. However, Krug (1978) obtained data on a much broader and more representative sample, and he finds one major difference in the cutoff scores. Krug's sample included 2,579 men and 2,215 women. On the faking-good scale, scores ranged from 0 to 15, with a mean of 6.36 and a standard deviation of 2.87 for men, while women's scores ranged from 0 to 14, with a mean of 5.71 and a standard deviation of 2.72.

Krug's data suggest that the cutoff score of 6 for the faking-good scales, as suggested by Winder et al., is much too liberal, since in using this cutoff score, almost 55 percent of those people who are routinely screened would be labeled as faking-good, instead of the approximately 7 percent that Winder et al. report. Krug's data would suggest that a raw score of 10 on the faking-good scale would be a much more appropriate cutoff point. Only about 15 percent of people taking the test would attain a score this high.

On the faking-bad scale, men ranged from 0 to 12, with a mean of 2.45 and a standard deviation of 2.27, while women scored from 0 to 11, with a mean of 2.24 and a standard deviation of 2.04. Winder's suggestion of a cutoff score of 6 for the faking-bad scale is supported by Krug. Both report that fewer than 10 percent of those taking the test will score above 6 on this scale.

It should be noted that, in general, college students show lower average scores than the adult population on both of the faking scores, and high school students score even lower than college students; hence an age factor may be operating.

Those who are attempting to fake-good and deny anxiety score very low on O and Q_4, and in general, those who are faking-good score in the following directions: C+, H+, L–, O–, Q_3+, Q_4–, and G+. Those who are faking-bad tend to present a mirror image of these data.

Krug offers the following rules to be used for making the profile more accurately interpretable when scores range from 6 upward:*

FOR FAKING GOOD:

1. If the score is 7, subtract 1 sten score point from C and add 1 point to Q_4.
2. If the score is 8, subtract 1 point from A, C, G, and Q_3 and add one point to L, O, and Q_4.
3. If the score is 9, subtract 1 point from A, C, G, and Q_3 and add 1 point to F, L, O, and Q_4.
4. If the score is 10, add 1 point to F, L, and O, add 2 points to Q_4, subtract 1 point from A, G, H, and Q_3, and subtract 2 points from C.

FOR FAKING BAD:

1. If the score is 7, add 1 point to C.
2. If the score is 8, subtract 1 point from O and Q_4 and add 1 point to C.
3. If the score is 9, subtract 1 point from L, O, and Q_4 and add 1 point to C, H, I, and Q_3.
4. If the score is 10, subtract 1 point from L and Q_4, add 1 point to A, H, I, and Q_3, and add 2 points to C.

Individuals who randomly mark the 16 PF answer sheet show a very flat profile, with a low score on scale B.

RORSCHACH TEST

A major problem with the use of the Rorschach (as well as other projective techniques) in the detection of deception—the apparent susceptibility to fake psychosis on the test—is evident in a classic study by Albert et

* S. Krug, "Further Evidence on the 16 PF Distortion Scales," *Journal of Personality Assessment, 42* (1978), 513–18. Printed with permission of the Society for Personality Assessment and the author.

al. (1980). Albert and his colleagues studied four different groups of Rorschach protocols. The first group, the Psychotic protocols, were obtained from actual mental hospital inpatients who were administered the Rorschach with standard instructions. The second group, labeled Uninformed Fakers, were obtained from college students who were given the instruction to malinger paranoid schizophrenia (that is, "you want the test result to show that you are a paranoid schizophrenic and not show that you are faking") with no other instructions. The third group, the Informed Fakers, were given the same instructions as the Uninformed Fakers, but additionally they heard a twenty-five-minute audiotape describing paranoid schizophrenia, which included actual examples of paranoid delusional thinking. However, at no point did the tape mention the Rorschach test or provide any specific suggestions as to how to fake psychosis. The fourth group, the Control group, consisted of college students on whom the protocols were obtained under standard instructions.

The protocols were sent for judging to clinicians experienced in the use of the Rorschach. Each judge was sent a randomly selected set of four Rorschach protocols and asked to provide a psychiatric diagnosis, to indicate certaintly of the diagnosis, and to rate protocols on dimensions of psychopathology and malingering. Results suggested that these experts were unable to discriminate the fakers from the actual psychotic individuals, although they did discriminate all psychotic groups from the normal group. The group most often seen by these experts as psychotic was the Informed Fakers. This study suggests that while the Rorschach is effective in pointing to psychotic psychopathology, reliable cues for distinguishing malingering from other psychopathology have not been found. The relatively small N in the above study is noted. However, other studies have supported the "fakeability" of both the Rorschach, TAT, most neuropsychological tests, and figure drawings, especially by sophisticated and/or prepared persons (Landis and Meyer, 1989; Rogers, 1986, 1988a).

With the above in mind, it is generally agreed that malingering clients (especially if unsophisticated) will respond to the Rorschach with a reduced number of responses and will also show slow reaction times, even when they do not produce particularly well integrated or complex responses. They take a cautious attitude and thereby produce few responses primarily determined by color. There are high percentages of pure F and popular responses. They easily feel distressed by the ambiguity of the stimuli and will subtly try to obtain feedback from the examiner as to the accuracy of their performance. Also, Seamons et al. (1981) note that if the F%, L, and X+% variables are in the normal range and there are a high number of texture, shading, blood, dramatic, nonhuman-movement, vista, or inappropriate-combination responses, malingering to cause a false appearance of a mentally disordered state should be considered.

☐   OTHER METHODS

It is ironic that clinicians have not carried out much research on the detection of deception, since it is a critical issue in many diagnostic decisions. In addition, most clinicians have not become sophisticated in methods other than psychological test measures of deception, and even here, testing has largely been restricted to the MMPI. Many people who use the 16 PF have been unaware of the deception scales that have been derived from it.

Only recently have clinicians shown an interest in adding physiological methods of deception-assessment to their armamentarium. At the same time, most states are passing laws that permit use of the titles "polygrapher" and "lie detection examiner" only by individuals who have training restricted to certain physiological tests. And, as Balloun and Holmes (1979) demonstrate, the less efficient assessment modalities are often the ones used in the standard examination format and may even be mandated by state law.

Several consistent behavioral cues have been noted in individuals who present a dishonest portrayal of themselves (Ekman, 1985; Bull and Rumsey, 1988). For example, on the average, such individuals nod, grimace, and gesture more than honest interviewees do, and they have less frequent foot and leg movements. They also talk less and speak more slowly, though they make more speech errors and smile more often. In addition, the dishonest interviewees tend to take positions that are physically farther from the interviewer. High voice pitch and many face and hand movements, relative to the individual's standard behavior, are also indicative of deception.

There is no real support for the idea that people who are deceiving will necessarily avoid eye contact (Ekman, 1985). There is some evidence that females will look longer into the eyes of male examiners while lying but usually not into a female examiner's eyes. These same cross-sex results hold for males as well, but not as clearly.

Clinicians also do not make much use of systematized interview observations or techniques that change the set of the person taking the test in order to gain a more truthful response. With reference to the set in which the test is taken, Macciocchi and Meyer (1981) told people that the test that they were going to take had built-in scales to detect deception. These subjects provided more-honest and less socially desirable response patterns than those who were told nothing except to be honest in their responses. Of even more importance, a group of subjects was told that if there was any hint in the psychological tests that they might have been deceptive, they would be given a lie detection examination. They were then even more honest and self-disclosing in their response patterns, compared to when the threat of detection was only by allegedly embedded psychological test scales designed to measure deception. More research in this area is needed to set test conditions more effectively so as to gain more-honest responses.

Clinicians also need to look more to specific tests if there is any question of dishonesty. For example, scales that tap a social-desirability response set, such as the Marlowe-Crowne Social Desirability Scale (Marlowe and Crowne, 1964), give an idea of the direction of a client's response set. A validated short version of the Marlowe-Crowne (Zook and Sipps, 1985) can easily be included in a standard screening battery, such as the Meyer Information Battery, which is found in Appendix A of this book. This Marlowe-Crowne scale and other scales of a similar nature—such as the M scale of Beaber et al. (1985)—are also helpful in conjunction with the other more standard detection scales built into such tests as the MMPI and 16 PF. Rogers (1988a, 1988b) is in the process of developing such a procedure (Structured Interview of Reported Symptoms, the SIRS). But as yet, it has not shown compelling validity data and should still be considered experimental. The Personality Inventory for Children-Revised, Shortened Format has been found to be effective in assessing deception in children (Daldin, 1985).

The Schedule for Affective Disorders and Schizophrenia (Spitzer and Endicott, 1978), a semistructured interview technique, is also of potential help here. A drawback of its use with malingerers is that it takes up to four hours to complete, although its length makes it easier to trip up a malingering client on inconsistent responses. Malingering is suggested if (1) sixteen or more of the "severe" symptoms are subscribed to, (2) forty or more symptoms are scored in the "clinical" range—a score of 3 or greater, or (3) four or more "rare" symptoms are subscribed to. These rare symptoms are each only found in 5 percent of a sample of 105 forensic patients, and only about 1 percent of this population showed five or more of these symptoms: (1) markedly elevated mood, (2) much less sleep in the previous week, (3) significantly increased activity level in the previous week, (4) thought withdrawal—something or someone is "pulling" thoughts from them, (5) delusions of guilt, (6) marked somatic delusions, (7) evident and recent loosening of associations, (8) incoherence at some point during the previous week (9) poverty of speech, or (10) neologisms. These rare symptoms could probably be effectively included in a short screening procedure.

☐ AMNESIA

Amnesia (see Chapter 7) is a commonly malingered symptom, probably because it is seemingly easy to carry off and acts to void responsibility while leaving the person otherwise fully functional in their world. True psychogenic amnesia is typically focused on personal memory, particularly those memories directly relevant to the traumatic event. Psychogenic amnesia can usually be differentiated from organic amnesia and faked amnesia by the sudden onset, shorter course and sudden recovery, anterograde direction (continued ability to learn new information), recoverability under hypnosis, personal focus, and unimpaired ability to learn new information that are characteristic of psychogenic amnesia (Wiggins and Brandt, 1988; Rogers, 1986; Schachter, 1986).

It's worthwhile for clinicians to first remember that vigor and/or apparent sincerity of presentation are not indicators of true amnesia. Indeed, there seems to be no clear correlation here. It's also worthwhile to remember that there may be both true and malingered amnesia in the same case. However, there are cues that indicate malingered rather than true amnesia:

1. True amnesia for situation is seldom either total or very specific. The manifestation of such patterns should cue one to possible malingering.

2. True amnesiacs have shown lower scores on MMPI scales 1, 2, and 3 than malingering amnesiacs (Parwatikar et al., 1985).

3. Malingering amnesia often results in inconsistencies between reports, as well as with usual psychogenic or organic syndromes.

4. True amnesiacs rate themselves higher on the ability to recall information if they are told they will be given extra time or prompting, and indeed, they do function better if primed. Malingerers are more likely to indicate the improbability of change in their amnesia; they then do not show much change even if prompted.

5. Malingerers show amnesia as "characterized by recall performance better than, and recognition performance worse than, that of brain-damaged memory-disordered subjects" (Wiggins and Brandt, 1988, p. 74). In addition, malingerers' serial-position pattern resembles that of normals rather than that of amnesiacs.

RULING OUT HYPOCHONDRIASIS, FACTITIOUS DISORDER, OR MALINGERING

There are three probable specific statuses that a clinician must invariably take into account where malingering or other distorted response sets are suspected. These three patterns are hypochondriasis (discussed in Chapter 6), factitious disorders, and true malingering. As noted, hypochondriasis is one of the somatoform disorders (along with the somatization disorder, conversion disorder, and psychogenic pain disorder), all of which are denoted by complaints of physical symptoms that have no identifiable physiological base and are *not* under voluntary control. The factitious disorders are discussed in the next section of this chapter.

Clinicians are often called upon to determine if any of these three conditions exist. Figure 12.1 shows an appropriate decision tree to apply to such a situation.

In order to facilitate this decision process, the following checklists for each of the three categories were developed by Elizabeth Salazar and

FIGURE 12.1   Symptom Decision Tree

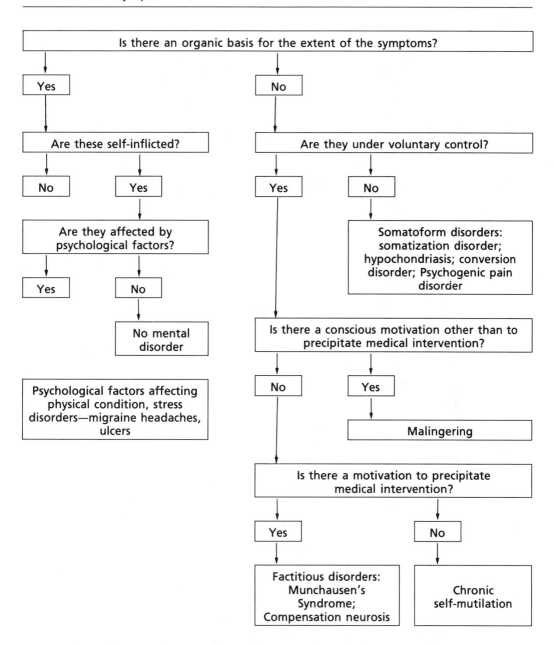

me. In the great majority of cases, a high percentage (75 percent or more) of positive answers will occur on predominately one checklist, indicating support for that pattern. If no condition clearly predominates, these three patterns can usually be ruled out. There are some cases in which two (or even, in very rare cases, all three) of these patterns will occur.

☐   HYPOCHONDRIASIS CHECKLIST

1. Is there a morbid preoccupation with the body, or a part of the body, that is felt to be diseased or functioning improperly?

2. Is there a long-term pattern of social or occupational impairment?

3. Are normal bodily functions/fluctuations exaggerated as indications of disease?

4. Are beliefs about the issue sustained in spite of consistent medical information to the contrary?

5. Is there a general indifference to the opinions of people in the client's environment?

6. Is the client anxious, worried, and concerned about this "illness"?

7. Does the client dwell excessively on symptoms, turning interviews into monologues—an "organ recital"?

8. Does the speech content consist almost solely of symptoms, their effect on his or her life, and the difficult search for a cure?

9. During conversation, does the client frequently point out afflicted areas of the body?

10. Is there an expression of obsessive-compulsive traits, such as defensiveness, obstinacy, miserliness, or conscientiousness?

11. Is there an indication of narcissistic traits, such as egocentrism or oversensitivity to criticism or slight?

12. Is there a lack of sense of inner worth, self-esteem, or adequacy?

13. Does the client appear to have a preference for being ill, showing positive emotions if any real sickness is found?

14. Are there indications of an affective disorder, such as significant depressive tendencies?

15. Is there a history of frequent doctor visits, with one physician or thorough "doctor shopping"?

16. Is there an unusual and wide-ranging familiarity with psychological or medical terms and jargon?

17. Is there an apparent addiction to reading medical journals, health magazines, and other related materials?

18. Does the client follow unusual health fads, diets, or exercise plans?

19. Has the client often made appeals for extensive tests, examinations, and prescriptions?

20. Do the symptoms commonly deal with the head, neck, abdomen, chest, gastrointestinal system, or generally the left side of the body?

21. Are there indications of a dependent relationship in which affection is not effectively displayed outside of sickness situations?

22. Do the symptoms seem to fulfill an ego-defensive purpose?

23. Do the symptoms ease an intolerable personal situation, avoid anxiety or personal responsibility, or gain needed attention?

24. Do the symptoms appear to be an attempt to control a situation that seems to be getting out of the client's control?

25. Did the pattern appear to have an early onset?

26. Did the client grow up in an "atmosphere of illness," e.g., with a bedridden, chronically ill, or terminally ill family member or a family member in the medical field who brought work home in some fashion?

27. Were the client's parents, especially the mother, overprotective, strict, or overly sanitary in health tendencies?

28. Did the client grow up without parents for a substantial period, or was there a pattern of self-mothering?

□   FACTITIOUS DISORDER CHECKLIST

1. Is there an absence of evident or obvious gain that the client would achieve as a result of the presented disorder pattern?

2. Is there a gut-level sense that the client has been inducing the symptoms?

3. Could the problem fulfill a masochistic need, such as relieving guilt, or a need to identify with the "sadistic" doctor?

4. Does the client show any counterphobic responses to other disorder patterns or syndromes?

5. Are there indications that deceiving others acts as a defense mechanism, e.g., against low self-esteem or a sense of powerlessness?

6. Are there indications that the presented disorder provides distance from frustrating objects, internal conflicts, or anxieties or provides a temporary identity while ego-dysfunctions are reorganized?

7. Is there any evidence that dependency needs are being gratified in the pattern?

8. Was childhood marked with institutional placement or sadistic, abusive, or rejecting parents?

9. Did the patterns apparently start in adolescence or early adulthood?

10. Is there a history of multiple hospitalizations?

11. Is there any evidence of multiple surgeries?

12. Do the symptoms appear to have symbolic meaning or to have been derived from a previously suffered disorder?

13. Does the client have a background in the health professions or some other access to medical knowledge?

14. Did the client grow up in an "atmosphere of illness"?

15. Is there any indication of wandering to many different hospitals or clinics?

16. Has the client accumulated diagnostic labels, medical biographies, radiographs, or thick hospital folders?

17. Is the medical history inconsistent with known pathophysiological courses?

18. Have there been any inconsistent lab or test results?

19. Have there been any unusual recurrent infections?

20. Has the client failed to respond to therapy as expected?

21. Has the client falsified his or her history in any manner?

22. Does the client dramatically present one or more symptoms with elaborate stories, while interacting on a narcissistic level?

23. Is the client's attitude toward staff threatening, aggressive, hostile and/or impatient?

24. Are there frequent requests for surgery, direct patient observation, or invasive procedures?

25. Does the client impassively or even eagerly submit to agonizing examinations and treatments, expressing high pain tolerance and/or exhibitionist traits?

26. Does the client show *pseudologia phantastica,* attention seeking, or restlessness?

27. Has the client ever discharged himself or herself or retreated indignantly when confronted?

28. Are there indications of any underlying histrionic, antisocial, and/or narcissistic personality disorder patterns?

☐   MALINGERING CHECKLIST

1. Would the client obtain any obvious gain by being considered ill or disordered?

2. Does the client seem to perceive interviews as a challenge or threat?

3. Does the client appear to be annoyed at what he or she considers to be unusual tests?

4. Does the client appear suspicious, overly evasive, vague, or unusually lacking in comprehension of issues?

5. Are there seemingly exaggerated concerns for the symptoms?

6. Is there an easily expressed pessimism about recovery?

7. Is there a relative lack of concern about treatment for the presented disorder?

8. Is the client quickly or especially explicit in denying concern for financial (or other goal-oriented) matters?

9. Is there a focused rather than wide-ranging familiarity with medical or psychological terminology?

10. Does the client show an overly self-confident or assertive manner?

11. Are there any indications of antisocial or psychopathic personality traits?

12. Are there any indications that either of the parents showed manipulative or psychopathic patterns?

13. Do some symptoms seem to contradict symptomatology the client should have?

14. In cases that should supposedly show a long-term deficit or problem, is there an unusual lack of previous exams?

15. Are there other discrepancies, contradictions, omissions, or odd exaggerations?

16. Is there poor test-retest reliability in testing or interview patterns?

17. Whether or not there are discrepancies, exaggerations, etc., do some portions of the client's presentation just seem too "neat," as if coming out of a textbook?

■ Factitious Disorders

Factitious means "not genuine" and refers to symptoms that are under voluntary control of the individual, a syndrome first clearly defined by Asher in 1951. At first, this syndrome may sound like malingering. The difference is that in a factitious disorder the goal or reinforcement sought is not obvious or inherent in the apparent facts of the situation. Instead, the motivation is understandable only within the person's individual psychology. These patterns have been traditionally confused with the conversion disorders, but in both the somatoform and conversion disorders of DSM-III-R, the symptoms are not under voluntary control. Also, in a conversion disorder, symptoms seldom follow a pattern that is true to the factitious disorders: Although the symptoms are not under voluntary control, they are usually associated with a degree of anxiety and have occurred more frequently in the person's history.

Factitious disorders are rare, and, according to Spitzer et al. (1979), they comprise the most difficult DSM category to diagnose, in part because the feigned symptoms are often accompanied by a more subtle, though actual, physical disorder. When diagnosticians become aware of what they perceive as deception, they are inclined to make a diagnosis of an antisocial personality instead of a factitious disorder and then give the person little attention (Landis and Meyer, 1989).

The factitious disorders are subdivided into: (1) Factitious Disorder with Psychological Symptoms (300.16), and (2) Chronic Factitious Disorder with Physical Symptoms (301.51), the latter often referred to in the literature as Munchausen's syndrome. The general DSM-III-R requirements in each syndrome are the intentional production or feigning of symptoms and a psychological need to assume the sick role, with an absence of external incentives as primary. There have also been a few isolated reports of "Munchausen's by proxy"—e.g., where a mother has induced multiple hospitalizations in her child by administering laxatives—but this pattern is not yet common enough or so clearly recognized as to warrant inclusion in DSM-III-R.

In the factitious psychological syndrome, the symptoms are mental rather than physical and therefore are often less well defined. These people usually talk around a point or give approximate though evasive answers to direct questions, a pattern referred to as *vorbereiten*. For example, if asked an arithmetic question (such as "How much is 35 minus 12?"), they may respond with only an approximate answer ("20 or 25"). In that sense, they are not unlike persons with Ganser's syndrome, though that pattern usually lasts no more than a few weeks, even if treatment is no more sophisticated than supportive therapy. The factitious disorders, on the other hand, are chronic.

The factitious disorders are thought to be more common in males. This may only reflect a more ready acceptance of verbalizations of sickness from females, so that the diagnostician would be less inclined to recognize a factitious disorder in females.

Munchausen's syndrome (Chronic Factitious Disorder with Physical Symptoms in DSM-III-R) was named after Baron Munchausen, an eighteenth-century German equivalent of our Paul Bunyan, both of whom are associated with tales of exaggeration.

The all-time champion victim of Munchausen's syndrome appears to be Stewart McIlroy, whose path through 68 hospitals (with at least 207 separate admissions) in England, Scotland, Ireland, and Wales was retraced by Pallis and Bamji (1979). Though McIlroy used false names and different complaints, he was eventually identified by scar patterns (i.e,, the "gridiron stomach," a pattern seen in a number of these individuals) and other permanent medical characteristics.

McIlroy is an excellent example of one who suffered mightily to satisfy his addiction. Pallis and Bamji (1979) estimate that over the years of his disorder, he was subjected to thousands of blood tests and X rays, his spine had been tapped at least forty-eight times, and his abdomen and body parts were crisscrossed with many scars from exploratory surgeries. It is probable that he cost the British Health Services the equivalent of several million dollars.

The range of symptomatology is limited only by the client's imagination and degree of sophistication about medical information. Some experience with hospitals or medical situations, either through prior hospitalizations or through knowledge from family members involved in the medical profession, often contributes to this disorder. It is highly refractory to intervention, in part because the person can often find another cooperative physician. Ironically, the disorder can take a high physical toll on the person, as seen in the case of Mr. McIlroy.

☐   TEST-RESPONSE PATTERNS

The functional performance of individuals with these disorders is that of malingering, though the psychology that generates the behaviors is somewhat different. However, the patterns and symptom picture described in the prior section on malingering is appropriate, especially as regards malingering used to gain admission to a hospital. It is unfortunate that clinicians have not paid more attention to the issue of the detection of deception, as it is relevant to so many disorders. The clinician is advised to depend on more than one test for indications of malingering. Also, the careful gathering and evaluation of past records, which is important in all disorders, is critical here (Landis and Meyer, 1989).

The factitious disorder with psychological symptoms generally parallels the classic signs of neurasthenia (Golden, 1979), in which the clinician can expect high 2, 7, 1, and 3 scales, in that order of elevation. The deception and sophistication found here would also suggest high 6 and 4 scales. A person with Munchausen's syndrome is more likely to show greater elevations on 1 and 3 than a person with psychological symptoms.

On the MCMI, elevations on 3 and C between 75 and 85 may occur. The submissive personality (elevation on 3) may use physical symptoms as a way to maintain nurturing and care-giving by others. Scale H may or may not be elevated, depending on the specific patterns of symptoms. It's important to note that the Rorschach and other projective tests are helpful because they present a situation in which it is hard to decipher the situational demands. Thus, such tests disrupt the sophistication and polish of deceptive clients in their presentation of symptoms. For that reason, it is advisable to use a projective test early in the battery; disturbing their sense of surety about performance may spill over into the tests that follow (Newmark, 1985).

☐   TREATMENT OPTIONS

Biofeedback and allied techniques are useful for any physiological disorder, regardless of the source, even including a physiological disorder that is a direct result of psychological conflicts (Schwartz, 1987). The factitious disorder is a different story, though, because the essential aspect is deception. Not surprisingly, such persons are going to be openly hostile and avoidant of treatment. Thus, unless they are coerced by a significant other, they are not likely to become involved in treatment. If they are coerced and are willing to participate, at least initially, many of the principles that hold for the paranoid disorders are applicable here.

Variations on reality therapy (Glasser, 1980) are also an appropriate therapeutic focus here. These emphasize that the person must accept responsibility for his or her behavior and, most importantly, for the consequences of that behavior. To the degree that reality therapy is effective, clients are more likely to come into contact with the conflicts central to their disorder. At that point, more traditional psychotherapeutic modes are appropriate.

☐ COMMENTS

It would be useful if graduate training programs in the mental health professions emphasized more the use of physiological measures in detecting deception. For example, the psychologist's extensive background in the study of human behavior and expertise in interviewing and psychological testing could easily be supplemented by this specific training. This not only would facilitate the accuracy of general psychological testing, it would also provide our court system with a much more expert and effective effort toward the detection of deception than is available from the usually minimally trained polygrapher (Landis and Meyer, 1989).

CHAPTER 13

Aggression Potential, Child Abuse, and Suicide Potential

■ ## Aggression Potential

A major issue in many psychological referral situations is the potential for acting-out, toward either others or oneself. Given the low base rates of such behaviors, making a highly accurate prediction to actual behavior is virtually impossible (Landis and Meyer, 1989; Monahan, 1981, 1984). Monohan has pointed to the eight most critical demographic predictor variables for aggression. It is more common if the potential perpetrator (1) is young (this variable correlates strongly up until the thirty to thirty-five age range, after which the correlation is random), (2) is male, (3) is of a lower socioeconomic class, (4) is from a disadvantaged minority (5) is less educated, (6) has a lower intellectual level, (7) has an unstable school and/or vocational history, and (8) has a history of alcohol and/or drug abuse. Other demographic indicators of a potential for violence that have been noted throughout the literature are (1) a prior history of violent behaviors, (2) a prior history of suicide attempts, (3) a history of family violence, (4) histrionic personality traits, (5) a pattern of cruelty to animals as a child or adolescent, (6) a rejecting or depressed father, and (7) recent stress, especially if associated with low levels of serontin. In addition to these predictors, assaultiveness on the ward by inpatient psychiatric patients is correlated with hallucinatory behavior, emotional lability, and a high level of activity. Additionally, there are test data that can help the clinician to make predictions at a higher level than that allowed by impressionistic data or chance.

□ ### MMPI

There are several indicators of potential for aggression against others in the MMPI (Kalichman, 1988). As in all areas of psychopathology, certain scales have been developed specifically to assess aggression potential. Ironically, in the general testing situation, the examiner would have to know the "answer" already, at least to a degree, to employ such scales. They are of help when there are prior cues, and it is worthwhile for the clinician to keep a range of specific tests available for such situations. A classic example in this area is the overcontrolled-hostility (O-H) scale, devised and refined by Megargee and his colleagues (Megargee and Cook, 1975). This scale is a subset of MMPI items and effectively identifies a subgroup of assaultive criminals who are generally overcontrolled in their response to hostility but who sporadically are extremely assaultive.

The type of individual discovered in this scale is similar to the one with the 4-3 profile type described by Davis and Sines (1971). The profile peak is on scale 4, the second highest elevation is on scale 3, and there is little significant elevation elsewhere. This profile is characteristic of men who maintain an ongoing quiet adjustment, yet who are prone toward hostile, aggressive outbursts. They may or may not fit the aforementioned criteria for the intermittent-explosive disorder. Davis and Sines hypothesize that those with the 4-3 profile type are constitutionally predisposed to this behavior by some kind of a cyclical internal mechanism that occasionally causes acute emotional outbursts. Later research, for the most part, confirmed the validity of this profile as suggestive of aggression potential across a number of settings, and among females as well as males (Gearing, 1979).

To the degree that both 4 and 3 are highly elevated in a typically nonaggressive person, the likelihood of an occasional aggressive outburst increases. In general, when scale 4 is greater than scale 3, control decreases. Conversely, as scale 3 increases over scale 4, potential for more ability to control and inhibit aggressive impulses increases. In females, the 4-3 pattern has also been commonly associated with promiscuity. This is probably true with males, but because of traditional sex role expectations, such behavior in males is not as commonly a focus in assessment.

Consistently assaultive individuals, whose overt interpersonal patterns are more consistent with this behavior, have high scores on scales F, 4, and 9, with secondary elevations on 6 and 8. All five of these scales have been classically regarded as scales that suggest a lack of impulse control. Persons with high scores on these scales combine social resentment and hostility, a lack of moral inhibitions, suspiciousness of and resentment toward authority and the world in general, and a lack of impulse control. Such a combination easily engenders hostility, even with minimal environmental stimulation. General problems in social adjustment also occur and combine with social resentment and envy of others to elevate the 0 scale. A high scale 5 score is generally indicative of ability to suppress aggression, though Graham (1987) notes that the 4-5/5-4 profile in women is correlated with aggression.

A specific criminal subgroup, Charlie, with elevations on these scores, is described by Megargee and Bohn (1979). Charlies—who are hostile, paranoid, and dangerous—showed characteristic elevations on scales 8, 6, and 4, in that order, with distinctly low scales on 1, 2, and 3. From an overall perspective, high scores on F, 6, 7, and 8 predict to violent incidents in a prison setting.

The subgroup How, also studied by Megargee and Bohn (1979), seeks interpersonal contact but is consistently rejected and builds up much anger, hostility, and anxiety. In that subgroup, scale 8 is usually highest, followed by scales 2, 4, and 1. The overall profile is distinctly elevated, with higher elevations on the above scales in a noteworthy jagged pattern.

The "double-M profile," with distinct elevations on 2, 4, 6, and 8, refers to individuals who are very unstable and dangerous to self or, more likely, to others. It is hard to bring them into a therapy situation, and if they appear, they are difficult to change.

☐   16 PF

There has not been as much research on the prediction of aggression with the 16 PF as there has been with the MMPI. However, several scales considered together do modestly predict aggression. Scales that tap aggression potential per se are E, L, and Q_1, and in each a high scale is predictive. General impulsiveness is reflected in high scores on F and H. Low scores on G, O, and Q_3, along with a high score on F, are thought to be predictors of low ego control and thus to contribute to a prediction of acting-out.

☐   OTHER TEST-RESPONSE PATTERNS

Persons who are inclined toward easy aggression seem less able to deal with their concerns by articulating them verbally (Goldstein and Keller, 1987); this may be reflected in the WAIS-R, since they usually obtain a verbal score that is lower than the performance score. Kunce et al. (1976) found a specific instance of this effect: Individuals prone to aggression were low on the similarities score relative to all other scales. Kunce and his colleagues suggest that a low ability to discuss abstract issues verbally is related to problems in impulse control. While this very specific prediction of the overall conceptual scheme has not been replicated, clients who act out aggressively tend to score lower on the similarities, vocabulary, and block design subtests.

Problems in aggression control are usually correlated with present or previous difficulties in adjusting to school (Mash and Terdal, 1988). Hence, within the verbal section of the WAIS-R, scores tend to be lower on information, arithmetic, and vocabulary relative to the other three scales taken as a whole. Quiet but hostile and explosive individuals attain low picture arrangement scores, relative to the more extroverted and consistently aggressive type.

An elevation on MCMI scales 6 of 85 or higher should alert the clinician to aggression potential. The 5-6/6-5 codes also occur frequently in the context of the antisocial personality diagnosis and may therefore be predictive of aggression. The deficient social conscience and interpersonal exploitiveness of a high 5 (narcissistic), combined with the hostile affectivity and interpersonal vindictiveness of a high 6 (antisocial), would seem to be indicative of a potentially dangerous individual. To the extent that elevations on B and/or T occur, in conjunction with elevated 6, aggression potential increases. As P and PP become more elevated, aggression potential may increase.

Persons who exhibit patterns of intermittent-explosive behavior certainly have potential for aggression, though predicting these episodes may be considerably more difficult (Monahan, 1984). (The reader is referred to Chapter 11 for discussion of disorders of impulse control.)

On the Rorschach, individuals who are prone to aggressive behavior typically show short reaction times, do not provide extensive response records, and may give quick responses to card I and the color cards (Beck, 1951). They tend to be low in the number of FC responses and high in C, CF, and popular responses (Phillips and Smith, 1953). Responses associated with fighting (swords, guns, blood) or aggressive animals (crabs, tigers) are expected in those individuals who consistently act out aggressively: assaultive psychopaths. The explosion-oriented response is more characteristic of the person who is making an attempt to control aggression: the explosive personality. Conversely, the potential for assault is contraindicated by a high number of F+, D, and FC responses, a high amount of abstraction content, and/or a higher number of popular and original responses (Exner, 1986; Phillips and Smith, 1953).

A number of specific contents on the Rorschach are often considered signs of aggression. On card I, in reference to the central light-gray detail on the midline, the responses "tomahawk" or "hammerhead" are given mainly by aggressive psychopaths. A response on card II like "two bears fighting with blood splashed around" is significant for the type of psychopath who entertains aggressive fantasies and is hostile toward the outer world. When card III, lower central light-gray detail, elicits a response like "jaws closing" cojoined with "blood," there is a possibility of latent hostility and sadistic aggressivity.

Potential for aggression is occasionally seen in frank, unsublimated expressions of aggressive impulses. More-subtle clues are drawings that seem to press out against the edges of the page, heavy pencil pressure, short and/or jagged strokes, transparencies, unrelieved areas of white space, teeth, long spikelike fingers, and a same sex-person depicted in an explicitly aggressive posture (Oster and Gould, 1987).

The reader is referred to the previous sections on the antisocial personality disorder, conduct disorder, and the passive-aggressive personality disorder, since these disorders in particular contain the potential for ongoing aggression, and the criteria described there are applicable here as well. With regard to periodic aggression, the reader is referred to the sections on the explosive personality and on the paranoid disorders.

■ Child Abuse

The physical and sexual abuse of children has been clearly documented throughout history across cultures (Gelles, 1986; Nelson, 1984). Although such abuse is frequently abhorred, few actual preventive measures have been taken. It is ironic that the first formal legal intervention in a child abuse case, that of Mary Ellen in New York in 1975, had to be prosecuted through animal protection laws and with the efforts of the Society for the Prevention of Cruelty to Animals. However, in the spectacularly short time of about five years, child abuse in the United States went from being virtually a nonissue to being the focus of national political concern (Nelson, 1984). All fifty states, partly spurred by the federal Child Abuse Prevention and Treatment Act, have established legal routes to identify and intervene in abusive families. As a result, the number of identified cases continues to grow enormously. Yet, because of the private nature of abuse and the reluctance of both perpetrators and victims to reveal its occurrence (Eckenrode et al., 1988), clearly identified cases of child abuse are generally believed to represent only a portion of the actual cases.

☐ DIAGNOSTIC CONSIDERATIONS

In the vast majority of cases, the first diagnostic cue emanates from the child. There are a number of common physical signs of physical abuse. A way of remembering them are the "four Bs": unexplained or unusual bruises, burns, bald spots, or bleeding.

Look for bruises around the head or face or in easily protected areas, such as the abdomen; multiple bruises, especially if spread over the body; or bruises in the shape of an object, such as a hand or a belt. Likewise, burns of all types should cause concern, especially cigarette burns; burns with a specific shape, such as an iron; and burns that suggest that a hand has been immersed in liquid. Concern should be heightened if the child provides an explanation that does not fit the injury.

Behavioral signs of physical abuse include accident-proneness, problems with schoolwork and peers, shrinking from physical contact, and wearing clothes that seem designed more to cover the body than to keep one warm. Be especially on guard if any of these symptoms represent a change in the behavior pattern of the child. Over and above these signs, delinquency, drug abuse, anorexia nervosa, and excessive avoidance of parents may reflect on abuse situation in older children and adolescents.

Along with physical abuse, there has been increasing attention to the sexual abuse of children. The behavioral signs noted above also are found in cases of sexual abuse. Additional signs include extreme secrecy, excessive bathing, indications of low self-worth, provocative or promiscuous sexual patterns, appearing more worldly than friends, or suddenly possessing money or merchandise that could have been used to bribe the child to keep quiet.

Specific physical signs of sexual abuse are pain, rashes, itching or sores in the genital or anal areas, enuresis, frequent urinary infections, or frequent vomiting.

On the MMPI, the 4/8 code has been shown to predominate in the victims of father-daughter incest, when they are either later-adolescent or adult clients (Scott and Stone, 1986). Adult victims may have significantly elevated 1, 2, and 5 scales, suggesting that depression is a feature. Adolescents show higher elevations on scale 9, suggesting acting-out behaviors.

General diagnostic considerations flow from an understanding of the many factors that contribute to the ultimate emergence of an episode of physical and/or sexual child abuse (Finkelhor, 1985; Gelles, 1986). These factors are found within three contributing systems: sociocultural, familial, and individual. To the degree these factors are present, the probability of an occurrence of child abuse is increased. At the most basic level are the following *sociocultural* factors that facilitate an increase in child abuse episodes:

1. Lack of affirmation and support of the family unit.
2. Lack of emphasis on parent-training skills as a prerequisite to parenting.
3. Acceptance of and high media visibility of violence.
4. Acceptance of corporal punishment as a central child-rearing technique.
5. Emphasis on competition rather than cooperation.
6. Unequal status for women.
7. Low economic support for schools and day-care facilities.

These sociocultural factors heighten the probability of abuse in conjunction with the following *familial* factors:

1. Low socioeconomic and education level.
2. Little availability of friends and extended family for support.
3. Single-parent or merged-parent family structure.
4. Marital instability.
5. Family violence as common and traditionally accepted.
6. Low rate of family contact and information exchange.

7. Significant periods of mother absence.
8. High acceptance of family nudity.
9. Low affirmation of family-member privacy.
10. "Vulnerable" children (to the degree they are young, sick, disturbed, retarded, or emotionally isolated).

The probability of abuse in a specific instance is in turn increased by the following *individual* factors:

1. History of abuse as a child.
2. Low emotional stability and/or self-esteem.
3. Low ability to tolerate frustration and inhibit anger.
4. High impulsivity.
5. Lack of parenting skills
6. High emotional and interpersonal isolation.
7. Problems in handling dependency needs of self or others.
8. Low ability to express physical affection.
9. Unrealistic expectations for child's performance.
10. Acceptance of corporal punishment as a primary child-rearing technique.
11. Presence of drug or alcohol abuse.

In most cases, many (though not all) of the above factors are found. Some predict more to physical abuse and some to sexual abuse, but most factors predict to either type. Other specific diagnostic considerations (including test correlates) and treatment considerations can be found in the prior section on aggression potential, and in the sections on pedophilia and incest (see Chapter 8) and the personality disorders (see Chapter 9).

☐ ___ TREATMENT OPTIONS _____

In addition to individual psychotherapy, there are three core approaches that are potentially useful in almost all such cases (Brigham, 1988; Goldstein et al., 1986; Nelson, 1984):

1. *Family therapy.* Since the family is virtually always disrupted, family therapy is necessary. Even where the family system eventually changes, family therapy can help to mute the damage to all concerned.
2. *Parent training.* When the abuse comes from a parent, parent training is necessary to deal not only with the problems that led to the abuse, but to those generated by the abuse as well. Parent training to deal with

this latter factor is also important when the source of abuse is external to the family.

3. *Support systems.* Abuse often comes where there has been a sense of emotional isolation. In this vein, a community-based counseling and support group is available to abusing parents in Parents Anonymous. This organization works in the samer manner as Alcoholics Anonymous or Gamblers Anonymous. A similar group is Parents United. Contact with other abusers and the opportunity to share problems with sympathetic and understanding others are helpful for parents for whom abusive behaviors are triggered by psychosocial stressors and a sense of emotional isolation. There are also support groups for the victims of child abuse, which are especially useful with older abuse victims.

The above can also be supplemented by other interventions, for instance, attempts to change the person's employment possibilities or social skills. Where there is a couple involved, marital therapy is likely to be necessary if the marriage is to continue.

While treatment may help in a specific case, the greatest changes will come with efforts at prevention (parent training *before* becoming parents, reduction of the percentage of very young and/or single parents without skills or resources, educational programs in schools) or cultural change (efforts to reduce the acceptance of physical discipline) (Nelson, 1984; Finkelhor, 1985; Eckenrode et al., 1988).

■ Suicide Potential

As with aggression, the clinician is often called on the make predictions about suicide potential, and it is an equally difficult task (Landis and Meyer, 1988; Monahan, 1981). Though suicide is still an issue of concern in legal areas, it is no longer considered a crime. Only in recent times has our legal predecessor, England, stopped responding to a suicide attempt with hanging. But hanging had superseded an even more flamboyant approach: driving a stake through the heart of one who attempted suicide. Though Edward Phillips claimed in his 1662 dictionary to have invented the word "suicide," the British poetry critic Alfred Alvarez reported in 1971 that he had found the word used even earlier, in Sir Thomas Brown's *Religio Medici*, written in 1635 and published in 1642 (Schneidman, 1985).

Most authorities believe that the suicide rate has been rising, but it is still not clear whether this is because of a greater willingness on the part of coroners and police officers to use the term or because there is a true increase in the incidence of suicide. The research of Murphy and Wetzel (1980) suggests that the suicide rate significantly increased throughout the years 1949–1974; there is good reason to believe that this increase has not since abated (Kreitman, 1986). However, they point out that before these findings are used to authorize an expansion of traditional efforts to increase the number of suicide prevention centers, one should note that the rise in the suicide rate has coincided with a rise in the distribution and visibility of these centers in the United States. Interestingly, the opposite effect has been noted in England.

Suicide appears to be increasing among young adults; at present, it is the second highest cause of death for white males aged fifteen to nineteen (approximately 88 per 100,000). For many years, the reported rate of suicide in the United States has been approximately 10–12 per 100,000 population. In several European countries, notably Sweden and Switzerland, rates of approximately 25 per 100,000 have been reported. However, it is not clear whether this reflects truly differential rates.

More men than women actually kill themselves (at approximately a ratio of 3:1), although more women than men *attempt* suicide, again at approximately a 3:1 ratio (Schneidman, 1985). The majority of suicides, approximately 90 percent, are committed by whites, and most of the data about suicide concern whites.

Suicidal individuals tend to give clues to those around them. Seriously suicidal individuals tend to perceive life in a negative manner and associate many attractive concepts with death; the reverse is true for those who are not so intent on self-destruction. Such measures as the semantic differential could be helpful in this regard. Approximately 80 percent of those who have made a suicide attempt discussed their intent to do so with persons around them, and they are usually open to discussing their suicidal concerns with clinicians.

In addition to being depressed, with feelings of hopelessness, helplessness, a loss of a sense of continuity with the past and/or present, and loss of pleasure in typical interests and pursuits, suicidal persons are more likely to (1) have had a parent or other important identity figure who attempted or committed suicide, (2) have a history of family instability and/or parental rejection, (3) be socially isolated, (4) have a physical illness, (5) have a history or self-damaging acts, often previous suicide attempts (in this context, the first axiom of psychology could well be "Behavior predicts behavior," and the second axiom could be "Behavior without intervention predicts behavior"), (6) show a preoccupation with death and/or make statements of a wish to die, especially statements of a wish to commit suicide, (7) manifest *consistent* life patterns of leaving crises rather than facing them (in relationships: "You can't walk out on me, I'm leaving you"; or in jobs: "You can't fire me, because I quit"), (8) show a family history of self-damaging acts, (9) are involved (married or similarly occupied) with a loved mate who is competitive and/or self-absorbed, (10) show sudden cheerfulness after a long depression, (11) are noted to be putting their affairs in order, e.g., giving away favorite possessions, revising wills, or (12) show some abrupt atypical behavior change, e.g., withdrawal from family or friends.

At the biological level, depressions marked by low levels of 5-HIAA, as well as high levels of cortisol and a high ratio of adrenaline to noradrenaline, increase the probability of suicide attempts. Also, suicide completers' brains show one half to two thirds the number of receptical, or "binding," sites for the chemical imipramine than do normal brains. The initiation of the suicidal event is especially likely to be triggered by a major life stress or, for example, the experience of a chronic debilitating illness or the loss of an important social support, such as a confidant (Rutter, 1988; Fawcett et al., 1987; Kreitman, 1986; Schneidman, 1985).

The following factors can then increase this potential:

1. A cognitive state of constriction, that is, an inability to perceive any options or way out of a situation that is generating intense psychological suffering.
2. Easy access to a lethal means.
3. Absence of an accessible support system (family and good friends).
4. Life stresses that connote irrevocable loss (whether of status or of persons), such as the relatively recent death of a favored parent. This factor is particularly important if the person at risk is unable to mourn the loss overtly.
5. High physiologic responsiveness: cyclical moods and a high need for stimulation-seeking in spite of suicide thoughts.
6. Serious sleep disruption and abuse of alcohol or drugs.

The clinician should be especially and immediately alert to the person's access to lethal instruments and take direct steps to change that situation. It's been found that the highest suicide rates occur among police officers and physicians. And while it could be argued that the high level of frustration in the work of both of these groups may be an important variable, most suicide experts believe the critical variable is their high access to lethal means, guns and poisonous drugs, respectively.

In general, most people who are severly depressed and suicidal are more dangerous to themselves when they begin an upswing out of the depths of depression. If successive testings by an MMPI or specific depression scale reveal an initial upswing in a depressive who has discussed the possibility of suicide, precautions should be emphasized at that time. There are various types of suicide, as shown below, and type of intervention will depend upon the motivation for the suicide in the individual case (Kreitman, 1986; Schneidman, 1985):

☐   TYPES OF SUICIDE

1. Realistic.
   These are suicides precipitated by such conditions as the prospect of great pain preceding a sure death.

2. Altruistic.

The person's behavior is subservient to a group ethic that mandates or at least approves suicidal behavior, like kamikaze pilots in World War II.

3. Inadvertent.

The person makes a suicide *gesture* in order to influence or manipulate someone else, but a misjudgment leads to an unexpected fatality.

4. Spite.

Like the inadvertent suicide, the focus is on someone else, but the intention to kill oneself is genuine, with the idea that the other person will suffer greatly from consequent guilt.

5. Bizarre.

The person commits suicide as a result of a hallucination (such as voices ordering the suicide) or delusions (such as a belief the suicide will change the world).

6. Anomic.

An abrupt instability in economic or social conditions (such as sudden financial loss in the Great Depression) markedly changes a person's life situation. Unable to cope, the person commits suicide.

7. Negative self.

Chronic depression and a sense of chronic failure or inadequacy combine to produce repetitive suicide attempts, eventually leading to death.

A dimension that is especially useful to most clinicians in the concept of manipulative versus "genuine" suicide (Schneidman, 1985). Both types will be discussed below.

☐ MMPI

The prototypical pattern for a suicidal individual is the 2-7/7-2 combination. This code particularly reflects suicidal ideation, and any time 2 is elevated above 80 T, the clinician should pursue the question of possible suicidal ideation. Reflecting the dictum "If you want to know something specific about clients, you should ask them about it," the critical items concerning suicide should always be checked. The likelihood of this ideation's being actualized increases as scores on scales 4, 8, and 9 rise. Such a rise reflects an increasing loss of control over impulses, a rise in the energy available for behavior, and an increasing sense of isolation and resentment toward other people. A rise in scale 8 also reflects poor judgment; hence, suicidals who are not totally genuine in their suicide motivation may actually kill themselves whether they want to succeed or not, as the judgment may bring inadvertent "success."

Some people are suicidal for only a short period of time, usually when there is a severe loss in their psychological world that has not yet been integrated (Fawcett et al., 1987). Such people are temporarily suicidal, and if they can be restricted during this period of time and treated, they are likely to reintegrate and more away from the suicidal ideation. A high spike on scale 2 is characteristic here.

The 2-4/4-2 code is more likely to reflect a manipulative suicide. Where both scales 4 and 6 are elevated, in addition to at least a moderate elevation on scales 2 and 7, repressed anger and interpersonal hostility are basic to the suicide attempt as manipulation. It is an attempt to inflict punitive guilt and consequent behavior control on another.

Several observers have noted that an additional pattern, at least in women, has been associated with suicide attempts. The major features are a low K scale and a high 5 scale (both suggesting a strong, almost counterphobic rejection of feminity); a paradoxically high score on scale 3, indicating a histrionic component; and a high score on scale 0, reflecting a sense of social isolation and rejection. These women feel alienated and disturbed in their self-identity, yet they have no sense of a possible alternative to deal with this distress. Since they are impulsive as well, the potential for an acting-out behavior is heightened.

16 PF

On the 16 PF, attempters consistently show themselves to be more tense, expedient, shy, suspicious, emotionally unstable, apprehensive, self-sufficient, extremely anxious, and somewhat introverted. Translated into 16 PF scales, this means high scores on Q_4, O, 1, Q_2 and lower scores on G, H, and C. Furthermore, repeated attempters typically score lower on scales Q_3 and C than do first-time attempters, indicating less stability and more impulsivity.

OTHER TEST-RESPONSE PATTERNS

Exner (1978, 1986) has provided the most elegant and effective research on the use of Rorschach in the prediction of suicide. In 1978, he offered eleven variables that together form a prediction for suicide potential. The variables he first cited as important are as follows:*

1. FV + VF + V + FD is greater than 2.
2. An occurrence of a color-shading blend response.
3. Zd is greater than $\pm$ 3.5.

---

* J. Exner, *The Rorschach: A Comprehensive System,* Vol. 2: *Current Research and Advanced Interpretation.* New York: Wiley, 1978, p. 204. Used with permission of the publisher.

4. 3r + (2)/R is less than 0.30.

5. Experience Potential is greater than Experience Actual.

6. CF + C is greater than FC.

7. S is greater than 3.

8. X+ % is less than 0.70.

9. Pure H is less than 2.

10. P is greater than 8 or less than 3.

11. R is less than 17.

In addition to the eleven criteria used in the original constellation, two new criteria have been established (Exner, 1986). By adding an upper range for the egocentricity scale (3r+(2)/R greater than 0.45 or less than 0.30) and incorporating the Morbidity Index (MOR greater than 3) the accuracy of the index has significantly improved. The original criterion (eight of eleven variables) could accurately predict 75 percent of suicides, categorizing 20 percent of depressed inpatients and 12 percent of schizophrenics as false positive errors. The new criterion (eight of thirteen variables) can predict 83 percent of suicides accurately, only classifying 12 percent of depressed inpatients and 6 percent of schizophrenics as false positives. Neither of the two scales made false-positive errors in classfying non-suicidal controls as suicides. This change represents a significant increase in power.

Other authors have supported Exner's concepts that the number of responses is low in suicidals, especially when they are depressed, that less integrated color responses are more common, and that the number of popular responses are either very high or low (Swiercinsky, 1985). Also, there is some indication that transparency responses (such as light bulbs) or cross-sectional responses (such as X rays) are found more commonly in potential suicides than in other persons; and the greater the number of vista and shading responses, the greater the depression-based suicide potential.

Phillips and Smith (1953) state that content suggesting decay or geographic depression (e.g., canyons) is indicative of suicidal ideation. Others have argued that landscape or serenity associations are indicative of suicides who have not yet communicated their intent. Responses that suggest hanging or drowning or other direct means of suicide should obviously alert the examiner to further consideration.

As might be expected, elevations on the MCMI of 85 or higher on D and CC would be indicative of suicide potential. If N begins to increase and a very high D begins to decrease on repeated testing, the patient may be acquiring the necessary resolve and energy to complete the act; thus, suicide potential may be high. Those personality patterns most likely to exhibit suicide potential are indicated by elevated scores on

2, 8, 5, and/or C. These patterns represent the most inconsistent patterns and they are particularly susceptible to poorly developed support systems. High scores on scale 8 are particularly associated with manipulative suicide potential.

Since completed suicides are more often psychotic, while attempters are more often neurotic, greater elevations on pathological-personality scales S, C, and P than on scales 1–8, along with greater elevations on SS, CC, and PP, are found in those who are more likely to complete bizarre suicide gestures.

Beck et al. (1983) found that a score of 10 or more on the Hopelessness Scale, devised by Beck, correctly identified 91 percent of later actual suicides. Also, the pessimism item of the Beck Depression Inventory was quite predictive of later suicides.

Extra data may be available if an individual has already attempted suicide but has been prevented from completing it: the suicide note. The work of Edwin Schneidman and Norman Farberow (Schneidman, 1985) over many years has found that people who attempt suicide and genuinely mean to kill themselves write notes that are matter-of-fact and practical in their content. They may ask the target of the note to pay back small debts, return small items, or otherwise show seemingly trivial concerns, and they do not show much emotional content. It is as if they have already integrated the idea that they will be dead, so emotion is no longer directly tied to living relationships. Those individuals who attempted suicide yet apparently had no real intent to kill themselves left romantic, emotion-laden notes, thus attempting to institute guilt in the others and pressure them to change their behavior. Obviously, they believed they would be around to reap the fruits of that change.

☐   PREVENTION

Suicide prevention techniques have been developed at both the societal and individual level, but implementing them is not alway easy. The following dialogue from the old television show *Mary Hartman, Mary Hartman* shows the difficulty most people have in responding effectively to a potential suicide's questions.

HEATHER (Mary's twelve-year-old daughter): I have nothing to live for.
MARY: Sure you do.
HEATHER: Like what?
MARY: Well . . . wait and see.

☐   SOCIETAL PREVENTION

Several things can be done on a societal level to lower the incidence of suicide (Phillips, 1986; Schneidman, 1985). Educating the public on the myths and facts of suicide is an important first step. Second, there is evidence that suicide-prevention center and telephone hotlines can slightly decrease the suicide rate. A third step in suicide prevention (and analogously, in lowering the incidence of aggressive acts) may involve some restriction on media publicity about suicides (and violent aggression). Phillips (1986) documents the correlation between a rise and fall in suicide rates and the amount of newspaper publicity given to suicides in that locality. Such self-imposed restriction is a thorny ethical issue for newspapers and television, especially because rates of all externally directed violence (murder, rape) may also be increased by publicity about similar incidents (Phillips, 1986).

INDIVIDUAL PREVENTION

Clinicians can be effectively involved in suicide prevention education by promoting and emphasizing those precautions that can be taken at the individual level by laypersons, such as :

1. Attending seriously to people who voice a desire to kill themselves or "just go to sleep and forget it all."
2. Attending especially to depressed individuals who speak of losing hope.
3. To the degree possible, keeping lethal means (guns, large prescriptions of sedatives) away from suicidal individuals.
4. Generating a personal concern toward a suicidal person; a suicide attempt is most often a cry for help. Suicidal individuals need a temporary "champion" who can point them toward new resources, suggest new options, and at least in a small way can diminish the sense of hopelessness.
5. Trying to get the person to perform some of the following behaviors: (a) engage in regular physical exercise, (b) start a diary, (c) follow a normal routine, (d) do something in which he or she has already demonstrated competence, (e) confide inner feelings to someone, (f) cry it out. Trying to get the person to avoid self-medication and other people inclined toward depression.
6. Making every effort to guarantee that a suicidal person reaches professional help. Making an appointment is a good first step; getting the person to the appointment is the crucial step.

CHAPTER 14

Central Nervous System Impairment, Attention-Deficit Hyperactivity Disorder, and Retardation

■   ## Central Nervous System Impairment

Clinicians often face the issue of whether there may be central nervous system impairment (CNSI) in a client (Orsini et al., 1988). Earlier in this book, I used the traditional and less accurate terms "organic dysfunction" and "organic brain damage" because they are so commonly used by clinicians; throughout this chapter, I'll simply refer to it as CNSI. The intricacies of a broad, thorough CNSI evaluation will not be discussed here because this would require more material than is appropriate for this book. If there is reason to think there is CNSI and there is a request or need for a more certain and/or localized diagnosis, it is important to have a full evaluation carried out by a clinical neuropsychologist and/or a neurologist.

The types and the range of information needed for a full neuropsychological assessment are embedded in the model report format in Chapter 16. It is evident from that format that a good history is always critical. Sudden onset of symptoms, whatever their nature, should alert the clinician to possible CNSI. Changes in functioning of any sort are important data, so information from family and friends is helpful.

Close observation of speech quality and problems, dress, grooming, gait and coordination while walking to and from the office, and affect can all provide clinical signs to help the clinician. Any signs of asymmetry should particulary be noted. For example, one client with visual-field deficits neatly shaved one side of his face, but only roughly and sloppily shaved the other side. Obtaining some subject-as-own-control data is also useful, such as grip strength, finger-tapping tasks, or having the person touch various body parts with either hand with the eyes closed. Deficits may be especially meaningful if a short-form measure of IQ, such as the Shipley Institute of Living Scale (Jacobsen and Tomkin, 1988), indicates average-or-better general intelligence. In addition to the these specific performance tasks, there are also normative or test data, the focus of this section. Test-retest data—say, at six-month intervals—can also be useful.

If the clinician is to carry out a substantial neuropsychological assessment, extensive methods of obtaining normative data, such as the Halstead-Reitan, Luria-Nebraska, or Smith-Michigan batteries, are appropriate here. It is worth noting that for many years the Halstead-Reitan battery, which includes a WAIS-R or WISC-R and requires four to five hours test time, was seen as the "benchmark" battery by clinicians. In recent years, however, much more diversity has emerged. Such batteries are prognostic as well as diagnostic and can be extremely useful in other applications, such as evaluating the effects of drug trials. A good intermediate-level screening battery for CNSI might include a WAIS-R (or a validated short form such as the Satz-Mogel), MMPI, specific tests for lateralization (such as grip strength), the Purdue Pegboard and/or tapping tests, tests for sensory response, and at least some of the other tests that help cover the required variety of modalities and functional domains (e.g., Reitan Aphasia Screening Test, Word Finding Test, Indented-Paragraph Reading Test, Benton Visual Retention Test, Wechsler Memory Test, Trail-Making Test Part B, Boston Naming Test, Rey Auditory Verbal Learning Test, Symbol Digit Modalities Test) (Orsini et al., 1988; Richardson-Klavehn and Bjork, 1988; Caplan, 1987; Salmon and Meyer, 1986).

The Trail-Making Test B is one of the most sensitive indicators of CNSI in the Halstead-Reitan Battery. For young to middle-age adults, a time of 0–26 seconds is considered normal, 27–39 seconds is in the mild range, 88–120 seconds is moderate, and over 120 seconds is in the severe range. On Trails B, age is a factor in performance. Respective borderline deficit and critical deficit performance in seconds, for the following ages, are: age 40 (+95 seconds, +125 seconds); 40–49 (+100, +150); 50–59 (+135, +175); 60–69 (+170, +280); 70+ (+280, +425), though an important confounding variable is IQ and responsiveness to the test situation (see Table 14.1). The Indented-Paragraph Reading Test (Caplan, 1987), a test with an uneven left border, has proven effective in helping pinpoint right-hemisphere damage.

The CNSI literature often discusses the value of fixed versus flexible batteries. In many ways, this is a false issue because one can simply use one of the fixed batteries, e.g., The Halstead-Reitan, and then supplement it with whatever other specific tests are viewed as helpful in a particular case. In clinical situations, it's certainly arguable that an individualized battery might be optimal, as it is more directly tailored to the referral question, and should be more flexible and cost-efficient. However, one minor advantage of the fixed battery, i.e., norms for the battery as a whole, is not available, and this cost has to be factored into the decision. In forensic situations, some clinicians may feel the defensibility and protection of fixed-battery norms may tip the scales in this decision.

More importantly, any diagnostician must be aware of the common signs of CNSI in the standard tests and in behavior, particularly in the event that no one has yet asserted the possibility of CNSI. For example, the interaction of type of symptoms with rapid-versus-gradual onset can distinguish between cerebral impairment and such psychopathology as the affective disorders. When a syndrome with a gradual onset of a wide range of affective symptomatology is accompanied by neurological and cognitive deficits, along with aphasia and agnosia and/or a loss of sphincter control, irreversible CNSI is probable, though reversible conditions such as normal-pressure hydrocephalus could cause this. If the affective symptomatology is unaccompanied by the latter symptomatology and the depression and/or mania are severe and possibly accompanied by persistent delusions, an affective or bipolar disorder is more probable, though CNSI later in life can produce such symptoms.

If instead, there is a rapid onset of symptoms focusing on confusion, agitation, attentional problems, and disrupted sleep patterns, along with problems in self-care (including impaired sphincter control), and a focus primarily on visual hallucinations, there is a high probability of acute CNSI. If death does not occur, recovery is often reasonably rapid. But if symptoms do not include such evident self-care problems but instead include delusions or auditory hallucinations, then an affective or schizoaffective disorder is probable.

The discrimination between right- and left-cerebral-hemisphere impairment has fascinated clinicians for a long time. As an overall rule, specific deficits in spatial orientation and perceptual and/or organizational functions point to right-hemisphere disorder, whereas specific problems in language, motor, and executive functions suggest left-hemisphere and/or frontal impairment. Right-hemisphere impairment is more likely to be manifest in a disruption of emotion-laden knowledge and a disruption of the nuances of speech.

Difficulties in right-left spatial-orientation problems have traditionally been seen as suggestive of disorder in the right hemisphere. But language is a critical factor in such discriminations, and so attention to the quality of a client's difficulty may lead to a hypothesis that there is left-hemisphere disorder instead.

Benton (1980) has commented on the ability to make facial recognition as a diagnostic sign. His data, as well as those of others, suggest that specific facial agnosia, that is, the loss of ability to recognize familiar friends and family, is a good indicator of bilateral lesion. On the other hand, consistent problems in facial discrimination, such as in identifying new acquaintances, point to right-hemisphere impairment, and if the lesion turns out to be even more localized, it is probably posterior rather than anterior.

A clinician might consider including a test like the Reitan Aphasia Screening Test, a shortened version of Halstead and Wepman's Aphasia Screening Test (Reitan and Wolfson, 1986), in a routine test battery. It takes only about ten minutes to administer and a rough assessment of spatial and verbal factors, as well as aphasia. It is a good gross screening measure for significant cerebral impairment, as normals seldom make errors and perform effortlessly. It is very important to elicit the best possible performance the person can honestly give, to the point of allowing extra trials, and never immediately accept "I don't know" responses. If a client then makes even two or three errors, it is worthwhile to take a deeper look for more signs of cerebral impairment. An excellent item on the Reitan Aphasia Screening Test is the request for the client to produce a Maltese cross. Clinicians could add some version of the Maltese cross in conjunction with a few other figures, perhaps similar to cards A and 7 of the Bender-Gestalt, to the routine self-administered battery in Appendix A. Some specific measure of memory is also useful (Richardson-Klavehn and Bjork, 1988).

The clinician can also include a finger-tapping test, using a simple event counter. The general assumption is that performance will be about 10 percent better with the dominant hand (thus the opposite hemisphere), so any substantianl deviation from this pattern can be suggestive of disorder in one hemisphere. A test of grip strength is also advised. In these tests, a result wherein the left hand is twenty percent or more deficient in comparison with the right hand in right-handed clients or the left hand is no better than the right in a left-handed client is suggestive of right-cerebral damage. If performance on these tests has the reverse results, this is suggestive of left-cerebral damage. With syndromes in which dementia is suspected, especially in older individuals, the Boston Naming Test is useful, as language-naming deficits are often an early sign. Van Gorp et al. (1986) provide normative data on this test for individuals over 59 years of age. When testing older individuals, the data on normal, healthy older adults, provided in Table 14.1, should be of help.

□   MMPI

There is no modal MMPI profile for CNSI, and for good reason: There is no modal CNSI pattern of deficit. In this area, the dominant axiom should be that individual differences are determinative (Gass and Russell, 1986). Yet there are a number of patterns that should alert the clinician to consider possible CNSI. An obvious first sign is not a code type but an examination of how the person completed the form. For example, persons with visual-field deficits may neglect portions of the answer form, thus invalidating the profile. Extremely erratic profiles will show up in the validity scale elevations; confusion or dementia may be causal, though the reader should also consult the section on malingering for relevant information.

TABLE 14.1 Normative Data on Neuropsychological Tests for 156 Healthy, Well-Educated ($\bar{X}$ = 14–15 Years), Elderly People

	VERBAL IQ	PERFOR-MANCE IQ	WMS* LOGIC PROSE IMMED	WMS VISUAL REPROD.	WMS LOGIC PROSE DELAY (45 MIN.)	WMS VISUAL REPROD. DELAY (45 MIN.)	TRAILS A	TRAILS B	BOSTON NAMING TEST
58–85 (N = 156)									
Mean	117.650	110.617	8.925	7.633	6.233	4.733	48.700	107.550	54.017
STD DEV	13.527	13.493	2.752	3.498	2.733	3.741	14.468	45.631	5.391
58–65 (N = 28)									
Mean	117.200	109.200	9.750	9.600	7.800	6.600	41.500	84.400	55.500
STD DEV	11.331	11.555	2.395	2.757	2.163	2.459	7.832	24.600	4.528
66–70 (N = 45)									
Mean	114.800	111.467	8.467	8.667	5.733	6.333	43.200	105.200	55.467
STD DEV	17.034	16.831	2.649	3.811	2.235	3.830	14.982	43.432	3.944
71–75 (N = 57)									
Mean	122.875	115.083	9.271	7.792	6.313	4.375	50.083	97.791	53.875
STD DEV	11.380	11.938	3.148	2.992	3.158	3.932	12.884	30.404	5.728
76–85 (N = 26)									
Mean	110.545	101.000	8.045	4.091	5.318	1.636	59.727	153.090	51.000
STD DEV	11.246	8.775	2.185	2.256	2.483	1.690	15.950	62.603	6.356

* Wechsler Memory Scale
Table adapted from data provided by Wilfred Van Gorp, Ph.D., of the West Los Angeles VA Medical Center.

In general, persons with a left-hemisphere dysfunction (especially to the degree that this is the dominant hemisphere) will show a "catastrophic response" pattern on the MMPI; those with right-hemisphere dysfunction are more likely to appear "indifferent" (Meier et al., 1987). To the degree a lesion to the dominant hemisphere has produced aphasia, higher scores on F, 6, 7, and 8 are likely to occur (Gass and Russell, 1986). Lachar (1974) notes that the relatively rare 1-9/9-1 code, with a low scale 2, is found in a number of persons with acute CNSI. This most commonly occurs where there is a dawning awareness in clients that they have suffered a loss of function and where they are dealing with it in a counterphobic manner. As they lose the will to fight in response to the loss and depression emerges, the 2-9/9-2 code is more common. When their personality functions begin to fall apart, accompanied by activity levels raised against their phobia, the 9-8/8-9 profile may occur (Gynther et al., 1973a). While scale 8 is often the highest scale in epileptic patients, scales 1, 2, and 3 are more likely to be elevated in clients with multiple sclerosis. Scale 8 is also often elevated as aphasic clients begin to withdraw.

Persons with CNSI from a toxic substance are likely to show a generally elevated MMPI profile with a particularly high score on scale 8 and scores on most other scales (excluding the 5 scale) at about 70 T. Scales that tend to be higher in this profile are 1 and 2. When CNSI occurs as a result of senility or a neurological degenerative process, elevations are more likely on scales 2 and 8, both around the 70 T mark. The senile group tends to have a slightly higher elevation overall in the other scores, with scale 1 being particularly higher than in the neurological degenerative group (Pennington et al., 1979).

According to Lachar (1974), the classic signs of chronic CNSI are scores elevated about 70 T on scales 8, 6, 4, and 2. Scales 1 and 3 are usually lower, except with those who have multiple sclerosis and similar disorders. In one sample of neurological clients, scales 1, 2, and then 4 were the highest (Dahlstrom et al., 1986). Watson et al. (1978) find that the scale-1: scale-7 ratio is much higher for CNSI clients than other groups with psychopathology. Also, the F scale is high, particularly if damage is severe. In chronic CNSI, the 9 scale is often a barometer of the person's reaction to it; a lower 9 score indicates either acceptance or a lack of reaction to it, while a high 9 suggests an attempt to cope, poorly at times. When scales 8 and 6 are very high and there are other solid indications of CNSI, the CNS disorder is possibly accompanied by schizophrenia.

When dealing with possible CNSI cases, particularly in the aged, the MMPI may have to be administered over several sessions because of fatigue and/or attention problems, or it may only be possible to use a short form (Meier et al., 1987).

☐   16 PF

Because of the variety of reactions subsumed under the term " central nervous system impairment," a modal 16 PF profile for CNSI is not available. However, persons with CNSI are generally high on scales O and Q_4, reflecting their sense of insecurity and anxiety. Those individuals who have moved into depression would probably not score so high. Q_3 is low, reflecting the degree of personality disintegration, and scale B is lowered, indicating the correlated loss of intellectual functioning. Moderately low scores on Q_2, F, and H are also standard. The scores on scale E vary markedly, depending on the reaction to the awareness of loss. If persons have become depressed and submissive to a hospital environment, E is low, whereas if they are attempting counterphobic mechanisms, it is elevated. G tends to vary markedly as well, but usually it is at least moderately high.

☐   OTHER TEST-RESPONSE PATTERNS

Before looking at possible cues from specific WAIS-R subtests, several overall perspectives that can aid the clinician in this type of assessment must be stated.

1. On the WAIS-R, the general rule has been that low verbal scales relative to performance scales indicate left-hemisphere lesions (if it has been determined that the left hemipshere is the dominant one). To a lesser degree, the converse is true: low performance scores relative to verbal scores indicate a right-hemisphere lesion, especially to the degree that this discrepancy is determined by low scores on picture arrangement and block design. Unfortunately, these discrepancies are not always clear-cut or perfectly correlated, but it is a good first rule. Left-hemisphere damage may produce a very low profile, and such clients may be difficult to differentiate from those with mental retardation (Matson, 1987). Persons with right-hemisphere damage do better on comprehension, similarities, and vocabulary than on other verbal tests, and better on picture completion within the performance tests. Those clients with diffuse CNSI do somewhat better on verbal tests than performance tests, particularly on vocabulary and information, but they also do well on picture completion in the performance tests. They do particularly poorly on digit symbol, as do most CNSI groups, as well as on arithmetic and usually on block design.

Overall, it is reasonable to assert that a low-performance/high-verbal pattern is more suggestive of overall CNSI than is the high-performance /low-verbal pattern. Also, it's worthwhile to remember that traumatic head injuries clearly to one side produce patterns more similar to diffuse CNSI than one would find in unilateral CNSI produced by processes other than acute trauma.

2. In general, marked verbal-performance splits are likely to indicate intracerebral tumors or cerebrovascular accidents. Clients with cerebrovascular accidents are then more likely to show disrupted differential performance on grip strength and tapping tests than do clients with tumors.

3. In verbal subtests that require a high level of verbal precision and identification (the vocabulary scale), expressive-speech problems are suggested by hesitating and circuitous speech–the patient cannot find the precise word.

4. The picture completion subtest can also be helpful in assessing the difficulties in expressive speech. It is important that the clinician create very specific demands. If the clinician's style is to accept approximate answers easily, or pointing rather than naming, for example, the client is not adequately pressed to make the precise designation.

5. The similarities subtest and the proverbs on the comprehension subtest test general intellectual and abstracting ability, and thus identify either more diffuse cerebral impairment or at least cerebral trauma that leads to a wide range of impairment.

6. The overall range between lowest and highest WAIS-R subscales is a good indicator of general impairment. When the range between scale scores is greater than five in persons without another handicap (such as lack of education), the clinician should consider the possibility of CNSI.

7. The highest WAIS-R subscale scores provide a reasonably good index of premorbid intellectual functioning in cases of cerebral impairment, but only when they are scales that correlate reasonably well with the full-scale WAIS-R, as in the vocabulary subtest. When digit span is the highest postmorbid scale, it would not be an especially efficient predictor.

8. Within-subtest scatter (consistently missing easy items while answering hard ones accurately) is an important indicator of the ability to maintain set. Clients with certain cerebral impairments find it hard to keep the program in mind and to process the data at the same time. For example, they may keep in mind the general problem on the arithmetic subtest but forget the exact numbers in the process–or the reverse.

Digit symbol is commonly low in all brain-injured persons. Arithmetic is almost as consistently low, especially in those with left-hemisphere injuries. In combination with digit span, arithmetic is an excellent measure of the degree of transient anxiety and depression, though the CNSI can affect digit span as much as or more than depression can. Information may be low in persons who are suffering early CNSI in the left hemisphere, but it remains reasonably high in most CNSI cases, as do comprehension and similarities. Picture arrangement most often reflects right-hemisphere disorder (especially right anterior temporal lobe), as do object assembly and block design. The diagnostician may see unusual placements in block design and object assembly, placements that the client finds difficult to explain. Picture completion and similarities are rarely affected, except in chronic CNSI. Most schizophrenics do better on information than on similarities; this can be one cue to distinguish between them.

Block design also helps in the discrimination between CNSI and schizophrenia. It usually remains relatively high in schizophrenia, whereas it is virtually always affected to some degree in CNSI. It is consistently low in diffuse brain injuries and in injuries involving the right temporal and parietal lobes. In another important discrimination, object assembly is often one of the higher scores in mentally retarded persons, whereas both CNSI and schizophrenics, as well as depressives, are prone to do poorly (Golden, 1979).

Fuld (1984) has provided further validation data of a marker of dementia of the Alzheimer type that was occasionally noted earlier in the literature. This WAIS-R subtest profile marker, indicating the probable presence of this dementia, is defined by the following formula:

$$A > B > C < D, A > D$$

in which A is the mean of the information and vocabulary subtest scores, B is the mean of the similarities and digit span scores, C is the mean of the digit symbol and block design scores, and D is the object assembly score. All subtest scores are age-corrected. This marker was positive in approximately 50 percent of actual Alzheimer-dementia cases and in only 11 percent of non–Alzheimer-dementia cases in two separate studies (Fuld, 1984; Brinkman and Braun, 1984). A further validation by Paul Satz and his colleagues (Satz, 1987) found the marker gives an equally effective discrimination between Alzheimer-dementia cases and the normal elderly.

On the Wide-Range Achievement Test-Revised (WRAT-R), disorders in reading ability should cue the clinician toward the possibility of temporal-occipital left-hemisphere disturbance or long-standing learning disability in the presence of average or above average IQ. A significant loss of spelling ability should suggest the possibility of parietal and/or occipital dysfunction (Cantwell and Baker, 1987).

The classic signs of CNSI on the Bender-Gestalt are perplexity, impotency, distortions, perseveration, significant rotation of designs, and peculiar sequencing. Impotency, or statements indicating dissatisfaction with one's performance, is common throughout all the tests when such a client runs into difficulty. Also common is the element of perplexity, wherein a person overtly indicates confusion and uncertainty about handling the task given.

On the Benton Visual-Retention Test, signs similar to that on the Bender-Gestalt are evidence of CNSI. More specifically, Golden (1979) states that persons with CNSI are most likely to make three types of errors here: the omission of a peripheral figure, rotation, or size error (a loss of the size relationship between the major and peripheral figures). It is important to note that even though rotations do occur in normals, they are more likely to be stabilizing errors: when a figure that is presented as at an angle is then rotated so that it sits flat. Alexias or aphasias may be involved if the client has difficulty recognizing previously learned configurations (circle, square) (Bender, 1938).

As with the other drawing tests, distortions, perplexity, impotency, and perservation in response to the Draw-A-Person Test are classic signs of cerebral impairment. The clinician might find it useful to have clients routinely write their name as well as a novel sentence (e. g., "The shed is next to the house") on the same page with the person they have drawn. In general, clients with left-hemisphere impairment can often do the overlearned task—that is, write their name—reasonably well. But at the same time, they have marked difficulties with the novel sentence. Also, as a general rule, if the drawing is adequate but the writing is bad, the left hemisphere may be impaired, whereas if the drawing is poor and the writing is acceptable, the localization, if any, may be in the right hemisphere. Differences in the general style of drawings between those with right-hemisphere CNSI and left-hemisphere CNSI are reflected in the following contrasts:

RIGHT-HEMISPHERE CNSI	**LEFT-HEMISPHERE CNSI**
Loss of adequate gestalt relationships	Sequential relationships impaired
Scattered and fragmented individual responses	Simple and coherent individual responses
Loss of adequate spatial relationships	Spatial relationships are adequately retained
Corrective lines are added	Gross lack of detail
Drawings are made energetically, almost driven	Drawings are made slowly and laboriously, haltingly at times
Orientation to the general task is faulty or lost	Orientation to the general-task structure is reasonably accurate

It is important to look for perseveration in the drawing tests, as well as in a wide range of performance areas. One cerebrally impaired client kept doing an infinite division problem almost to a point of exhaustion, at which time he simply said, "There's too much of this."

On the Rorschach, perplexity, repetition, and impotency are also common, which is not surprising in light of the ambiguity of the stimuli. There is often a delayed reaction time to the cards, and persons may turn the cards in a confused manner, indicating an attempt to cope with a task in which they lack confidence (Exner, 1986).

Overall, there are a low number of responses, with the average time per response quite high, and a deterioration of the response quality as clients proceed through the cards. Constriction, being bound to stimuli (e.g., "This is where some ink has been splashed"), fragmented responses, and a high need for more structure are common. Positional responses are more common than normal. Occasional perseveration of content occurs, sometimes even to the point where there is a repetition of automatic phrases. In particular, there may be a perseveration of CF responses in the last three cards. "Color naming" and crude CF and C responses are given, in contrast to a low number of M responses and a low $F+\%$. Vague W responses, with good form Dd responses, may be found. Responses about anatomy content and those in which humans or animals are mutilated reflect the client's concerns about his own deterioration.

Bellak (1986, pp. 215–18) points to the following consistent features found in the TAT stories of persons with CNSI (some of these apply equally well to other tests, such as the Rorschach).

1. Use of fewer ideas and words
2. Longer response times, often with punctuating pauses
3. Concrete, simple descriptions; occasionally a listing of items in the picture
4. Trite stories with little action
5. Confusions and misinterpretations
6. Proportionately fewer common themes
7. Perseveration of themes; repetition of words and phrases
8. Difficulties in providing an adequate response (especially to more complex or vague cards) or in changing an inadequate response
9. Expressions of self-doubt
10. Missing the most salient objects in a card, e.g., the violin in card 1 of the TAT
11. Stereotypical stories from TV or popular stories
12. Inability to focus on one central character throughout
13. Problems in developing any parallel plot or bringing the story to a reasonable conclusion
14. Lack of coordinated plot or action sequences
15. Themes of problems in learning, dependency on others in everyday behaviors, being isolated from peer situations, or of impulsive unplanned actions.

Before moving on to the next section, take note of several "uniformity myths" that have unfortunately been pervasive in the traditions of CNSI assessment (Meier et al., 1987; Salmon and Meyer, 1986).

☐   UNIFORMITY MYTHS

The term "brain damage" is an accurate description of the effects of central nervous system impairment.

Individual differences do not significantly affect the manifestation, course, or outcome of CNS impairments.

Lesions of CNS tissues constitute a homogeneous class of phenomena.

Brain injuries are relatively static events and are comparatively insensitive to the effects of time.

The clinician's role in neuropsychological investigations is confined primarily to diagnostic activities.

The rehabilitation of CNSI must be concerned with building upon remaining strengths rather than rebuilding deficits (or vice versa).

■   # Attention-Deficit Hyperactivity Disorder

Attention-deficit disorder (ADD) refers to a condition that involves the persisting inability to keep one's attention focused. Children and adolescents with attention-deficit disorder are presumed to possess adequate basic cognitive capabilities, but they are typically unable to focus themselves effectively enough to get things done. DSM-III-R recognizes two forms of ADD: with or without hyperactivity. The latter is termed Undifferentiated Attention-Deficit Disorder (314.00). Attention-Deficit Hyperactivity Disorder (ADHD) (314.01) involves behavioral manifestations of attentional problems, including persistent symptoms of restlessness, fidgeting, and constant activity. ADHD occurs at an incidence rate of about 6–8 percent with about a 5:1 ratio of males to females and an even higher ratio for the more active and aggressive forms (Gillberg and Gillberg, 1988; Lambert et al., 1987; Robe, 1987).

DSM-III-R requires disturbances of at least six months, with onset before age seven, during which at least eight of the following are observed: (1) fidgets or squirms, (2) has difficulty in remaining seated, (3) is easily distracted, (4) has difficulty awaiting one's turn, (5) blurts out responses, (6) has difficulty completing tasks, (7) has difficulty sustaining attention, (8) often shifts to other activities, (9) seldom plays quietly, (10) interrupts or intrudes, (11) talks excessively, (12) does not pay attention, (13) often loses things essential to tasks, or (14) takes risks or seeks thrills.

Current recognition of ADHD in the DSM-III-R reflects the belief of physicians, teachers, and psychologists over the years that persisting problems in regulating both attentional processes and motor behavior comprise a distinct syndrome frequently seen in clinical settings. Originally, terms such as "hyperactivity," "hyperkinesis," and "minimal brain dysfunction" were used to characterize the condition, which was believed to involve various forms of mild central nervous system impairment

(CNSI). So strong was the association between excessive activity and underlying brain impairment that the corresponding diagnostic terms were used interchangeably for years. In practice, the nature of this deficit was seldom specified, owing to the wide range of disorders and conditions that may have hyperactivity as an associated symptom. This caused endless confusion among professionals and considerable anxiety on the part of parents whose children were labeled as having "minimal brain damage" or the "hyperkinetic syndrome."

Recent research, however, strongly suggests that neither attentional problems nor hyperactivity should *necessarily* be assumed to involve CNS damage. Because of these findings, the popularity in particular of the term "hyperactive" has declined. Its inclusion in the DSM-III-R as an auxiliary condition used only in conjunction with ADHD is consistent with its diminished status from a distinct diagnostic entity. Current research has amply documented the fact that genetic, physiological-dysfunction, nutritional, motivational, social, and environmental factors all may play important roles in the regulation and allocation of attentional capabilities (Gillberg and Gillberg, 1988; Kirby and Grimley, 1986; Henker et al., 1986).

☐   INDIVIDUAL HISTORY VARIABLES OFTEN NOTED IN HYPERACTIVE CHILDREN

Family history of hyperactivity or learning disability

Mother's trauma or illness during pregnancy

Mother's substance abuse

Oxygen disruption during delivery

Problems or trauma during delivery

Perceived from early on as "overactive"

Slow development

High fevers

Head banging, knee-elbow rocking

Hyperkinesis

Reduced attention

Poor coordination

Difficulties with speech, writing, reading, spelling

Conduct problems in general, especially if little evidence of guilt or remorse

Preference for very bland or overly spiced foods

Tendency toward food "addictions" and/or allergies

Transfixed by high action TV or movies

Behavior problems in school

Left-handedness

Easily distracted

Disturbed by bright lights

Disturbed by loud noises

Mirror writing

Letter reversals

Visual disturbances

Severe headaches

Fainting

Impulsivity

Aversive to peers and/or caretakers

Migraines

Convulsions

Epilepsy

EEG abnormality, or if "normal" some non-specific abnormalities

☐   DIAGNOSTIC CONSIDERATIONS

In many ADHD cases, a neuropsychological evaluation (see preceding section) and/or an evaluation for possible retardation (see upcoming section) are indicated. In any case, a thorough assessment for ADHD includes an evaluation of the following factors: (1) the client's overall behavioral repertoire and patterns of interaction with the environment, (2) patterns of motor activity, and (3) how the person typically approaches and works through tasks. By the time an evaluation has been completed, a person with ADHD may well have been assessed by pediatricians, teachers, psychologists, and parents. Each of these individuals has relevant information to the overall decision.

☐   TYPES OF HYPERACTIVITY

There are four major types of hyperactivity (Gillberg and Gillberg, 1988; Lambert et al., 1987; Robe, 1987). The least common is environmentally generated hyperactivity, about 5–10 percent of all hyperactive children. This type may even be labeled "pseudohyperactivity," as it has no significant biological component, unlike the three other forms of hyperactivity.

The two major causes of environmentally generated hyperactivity are a severe stress, such as loss of a parent or child abuse, and the child who has been spoiled in such a way that he or she has never learned to deal with limits on activity. Not surprisingly, the parents of the latter type of hyperactive child don't see the behavior as nearly the problem that teachers and day-care workers do.

A common characteristic of such children is an absence of hyperactivity before the trauma or hyperactive behavior only in certain situations, e.g., where limits are not clear or are not enforced. Treatment for such children includes anxiety reduction techniques if stress is involved and school consultations and family therapy to teach the teachers and parents how to more effectively set limits.

A second pattern is stimulant- or food-induced hyperactivity. Some people have argued that certain foods or food additives cause the great majority of hyperactive cases. It soon became apparent to most experts that this was erroneous, but many experts do agree that these factors are the major cause in about 10–15 percent of hyperactive cases. Such children often manifested food allergies as early as infancy and may show standard allergy patterns.

Such children also show more unpredictable outbursts of hyperactivity than do the other forms of hyperactivity, though they are especially likely to increase their hyperactivity after certain meals. Commonly suspected culprits here are foods high in simple sugars, foods high in additives and preservatives, chocolate, and milk, egg, or wheat products. It's important to note that the range of foods that could be the cause of such behavior is wider than originally imagined.

Naturally, the focus of treatment is to eliminate those foods that generate the hyperactivity. However, this should only be done after an exhaustive survey of food intake and related behaviors. For example, for a minimum of two weeks, and often longer, parents should keep a log of all foods the child eats, including the lists of ingredients. An hourly behavior chart is also kept. These are very time-consuming tasks, but if they are not diligently carried out, the problem substance will escape discovery. All of this should be done in consultation with the child's pediatrician.

If the hyperactivity is food-generated, certain consistent patterns should become clear. Those foods can then be systematically eliminated, and the hyperactivity should diminish. If the hyperactivity does not lessen, one of the more common hyperactivity patterns should be con-sidered—overstimulated (overactive) hyperactivity, about 30 percent of all cases of hyperactivity; and understimulated (underactive) hyperac-tivity, which accounts for approximately half of all cases of hyperactivity.

In spite of the opposite labels, children in both of the latter patterns show high levels of activity and distractibility. Also, unlike environmen-tally generated hyperactivity, both patterns start becoming evident even in early childhood. The following chart highlights the characteristics and differences between these two major hyperactive patterns.

OVERACTIVE (OVERSTIMULATED) HYPERACTIVITY (30%)	UNDERACTIVE (UNDERSTIMULATED) HYPERACTIVITY (50%)
Child carries a high level of neurophysiological arousal, so is highly "stimulation-respondent."	Child carries a low level of neurophysiological arousal, relative to psychological needs, so is highly "stimulation-seeking."
Responds reasonably well to "quiet time" or stimulus reduc-tion methods; responds to stan-dard "time-out" wherein stimuli are highly restricted.	Has difficulty calming down at "quiet time"; needs some struc-tured activity even during "time-out" or will quickly be disruptive or destructive; liable to be excessively spanked, as they show little response to it.
Becomes somewhat calmer as evening progresses; will usually fall asleep easily enough, but is a restless sleeper, and hard to awaken.	Has difficulty going to bed and to sleep—"the tireder they get, the worse they are"—but usually sleeps soundly. Often awakens early and is ready to go right away.
Likes TV, but can be easily overstimulated by it. Often has to do other things while watch-ing TV. Is overstimulated and	Likes TV, especially highly stimulating programs, but can sit for hours in front of such programs, as if hypnotized. Can

has difficulty "coming down" from periods of physical activity.

Is finicky eater. Doesn't like green vegetables or strong-flavored foods, like broccoli, curry, etc. Favorite foods are bland, like macaroni and cheese, meat, potatoes; often will use cheese or sauces to mask flavors.

Often shows hyperactive response in new situations or to changes in routine. The more consistent, structured, and calm the home and school environment, the better the child behaves.

Stimulant medications (e.g., Ritalin, Cylert) are seldom markedly effective, and moderate to high doses may make matters worse. Small doses of mild tranquilizers or sedatives help in some cases. May show sedation from over-the-counter medicines containing codeine or antihistamines.

be calmed by long periods of intense physical activity.

Usually enjoys a number of strong-flavored foods; will quickly overseason and over-sugar foods. Loves colorful, over-sweetened, novelty breakfast cereals. (These children are the perfect target for the Saturday morning cartoon advertisement.)

Often is well-behaved in new situations, but gets progressively worse as newness wears off (so clinicians may need to schedule several sessions in order to see the problem behavior emerge). Constantly seeks more-stimulating environments.

Stimulant medications are usually effective (such children may even be calmed by coffee or tea) as preparation for therapy and retraining. When high doses are needed to control behavior, ability to effectively learn may be impaired.

☐   OTHER TEST-RESPONSE PATTERNS

For a young adult who is still diagnosable as ADHD, elevations on the MMPI on scales 4, 6, 8, and 9 are probable. The expectations for those in the population that would come to clinical detection would be that about half would fit in the category of conduct disorder. If there is a lack of reported violent behaviors, expect a 4-9/9-4 profile. A 2-4/4-2 profile would also be a possibility. The high 9 should be especially prominent in those patients who are still experiencing an active episode.

On the 16 PF (or more likely the HSPQ, since this type of referral question is more likely to occur in adolescents), low scores on Q_3 and B are most probable, with high scores on O, L, and M also being likely. On the MCMI, scale N is most likely to be high, with V high to the degree the attention span is actually limited. To the degree an antisocial component has developed, scale 6 would be high.

On both the Rorschach and TAT, ADHD clients are likely to show the general affects of impulsivity and distraction (see Chapter 11). They may end out with long response times, show a confused sequential analysis of the blot or picture, and tend to stay with popular responses or stories. Boundary/containment response issues are common. Parts may be missed: For example, Bellak (1986) noted that the failure to even identify the violin in TAT card 1 has been observed in ADHD cases. On the Rorschach, a higher number of animal responses and delayed response to the color cards is expected.

In performance drawings, the ADHD adolescent is likely to attempt them in a brusque and rapid manner (Oster and Gould, 1987). Where there is an associated spatial dyslexia, drawings of a face tend to be "neolithic" (there is no separation of the nose from the forehead and no suggestion of a nose bridge). To the degree he is also emotionally disturbed, he is likely to show a confused order of drawings, overly large drawings, and boxed figures (Rossini and Kaspar, 1987). Watching him attempt the drawings may be at least as instructive as what the drawings actually produce. He may be distracted easily and may make this apparent by glancing around the room, investigating distracting objects, fidgeting, or drawing objects that are different from those requested. Because ADHD tends to result in a lower school performance, related concerns may lead such individuals to draw figures that reflect strong feelings of inadequacy and guilt, and they sometimes describe their drawings as stupid or crazy.

☐   TREATMENT OPTIONS

Therapy of some sort is critical for these cases as the long-term effects of hyperactivity on both academic and social adjustment are negative. Hyperactivity is of course a precursor to academic failure, but it can also be a precursor to a wide variety of other patterns, such as schizophrenia and criminality (Lambert et al., 1987; Gillberg and Gillberg, 1988). Both family therapy and parent-training technques are necessary for most cases (Dangel and Polster, 1986). Part of the family therapy should be directed toward helping parents and siblings reduce the stress, guilt, and wear-and-tear these children generate in the family. The parents of such a child are apt to heartily agree with the following classic quip, "Life begins when the children leave home and the dog dies."

Chemotherapy with methylphenidate (Ritalin) and related substances (e.g., Cylert) is a common approach. Clonidine, an alpha-adrenergic stimulating agent whose action consists of inhibiting noradrenergic activity, has been increasing in popularity. All of these medications have significant side effects, including inhibition of growth in height and weight, if used for any significant length of time. Yet, they do lead to improvement in many ADHD children and adolescents (Henker et al., 1986), which leads to some difficult cost-benefit clinical questions.

A variety of behavioral and cognitive-behavioral techniques have proven helpful for ADHD (Davey and Cullen, 1988). The drawbacks with these techniques are the high cost in personnel time and the problems of generalization of effects. If there is a neuropsychological problem, specific rehabilitative efforts are usually required (Meier et al., 1987). For older children and adolescents with ADHD, a support therapy group can be helpful (Brigham, 1988).

■ Mental Retardation

Mental retardation is another common referral problem for the clinician; it is generally agreed that about 1 percent of the population falls into this category (Berk, 1989). The DSM-III-R requires indication of subaverage intellectual functioning (an IQ of 70 or below) in an individually administered test, correlated problems in adaptive coping behaviors, and onset before the age of eighteen. If onset is later than age eighteen, the term "dementia," subcoded as an organic mental disorder, is appropriate. The criteria for severity are noted in the following four subcategorizations.

Mild Mental Retardation (317.0x) is designated by IQ scores of 50-55 to approximately 70. This is the largest group of retarded individuals, comprising about 85 percent of the overall retarded population; such persons are commonly referred to as "educable." Many of these individuals develop sixth- or seventh-grade academic skills by the time they are in their middle adolescence.

Moderate Mental Retardation (318.0x), approximately 10 percent of the retarded population, is classified by an IQ score of 35-40 to 50-55. This group usually requires at least moderate supervision, particularly in financial matters and/or when under stress. They seldom progress beyond the third-grade achievement level, but they can often communicate adequately.

Severe Mental Retardation (318.1x), classified by an IQ score of 20-25 to 35-40 comprises about 3–4 percent of the retarded population. This group is not likely to profit from any vocational training, though they can usually learn elementary self-care skills.

Profound Mental Retardation (318.2x), 1–2 percent of the retarded population, is designated by an IQ score of 20-25 or less.

If there is good reason to believe that significant intellectual retardation is present with functioning at least below an approximate IQ of 70, and for some reason the individual is untestable, the term Unspecified Mental Retardation (319.00) is used. The diagnosis of Borderline Intellectual Functioning (V40.00) requires evidence of problems in adaptive coping and an IQ of 71–84.

Since the MMPI requires approximately a sixth-grade reading level, it is seldom administered to most mentally retarded persons. The

Improved Readability Form (IRF), derived by Ward and Selby (1980), can occasionally be used effectively here (the reader is referred to the initial portion of the chapter on the clinical correlates of the MMPI and 16 PF). Regardless of which method of administration is used, such clients sometimes respond with a random response pattern (Matson, 1987) (see the section on malingering).

Aside from the overall scores obtained on the WAIS-R, there are certain trends in the subtest patterns of mentally retarded individuals, First, they score relatively high on object assembly, whereas persons with CNSI score low. Performance subtests may exceed the verbal subtests, but this is not always the case. Academically oriented tests, such as information and arithmetic, are usually low. Also, the similarities test is relatively low, while comprehension, picture completion, and digit span are higher.

On the Rorschach, a low number of overall responses are usually obtained, containing a low F+%, a high F%, few or poor M responses, and a high percentage of animal responses. When W responses are made, they are of poor quality. Repetitive and perseverative content occurs, and apparently impulsive inferences to content from the stimuli of the blots are common. On the Bender-Gestalt, changes in angulation, closure difficulty, irregular use of space and sequence, a probability of rotations, and collision tendencies are noted. Simplistic drawings, such as attachment of the appendages to the head, are seen on the Draw-A-Person Test in more severely retarded persons (Newmark, 1985).

CHAPTER 15

Criminal Responsibility (Insanity), Civil Commitment, and Competency

Forensic issues are becoming increasingly important to mental health professionals. The clinician can be brought into the forensic arena in a number of ways, as is evident in the list on the following page.

However, most of these roles only come about if the clinician chooses to enter the forensic arena, e.g., helping to decide if parole should be granted, taking on child-custody or personal-injury cases, etc. Yet, any clinician, because of the status of one of his or her clients, can easily become involved in three of the broad traditional areas on the interface of law and mental health: criminal responsibility, civil commitment, and competency.

■ Criminal Responsibility (Insanity)

The tests and standards used to assess insanity, or, more broadly, criminal responsibility, vary somewhat from state to state. The traditional formulation, referred to as the M'Naghten Test, is again influential in many states, though it has typically been modified in some form. This in large part reflects the effect of the trial of John Hinckley, Jr. for his attempted assassination of President Reagan (Low et al., 1986). In its purest form, the criterion is whether or not a person committed an unlawful act as a result of "defect of reason" arising out of "a disease of the mind" that results in not "knowing the nature of the act" or, if the individual was aware it it, not knowing that it was wrong. This is often referred to cryptically as the "knowing-right-from-wrong standard."

In 1954, the Durham Rule, whose primary author was Judge David Bazelon, focused chiefly on the issue of whether the unlawful behavior was "the product of mental disease or mental defect" (*Durham* v. *United States,* 214 F.2d 862 D.C. Cir., 1954). However, though this rule received initial acclaim, it has seldom been followed since.

The Various Potential Roles of the Forensic Clinician as Fact-Finder in the Legal Arena

CLIENT		ISSUE
Criminal Defendant (Client)	_____	Criminally responsible, or "insane"?
Witness to Event	_____	Adequate enough in perception and information processing?
Child Witness	_____	Mature enough to testify?
Rape Victim	_____	Credible, or psychotic fantasy?
Offender	_____	Dangerous to release?
Juvenile Offender	_____	Emotionally and cognitively mature enough to stand trial as an adult? Dangerous to be released?
Parole Candidate	_____	Rehabilitated? Dangerous to release?
Mental Patient (Client)	_____	Dangerous to community or to self?
Parent	_____	Responsible enough to have custody of child?
Criminal Defendant (Client)	_____	Competent to stand trial?
Criminal Defendant	_____	Competent to be executed?
Testator (Client)	_____	Competent to make a valid will?
Contracting Party (Client)	_____	Competent to make binding contract?

Adapted from W. Curran and S. Pollack, "Mental Health and Justice." In W. Curran, A. L. McGarry, and S. Shah, Eds., *Forensic Psychiatry and Psychology*. Philadelphia: F. A. Davis, 1986.

A legal definition of insanity that has been especially influential on legal theorists—and to a somewhat lesser degree, on the state laws—was formulated by the American Law Institute (ALI) and is included in the Model Penal Code. It is comprised of two major sections:

1. Persons are not responsible for criminal conduct if, at the time of such conduct, as a result of mental disease or defect they lack substantial capacity either to appreciate the criminality (wrongfulness) of their conduct or to conform their conduct to the requirements of law.

2. The terms ("mental disease" or "defect") do not include an abnormality manifested only by repeated criminal or otherwise antisocial conduct.

The rationale for the adoption of the ALI is best exemplified in the case of *People* v. *Drew* (Sub., 149 Cal. Rptr 275, 1978):

First, the ALI test adds a volition element, the ability to conform to legal requirements, which is missing from the *M'Naghten* Test. Second, it avoids the all-or-nothing language of *M'Naghten* and permits a verdict based on lack of substantial capacity. . . . Third, the ALI Test is broad enough to permit a psychiatrist to set before the trier of facts a full picture of the defendant's mental impairments and flexible enough to adapt to future changes in psychiatric theory and diagnosis. Fourth, by referring to the defendant's capacity to "appreciate" the wrongfulness of his conduct the test confirms our holding . . . that mere verbal knowledge of right and wrong does not prove sanity. Finally, by establishing a broad text of nonresponsibility, including elements of volition as well as cognition, the test provides the foundation on which we can order and rationalize the convoluted and occasionally inconsistent law of diminished capacity (p. 282).

Criticisms of the ALI Rule focus on its alleged too-great-flexibility and the difficulties in determining what is specifically meant by "appreciate" and by "substantial capacity." Also, some jurisdictions used the phrase "appreciate the criminality," while others used "appreciate the wrongfulness," and they seem to communicate different concepts (Finkel, 1988; Rogers, 1986). Lastly, many states have dropped or ignored the "conform" or volitional element, thus rendering the ALI Rule very similar to the M'Naghten Rule.

Before proceeding, it should be remembered that the expert witness, the clinician who offers an opinion in this area, does not make the ultimate decision, as stated in *United States* v. *Freeman* (357 F.2d 619):

At bottom, the determination whether a man is or is not held responsible for his conduct is not a medical but a legal, social, or moral judgment, . . . it is society as a whole, represented by a judge or jury which decides whether a man with the characteristics described should or should not be held accountable for his acts (pp. 619–620).

Inherent in all of this is the fact that insanity is not a psychological/medical term, but is instead a legal term (Smith and Meyer, 1987). Hence, the expert has the problem of transforming and explaining clinical data in such a way as to facilitate the jury's opinion about whether the individual is insane. Although the judge and jury ultimately decide the issue, it is not uncommon for the expert to be asked indirectly, and sometimes directly, whether the individual is "insane." Also, even though a subsequent term, "incompetency," refers to the person's mental status at the time of the examination, there is an extra difficulty in that insanity requires an inference to mental status at the time of the alleged act (Szasz, 1987). This extra difficulty may be another reason why the insanity defense, in whatever form it is put forth, is not often effective as a defense.

Until the Durham decision in 1954, there was a fairly high correlation between the legal concept of insanity and the concept of psychosis. However, the Durham decision allowed the inclusion of "sociopathic personality," the DSM-I term in use at that time, as a mental disease included under "insanity." The second clause in the ALI Rule noted earlier was directed at eliminating this exception.

Under the influence of the ALI standard, it seems reasonably clear that several conditions in DSM-III-R can be considered to fit with the concept of insanity. First, the presence of delusions, hallucinations, or other significant interference with cognitive functioning should be enough to warrant an assertion of insanity. Hence, most of schizophrenic disorders and those dissociative disorders in which the behavior is relevant to the criminal act would be considered appropriate. Also, in most instances, the delusional (paranoid) disorders and some of the severe affective disorders, such as manic episode and depressive episode, would fit these criteria. Some juries readily accept the idea that hallucinations and delusions void criminal responsibility. However, a true connection has to be made between these phenomena and the alleged offense. Appropriate sections in this text deal with the specific diagnostic criteria commonly associated with these categories.

Juries are also usually more willing to see organic conditions that are coincident with the alleged offense as both more "real" and more causal, even when there is little reason to argue cause rather than correlation (Smith and Meyer, 1987). For example, there was some evidence of a causal link in a case of hypothyroid psychosis, commonly referred to in the literature as "myxedema psychosis," during which a young man allegedly commited a murder (Easson, 1980). He was held to be incompetent at the time of the trial. Later, after a two-month course of thyroid medication returned him to a status of competency, he stood trial and was found to be not guilty by reason of insanity, even though he was clearly sane at the time of his trial. Myxedema psychosis is rare, and it is marked by both paranoid symptoms and cognitive deficits. In this case, the person had referred himself for hospitalization because of his mental symptoms several months before the murder, and despite the fact that his scar for a prior thyroid operation had been noted, no effort was made to evaluate further for hypothyroidism.

IRRESISTIBLE IMPULSE

Because of the narrow cognitive focus of the M'Naghten Rule, there have been a variety of attempts to establish "irresistible impulse" as an additional rule, essentially beginning with State v. Thompson in 1834

(Rogers, 1986) and then evolving in the United States in *Parsons* v. *State* (1887) and its federal counterpart, *Davis* v. *United States* (1897). Of course, the central problem for both courts and clinicians has been to differentiate between an impulse that is irresistible and one that has not been resisted. In that regard, the reader is referred to Chapters 11 (Disorders of Impulse Control) and 12 (Malingering). In practice, this variation of criminal responsibility has received little support from either courts or clinicians, so it is recognized in only a few states. The Supreme Court has specifically curtailed its applicability to compulsive gambling (*United States* v. *Tonero*, 735 F. 2d 725, 1984) and to the addictions (*United States* v. *Lions*, 731 F.2d 243, 1984), and when it has received any support, it is usually with "command hallucinations" in schizophrenia and in severe obsessive-compulsive disorder cases.

□ ## EXCEPTIONS TO INSANITY JUDGMENTS

There are two major exceptions to a judgment of insanity. The first is those conditions resulting from substance abuse, particularly if the substance was voluntarily ingested. As asserted in *Barrett* v. *United States* (377 A.2d 62, 1977):

Temporary insanity created by voluntary use of alcohol or drugs will not relieve an accused criminal of responsibility even if that mental condition would otherwise meet the applicable legal definition of insanity (p. 62).

However, there are occasions when this is not so clearly applicable. First, insanity may be argued if the substance abuse was caused by another person without the victim's awareness, e.g., where someone spikes the victim's drink. Second, when "insanity" continues well beyond the actual effect of the drug use that was a catalyst for it, as stated in *State of New Jersey* v. *Stasio* (78 N.J. 467, 1979):

Insanity is available when the voluntary use of the intoxicant or drug results in a fixed state of insanity after the influence of the intoxicant or drug has spent itself (p. 467).

The second exception to a judgment of insanity, under either the M'Naghten or ALI rules, is articulated in the secondary paragraph of the ALI Rule in stating there is no insanity defense available where there is an "abnormality manifested only by repeated criminal or otherwise antisocial contact." This would usually disallow the antisocial-personality syndrome.

Two of the newer developments as regards criminal responsibility are guilty but mentally ill (GBMI) and diminished capacity. GBMI, which essentially allows a finding of both insanity and guilt, has received much attention, probably because it gives the jury a way out of an especially difficult decision. But the criteria and techniques for the insanity decision component are often the same as in other insanity formulations.

Diminished capacity is a potential, partial defense to a criminal charge. It permits a reduction of the level of offense upon a showing that the defendant is actually incapable of forming the required intent. Most of the experience with this defense has occurred in Michigan, and attorneys seem to view it as an updated version of the "intoxification defense." Ironically, of the many and varied referrals to the Center for Forensic Psychiatry in Ann Arbor, Michigan for consideration of this defense, it has almost never been found to be viable in practice (Clark, 1988).

☐   ASSESSMENT OF INSANITY

Kurlychek and Jordan (1980) present an interesting study that compared the MMPI profiles of thirty male defendants who were found to be criminally responsibile and those of twenty male defendants who were determined to be criminally not responsible. The modal code in the non-responsible group was the 8-6 code. Six nonresponsibles obtained that code, and only two responsibles did. Three responsibles each obtained 2-3 and 2-7 codes, but no nonresponsibles scored in that pattern. The modal code for the responsible group was 8-7 (six subjects), though three nonresponsible subjects also obtained that pattern. The high incidence of the 8-6 code in the nonresponsible clients suggested to the authors that highly delusional thought processes are a prevalent factor in non-responsible defendants. The common scales in the responsible group (8-7, 2-3, 2-7, and 2-0) indicate that more neurotic and inhibitory effects on any psychotic tendencies are found in responsible individuals.

Since faking-bad is particularly likely to be an issue in a decision about insanity, the reader is referred to Chapter 12. All reasonable precautions should be taken to prevent this. At the same time, clients should always be clearly told of the reason for the evaluation, what kind of decisions the information will be used for, and to whom it will be disseminated. To buttress the credibility of testimony, a number of clinicians argue that it is helpful to have protocols scored and interpreted by computer. Although this only offers part of the information a clinician needs to interpret the profile, they assert this lends support and apparent credence to testimony. On the other hand, introducing computer-generated reports into court easily leaves one "locked into" many of the comments in the report that the clinician may disagree with, as well as the potential ploy then available to a cross-examining attorney of asserting that the clinician has to rely on such a report because of a lack of expertise with that test.

As yet, effective "tests" specific to the assessment of insanity have not been developed, in contrast to those tests used to efficiently evaluate competency to stand trial (Meyer et al., 1988). However, there is data to suggest that the Rogers Criminal Responsibility Assessement Scale (R-CRAS) is useful as a decision tree (Rogers et al., 1981; Rogers 1986, 1988a). Twenty-three variables are rated to give scores on five discrete scales (the client's reliability, evidence of possible CNSI, psychopathology, cognitive control, and behavioral control). A hierarchical decision model, based on the ALI Rule, is then applied to these data.

Several studies have assessed the reliability and validity of the R-CRAS. Rogers (1986) reports that, overall, "reliability findings indicated a moderate degree of reliability for the individual variables (mean reliability coefficient was .58) and much higher reliability coefficients for the decision variables (average kappa coefficient was .81). Most important, clinical opinion regarding sanity was in almost perfect agreement, with a 97 percent concordance rate and a kappa coefficient of .94" (p. 168). Construct validity studies produced a .88 concordance rate, and a moderate degree of internal consistency (mean alpha of .60) was obtained. Grisso (1986) is generally positive about the value of the R-CRAS, only citing as negative the low reliability of several individual criteria and the absence of factor-analytic studies to statistically assess the structure of the R-CRAS.

Another scale, the MSE, devised by Slobogin et al. (1984) is especially effective in one direction and, in that sense, is a very good screening device. Those who are found on the MSE to have no significant mental abnormality almost uniformly are found in later court dispositions to be seen similarly. However, a finding of mental abnormality on the MSE has little predictive validity to subsequent court decisions.

■ Civil Commitment

Clinicians are becoming increasingly involved in assessments of dangerousness to self or others as this relates to civil commitment cases (Grisso, 1986). During the 1970s and early 1980s, the requirements for civil commitment were tightened considerably. Also, in the celebrated Donaldson case (*O'Connor* v. *Donaldson,* 95 S. Ct. 2486, 1975), commitment without some form of treatment was held to be unconstitutional.

At present, the basic requirements in most states for civil commitment are presence of mental illness or disorder, leading to dangerousness. This dangerousness is usually further interpreted as being physically dangerous to others or unable to provide the basics of life for oneself. In addition (particularly following the Donaldson case), some form of effective treatment must be available where the client is to be committed, and the least restrictive alternative should be used. There is now a clear trend toward expanding the scope of civil commitment, usually under doctrines that sound very much like *parens patriae*. One problematic consideration in commitment is that, according to *Buchanan* v. *Kentucky,* 107 S. Ct., 115 55 L.W. 5026, 1987, evidence gathered by clinicians during involuntary civil commitment evalutions may in some circumstances be used against the person in a related criminal proceeding.

The prediction of dangerousness is one of the most difficult assessment questions a clinician must face (Monahan, 1981, 1984) (see chapter 13). The decision has to focus on reasonably immediate dangerousness to self or others, and the clinician must come to a decision under the standard of "reasonable probabilty." On the first point, the clinician could act on the most accurate available prediction of dangerousness by simply collecting all persons who had been incarcerated for a severe assault just as they left a penitentiary and then commit them, since in the long run it is reasonably certain that a high proportion of these individuals will endanger others. Of course, most of them do not provide an immediate threat of dangerousness—the issue at hand.

With regard to the clinician's prediction of dangerousness in an individual client, the reader is referred to the sections on aggression and suicide potential. Also, assessments for mental retardation are appropriate, since in some cases there is an inability to provide for one's basic life care (Matson, 1987). Consideration of organic dysfunction (or CNSI) may also be relevant, as in the senile individual who is a diabetic. Such persons would probably not be able to take medication as required and in that sense would endanger their own life. The clinician must recall, however, that the ability to predict specific dangerousness in any reasonably circumscribed period of time is very low, and, in most cases, probably not at a level to warrant the cost, that is, the restriction of a person's freedom and civil liberties.

■ Competency

Competency refers to a variety of legal doctrines—most notably, standing trial, managing one's own affairs (guardianship), the contesting of a will—and the criteria differ for each of these (Smith and Meyer, 1987). There is even an increasing interest in "competency to be executed," evolving from the 1987 Supreme Court case of *Ford* v. *Wainwright* (477 U.S. 399). With the exception of competency to stand trial, clinicians traditionally are not commonly involved. However, some attorneys are now asking psychologists or other clinicians to assess their clients at the time they write a will if the attorney thinks there might be any future contesting of the will on the basis of competency. The clinician's report, made at the time of the writing of the will, is then filed with the will. This serves to make any later challenge rather absurd since the original assessment will be based on far more data than will be available following the individual's death. The procedure can be further strengthened by having the signing of the will and/or part of the evaluation videotaped as a record for later queries.

In general, competency to stand trial requires that these people have adequate mental ability to understand the charges and to participate in his or her own defense (Grisso, 1986). Insanity refers to the mental condition at the time they allegedly committed the crime, whereas incompetency to stand trial refers to their mental condition at the time of the trial. In addition, and more specifically, the Supreme Court has stipulated that "the test must be whether he has sufficient present ability to consult with his lawyer with a reasonable degree of rational understanding–and whether he has a rational as well as a factual understanding of the proceedings against him" (*Dusky* v. *United States,* 362 U.S. 402, 1960). They have to understand the nature of the proceedings with which they are involved and the consequences of those proceedings and manifest an ability to cooperate with the attorney in the preparation of their defense. Ironically, as held in *Colorado* v. *Connelly* (1987) 107 S. Ct. 115, 55 L.W. 4043, severe mental illness (and apparently, incompetency to stand trial) does not make a confession involuntary and therefore inadmissible.

These are clearly different criteria from any of the notions relating to insanity. These are much more specific and more related to actual behavior than to inferred mental status. Yet many clinicians who testify regarding incompetency do not realize this differentiation and as a result often confuse the issue of competency with that of either "psychosis" or "responsibility."

One of the major ways an individual can be incompetent is as a result of inadequate intellectual ability; the reader is referred to the prior section on mental retardation. However, the clinician should not make a decision by using a strict transition from any particular IQ to an arbitrary cut-off point for competency. The IQ is a critical variable, but the final decision should also take into account other factors, such as history of adaptation, common sense (both in the client and in the clinician), and any already observed ability to cooperate with the attorney and discuss the issues of law. Most individuals with mild mental retardation can cooperate effectively, although not always. As one proceeds through the levels of moderate, severe, and profound mental retardation, the proportion of those persons who cannot competently assist in their trial rises quickly (Matson, 1987).

If clinicians do any significant number of competency screenings, it is strongly recommended that they become familiar with and use the various competency screening instruments that are available (Grisso, 1986). An excellent set was devised by the Laboratory of Community Psychiatry (1973) at Harvard, particularly the Competency Assessment Instrument (CAI) and the Competency Screening Test (CST). That group also attempted to develop a projective test for competency, similar in design to the TAT, but so far have not found adequate reliability and validity.

The CAI attempts to standardize and structure the interview

procedure. It is formulated as a set of thirteen areas of ego awareness, covering virtually all of the legal grounds required of defendants if they are to cope effectively with such proceedings. Some of the areas assessed by the CAI are: awareness of available legal defenses, understanding of court procedures, appreciation of charges, range and nature of possible penalties, appraisal of possible outcome, capacity to inform the attorney adequately, and capacity to testify. The client is then evaluated on a scoring system of one (total incompetency) to six (totally competent) on the degree of ability in each area, based on an extensive interview as well as the history data. For example, in the ego function of "quality of relating to attorney," some of the suggested questions are: "Do you think your attorney is trying to do a good job for you?" or "Do you agree with his plans for handling your case?"

Interrater reliability on the scoring of responses to the items in the latest version of the CAI is .87, definitely an acceptable figure. The authors make the point that the efficacy and reliability of this instrument, as well as the CST, are directly correlated with experience with the instrument and with the competency process itself. Reliability increased dramatically from the point of the clinician's first experience with the CAI to its fourth or fifth use. Before using these instruments, a test use with some colleague consultation is advised. Persons can obtain a full report of this project, entitled *Competency to Stand Trial and Mental Illness,* from the National Institute of Mental Health, Center for Crime and Delinquency, 5600 Fishers Lane, Rockville, MD 20852, or can get in touch with the Laboratory of Community Psychiatry at Harvard University.

The Competency Screening Test is a sentence-completion technique that has been copyrighted by the project's psychologists, Paul Lipsitt and David Lelos. It consists of twenty-two sentence items, such as "When Phil was accused of the crime, he . . . ," and the like. A handbook in the appendix of the report gives differently scored answers for each item, as they are scaled as either 0, 1, or 2, with higher scores indicating higher levels of competency.

The five items that were found to be particularly predictive of competency are:*

9. When the lawyer questioned his client in court, the client said . . .

13. When the witness testifying against Harry gave incorrect evidence, he . . .

14. When Bob disagreed with his lawyer on his defense . . .

19. When I think of being sent to prison . . .

22. If I had a chance to speak to the judge . . .

---

* P. Lipsitt and D. Lelos, *Competency Screening Test,* copyright 1970 by authors. Used with permission.

The scoring emphasizes degrees of legal understanding and psychological integration. For example, for No. 9 above, answers such as "I am not guilty" or "I did not do anything" are assigned a 2, whereas an overspecific, vague, or hesitant response, such as "He had no knowledge of it" or "I don't know why—I guess I'm not guilty," brings the score down to 1. Irrelevant answers such as "He was too nervous to talk" or "The obvious thing" are scored zero. Similar scoring procedures are used with the other five items.

An impressive level of interrater reliability of .93 was obtained for the CST, using standard Z scores. Also, the overall predictive accuracy of the CST "in agreement with subsequent court determinations of competency," was 89.7 percent. By combining the CST predictive information with the validity scales of the MMPI and the female and male Draw-A-Person test, an accuracy rate above .90 is obtained.

There is some evidence that the CST screening was more valid than the highly structured and practiced judgments made by their trained raters. For example, some persons who were eventually designated as incompetent by the raters, based on overall data, actually showed clear evidence of competence throughtout all the tests. However, these particular individuals had a history of markedly aggressive behavior, and their crimes were repugnant to the community. Hence, the raters may have been swayed by those considerations.

Shatin (1979) found that a brief form of the CST (again, items 9, 13, 14, 19, 22) correlated .92 with the full-scale version in twenty-one female patients in a forensic psychiatric service examined for mental competency to stand trial, a result consistent with some data collected by the test's authors. This brief form also classified seventeen of the twenty-one patients in direct agreement with the results of a full clinical evaluation. Thus, there is good reason to believe that these five items will be useful and applicable to preliminary competency evaluations, possibly by incorporation into the Meyer Information Battery found in Appendix A.

An alternative competency instrument has been presented by Golding et al. (1984). Based on their earlier work showing that elaborate live-in assessments for competency are not cost-effective, these authors developed the Interdisciplinary Fitness Interview (IFI). In this original version, the IFI involves a semistructured interview coupled with anchored rating scales and is designed to involve a joint interview by a legal and a mental health professional. The manual and training procedures are more explicit than those for the CAI. There are three major sections: legal issues, psychopathological issues, and overall evaluation. The section on legal issues is divided into five areas that are somewhat different from the four factors described above. In a partial reversal of the trend started by the CAI, the authors have taken the position that psychopathological questions should be explicitly assessed in addition to purely legal questions and that both should contribute to the overall judgment of competency. The preliminary reliability and validity data presented by Golding et al. suggest that the IFI has potential for use either as an efficient screening device or as a full-scale assessment.

An excellent competency examination would include the CAI as a means of structuring the interview, the CST, a WAIS-R, an MMPI, and further assessments specific to potential malingering and personality functioning, such as the 16 PF and the Marlowe-Crowne Social Desirability Scale (Smith and Meyer, 1987; Grisso, 1986).

CHAPTER 16

Professional Case Preparation and Presentation: For Office or Courtroom

This chapter presents guidelines for more effective case preparation. By following these guidelines, the clinician will not only function more efficiently, but will significantly lessen the probability of being accused of malpractice. After discussing malpractice in general, the first set of guidelines is concerned with case preparation in general, followed by a model case report format that can easily be adapted to most clinical, neuropsychological, or forensic case situations. After that, I present guidelines for entering into a case as an expert witness, preparing for a deposition, and preparing for the actual courtroom appearance, if that is actually required. The chapter concludes with an examination of some of the major role conflicts a clinician often encounters in the forensic area.

Some of this material was touched on in the earlier edition of this handbook but was more extensively developed in Smith and Meyer (1987) and Meyer et al. (1988). The author was influenced by the notable contributions of such experts in the area as Monahan (1981), Ziskin (1981), Shapiro (1984), Blau (1984), Kennedy (1986), Grisso (1986), Melton et al., (1987), Weiner and Hess (1987), and others, so they will not be repeatedly cited throughout the chapter.

■ Malpractice

Malpractice considerations have been increasing for all mental health professionals. Claims are much higher against psychiatrists, in large part because they prescribe medication and use a number of instrusive techniques, such as ECT and psychosurgery. However, claims are increasing in every mental health sector. For example, during the first ten years (1961–71) of the malpractice insurance program of the American Psychological Association, only a few malpractice claims were made, and none were paid. During the 1976–80 period, however, 122 claims were processed, with estimated payments totaling $435,642, and both claims and payouts have continued to increase.

While some malpractice claims have been based on intentional torts (e.g., battery, false imprisonment, or intentional infliction of mental distress), most are based on the torts of negligence and/or contract liability. Overall, claims commonly arise from concepts such as unfair advantage (e.g., sexual improprieties), incorrect or inadequate treatment or diagnosis, failure to obtain informed consent, breach of confidentiality, wrongful involuntary commitment, failure to prevent suicide, nonfulfillment of contract (implicit or explicit), defamation, or failure to refer and/or to avoid practicing in a specific area where competence is lacking. As regards actual claims, sexual-impropriety claims and payouts and those for incorrect treatment are the most common.

As noted above, the guidelines that are discussed throughout this chapter will help avoid the spector of malpractice, in addition to promoting their primary purpose: effective and efficient clinical functioning. In addition, several specific steps may be taken to lessen malpractice probabilities: (1) think of records as eventual legal documents, (2) avoid touching clients, especially of the opposite sex, (3) get written releases, (4) don't collect overdue bills from clients who you could reasonably expect to be litigious and/or who expressed disappointment with their treatment, (5) avoid high-risk clients, e.g., paranoid, borderline, or narcissistic clients, chronic legal offenders, sexual problems in a fragmenting marriage, seriously depressed and/or suicidals, et al. These will help, but the flip side is that your practice will be restricted. In any case, using the following guidelines should help you avoid malpractice and practice more effectively.

■ General Principles for Case Preparation

Clinicians can take a number of measures to insure that their procedures are ethical, appropriate, and expert. This first set of suggestions concerns general issues with which most professionals in these areas would concern themselves; later, we will discuss the preparation of reports, the preparations for depositions, and the active courtroom appearance. The general suggestions for case preparation are as follows:

1. Don't take on a case in which you do not have a reasonable degree of expertise. There are numerous examples of mental health professionals taking on cases in which they only have a passing awareness of the issues or the requirements of practice. If you are trying to branch into a new area, make sure that you receive appropriate background education and supervision. After all, even the best and most experienced clinicians continue to use colleague consultation throughout their careers. It is also appropriate to inform the client, in a nonthreatening fashion, that this is a new area for you and to tell the client what the limits are that can be expected from your participation.

2. Establish a clear contract with your client. At the very least, make a thorough oral presentation in a contractual manner of what the client can expect from you and also of what you will expect from the client. It is probably advisable to put this in writing. The contract should cover the issue of compensation.

3. Keep meticulous notes on your encounter with the client and on related events. This is especially true in diagnostic cases, because these often will have implications in the forensic area or in other decision-making agreements. Make sure that when you return to the case after a lengthy period of time that you will be able to clearly reconstruct what occurred between you and the client and that you can report clearly what the client told you. Additionally, it is worthwhile to record your overall impressions at the time in which you first summarized the data in your own mind.

4. Make sure your history is a thorough one. Many cases have related issues that occur in the history of the client. The relevance of these issues may not be apparent at the time. Make sure that you have looked at all of the potential issues that are possibly relevant.

5. Use standard procedures and tests. Your results will be more acceptable to other professionals and to the courts. This does not preclude using some unusual techniques, but do so in a context of commonly accepted procedures and tests.

■ A Model Report Format

Whether the clinician is communicating with agencies, other professionals, attorneys, or the court, a formal report is often required. The following general outline has been found to be useful in such report writing. The clinician collects all relevant data and then goes through the sequence point by point as the report is dictated or written. Exclusion of subsections or inclusion of other information sections is easily accomplished, to meet the requirements of an individual case and/or the court's request.

In order to be most effective here, the clinician should use a combination of information sources (Grisso, 1986). These generally consist of (1) psychometric approaches, (2) observational approaches, (3) clinical interviews, (4) psychophysiological measures (possibly even polygraph examinations), and (5) peripheral methods, such as hypnosis and sodium amytal. Documentation of those sources that were used is especially important if the clinician must take this report into the legal arena. As noted in the last chapter, there are numerous ways the clinician can be brought into the legal system.

Name of Client:

Name of Examiner:

Date of Examination: Date of Report:

A. Introductory Variables

    1. Age
    2. Sex
    3. Educational background
    4. Socioeconomic status
    5. Occupational status, responsibilities

B. Referral Source and Related Information

C. Circumstances of Examination

    1. Place of examination
    2. Length of exam
    3. Present medications and last time used
    4. Tests administered

D. General Appearance

    1. Physical characteristics
    2. Dress and grooming
    3. Unusual behavior or mannerisms

E. Level of Response

    1. Answers questions fully?
    2. Volunteers information?
    3. Protocols adequate?
    4. Attitude toward testing and examiner

F. Presenting Problem and Dimensions of that Problem

    1. Duration
    2. Pervasiveness
    3. Severity
    4. Frequency

G. Consequences and Implications of Presenting Problem

    1. Functional aspects of impairment regarding
       a. job
       b. family
       c. school
       d. social milieu

    2. Legal status (e.g., pending litigation) of this incident or others
    3. Necessary changes in habits, roles (especially if acute)
    4. Adoption of coping skills or defense mechanisms, both healthy and unhealthy

H. Historical Setting

    1. Was the onset of any symptoms acute or gradual?
    2. Circumstances surrounding onset of symptoms
    3. Evidence of data re premorbid functioning in these areas

I. Other Historical Factors

    1. Level of adjustment as a child
    2. Level of adjustment as an adolescent
    3. Prior hospitalizations and diagnoses
    4. Parental relationships, then and now.
    5. Sibling relationships, then and now.

J. Other Present Situational Factors

    1. Marital relationship
    2. Children
    3. Job or School
    4. Other maintaining factors

K. Current Physical/Physiological Condition

    1. Medication, types and dosages
    2. Medical complications (e.g., removal of limb)
    3. Other factors not directly related to presenting problem

L. Type of Affect and Level of Anxiety

    1. Amount
    2. Appropriateness
    3. In-session versus ongoing functioning
    4. General mood
    5. Effects on testing and interview behavior

M. IQ Level

    1. Subtest variability
    2. Pre-incident versus present level
    3. Educational preparation versus inherent ability
    4. Potential functioning
    5. Personality inferences

N. Organic Involvement

   1. Any significant indicators
   2. Degree, if any
   3. Specific or global
   4. Cause: alcoholism, birth or prenatal factors, trauma
   5. Cause of or coincidental to other disorder

O. Thought Processes

   1. Hallucinations or delusions
   2. Paranoid traits
   3. Degree of insight
   4. Adequate social judgments
   5. Adequate abstracting ability
   6. Orientation to environment

P. Overall Integration and Statement of Personality Functioning—Diagnosis

Q. Evaluation of Patient's Current Overall Attitudes Toward His/Her Situation

   1. Expectancies about recovery
   2. Attitude toward disorder
   3. Motivation for treatment
   4. Understanding of status/condition
   5. Coping skills, responses to stress and crisis

R. Identification of Any Need for Further Referral or Consultation

S. Identification of Targets for Modification, Intervention

T. Treatment Recommendations

   1. Individual, family, and/or group therapy
   2. Chemotherapy
   3. Hospitalization
   4. Predictions of dangerousness to self or to others
   5. Interest in change
   6. Probability of maintenance in treatment

U. Priority of Treatment Recommendations (Including Reevaluation and Follow-up), Based on Available Resources

V. Judgment Regarding Prognosis, Based on

   1. Age at time of onset
   2. Phase of disease or disorder

3. Known morbidity rates
4. Severity of affliction
5. Accessibility of family, other social-support systems
6. Test results
7. Patient's attitude

W. Other Summary Formulations and Conclusions

Expert Witness Case Preparation

While these suggestions and principles are important for virtually any professional in the mental health area, there are several other suggestions that are important if you eventually become directly involved in the judicial process in a client's case:

1. Take some time to observe courtroom procedures in general and try to observe various mental health professionals in the role of an expert witness. This will allow you to become familiar and comfortable with courtroom process.

2. Even though mental health experts who are called by one party should be an advocate for their opinions and not for the party, they still must operate within the adversary legal system. Therefore, you should not discuss the case with anyone other than the court or the party for whom you have conducted an evaluation without the knowledge or permission of the court or that party.

3. Once the opinion has been formed, insist that the attorney who employs you provide the basic facts of the case, the relevant statutory and case law, and that he or she explains the theory under which the case is to be pursued. Understanding of these issues is crucial to your preparation for the case, and reports and testimony should specifically address these legal issues.

4. Prepare your case in language that will be meaningful to the court. Remember that jurors are going to be put off by jargon, or they will misunderstand and, thus, not give proper weight to your testimony.

5. Prepare yourself to give a thorough overview of all the examination devices that you will be referring to. In the courtroom, you may be asked about the reliability and validity of these devices, about how they were derived, or about what they are purported to measure. You should be ready to answer this in a crisp and efficient fashion, in a language that people will find understandable and useful

6. Make sure ahead of time of the role you will take in the courtroom situation and communicate this to the attorney who has brought you into the case.

7. When you are close to actually presenting the case in deposition or in court, make sure you can be comfortable with your knowledge of the client. This may entail bringing the client in for visits shortly before the court testimony. In many court cases, the professional may do the evaluation years before actually going into court. In such a case, you really ought to see the client again, if at all possible, to check on prior data that was collected and to update your impressions and inferences.

■ Deposition Preparation and Presentation

In virtually every case that takes on a legal dimension, there is a strong likelihood that the clinician will be deposed. Indeed, in many case there may be no courtroom appearance after a deposition, either because the case is settled out of court or the material that came to light in the deposition eliminated the need or desire to have the clinician testify in person.

Many of the suggestions already mentioned as critical in general and in expert-witness case presentation—or that will be mentioned shortly as important in preparing for a courtroom presentation—are relevant to the deposition as well. However, the following are more specific to preparation for a deposition.

1. Organize and review all materials pertinent to the case and request a predisposition conference with the attorney.

2. Bring to the deposition only those records, notes, etc. that you are willing for all involved parties to be aware of or, in many cases, to gain access to.

3. Be aware that there are two types of subpoenas. The first, the *subpoena ad testicandum,* is what most people assume, a summons to appear at court at a specified date and time. The second, the *subpoena duces tecum,* requires the clinician to bring specific materials to the court.

4. Remember that just because a particular set of records has been requested, or even subpoenaed, does not mean they must be released. If in doubt, the clinician should (a) insist that the attorney requesting the information provide a valid authorization from the affected person, (b) request a court order before releasing the information (in some jurisdictions, even a court order is not sufficient), and (c) seek independent legal counsel before acting.

5. Bring an extra copy of your curriculum vitae, as it is likely it will be incorporated into the record at this time.

6. Be courteous and speak in a voice that is audible to everyone, especially the stenographic reporter.

7. Be honest in all responses, but do not provide information that is not requested. Avoid any elaboration.

8. Think before you respond. You can take as much time as you wish to think out your response, since there is no issue of conveying a confused or tentative image to the jury, as there may be in the courtroom.

9. If an attorney objects, stop talking. It is best to let the attorneys deal with the point in question.

10. Remember that the opposing attorney will be evaluating you as a witness and may try many things in deposition that won't be used in trial.

11. Thoroughly read and check the deposition when a copy is sent to you for your signature; do not waive your right to sign it. Correct any errors in it as your attorney instructs. Keep a copy of the deposition with your other records pertaining to that case.

12. Prior to going to court, review your copy of the deposition and take it with you to the witness stand.

■ Courtroom Presentation

While all cases in which the clinician is deposed do not result in a court appearance, many do. The following suggestions are useful when it actually comes to presenting testimony in the courtroom.

1. First and foremost, be honest in all of your testimony. If you do not know the answer, say so, and offer to give related information that may clarify the question. But do not try to answer questions when you really do not know the answer. Aside from the ethical issues involved, it is very likely that you will be tripped up later in the cross-examination.

2. Don't be overly reluctant to admit limitations in your expertise or in the data that you have available. If the cross-examining counsel presents a relevant and accurate piece of data, acknowledge this in a firm and clear fashion and do not put yourself into a defensive position.

3. Acknowledge, by eye contact, the person who has requested your statement, be it the judge or one of the attorneys. But at the same time, as much as possible, maintain eye contact with the jury.

4. Be aware of the three classic errors of the expert witness: becoming (a) too technical, (b) too complex in discussion, or (c) condescending and too simplistic. Any of these approaches is likely to lose the attention of the jurors and may also turn them against you and the content of your testimony.

5. Avoid long, repetitive explanations of your points. If at all possible, keep your responses to two or three statements. If you feel more is needed, try to point out that you cannot fully answer the question without elaborating.

6. Never answer questions that you do not really understand. If you are uncomfortable with the wording of the question, ask to have it restated and, if need be, describe your problems with the question as originally posed.

7. Similarly, listen carefully to what is asked in each question before you answer. If there is a tricky component to the question, acknowledge that and then try to deal with it in a concise fashion. If the attorney has made an innuendo that is negative to the case or to you, respond, if you feel it is appropriate, without becoming adversarial. Keep your response unemotional. This *may* be a good time to bring in a bit of humor. However, the use of humor requires *great* caution.

8. If you feel the attorney has misstated what you have just said, when he or she asks a follow-up question, take the time to unemotionally clarify what you actually did say, and then go on and answer the next question.

9. Speak clearly, fluently, and somewhat louder than you would normally speak. Make sure the jury hears you. Speak when spoken to, and avoid smoking or chewing. Avoid weak or insipid speech patterns, commonly marked by (a) hesitation forms, such as "Uh," "You know," "Well," (b) formal grammar, (c) hedges, such as "sort of," "I guess," "I think," (d) overly polite speech, (e) the use of a questioning form of sentence structure rather than straightforward sentences. Communicate a confident, straightforward attitude.

10. Avoid using any graphs, tables, or exhibits that are not easily visible, readable, and comprehensible by the average juror.

11. Be prepared for questions about journal articles, books, etc., relevant to issues in this particular case. This is more important now than it was at the deposition stage. You can't check up on all of the relevant literature, but by familiarizing yourself with some key recent articles, you can more easily blunt an attack.

12. Be prepared to be questioned about the issue of fees. Attorneys may ask questions like, "How much are you being paid to testify for this client?" You need to correct that and state that you were asked to do an evaluation, then give your full and honest opinion to the best of your knowledge, and that it was then up to the attorney to decide whether he or she wanted to go ahead and use you in the courtroom. Also, make sure that you state that you are not being paid for your testimony, but that you are being paid for the time that you put into this trial, no matter what testimony would emerge from that time spent. For that reason, you probably will look better to the jury if you charge by the hour rather than charging a flat fee for a case.

13. Be professional in both your dress and demeanor. Informal dress is seldom appropriate in a courtroom. Reasonably conservative attire makes a more positive impression on the jury. Similarly, your demeanor should be professional, and you should avoid becoming involved in any kind of tirade or acrimony.

14. Never personalize your interactions with an attorney who is attempting to disrupt you. If you become emotional and make any kind of personal attack, you will likely taint the value of your testimony. There may be times when you do need to express some emotion in giving an opinion in order to emphasize that opinion. But make sure the emotion is properly placed on the opinion and not as a defensive or attacking response toward the court, jury, or a cross-examining attorney.

Just as the clinician is organizing to make an effective presentation to the court, the attorneys are preparing to devalue any or all parts of the clinician's testimony. The well-prepared clinician reminds himself or herself of the strategies that he or she is likely to encounter.

■ Anticipating Cross-Examination

Cross-examination is designed to challenge or discredit those data and opinions that have been presented by the clinician that are inconsistent with that attorney's case. There are a variety of ways in which the cross-examining attorney will attempt to challenge this testimony:

1. A primary target for examination is the expert's qualifications. Two kinds of questions concerning qualifications are: (a) whether a witness is sufficiently qualified to be permitted (by the judge) to testify as an expert, and (b) the "weight" that should be given (by the judge or jury) to the expert's opinion. Presumably, the more highly qualified the expert, the greater the weight should be given that professional's opinion. The expert's experience in the area and the level of relevant education are common targets. More often, the critique is directed toward the specialization that is important in this particular case. For example, an expert clinical psychologist may have had little involvement in the area of neuropsychology, and yet the critical point in the case may involve a neuropsychological issue. This, of course, would appropriately reduce the credibility of the expert.

2. Another common way to challenge the expert witness is through contradictory testimony from other experts in the field. These experts may testify in the trial, or the challenge may be in the form of a book or article submitted as written authority. A favorite approach is to attempt to lead the witness down the garden path by asking if such-and-such a source is authoritative, etc., and then presenting the contradictory testimony from that source. So when an expert is asked if this book or person is authoritative, it may be wise to make a disclaimer like "Dr. _____ does write in this field. Other experts might agree with some of the things he says, but he's not my authority [or the only authority]."

3. A third technique is to attack the procedures that are used by the expert witness. A classic instance is the discovery that the expert spent a very short period of time with the client. An expert who so cavalierly comes to such an important decision should be vulnerable in the cross-examination.

The particular tests used in an evaluation are also important. For this reason, most mental health expert witnesses prefer to use a variety of objective psychological tests in their examination. It is debatable whether having the tests computer-scored and interpreted adds something to the testimony. It can be argued that this adds a validation by an "apparently objective other." At the same time, sending off a test for scoring or interpretation can be construed, through the presentation of the cross-examining attorney, as dependency on outside opinions because of a lack of expertise. Also, one is prone to be "locked into" all of the statements made in the computer-generated report. Some may clearly not fit this individual case, and the clinician may disagree with a number of the statements (Butcher, 1987).

Projective tests can, of course, be used in court, but they are much more vulnerable to cross-examination. A sophisticated attorney is likely here to pull out an ink blot and ask for the expert's response, or a typical response, and then try to get a statement from the expert as to what is the appropriate idea here or what can be made of a response the client made. This is one of those times when it is very critical for the expert witness to communicate that the opinions and inferences have been based on a variety of data and not from any individual piece of datum.

4. Another area in which the clinician can be impeached is through bias, for example, by attacking the expert witness as a "hired gun" and asking a variety of questions about how the individual has been paid. As noted elsewhere, it is probably wise for the expert to bill on an hourly basis, rather than through a flat fee, because this seems to communicate to jurors a more professional approach. Also, the expert should be prepared to note that it was his or her evaluation that was paid for, not any outcome or particular slant to the testimony, and that it was stated up front, "I will make my evaluation and give you my honest opinion."

5. Another possibility here is to attack the expert as a "professional witness," one who spends virtually his or her entire career going from courtroom to courtroom. People who do a lot of forensic work are vulnerable to this characterization, and they need to be ready to present a picture of how they became involved in court cases and why they appear frequently.

6. Another potential point of attack is any special relationship to the client. If there is any sense in which the expert is a friend of the client, is doing the client a "favor," or in turn is receiving "favors" for the testimony, the expert's testimony is likely to have little positive impact on the jury.

7. Expert witnesses are occasionally cross-examined on their personal vulnerabilities or deficiencies. Any general indications of instability or deviation in the history of the expert witness may be brought out if they can be discovered. Persons who have obvious vulnerabilities, possibly a history of alcoholism or hearing or vision problems (which may in some instances be relevant), should consider means of handling such an attack.

8. Just as the attorney will try to challenge the sources of an inference, they will also try to impeach the process of deriving the inference or opinion. They may try to introduce at least apparently contradictory data or they may just simply ask "Isn't this alternate idea *possible*?" It is important for the expert witness not to become too defensive here. There may be a reasonable admission that other interpretations are possible. The expert witness needs to define that we are in a world of probabilities, possibly stating something to the effect that "Yes, almost anything is possible, but I feel that the bulk of evidence supports the opinion I have rendered."

9. An excellent way to impeach an expert witness is to disclose prior reports or transcripts of court testimony given by the same expert that are contradictory to the present testimony. The expert should be aware of this possibility, and experts who publish a great deal are even more vulnerable. They need to be able to explain this situation reasonably, e.g., that opinions do change over time and that they may have made a statement some time before in a book with which they do not wholly agree now, or they need to point out why the earlier comments do not exactly apply here. Again, defensiveness is a bad strategy here. Openness can be the best method of handling this type of attack.

Clinicians should remember that at its root, cross-examination is a process of searching for the truth by challenging the ideas and conclusions of the expert. In this sense, it compresses into a short time the long process of challenge to publication and research. Cross-examination is not a perfect process of truth-finding. The presentation of information to a lay jury may, in a few instances, cause obfuscation through cross-examination. Some attorneys unfairly attack or even badger witnesses. The fact that some attorneys try these tactics, however, does not mean that they have succeeded; such tactics often backfire. Juries probably resent trickery on credible experts. If a mental health expert has drawn reasonable conclusions based on full examination and has avoided exaggerated statements and emotional responses to cross-examination, the expert will have succeeded in making his or her point to the jury. A dry run, a practice cross-examination, can be especially helpful, particularly for the expert who has not testified before. It may also be instructional to review Ziskin (1981) on similar materials so that the approaches any sophisticated attorney may take in a cross-examination can be anticipated.

■ The Clinician's Role in Court

As an increasing number of clinicians enter the forensic arenas, they encounter ethical situations and practical problems that are seldom found in other areas of practice (Barrett et al., 1985). One of the most frequent dilemmas concerns being asked to take, in the same case, more than one of the following three roles: expert witness, consultant, advocate. Each has a different ultimate client focus: expert witness–court; consultant–client/attorney; and advocate–cause. Any one of these roles is proper for a clinician, but accepting more than one role in the same case, or even blurring the roles' boundaries, is inappropriate.

Pressure to take more than one role in a single case may come from either the clinician or the attorney. Pressure from within the clinician often comes when there is a late call for help with the case. Demand characteristics of the situation can readily couple with personal needs to put the clinician in the classical role of "rescuer." In the extreme, the unsuspecting clinician may soon be agreeing to testify as an expert witness, to suggest theories of defense, to offer advice on how to make the client more presentable to a jury, and to help select a jury.

A closer look at the three roles will make clear the reasons why the roles should not be combined or blurred. The expert is present to assist the jury with questions that it does not have the required special knowledge to address by itself. In that sense, the "client" is the court. The designation "expert witness" refers not only to the qualifications and expertise of the person in the role, but especially to the rules that will govern the person's testimony. Unlike other witnesses, the expert witness may render an opinion. Further, the expert witness may incorporate "hearsay evidence" that other witnesses may not use, and opinions may be based on this evidence. As Shapiro (1984) notes:

> Whenever one testifies in court, . . . one should not consider oneself an advocate for the patient, for the defense, or for the government. One is an advocate only for one's own opinion. When the expert witness allows himself or herself to be drawn into a particular position, because of a feeling that the patient needs treatment, that the patient should be incarcerated, or that society needs to be protected, the credibility and validity of one's testimony invariably suffers. . . . (pp. 77–98.)

It would be an abuse of process, as well as a way of diminishing the value of one's testimony, for the expert witness to use his/her unique role in order to advocate anything other than a professional opinion.

The role of consultant in forensic cases is also one that clinicians are occasionally called upon to take. The "client," in this case, is the side that retained the consultant. Jury selection, preparation of direct- and cross-examination questions, review of treatment records, procurement of appropriate expert witnesses, recommendations for packaging and sequencing of evidence, courtroom jury monitoring, and other consultant functions may be performed. However, the forensic consultant must maintain some distance from the advocacy role taken by the attorneys.

Keeping professional distance from the advocacy process is one of the most challenging tasks faced by the consulting clinician. However, it is essential that this task be completed successfully. The consultant role, *per se,* requires that one "call it as he/she sees it" and not as the client wants it. It is possible that one's client will perceive such professional detachment as coldness and lack of care about the case, but that risk must be taken. Focus must be, instead, on the rendering of the best possible consulting opinon, regardless of what effect it might have on the advocate's behavior or case. The consultant cannot be accountable for the use that the client makes of the opinion that is given, nor is the consultant accountable if the advocate fails to use the opinion.

The role of advocate is seldom a legitimate role for clinicians. This is fortunate, since this role is fraught with ethical implications. As an advocate, the clinician is a member of the team and, like other team members, has the goal of winning. The sciences and arts of the mental health professions are here used to achieve an end that the advocate defines as worthy. This may include conviction, acquittal, or modification of sentences in criminal cases. It is possible, and perhaps likely, that an advocate in a case will have personal motives that are not necessarily related directly to the case. For example, advocates for or against capital punishment may be more concerned with the issue of execution than with presentation of the most complete or accurate possible case to a jury.

It is important for the clinician to make it clear when an advocate role has been taken. Otherwise, juries or the media may mistake statements intended only to advance a cause for a reasoned, responsible professional opinion. Use of such expertise to promote a particular view that is not scientifically supported generally would be considered unethical.

Thus, as an expert witness, the clinician will find a primary allegiance to the opinion rendered to the court; as a consultant, to the best information rendered to the client; and as an advocate, to service to a cause or point of view. Again, it can be appropriate to take the role of either expert, consultant, or advocate, but each of these roles has limits and one should neither take more than one role per case nor blur the role boundaries. In difficult cases of this sort, colleague consultation can be especially helpful. But if doubt still persists, the old adage "If in doubt, don't" is the wisest course.

Appendix A:
The Meyer Information Battery

Name _____ Age _____ Sex _____ Date _____

Please finish each of the sentences and say as much as you can about how you feel. Use your true feelings in your answers. Try to complete every one and say as much as possible about yourself. Thank you.

My favorite kind of job would be _____

_____

Men think I _____

_____

I could be a better worker if _____

_____

Women think I _____

_____

My school grades _____

_____

My father _____

_____

When adapting this battery, more-adequate space for responses should be included.

Failure _____

_____

Most bosses _____

_____

My blood boils when _____

_____

My biggest fear is _____

_____

The best way to control pain is _____

_____

The best way to control anxiety or depression is _____

_____

My mother _____

_____

I like best the kind of work that _____

_____

My proudest time is _____

_____

I wish I could forget _____

_____

If things go badly for you, do you get angry or depressed? _____

_____

    What do you then do about it? _____

_____

Do you feel it would help to talk to anyone about your problems? _____

_____

Why or why not? _____

_____

What do you think the future holds for you and why? _____

_____

At what time in your life were you closest to panic? _____

_____

Why? _____

_____

When did you feel most guilty? _____

_____

Why? _____

_____

What does marriage mean to you? _____

_____

Explain in some detail what death means to you. _____

_____

_____

If I could be anything that I wished, I would choose to be _____

_____ because _____

_____

If I could have any three wishes in the world, I would wish

1. _____

2. _____

3. _____

If I could make any one change in other people, it would be _____

_____

because _____

The very earliest thing that I can remember as a child is _____

_____

_____

My most pleasant memory is _____

_____

_____

My most unpleasant memory is _____

_____

_____

Explain the four proverbs below. For example, the proverb _Large oaks from little acorns grow_ means that great things may have small beginnings. Say as best you can what each of these proverbs means.

While the cat's away, the mice will play. _____

_____

_____

It never rains but it pours. _____

_____

_____

Don't cry over spilt milk. _____

_____

The burnt child dreads the fire. _____

_____

_____

If the following people were asked to describe you in one word, what word would each probably use?

Mother _____

Father _____

Brother(s) _____

Sister(s) _____

Your spouse or most intimate opposite-sex friend _____

Your best friend now _____

Your boss _____

Your son(s) _____

Your daughters(s) _____

I would most strongly wish to raise my child to be _____

_____

_____

If there is one thing that I could go back and change about my life, it would be __

_____

_____

_____

_____

Briefly describe your history of arrests and convictions (either felonies or misdemeanors), including any moving violations while in an automobile.

_____

_____

_____

_____

Briefly describe any history of psychological or psychiatric treatment.

_____

_____

_____

_____

■   ## Draw-A-Group

Please draw a picture of any group scene that involves you and at least
two other people. I know that many people are not artists and may
seldom draw anything. However, simply go ahead and do your best. Use
first names or role names (e.g., Jack, Sue, Amy, friend, father, sister,
me, etc.) to label each of the figures in your drawing. Remember, I
understand that not everyone draws well or even likes to draw. All I
want is your best effort. Thank you.

■   ## Drawing Explanation

Use the space that follows to describe what is happening in the drawing you made. Describe what is going on; whether someone is talking to someone; what they are saying; or anything else that is important. Give all the details you can. Thank you.

What is your most serious physical problem at this time? _____

_____

What treatment are you receiving? _____

_____

What is your most serious emotional problem at this time? _____

_____

Why? _____

_____

How could other people help you change for the better? _____

_____

Do you prefer to live in the city, the suburbs, or the country? _____

_____

Why? _____

_____

Which man of the past or present do you most admire? _____

_____

Why? _____

_____

Which woman of the past or present do you most admire? _____

_____

Why? _____

_____

Who has been more meaningful to you, your father or your mother? _____

_____

Why? _____

_____

What is your favorite movie of all time? _____

Why? _____

_____

Who is your favorite male movie star? _____

Why? _____

Who is your favorite female movie star? _____

Why? _____

Do you believe in God? _____ Why or why not? _____

_____

Do you practice a religion? _____ Why and in what way? Or why not? _____

_____

Has your sexual history been good or bad? _____ Describe and say why it has

been good or bad for you. _____

_____

What has been the greatest injustice you have suffered? _____

_____ What did you do about it? _____

_____

Thank you for your cooperation

Appendix B

Major Groups of Psychotropic Chemotherapeutic Agents

EFFECT GROUP	CHEMICAL GROUP	GENERIC NAME	TRADE NAME
Minor Tranquilizers	Propanediols	Meprobamate	Equanil Miltown
	Benzodiazepines	Clorazepate dipotassium Alprazolam Diazepam Lorazepam	Tranxene Xanax Valium Ativan
Neuroleptics (Antipsychotics)	Phenothiazines	Chlorpromazine Trifluoperazine Thioridazine	Thorazine Stelazine Mellaril
	Butyrophenones	Haloperidol	Haldol
	Thioxanthenes	Chlorprothixene	Taractan
Central Nervous System Stimulants	Oxazolidine	Pemoline	Cylert
	Amphetamines	Dextroamphetamine	Dexedrine
		Methamphetamine	Desoxyn
	Piperidyls	Methylphenidate	Ritalin
Antidepressants	Tricyclics	Doxepin Hydrochloride (HCl)	Adapin Sinequan
		Amoxapine	Asendin
		Nortriptyline	Aventyl
		Trazodone	Desyrel
		Amitriptyline HCl	Elavil
		Imipramine	Janimine Tofranil
		Maprotiline HCl	Ludiomil
		Desipramine HCl	Norpramin
	Monoamine Oxidase Inhibitors (MAOs)	Phenelzine	Nardil
		Tranylcypromine	Parnate
		Isocarboxazid	Marplan

This is a list of the most commonly known and widely used chemical groups, and examples within each group.

Bibliography

Abel, G., Rouleau, J., & Cunningham-Rathner, J. (1986). "Sexually Aggressive Behavior." In W. Curran, A. L. McGarry, and S. Shah, Eds. *Forensic Psychiatry and Psychology*. Philadelphia: F.A. Davis.

Abramson, P., Perry, L., Seeley, T., Seeley, D., and Rothblatt, A. (1981) "Thermographic Measurement of Sexual Arousal: A Discriminant Validity Analysis." *Archives of Sexual Behavior, 10,* 171–176.

Adler, M. (1988). "Milieu therapy." In J. Lion, W. Adler, and W. Webb, Eds. *Modern Hospital Psychiatry*. New York: W. W. Norton.

Agras, W. (1987). *Eating Disorders*. New York: Pergamon.

Albert, S., Fox, H., and Kahn, M. (1980). "Faking Psychosis on the Rorschach: Can Expert Judges Detect Malingering?" *Journal of Personality Assessment, 44,* 115–119.

Allison, J., Blatt, S., and Zimet, C. (1988). *The Interpretation of Psychological Tests*. New York: Hemisphere.

Altman, J. and Wittenborn, J. (1980). "Depression-Prone Personality in Women." *Journal of Abnormal Psychology, 89,* 303–308.

American Psychiatric Association (1952). *Diagnostic and Statistical Manual of Mental Disorders (DSM-I)*. 1st ed. Washington, DC: APA.

_____ (1968). *Diagnostic and Statistical Manual of Mental Disorders (DSM-II)*, 2nd ed. Washington, DC: APA.

_____ (1980). *Diagnostic and Statistical Manual of Mental Disorders (DSM-III)*, 3rd ed. Washington, DC: APA.

_____ (1987). *Diagnostic and Statistical Manual of Mental Disorders (DSM-III-R)*, 3rd ed., revised. Washington, DC: APA.

Anastasi, A. (1987). *Psychological Testing,* 6th ed. New York: Macmillan.

Anderson, W., and Bauer, B. (1985). "Clients with MMPI High D-Pd." *Journal of Clinical Psychology, 41,* 181–188.

Andreasen, N., Schaftner, W., Reich, T., Hirschfield, R., Endicott, J., and Keller, M. (1986). "The Validation of the Concept of the Endogenous Depression." *Archives of General Psychiatry, 43,* 246–254.

Archer, R. (1987). *Using the MMPI with Adolescents.* Hillsdale, NJ: Lawrence Erlbaum Associates.

Arkes, H. (1981). "Impediments to Accurate Clinical Judgment and Possible Ways to Minimize Their Impact." *Journal of Consulting and Clinical Psychology, 49,* 323–330.

Armentrout, J., and Hauer, A. (1978.) "MMPI's of Rapists of Adults, Rapists of Children and Non-rapists Sex Offenders." *Journal of Clinical Psychology, 34,* 330–332.

Aronow, E., and Reznikoff, M. (1976). *Rorschach Content Interpretation.* New York: Grune and Stratton.

Ballenger, J., Burrows, G., DuPont, R., Lesser, I. et al., (1988). "Alprazolam in Panic Disorder and Agoraphobia." *Archives of General Psychiatry, 45,* 413–422.

Balloun, K., and Holmes, D. (1979). "Effects of Repeated Examintions on the Ability to Detect Guilt with a Polygraphic Examinatin: A Laboratory Experiment with a Real Crime." *Journal of Applied Psychology, 64,* 316–322.

Barbaree, H., Marshall, W., and Lanthier, R. (1979). "Deviant Sexual Arousal in the Rapist." *Behavior Research and Therapy, 17,* 215–222.

Barkley, R. (1987). *Defiant Children.* New York: Guilford.

Barnett, P., and Gotlib, I. (1988). "Psychological Functioning and Depression." *Psychological Bulletin, 104,* 97–126.

Barrett, C. (1981). Personal communication.

Barrett, C. (1986). "Use of Disulfiram in the Psychological Treatment of Alcoholism." *Bulletin of the Society of Psychologists in the Addictive Behaviors, 4(4),* 197–205.

Barrett, C., Johnson, P., and Meyer, R. (1985). "Expert Witness, Consultant, Advocate: One Role is Enough." *Bulletin of the American Academy of Forensic Psychology, 6,* 5.

Beaber, R., Marston, A., Michelli, J., and Mills, M. (1985). "A Brief Test for Measuring Malingering in Schizophrenic Individuals." *The American Journal of Psychiatry, 142,* 1478–1481.

Beck, A., (1976). *Cognitive Therapy and the Emotional Disorders.* New York: International Universities Press.

Beck, A., Steer, R., Kovacs, M., and Garrison, B. (1983). "Hopelessness and Eventual Suicide: A 10-Year Prospective Study of Patients Hospitalized with Suicidal Ideation." *American Journal of Psychiatry, 142,* 559–563.

Beck, S. (1951). "The Rorschach Test: A Multi-dimensional Test of Personality." In H. Anderson, H. Harold, and G. Anderson, Eds. *An Introduction to Projective Techniques.* Englewood Cliffs, NJ: Prentice-Hall.

Beck, S., and Beck, A. (1978). *Rorschach's Test: II. 1 Gradients in Mental Disorder. Third Edition of II. A Variety of Personality Pictures.* New York: Grune and Stratton.

Beck, S., and Molish, H. (1952). *Rorschach's Test: Advances in Interpretation,* New York: Grune and Stratton.

Bellak, J. (1986). *The T.A.T., C.A.T. and S.A.T in Clinical Use,* 4th ed. Orlando, FL: Grune and Stratton.

Belli, M. (1979). "Transsexual Surgery: A New Tort." *Journal of Family Law, 17,* 487–504.

Bender, L. (1938). *A Visual Motor Gestalt Test and Its Clinical Use.* New York: American Orthopsychiatric Association.

Benedikt, R., and Kolb, L. (1986). "Preliminary Findings on Chronic Pain and Post-Traumatic Stress Disorder." *American Journal of Psychiatry, 143,* 908–910.

Benton, A. (1980). "The Neuropsychology of Facial Recognition." *American Psychologist, 35,* 176–186.

Berk, L. (1989). *Child Development: Theory, Research and Applications.* Needham Heights, MA: Allyn and Bacon.

Berne, E. (1964). *Games People Play.* New York: Grove.

Bernstein, A., Riedel, J., Graae, F., Seidman, D., et al. (1988). "Schizohrenia Is Associated with Altered Orienting Activity, Depression with Electrodermal (Cholinergic?) Deficit and Normal Orienting Response." *Journal of Abnormal Psychology, 97,* 3–12.

Bertinetti, J. (1980). "Substance Abuse." In R. Woody, Ed. *The Encyclopedia of Clinical Assessment.* San Francisco: Jossey-Bass.

Beutler, L., Karacan, I., Anch, M., Salis, P., Scott, F., Williams, R. (1975). "MMPI and MIT Discriminators of Biogenic and Psychogenic Impotence." *Journal of Consulting and Clinical Psychology, 43,* 899–908.

Binder, A. (1988). "Juvenile delinquency." In M. Rosenzweig and L. Porter, Eds. *Annual Review of Psychology,* Vol. 39. Palo Alto, CA: Annual Reviews, Inc.

Blanchard, R., Steiner, B., and Clemmensen, L. (1985). "Gender Dysphoria, Reorientation and the Clinical Management of Transsexualism." *Journal of Consulting and Clinical Psychology, 53,* 295–304.

Blane, H., and Leonard, K. (1987). *Psychological Theories of Drinking and Alcoholism.* New York: Guilford.

Blatt, S. and Allison, J. (1981). "The Intelligence Test in Personality Assessment." In A. Rabin, Ed. *Assessment with Projective Techniques.* New York: Springer.

Blatt, S., Baker, B., and Weiss, J. (1970). "Wechsler Object Assembly Subtest and Bodily Concern." *Journal of Consulting and Clinical Psychology, 34,* 269–274.

Blau, T. (1984). *The Psychologist as Expert Witness.* New York: John Wiley.

Bloom-Feshbach, J., and Bloom-Feshbach, S. (1987). *The Psychology of Separation and Loss.* San Francisco: Jossey-Bass.

Boerger, A., Graham, J., and Lilly, R. (1974). "Behavioral Correlates of Single-Scale MMPI Types." *Journal of Consulting and Clinical Psychology, 42,* 398–402.

Bornstein, P., and Bornstein, M. (1986). *Marital Therapy.* Elmsford, NY: Pergamon.

Boudewyns, P., and Shipley, R. (1983). *Flooding and Implosion Therapy.* New York: Plenum.

Breggin, P. (1979). *Electroshock: Its Brain-Disabling Effects.* New York: Springer.

Brigham, T. (1988). *Working with Troubled Adolescents.* New York: Guilford.

Brinkman, S., and Braun, P. (1984). "Classification of Dementia Cases by a WAIS Profile Related to Central Cholinergic Deficiencies." *Journal of Clinical Neuropsychology, 6,* 393–400.

Brown, S. (1985). *Treating the Alcoholic.* New York: John Wiley.

Bruch, H. (1978). *The Golden Cage: The Enigma of Anorexia Nervosa.* Cambridge, MA: Harvard University Press.

Bruch, H., Czyzewski, D., and Suhr, M. (1988). *Conversations with Anorexics.* New York: Basic Books.

Budman, S., and Gurman, A. (1988). *Theory and Practice of Brief Psychotherapy.* New York: Guilford.

Buechley, R., and Ball, H. (1952). "A New Test of Test Validity for the Group MMPI." *Journal of Consulting Psychology, 16,* 299–301.

Bull, R., and Rumsey, N. (1988). *The Social Psychology of Facial Appearance.* New York: Springer-Verlag.

Burger, G., and Kabacoff, R. (1982). "Personality Types as Measured by the 16 PF." *Journal of Personality Assessment, 46,* 175–180.

Burke, H., and Mayer, S. (1985). "The MMPI and the PTSD in Vietnam Era Veterans." *Journal of Clinical Psychology, 41,* 152–156.

Butcher, J. (1987). *Computerized Psychological Assessment.* New York: Basic Books.

Butcher, J., Ed. (1979). *New Developments in the Use of the MMPI.* Minneapolis: University of Minnesota Press.

Butcher, J., and Graham, J. (1988). "Clinical Applications of the MMPI." Workshop. February 5–6, 1988, Cincinnati, OH.

Caine, T., Henley, S., Moses, P., Shamni, S., et al., (1986). "A New Projective Test: The Caine Marteau-Dympna Test (CMD)." *British Journal of Medical Psychology, 59,* 157–163.

Cantrell, J., and Dana, R. (1987). "Use of the MCMI as a Screening Instrument at a Community Mental Health Center." *Journal of Clinical Psychology, 43,* 366–375.

Cantwell, D., and Baker, L. (1987). *Developmental Speech and Language Disorders.* New York: Guilford.

Caplan, B. (1987). "Assessment of Unilateral Neglect: A New Reading Test." *Journal of Clinical and Experimental Neuropsychology, 9,* 359–364.

Cappe, R., and Alden, L. (1986). "A Comparison of Treatment Strategies for Clients Functionally Impaired by Extreme Shyness and Social Avoidance." *Journal of Clinical and Consulting Psychology, 54,* 769–801.

Carbonell, J., Megargee, E., and Moorhead, K. (1984). "Predicting Prison Adjustment with Structured Personality Inventories." *Journal of Consulting and Clinical Psychology, 52,* 280–294.

Cargonello, J., and Gurekas, R. (1988). "The WAIS-SAM: A Comprehensive Administrative Model of Modified WAIS Procedures." *Journal of Clinical Psychology, 44,* 266–270.

Carson, R. (1969). "Interpretative Manual to the MMPI." In J. Butcher, Ed. *MMPI: Research Developments and Clinical Applications.* New York: McGraw-Hill.

Cattell, R. (1965). *The Scientific Analysis of Personality.* Chicago: Aldine.

_____ (1973). *Personality and Mood by Questionnaire.* San Francisco, CA: Jossey-Bass.

_____ (1978). Personal communication.

_____ (1979). *Personality and Learning Theory*, Vol. 2: *The Structure of Personality in Its Environment*. New York: Springer.

_____ (1986). *Psychotherapy by Structural Learning*. New York: Springer.

Cattell, R., Eber, H., and Tatsuoka, M. (1970). *Handbook for the Sixteen Personality Factors Questionnaire*. Champaign, IL: IPAT.

Cattell, R., and Warburton, F. (1967). *Objective Personality and Motivation Tests*. Champaign: University of Illinois Press.

Cautela, J., and Wall, C. (1980). "Covert Conditioning in Clinical Practice." In A. Golstein and E. Foa, Eds. *Handbook of Behavioral Interventions*. New York: John Wiley.

Chambless, D. (1985). "The Relationship of Severity of Agoraphobia to Associated Psychopathology." *Behavior Research and Therapy, 23*, 305–310.

Chambless, D., Sultan, F., Stern, T., O'Neill, C., et al. (1984). "Effect of Pubococcygeal Exercise on Coital Orgasm in Women." *Journal of Consulting and Clinical Psychology, 52*, 114–118.

Cheek, D. (1965). "Emotional Factors in Persistent Pain States." *The American Journal of Clinical Hypnosis, 9*, 100–101.

Choca, J., Peterson, C., and Shanley, L. (1986). "Factor Analysis of the Millon Clinical Multiaxial Inventory." *Journal of Consulting and Clinical Psychology, 54*, 253–255.

Clare, A. (1985). "Invited Review: Hormones, Behaviour and the Menstrual Cycle." *Journal of Psychosomatic Research, 28*, 225–233.

Clark, C. (1988). "Diminished Capacity in Michigan: Factors Associated with Forensic Evaluation Referrals." Mid-Winter Meeting, American Psychology-Law Society, Miami Beach, FL.

Cleckley, H. (1964). *The Mask of Sanity*, 4th ed. St. Louis Mosby.

Clum G. (1989). *Coping with Panic*. Chicago: Dorsey.

Cofer, D., and Wittenborn, J. (1980). "Personality Characteristics of Formerly Depressed Women." *Journal of Abnormal Psychology, 89*, 309–315.

Cohen, M., Seghorn, T., and Calmas, W. (1969). "Sociometric Study of Sex Offenders." *Journal of Abnormal Psychology, 74*, 249–255.

Coleman, E. (1987). "Sexual Compulsivity: Definition, Etiology, and Treatment Considerations." *Journal of Chemical Dependency Treatment, 1*, 189–204.

Colligan, R., and Offord, K. (1988). "Contemporary Norms for the Wiggins Content Scales: A 45-Year Update." *Journal of Clinical Psychology, 44*, 23–32.

Colligan, R., Osborne, D., Swenson, W., and Offord, K. (1983). *The MMPI: A Contemporary Normative Study*. New York: Praeger.

Conley, J. (1981). "An MMPI Typology of Male Alcoholics: Admission, Discharge, and Outcome Data." *Journal of Personality Assessment, 45*, 33–39.

Cooper, S., Perry, J. C., and Arnow, D. (1988). "An Empirical Approach to the Study of Defense Mechanisms: Reliability and Validity of Rorschach Defense Scales." *Journal of Personality Assessment, 52*, 187–203.

Costello, R. (1978). "Empirical Derivation of a Partial Personality Typology of Alcoholics." *Journal of Studies of Alcoholism, 39*, 1258–1266.

Cox, D. (1980). "Exhibitionism: An Overview." In D. Cox and R. Daitzman, Eds. *Exhibitionism*. New York: Garland.

Cox, D., and Meyer, R. (1978). "Behavioral Treatment Parameters with Primary Dysmenorrhea." *Journal of Behavioral Medicine, 1,* 297–310.

Crabtree, A. (1988). *Multiple Man.* New York: Praeger.

Craig, R. (1988). "Diagnostic Interviews with Drug Abusers." *Professional Psychology: Research and Practice, 19,* 14–20.

Craig, R., Verinis, J., Wexler, S. (1985). "Personality Characteristics of Drug Addicts and Alcoholics on the Millon Clinical Multiaxial Inventory." *Journal of Personality Assessment, 49,* 156–160.

Craigie, F., and Ross, S. (1980). "The Use of a Videotape Pre-treatment Training Program to Encourage Treatment-Seeking among Alcoholic Detoxification Patients." *Behavior Therapy, 11,* 141–147.

Crisp, A., Burns, T., Bhat, A. (1986). "Primary Anorexia Nervosa in the Male and Female." *British Journal of Medical Psychology, 59,* 123–132.

Dahlstrom, W., and Dahlstrom, L., Eds. (1980). *Basic Readings on the MMPI.* Minneapolis: University of Minnesota Press.

Dahlstrom, W., Lachar, D., and Dahlstrom, L. (1986). *MMPI Patterns of American Minorities.* Minneapolis: University of Minnesota Press.

Dahlstrom, W., and Welsh, G. (1980). *An MMPI Handbook: A Guide to Clinical Practice and Research.* Minneapolis: University of Minnesota Press.

Dahlstrom, W., Welsh, G., and Dahlstrom, L. E. (1972). *An MMPI Handbook,* Vol. 1: *Clinical Interpretation.* Minneapolis: University of Minnesota Press.

———— (1975). *An MMPI Handbook,* Vol. 2: Research Applications. Minneapolis: University of Minnesota Press.

Daldin, H. (1985). "Faking Good and Faking Bad on the Personality Inventory for Children-Revised, Shortened Format." *Journal of Consulting and Clinical Psychology, 53,* 561–563.

Dam, H., Mellerup, E., and Rafaelson, O. (1985). "The Dexamethasone Suppression Test in Depression." *Journal of Affective Disorders, 8,* 95–103.

Dangel, R., and Polster, R. (1986). *Teaching Child Management Skills.* New York: Pergamon.

Davey, G., and Cullen, C. (1988). *Human Operant Conditioning and Behaviour Modification.* New York: John Wiley.

Davis, K., and Sines, J. (1971). "An Antisocial Behavior Pattern Associated with a Specific MMPI Profile." *Journal of Consulting and Clinical Psychology, 36,* 229–234.

Davison, G. (1978). "Not Can But Ought: The Treatment of Homosexuality." *Journal of Consulting and Clinical Psychology, 45,* 170–172.

Dawood, M. (1985). "Premenstrual Tension Syndrome." *Obstetrics and Gynecology Annual, 14,* 328–343.

Dejong, R., Rubinow, D., Roy-Byrne, P., Hoban, M., Grover, G., and Post, R. (1985). "Premenstrual Mood Disorder and Psychiatric Illness." *American Journal of Psychiatry, 142,* 1359–1361.

De Silva, P. (1987). "Obsessions and Compulsions." In S. Lindsay and G. Powell, Eds. *Handbook of Clinical Adult Psychology.* Aldershot, England: Gower.

Diaz-Buxo, J., Caudle, J., Chandler, J., Farmer, C., and Holbrook, W. (1980). "Dialysis of Schizophrenic Patients: A Double-Blind Study." *American Journal of Psychiatry, 137,* 1220–1222.

Donnelly, E., Murphy, D., Waldaman, I., and Reynolds, T. (1976). "MMPI Differences Between Unipolar and Bipolar Depressed Subjects: A Replication." *Journal of Clinical Psychology, 32,* 610–612.

Donovan, J. (1986). "An Etiologic Model of Alcoholism." *Archives of General Psychiatry, 143,* 1–11.

Duckworth, J. (1979). *MMPI Interpretation Manual for Counselors and Clinicians.* Muncie, IN: Accelerated Development.

Earls, C., and Prouix, J. (1986). "The Differentiation of Francophone Rapists and Non-rapists Using Penile Circumferential Measures." *Criminal Justice and Behavior, 13,* 419–429.

Easson, W. (1980). "Myxedema Psychosis: Insanity Defense in Homicide." *The Journal of Clinical Psyciatry, 41,* 316–318.

Eber, H. (1975). Personal communication.

_____ (1987). Personal communication.

Eckenrode, J., Powers, J., Doris, J., Munsch, J., and Bolger, M. (1988). "Substantiation of Child Abuse and Neglect Reports." *Journal of Consulting and Clinical Psychology, 56,* 9–16.

Edell, W. (1987). "Relationship of Borderline Syndrome Disorders to Early Schizophrenia on the MMPI." *Journal of Clinical Psychology, 43,* 163–174.

Edinger, J. (1979). "Cross-Validation of the Megargee MMPI Typology for Prisoners." *Journal of Consulting and Clinical Psychology, 47,* 234–242.

Edmonston, W. (1986). *The Induction of Hypnosis.* New York: John Wiley.

Ekman, P. (1985). *Telling Lies.* New York: W. W. Norton.

Ellis, A., and Dryden, W. (1987). *The Practice of Rational-Emotive Therapy.* New York: Springer.

Ellsworth, R., Collins, J., Casey, N., Schoonover, R., Hickey, R., Hyer, L., Twenlown, S., and Nesselroade, J. (1979). "Some Characterisitcs of Effective Psychiatric Treatment Programs." *Journal of Consulting and Clinical Psychology, 47,* 799–817.

Emmelkamp, P. (1988). "Phobic Disorders." In C. Last and M. Hersen, Eds. *Handbook of Anxiety Disorders.* Elmsford, NY: Pergamon.

Erickson, W., Luxemberg, M., Walbek, N., and Seely, N. (1987). "Frequency of MMPI Two-Point Code Types Among Sex Offenders." *Journal of Consulting and Clinical Psychology, 55,* 566–570.

Erlich, P., and McGeehan, M. (1985). "Cocaine Recovery, Support Groups and the Language of Recovery." *Journal of Psychoactive Drugs, 17,* 11–17.

Exner, J. (1974). *The Rorschach: A Comprehensive System,* Vol. 2. New York: John Wiley.

_____ (1978). *The Rorschach: A Comprehensive System,* Vol. 2: *Current research and advanced interpretation.* New York: John Wiley.

_____ (1986). *The Rorschach: A Comprehensive System,* Vol. 1, 2nd ed. New York: John Wiley.

Eysenck, H. (1985). "Incubation Theory of Fear/Anxiety." In S. Riess and R. Bootzin, Eds. *Theoretical Issues in Behavior Therapy.* Orlando, FL: Academic press.

Fabian, M., and Parsons, O. (1983). "Differential Improvement of Cognitive Fuctions in Recovering Alcoholic Women." *Journal of Abnormal Psychology, 92,* 87–95.

Fabry, J. (1980). "Depression." In R. Woody, Ed. *Encyclopedia of Clinical Assessment.* San Francisco: Jossey-Bass.

Fairbank, J., McCaffney, R., and Keane, T. (1985). "Psychometric Detection of the Fabricated Symptoms of PTSD." *American Journal of Psychiatry, 142,* 501–503.

Fairbank, J., and Nicolson, R. (1987). "Theoretical and Empirical Issues in the Treatment of PTSD in Vietnam Veterans." *Journal of Clinical Psychology, 43,* 44–53.

Faulstitch, M., Delatte, J., Carey, M., and Delatte, G. (1985). "Age Differences on Alcoholic MMPI Scales." *Journal of Clinical Psychology, 41,* 433–439.

Faucett, J., Scheftner, W., Clark, D., Hedeker, D., et al. (1987). "Clinical Predictors of Suicide Patients with Major Affective Disorders." *American Journal of Psychiatry, 144,* 35–40.

Fekken, C. G., and Holden, R. (1987). "Assessing the Person Reliability of an Individual MMPI Protocol." *Journal of Personality Assessment, 51,* 123–132.

Fersch, E. (1980). *Psychology and Psychiatry and Courts and Corrections.* New York: John Wiley.

Figley, C. A. (1988). "A Five-Phase Treatment of Post-Traumatic Stress Disorder." *Journal of Traumatic Stress, 1,* 127–141.

Finkel, N. (1988). *Insanity on Trial.* New York: Plenum.

Finkelhor, D. (1985). *Child Sexual Abuse.* New York: Free Press.

Fjordback, T. (1985). "Clinical Correlates of High Lie Scale Elevations Among Forensic Patients." *Journal of Personality Assessment, 49,* 252–255.

Fleming, M., Cohen, D., Salt, P., Jones, D., and Jenkins, S. (1981). "A Study of Pre- and Postsurgical Transsexuals: MMPI Characteristics." *Archives of Sexual Behavior, 10,* 161–170.

Foa, E., and Kozak, M. (1986). "Emotional Processing of Fear: Exposure to Corrective Information." *Psychological Bulletin, 99,* 20–35.

Foa, E., and Tillmanns, A. (1980). "The Treatment of Obsessive-Compulsive Neurosis." In A. Goldstein and E. Foa, Eds. *Handbook of Behavioral Interventions.* New York: John Wiley.

Follingstad, D., Rutledge, L., McNeill-Harkins, K., and Polek, D. (in press). "Factors Related to Physical Violence in Dating Relationships." *Victimology.*

Fordyce, W. (1979). "Use of MMPI in the Assessment of Chronic Pain." In J. Butcher, G. Dahlstrom, M. Gynther, and W. Schofield, Eds. *Clinical Notes on the MMPI.* Nutley, NJ: Roche Psychiatric Service.

Forgione, A. (1976). "Instrumentation and Techniques. The Use of Mannequins in the Behavioral Assessment of Child Molesters: Two Case Reports." *Behavior Therapy, 7,* 678–685.

Fowler, R. (1976). *The Clinical Use of the Automated MMPI.* Nutley, NJ: Roche Psychiatric Service.

———— (1981). *Advanced Interpretation of the MMPI.* Guadaloupe, French W.I.: SEPA Workshops.

Freud, K., Scher, H., and Hucker, S. (1983). "The Courtship Disorders," *Archives of Sexual Behavior, 12,* 369–379.

Friedman, R. (1988). *Male Homosexuality.* New Haven, CT: Yale University Press.

Fuld, P. (1984). "Test Profile of Cholinergic Dysfunction and of Alzheimer-type Dementia." *Journal of Clinical Neuropsychology, 6,* 388–392.

Fulkerson, S., and Willage, D. (1980). "Decisional Ambiguity as a Source of "Cannot Say" Responses on Personality Questionnaires." *Journal of Personality Assessment, 44,* 381–386.

Gackenbach, J., Ed. (1985). *Sleep and Dreams: A Sourcebook.* New York: Garland.

Gallucci, N. (1987). "The Influence of Elevated F Scales on the Validity of Adolescent MMPI Profiles." *Journal of Personality Assessment, 51,* 133–139.

Gardener, E. (1965). "The Role of the Classification System in Outpatient Psychiatry." In M. Katz, J. Cole, and W. Barton, Eds. *The Role of Methodology in Psychiatry and Psychopathology.* Washington, DC: U.S. Public Health Service.

Gardner, D., Lucas, P., and Cowdry, R. (1987). "Soft Sign Neurological Abnormalities in Borderline Personality and Normal Control Subjects." *The Journal of Nervous and Mental Disease, 175* (3), 177–180.

Garmezy, N. (1978). "Never Mind the Psychologists: Is It Good for the Children?" *The Clinical Psychologist, 31* (1), 4–6.

Gass, C., and Russell, E. (1986). "MMPI Correlates of Lateralized Cerebral Lesions and Aphasic Deficits." *Journal of Consulting and Clinical Psychology, 54,* 359–363.

Gearing, M. (1979). "The MMPI as a Primary Differentiator and Predictor of Behavior in Prison: A Methodological Critique and Review of the Recent Literature." *Psychological Bulletin, 86,* 926–963.

Gedo, J. (1986). *Conceptual Issues in Psychoanalysis.* Hillsdale, NJ: Analytic Press.

Gelles, R. (1986). "Family Violence." In R. Turner (Ed.) *Annual Review of Sociology,* Vol. 11. Palo Alto, CA: Annual Reviews.

Gilberstadt, H., and Duker, J. (1965). *A Handbook for Clinical and Actuarial MMPI Interpretation.* Philadelphia: Saunders.

Gilbert, J. (1978). *Interpreting Psychological Test Data.* New York: Van Nostrand Reinhold.

———— (1980). *Interpreting Psychological Test Data–II.* New York: Van Nostrand Reinhold.

Gillberg, I., and Gillberg, C. (1988). "Generalized Hyperkinesis: Follow-up Study from 7 to 13 Years." *Journal of the American Academy of Child and Adolescent Psychiatry, 27,* 55–59.

Gittelman, R. (1986). *Anxiety Disorders of Childhood.* New York: Guilford.

Glasser, W. (1980). "Two Cases in Reality Therapy." In G. Belkin, Ed. *Contemporary Psychotherapies.* Chicago: Rand McNally.

Golden, C. (1979). *Clinical Interpretation of Objective Psychological Tests.* New York: Grune and Stratton.

Golden, R., and Meehl, P. (1979). "Detection of the Schizoid Taxon with MMPI Indicators." *Journal of Abnormal Psychology, 88,* 217–233.

Goldfried, M., Stricker, G., and Weiner, I. (1971). *Rorschach Handbook of Clinical and Research Applications.* Englewood Cliffs, NJ: Prentice-Hall.

Golding, S., Roesch, R., and Schreiber, J. (1984). "Assessment and Conceptualization of Competency to Stand Trial: Preliminary Data on the Interdisciplinary Fitness Interview." *Law and Human Behavior, 8,* 321–334.

Goldstein, A., and Keller, H. (1987). *Aggressive Behavior.* New York: Pergamon.

Goldstein, A., Keller, H., and Erne, D. (1986). *Changing the Abusive Parent.* Champaign, IL: Research Press.

Goldstein, A., and Stein, N. (1976). *Prescriptive Psychotherapies.* New York: Pergamon.

Grace, W., and Sweeney, M. (1986). "Comparisons of the P>V Sign on the WICS-R an WAIS-R in Delinquent Males." *Journal of Clinical Psychology, 42,* 173–176.

Graham, J. (1977). *The MMPI: A Practical Guide.* New York: Oxford University Press.

_____ (1987). *The MMPI: A Practical Guide,* 2nd ed. New York: Oxford University Press.

Graham, J., and Strenger, V. (1988). "MMPI Characteristics of Alcoholics: A Review." *Journal of Consulting and Clinical Psychology, 56,* 197–205.

Greene, R. (1980). *The MMPI: An Interpretive Manual.* New York: Grune and Stratton.

Grisso, T. (1986). *Evaluating Competencies: Forensic Assesments and Instruments.* New York: Plenum.

Grob, C. (1985). "Single Case Study: Female Exhibitionism." *The Journal of Nervous and Mental Disease, 173,* 253–256.

Gross, W., and Carpenter, L. (1971). "Alcoholic Personality: Reality or Fiction?" *Psychological Reports, 28,* 375–378.

Guertin, W., Ladd, C., Frank, G., Rabin, A., and Hiester, D. (1966). "Research With the WAIS: 1960–1965." *Psychological Bulletin, 66,* 385–409.

_____ (1971). "Research with the WAIS: 1965–1970." *Psychological Record, 21,* 289–339.

Guertin, W., Rabin, A., Frank, G., and Ladd, C. (1962). "Research with the WAIS: 1955–1960." *Psychological Bulletin, 59,* 1–26.

Gynther, M., Altman, H., and Slettin, I. (1973a). "Replicated Correlates of MMPI Two-Point Types: The Missouri Actuarial System." *Journal of Clinical Psychology.* Monograph Supplement 39.

Gynther, M., Altman, H., and Warbin, W. (1973b). "Interpretation of Uninterpretable Minnesota Multiphasic Personality Inventory Profiles." *Journal of Consulting and Clinical Psychology, 40,* 78–83.

Gynther, M., and Green, S. (1980). "Accuracy May Make a Difference, but Does a Difference Make for Accuracy?: A Response to Pritchard and Rosenblatt." *Journal of Consulting and Clinical Psychology, 48,* 268–272.

Hall, G., Maiuro, R., Vitaliano, P., and Proctor, W. (1986). "The Utility of the MMPI with Men Who Have Sexually Assaulted Children." *Journal of Consulting and Clinical Psychology, 54,* 493–496.

Hare, R. (1986). "Twenty Years of Experience with the Cleckley Psychopath." In W. Reid, D. Dorr, J. Walker, and J. Bonner, Eds. *Unmasking the Psychopath.* New York: Norton.

Hathaway, S. (1947). "A Coding System for MMPI Profiles." *Journal of Consulting Psychology, 11,* 334–337.

Hathaway, S., and McKinley, J (1967). *The Minnesota Multiphasic Personality Inventory Manual.* New York: Psychological Corporation.

Hawk, G. (1983). "An Investigation of the Megaree MMPI Typology in a Forensic Setting." *Dissertation Abstracts International, 43* (11-B), 3732.

Haynes, S. (1986). "A Behavioral Model of Paranoid Behaviors," *Behavior
Therapy, 17,* 286–287.

Heath, D. (1986). "Drinking and Drunkenness in Transcultural Perspective."
Transcultural Psychiatric Research, 23, 7–42.

Hedlund, J. (1977). "MMPI Clinical Scale Correlates." *Journal of Consulting
and Clinical Psychology, 45,* 739–750.

Heilbrun, A., Blum, N., and Goldreyer, N. (1985). "Defensive Projection: An Investigation of Its Role in Paranoid Conditions." *Journal of Nervous and Mental
Disease, 173,* 17–25.

Heinrich, T., and Amolsch, T. (1978). "A Note on the Situational Interpretation
of WAIS Profile Patterns. *Journal of Personality Assessment, 42,* 418–420.

Heller, J. (1974). *Something Happened.* New York: Knopf.

Hendlin, H., and Haas, A. (1988). "Post-Traumatic Stress Disorder." In C. Last
and M. Hersen, Eds. *Handbook of Anxiety Disorders.* Elmsford, NY: Pergamon.

Hendrix, E., Thompson, L., and Rau, B. (1978). "Behavioral Treatment of an
'Hysterically' Clenched Fist." *Journal of Behavior Therapy and Experimental
Psychiatry, 9,* 273–276.

Hendrix, M., and Meyer, R. (1974). "Applications of Feedback Electromyography."
Journal of Biofeedback, 2, 13–21.

_____ (1976). "Toward More Comprehensive and Durable Client Changes: A
Case Report." *Psychotherapy: Theory, Research, and Practice, 13,* 263–266.

Henker, B., Astor-Dubin, L., and Varni, J. (1986). "Psychostimulant Medication and Perceived Intensity in Hyperactive Children." *Journal of Abnormal
Child Psychology, 14,* 105–114.

Herbert, M. (1987). *Conduct Disorders of Childhood and Adolescence.* New York:
John Wiley.

Hersen, M., and Breuning, S. (1986). *Pharmacological and Behavioral Treatment.* New York: John Wiley.

Hewett, B., and Martin, W. (1980). "Psychometric Comparisons of Sociopathic
and Psychopathological Behaviors of Alcoholics and Drug Abusers Versus a Low
Drug Use Control Population." *The International Journal of the Addictions, 15,*
77–105.

Higginbotham, N., West, S., and Donelson, R. F. (1988). *Psychotherapy and
Behavior Change.* Elmsford, NY: Pergamon.

Hoehn-Saric, R., and McLeod, D. (1988). "Panic and Generalized Anxiety
Disorders. In C. Last and M. Hersen, Eds. *Handbook of Anxiety Disorders.*
Elmsford, NY: Pergamon.

Hoffman, R., Stopek, S., and Andreason, N. (1986). "A Comparative Study of
Manic Versus Schizophrenic Speech Disorganization." *Archives of General
Psychiatry, 43,* 831–848.

Hogan, R. (1980). "Implosive Therapy in the Short-Term Treatment of
Psychotics." In G. Belkin, Ed. *Contemporary Psychotherapies.* Chicago: Rand
McNally.

Holcomb, W. (1986). "Stress Innoculation Therapy with Anxiety and Stress
Disorders of Acute Psychiatric Patients" *Journal of Clinical Psychology, 42,*
864–871.

Holland, T., Levi, M., and Watson, C. (1981). "MMPI Basic Scales Vs. Two-Point Codes in the Discrimination of Psychopathological Groups." *Journal of Clinical Psychology, 37,* 394–396.

Holland, T., and Watson, C. (1980). "Multivariate Analysis of WAIS-MMPI Relationships among Brain-Damaged, Schizophrenic, Neurotic, and Alcoholic Patients." *Journal of Clinical Psychology, 36,* 352–359.

Hovanitz, C., and Jordan-Brown, C. (1986). "The Validity of MMPI Subtle and Obvious Items in Psychiatric Patients." *Journal of Clinical Psychology, 42,* 100–108.

Hsu, L. (1986). "Implications of Differences in Elevations of K-Corrected and Non-K-Corrected MMPI T Scores." *Journal of Consulting and Clinical Psychology, 54,* 552–557.

Hsu, L., and Betman, J. (1986). "Minnesota Multiphasic Personality Inventory T Score Conversion Tables, 1957–1983." *Journal of Consulting and Clinical Psychology, 54,* 497–501.

IPAT Staff (1963). *Information Bulletin No. 8 to the 16 PF Handbook.* Champaign, IL: Institute for Personality and Ability Testing.

_____ (1972). *Manual for the 16 PF.* Champaign, IL: Institute for Personality and Ability Testing.

Jacobson, N., and Gurman, A., Eds. (1986). *Clinical Handbook of Marital Therapy.* New York: Guilford.

Jacobsen, R., and Tomkin, A. (1988). "Converting Shipley Institute of Living Scale Scores to IQ." *Journal of Clinical Psychology, 44,* 72–75.

Janov, A. (1980). "The Case of Gary." In G. Belkin, Ed. *Contemporary Psychotherapies.* Chicago: Rand McNally.

Jarvik, M. (1967). "The Psychopharmacological Revolution." *Psychology Today, 1,* 51–59.

Johnson, D., and Quinlan, D. (1980). "Fluid and Rigid Boundaries of Paranoid and Non-paranoid Schizophrenics on a Role-Playing Task." *Journal of Personality Assessment, 44,* 523–531.

Johnson, F., and Johnson, S. (1986). "Differences Between Human Figure Drawings of Child Molesters and Control Groups." *Journal of Clinical Psychology, 42,* 638–647.

Johnson, J., Klinger, D., and Gianetti, R. (1980). "Band Width in Diagnostic Classification Using the MMPI as a Predictor." *Journal of Consulting and Clinical Psychology, 48,* 340–349.

Johnson, M. (1966). "Verbal Abstracting Ability and Schizophrenia." *Journal of Consulting Psychology, 30,* 275–277.

Kalichman, S. (1988). "Empirically Derived MMPI Profile Subgroups of Incarcerated Homicide Offenders." *Journal of Clinical Psychology.* In Press.

Karon, B. (1976). "The Psychoanalysis of Schizophrenia." In P. Magero, Ed. *The Construction of Madness.* New York: Pergamon.

_____ (1981). "The Thematic Apperception Test." In A. Rabin, Ed. *Assessment with Projective Techniques.* New York: Springer.

Karson, S. (1959). "The Sixteen Personality Factor Test in Clinical Practice." *Journal of Clinical Psychology, 15,* 174–176.

_____ (1960). "Validating Clinical Judgments with the 16 PF Test." *Journal of Clinical Psychology, 16,* 394–397.

Karson, S., and O'Dell, J. (1976). *Clinical Use of the 16 PF.* Champaign, IL: IPAT.

Kaufman, A., McLean, J., and Reynolds, C. (1988). "Sex, Race, Residence, Region, and Education Differences on the 11 WAIS-R Subtests." *Journal of Clinical Psychology, 44,* 231–248.

Kay, S., and Lindenmayer, J. (1987). "Outcome Predictors in Acute Schizohrenia." *Journal of Nervous and Mental Disease, 175,* 152–160.

Keefe, F., and Gil, K. (1987). "Chronic Pain." In V. Hasselt, P. Strain, and M. Hersen, Eds. *Handbook of Developmental and Physical Disabilities.* Elmsford, NY: Pergamon.

Keiser, T., and Lowy, D. (1980). "Heroin Addiction and Wechsler Digit Span Test. *Journal of Clinical Psychology, 36* 347–351.

Keles, A. (1983). "Biopsychobehavioral Correlates and the MMPI." *Psychosomatic Medicine, 45,* 341–347.

Kellam, A. (1969). "Shoplifting Treated by Aversion to a Film." *Behavior Research and Therapy, 7,* 125–127.

Kelley C., and King, G. (1979a). "Cross Validation of the 2-8/8-2 MMPI Code Type for Young Adult Psychiatric Outpatients." *Journal of Personality Assessment, 43,* 143–149.

_____ (1979b). "Behavioral Correlates of the 2-7-8 MMPI Profile Type in Students at a University Mental Health Center." *Journal of Consulting and Clinical Psychology, 47,* 679–685.

_____ (1979c). "Behavioral Correlates of Infrequent 2-point MMPI Code Types at a University Mental Health Center." *Journal of Clinical Psychology, 35,* 576–585.

Kellner, R. (1986). "Somatization and Hypochondriasis." London: Praeger.

Kelly, G. (1955). *The Psychology of Personal Constructs.* 2 vols. New York: W. W. Norton.

Kelly, W., Ed. (1985). "Post-traumatic Stress Disorder and the War Veteran Patient. New York: Brunner/Mazel.

Kembler, K. (1980). "The Nosologic Validity of Paranoia (Simple Delusional Disorder)." *Archives of General Psychiatry, 37,* 695–706.

Kennedy, W. (1986). "The Psychologist as Expert Witness." In W. Curran, A. L. McGarry, and S. Shah, Eds. *Forensic Psychiatry and Psychology.* Philadelphia; F. A. Davis.

Kernberg, O. (1984). "Severe Personality Disorders. New Haven: Yale University Press.

King, G., and Kelley, C. (1977). "Behavioral Correlates for Spike-4, Spike-9, and 4-9/9-4 MMPI Profiles in Students at a University Mental Health Center." *Journal of Clinical Psychology, 33,* 718–724.

Kinsey, A., Pomeroy, W., and Martin, C. (1948). *Sexual Behavior in the Human Male.* Philadelphia: Saunders.

_____ (1953). *Sexual Behavior in the Human Female.* Philadelphia: Saunders.

Kirby, E., and Grimley, L. (1986). *Understanding and Treating Attenton Deficit Disorder.* New York: Pergamon.

Kirkley, B., and Janick, L. (1987). "Binge Eating in Obesity: Associated MMPI Characteristics." *Journal of Consulting and Clinical Psychology, 55,* 872–876.

Kirman, W. (1980). "The Modern Psychoanalytic Treatment of Depression." In G. Belkin, Ed. *Contemporary Psychotherapies.* Chicago: Rand McNally.

Kish, G., Hagen, J., Woody, M., and Harvey, H. (1980). "Alcoholic's Recovery from Cerebral Impairment as a Function of Duration of Abstinence." *Journal of Clinical Psychology, 36,* 584–589.

Kleinknecht, R. (1986). *The Anxious Self.* New York: Human Sciences Press.

Klingler, D., and Saunders, D. (1975). "A Factor-Analysis of the Items for Nine Subtests of the WAIS." *Multivariate Behavioral Research, 10,* 131–154.

Klopfer, W., and Davidson, H. (1962). *Rorschach's Technique: An Introductory Manual.* New York: Harcourt Brace.

Klopfer, W., and Taulbee, E. (1976). "Projective Tests." *Annual Review of Psychology, 27,* 543–576.

Kluft, R. (1987). "An Update on Multiple Personality Disorder." *Hospital and Community Psychiatry, 38,* 363–373.

Kolevzon, M., and Green, R. (1985). *Family Therapy Models.* New York: Springer.

Kopelmon, H. (1987). "Amnesia: Organic and Psychogenic." *British Journal of Psychiatry, 150,* 428–442.

Koss, M., and Butcher, J. (1973). "A Comparison of Psychiatric Patients' Self-Report with Other Sources of Clinical Information." *Journal of Research in Personality, 7,* 225–236.

Kozak, M., Foa, E., and McCarthy, P. (1988). "Obsessive-Compulsive Disorder." In C. Last and M. Hersen, Eds. *Handbook of Anxiety Disorders.* Elmsford, NY: Pergamon.

Kreitman, N. (1986). "The Clinical Assessment and Management of the Suicidal Patient." In A. Roy, Ed. *Suicide.* Baltimore: Williams and Wilkins.

Krishnan, R., Davidson, J., and Miller, R. (1985). "Trichotillomania: A Review." *Comprehensive Psychiatry, 26,* 123–128.

Krug, S. (1978). "Further Evidence on the 16 PF Distortion Scales." *Journal of Personality Assessment, 42,* 513–518.

————— (1980). *Clinical Analysis Questionnaire Manual.* Champaign: IL: IPAT.

————— (1981). *Interpreting 16 PF Profile Patterns.* Champaign, IL: IPAT.

Krug, S., and Johns, E. (1986). "A Large-Scale Cross-Validation of Second-Order Personality Structure Defined by the 16 PF." *Psychological Reports, 59,* 683–693.

Kunce, J., Ryan, J., and Eckelman, C. (1976). "Violent Behavior and Differential WAIS Characteristics." *Journal of Consulting and Clinical Psychology, 44,* 42–45.

Kurlychek, R., and Jordan, L. (1980). "MMPI Code Types of Responsibile and Nonresponsible Criminal Defendants." *Journal of Clinical Psychology, 36,* 590–593.

Laboratory of Community Psychology (1973). *Competency to Stand Trial and Mental Illness:* Rockville, MD: National Institutes of Mental Health.

Lachar, D. (1974). *The MMPI: Clinical Assessment and Automated Interpretation.* Los Angeles: Western Psychological Services.

Lachar, D., and Wrobel, T. (1979). "Validating Clinicians' Hunches: Construction of a New MMPI Critical Item Set." *Journal of Consulting and Clinical Psychology, 47,* 277–284.

Lambert, M., Hatch, D., Kingston, M., and Edwards, B. (1986). "Zung, Beck, and Hamilton Rating Scales as Measures of Treatment Outcome." *Journal of Consulting and Clinical Psychology, 54,* 54–59.

Lambert, N., Hartsough, C., Sassone, D., and Sandoval, J. (1987). "Persistence of Hyperactivity Symptoms from Childhood to Adolescence and Associated Outcomes." *American Journal of Orthopsychiatry, 57,* 22–32.

Landis, E. R., and Meyer, R. (1989). *Detecting Deception.* Chicago: Dorsey.

Landman, J., and Dawes, R. (1982). "Psychotherapy Outcome: Smith and Glass's Conclusions Stand Up under Scrutiny." *American Psychologist, 37,* 504–516.

Lane, J., and Lachar, D. (1979). "Correlates of Broad MMPI Categories. *Journal of Clinical Psychology, 35,* 560–566.

Lanyon, R. (1984). "Personality Assessment." *Annual Review of Psychology, 35,* 667–701.

Lasch, C. (1978). *The Culture of Narcissism.* New York: W. W. Norton.

La Torre, R. (1980). "Devaluation of the Human Love Object: Heterosexual Rejection as a Possible Antecedent to Fetishism." *Journal of Abnormal Psychology, 89,* 295–298.

Lazar, B., and Harrow, M. (1985). "Paranoid and Nonparanoid Schizophrenia." *Journal of Clinical Psychology, 141,* 145–151.

Lazarus, A. (1971). *Behavior Therapy and Beyond.* New York: McGraw-Hill.

Lazarus, A. (1987). Discussion. In J. Zeig, Ed. *The Evolutin of Psychotherapy.* New York: Brunner/Mazel.

Lerner, P., Ed. (1975). *Handbook of Rorschach Scales.* New York: International Universities Press.

Levine, S., and Stava, L. (1987). "Personality Characteristics of Sex Offenders." *Archives of Sexual Behavior, 16,* 57–79.

Levitt, E. (1980). *Primer on the Rorschach Technique.* Springfield, IL: Charles C. Thomas.

Lewy, A., Nurnberger, J., Wehr, T., Pack, D., et al. (1985). "Supersensitivity to Light: Possible Trait Marker for Manic-Depressive Illness." *American Journal of Psychiatry, 142,* 725–727.

Lieberman, R., Mueser, K., and Wallace, C. (1986). "Social Skills Training for Schizophrenic Individuals at Risk for Relapse." *American Journal of Psychiatry, 143,* 523–527.

Liebowitz, M., Gorman, J., Fryer, A., Levitt, M., et al. (1985). "Lactate Provocation of Panic Attacks." *Archives of General Psychiatry, 42,* 709–714.

Lo Piccolo, J. (1985). "Advances in the Diagnosis and Treatment of Sexual Dysfunction." Convention Workshop. Louisville: Kentucky Psychological Association.

Lo Piccolo, J., and Stock, W. (1986). "Treatment of Sexual Dysfunction," *Journal of Consulting and Clinical Psychology, 54,* 158–167.

Lorr, M., Nerviano, V., and Myhill, J. (1985). "Structural Analysis of the MMPI and the 16 PF." *Psychological Reports, 57,* 587–590.

Lorr, M., and Suziedelis, A. (1985). "Profile Patterns in the 16 PF questionnaire." *Journal of Clinical Psychology, 41,* 767–773.

Love, A., and Peck, C. (1987). "The MMPI and Psychological Factors in Chronic Low Back Pain: A Review." *Pain, 28,* 1–12.

Lovibond, S., and Caddy, G. (1970). "Discriminated Aversive Control in the Modification of Alcoholics' Drinking Behavior." *Behavior Therapy, 1,* 437–444.

Low, P., Jeffries, J., and Bonnie, R. (1986). *The Trial of John Hinckley, Jr.* Mineola, NY: Foundation Press.

Luria, Z., Friedman, S., and Rose, M. (1986). *Human Sexuality.* New York: John Wiley.

Lykken, D. (1957). "A Study of Anxiety in the Sociopathic Personality." *Journal of Abnormal and Social Psychology, 55,* 6–10.

Lyons, J., Rosen, A., and Dysken, M. (1985). "Behavioral Effects of Tricyclic Drugs in Depressed Inpatients." *Journal of Consulting and Clinical Psychology, 55,* 17–24.

MacAndrew, C. (1965). "The Differentiation of Male Alcoholic Outpatients from Nonalcoholic Psychiatric Patients by Means of the MMPI." *Quarterly Journal of Studies on Alcohol, 26,* 238–46.

Macciocchi, S., and Meyer, R. (1981). "Expectancy Mediated Behavior Change in a Detection Situation." Unpublished manuscript.

Magnusson, D. (1988). *Individual Development from an Interactional Standpoint.* Hillsdale, NJ: Lawrence Erlbaum.

Malamuth, N. (1986). "Predictors of Naturalistic Sexual Aggression." *Journal of Personality and Social Psychology, 50,* 953–962.

Mander, A. (1986). "Is Lithium Justified after One Manic Episode?" *Acta Psychiatrica Scandinavica, 73,* 60–67.

Marks, P., Seeman, W., and Haler, D. (1974). *The Actuarial Use of the MMPI with Adolescents and Adults.* Baltimore: Williams and Wilkins.

Marlatt, A., Baer, J., Donovan, D., and Kiviahan, D. (1988). "Addictive Behaviors: Etiology and Treatment." In M. Rosenzweig and L. Porter Eds. *Annual Review of Psychology,* Vol. 39. Palo Alto, CA: Annual Reviews.

Marlowe, D., and Crowne, D. (1964). *The Approval Motive.* New York: John Wiley.

Mash, E., and Terdal, L. (1988). *Behavioral Assessment of Childhood Disorders.* 2nd Ed. New York: Guilford.

Mason, B., Cohen, J., and Exner, J. (1985). "Schizophrenic, Depressive, and Nonpatient Personality Organization Described Rorschach Factor Structure." *Journal of Personality Assessment, 49,* 295–303.

Masters, W., and Johnson, V. (1970). *Human Sexual Inadequacy.* Boston: Little, Brown.

Masters, W., Johnson, V., and Kolodny, R. (1988). *Human Sexuality,* 3rd ed. Glenville, IL: Scott, Foresman, Little Brown.

Matarazzo, J. (1972). *Wechsler's Measurement and Appraisal of Adult Intelligence.* Baltimore: Williams and Wilkins.

Matson, J. (1987). "Mental Retardation–Adults." In V. Van Hasselt, P. Strain, and M. Hersen Eds. *Handbook of Developmental and Physical Disabilities.* Elmsford, NY: Pergamon.

Mattick, R., and Peters, L., (1988). "Treatment of Severe Social Phobia." *Journal of Consulting and Clinical Psychology, 56,* 251–260.

May, W., Barlow, D., and Hay, L. (1981). "Treatment of Stereotypic Cross-Gender Motor Behavior Using Convert Modeling in a Boy with Gender Identity Confusion." *Journal of Consulting and Clinical Psychology, 49*, 388–394.

McCann, J., and Suess, J. (1988). "Clinical Applications of the MCMI: The 1-2-3-8 Codetype." *Journal of Clinical Psychology, 44*, 181–186.

McInerney, J., Di Giuseppe, R., and Ellis, A. (1986). *Rational Emotive Approaches to the Treatment of Alcohol and Substance Abuse.* New York: Pergamon.

McKim, W. (1986). *Drugs and Behavior.* Englewood Cliffs, NJ: Prentice-Hall.

McNiel, K., and Meyer, R. (1988). "Detection of Deception and Diagnostic Accuracy of the Millon Clinical Multiaxial Inventory (MCMI)." Unpublished paper.

Meehl, P., and Hathaway, S. (1980). "The K Factor as a Suppressor Variable in the MMPI." In W. Dahlstrom and L. Dahlstrom, Eds. *Basic Readings on the MMPI.* Minneapolis: University of Minnesota Press.

Megargee, E., Ed. (1966). "Research in Clinical Assessment. New York: Harper and Row.

Megargee, E., and Bohn, M. (1979). *Classifying Criminal Offenders.* Beverly Hills, CA: Sage.

Megargee, E., and Cook, P. (1975). "Negative Response Bias and the MMPI O-H Scale: A Response to Deiker." *Journal of Consulting and Clinical Psychology, 43*, 725, 729.

Megargee, E., Cook, P., and Mendelsohn, G. (1967). "Development and Validation of an MMPI Scale of Assaultiveness in Overcontrolled Individuals." *Journal of Abnormal Psychology, 72*, 519–528.

Meichenbaum, D. (1985). "Cognitive Behavior Modification." In F. Kanfer and A. Goldstein, Eds. *Helping People Change.* New York: Plenum.

Meier,M., Benton, A., and Diller, L., Eds. (1987). *Neuropsychological Rehabilitation.* New York: Guilford.

Meissner, W. (1981). "A Note on Narcissism." *Psychoanalytic Quarterly, 50*, 77–87.

Meister, R. (1980). *Hypochondria.* New York: Taplinger.

Melton, G., Petrila, J., Poythress, N., and Slobogin, C. (1987). *Psychological Evaluations for the Courts.* New York: Guilford.

Mester, R. (1986). "The Psychotherapy of Mania." *The British Journal of Medical Psychology, 59*, 13–20.

Meyer, R. (1980). "The Antisocial Personality." In R. Woody, Ed. *Encyclopedia of Mental Assessment.* San Francisco: Jossey-Bass.

Meyer, R., and Freeman, W. (1977). "A Social Episode Model of Human Sexual Behavior." *Journal of Homosexuality, 2*, 123–131.

Meyer, R., Landis, E. R., and Hays, J. R. (1988). *Law for the Psychotherapist.* New York: W. W. Norton.

Meyer, R., and Osborne, Y. H. (1987). *Case Studies in Abnormal Behavior.* Boston: Allyn and Bacon.

Meyer, R., and Salmon, P. (1988). *Abnormal Psychology.* Boston: Allyn and Bacon.

Millon, T. (1981). *Disorders of Personality, DSM-III: Axis II.* New York: John Wiley.

Millon, T. (1985). "The MCMI Provides a Good Assessment of DSM-III Disorders: The MMCI-II Will Prove Even Better." *Journal of Personality Assessment, 49,* 379–391.

Millon, T. (1986). "The MCMI and DSM-III: Further Commentaries." *Journal of Personality Assessment, 50,* 205–207.

Mirsky, A., and Duncan, C. (1986). "Etiology and Expression of Schizophrenia: Neurobiological and Psychosocial Factors." In M. Rosenweig and L. Porter, Eds. *Annual Review of Psychology,* Vol. 37. Palo Alto, CA: Annual Reviews.

Mlatt, S., and Vale, W. (1986). "Performance of Agoraphobic Families Versus Nonagoraphobic Families on the 16 PF Questionnaire." *Journal of Clinical Psychology, 41,* 244–250.

Moldin, S., Gottesman, I., and Erlenmeyer-Kimling, L. (1987). "Searching for the Psychometric Boundaries of Schizophrenia." *Journal of Abnormal Psychology, 96, 354*–363.

Monahan, J. (1981). *Prediction of Violent Behavior.* Beverly Hills, CA: Sage.

Monahan, J. (1984). "The Prediction of Violent Behavior: Toward a Second Generation of Theory and Policy." *American Journal of Psychiatry, 141,* 10–15.

Money, J. (1987). "Sin, Sickness, or Status: Homosexual Gender Identity and Psychoneuroendocrinology." *American Psychologist, 42,* 384–399.

Money, J., and Weideking, C. (1980). "Gender Identity/Role Normal Differentiation and Its Transportations." In B. Wolman, Ed. *Handbook of Human Sexuality.* Englewood Cliffs, NJ: Prentice-Hall.

Montgomery, G., and Orozco, S. (1985). "Mexican Americans' Performance on the MMPI as a Function of Level of Acculturation." *Journal of Clinical Psychology, 41,* 203–212.

Moreland, K., and Orstad, J. (1987). "Validity of Millon's Computerized Interpretation System for the MCMI." *Journal of Consulting and Clinical Psychology, 55,* 113–114.

Morey, L. (1988). "Personality Disorders in DSM-III and DSM-III-R." *The American Journal of Psychiatry, 145,* 573–577.

Morey, L., Bloshfield, R., Webb, W., and Jewell, J. (1988). "MMPI Scales for DSM-III Personality Disorders." *Journal of Clinical Psychology, 44,* 47–50.

Munjack, D., Oziel, L., Kanno, P., Whipple, K., and Leonard, M. (1981). "Psychological Characteristics of Males with Secondary Erectile Failure." *Archives of Sexual Behavior, 10,* 123–132.

Murphy, G., and Wetzel, R. (1980). "Suicide Risk by Birth Cohort in U.S., 1949–1974." *Archives of General Psychiatry, 37,* 519–525.

Myers, J., Weissman, M., Tischler, G., Holzer, C., et al. (1984). "Six-Month Prevalence of Psychiatric Disorders in Three Communities." *Archives of General Psychiatry, 41,* 959–970.

Nasrallah, H., and Weinberger, D., Eds. (1986). "Handbook of Schizophrenia, Vol. 1: The Neurology of Schizophrenia. Amsterdam: Elsevier.

Nelson, B. (1984). *Making Child Abuse an Issue.* Chicago: University of Chicago Press.

Newcomb, M., and Bentler, P. (1988). "Impact of Adolescent Drug Use and Social Support on Problems of Young Adults: A Longitudinal Study." *Journal of Abnormal Psychology, 97,* 64–75.

Newmark, C., Ed. (1979). *MMPI Clinical and Research Trends.* New York: Praeger.

Newmark, C., Ed. (1985). *Major Psychological Assessment Instruments.* Boston: Allyn and Bacon.

Newman, C., and Hutchins, T. (1980). "Age and MMPI Indices of Schizophrenia." *Journal of Clinical Psychology, 36,* 768–769.

NIMH Staff (1977). *Lithium in the Treatment of Mood Disorders.* Rockville, MD: National Institutes of Mental Health.

Oas, P. (1984). "Validity of the Draw-A-Person and Bender-Gestalt Tests as Measures of Impulsivity with Adolescents." *Journal of Consulting and Clinical Psychology, 52,* 1011–1019.

Ogdon, D. (1977). *Psychodiagnostics and Personality Assessment: A Handbook.* Los Angeles: Western Psychological Services.

Olbrisch, M. (1977). "Psychotherapeutic Interventions in Physical Health." *American Psychologist, 32,* 762–777.

Oltmanns, T., and Maher, B. (1988). *Delusional Beliefs.* New York: John Wiley.

Orsini, D., Van Gorp, W., and Boone, K. (1988). *The Neuropsychology Casebook.* New York: Springer-Verlag.

Osgood, C., Luria, Z., Jeans, R., and Smith, A. (1976). "The Three Faces of Evelyn: A Case Report." *Journal of Abnormal Psychology, 85,* 247–286.

Oster, G., and Gould, P. (1987). *Using Drawings in Assessment and Therapy.* New York: Brunner/Mazel.

Otto, R., Lang, A., Megargee, E., and Rosenblatt, A. (1988). "Ability of Alcoholics to Escape Detection by the MMPI." *Journal of Consulting and Clinical Psychology, 56,* 452–457.

Pallis, C., and Bamji, A. (1979). "McIlroy Was Here. Or Was He? *British Medical Journal, 6169,* 973–975.

Parwatikar, S., Holcomb, W., and Menninger, K. (1985). "Detection of Malingered Amnesia in Accused Murders." *Bulletin of the American Academy of Psychiatry and the Law. 13,* 97–103.

Patalano, F. (1980). "Comparison of MMPI Scores of Drug Abusers and Mayo Clinic Normative Groups." *Journal of Clinical Psychology, 36,* 576–579.

Patrick, J. (1988). "Concordance of the MCMI and MMPI in the Diagnosis of Three DSM-III Axis I Disorders." *Journal of Clinical Psychology, 44,* 186–190.

Pauly, I. (1968). "The Current Status of the Change of Sex Operation." *Journal of Nervous and Mental Disease, 147,* 460–471.

Penk, W., Woodward, W., Robinowitz, R., and Parr, W. (1980). "An MMPI Comparison of Polydrug and Heroin Abusers." *Journal of Abnormal Psychology, 89,* 299–302.

Pennington, B., Peterson, L., and Barker, H. (1979). "The Diagnostic Use of the MMPI in Organic Brain Dysfunction." *Journal of Clinical Psychology, 35,* 484–492.

Peterson, R. (1978). "Review of the Rorschach." In O. Buros, Ed. *The Eighth Mental Measurements Yearbook.* Highland Park, NJ: Gryphon Press.

Phares, J. (1988). *Clinical Psychology,* 3rd Ed. Chicago: Dorsey.

Philips, J. and Ray, R. (1980). "Behavioral Approaches to Childhood Disorders: Review and Critique." *Behavior Modification, 4,* 3–34.

Phillips, D. (1986). "The Effects of Mass Media Violence on Suicide and Homicide." *Newsletter of the American Academy of Psychiatry and Law, 11,* 29–31.

Phillips, L. and Smith, J. *Rorschach Interpretation: Advanced Technique.* New York: Grune & Stratton.

Piotrowski, Z., Sherry, D., and Keller, J. (1985). "Psychodiagnostic Test Usage." *Journal of Personality Assessment, 49,* 115–120.

Piotrowski, Z. (1979). *Perceptanalysis.* Philadelphia: Ex Libris.

Price, W., Dimarzio, L., and Gardner, P. (1986). "Biopsychosocial Approach to Premenstrual Syndrome." *American Family Practitioner, 33*(6), 117–122.

Prien, R., and Klupfer, D. (1986). "Continuation Drug Therapy for Major Depressive Episodes: How Long Should It Be Maintained?" *American Journal of Psychiatry, 143,* 18–23.

Pritchard, D., and Rosenblatt, A. (1980). "Racial Bias in the MMPI: A Methodological Review." *Journal of Consulting and Clinical Psychology, 48,* 263–267.

Propkop, C., Bradley, L., Margolis, R., and Gentry, W. (1980). "Multivariate Analysis of the MMPI Profiles of Patients with Pain Complaints." *Journal of Personality Assessment, 44,* 246–252.

Quay, H., Ed. (1987). *Handbook of Juvenile Delinquency.* New York: John Wiley.

Quevillon, R., Landau, S., Apple, W., and Petretic-Jackson, P. (1986). "Assessing Adolescent Conduct Disorders and Oppositional Behaviors." In R. Harrington, Ed. *Testing Adolescents.* Kansas City, MO: Test Corporation of America.

Rabin, A. (1964). Lectures and personal communication.

———, Ed. (1968). *Projective Techniques in Personality Assessment.* New York: Springer.

——— (1972). "Review of the Rorschach." In O. Buros, Ed. *The Seventh Mental Measurements Yearbook.* Highland Park, NJ: Gryphon Press.

——— (1981). "Projective Methods: A Historical Introduction." In A. Rabin, Ed. *Assessment with Projective Techniques.* New York: Springer.

Rada, R., Laws, D., and Kellner, R. (1976). "Plasma Testosterone Levels in the Rapist." *Psychomatic Medicine, 38,* 257–268.

Rader, C. (1977). "MMPI Profile Types of Exposers, Rapists and Assaulters in a Court Services Population." *Journal of Consulting and Clinical Psychology, 45,* 61–69.

Rapaport, D., Gill, M., and Schafer, R. (1968). *Diagnostic Psychological Testing.* New York: International Universities Press.

Reed, G. (1985). *Obsessional Experience and Compulsive Behavior.* Orlando, FL: Academic Press.

Reitan, R., and Wolfson, D. (1986). *Traumatic Brain Injury: Recovery and Rehabilitation.* Tucson: Neuropsychology Press.

Retzlaff, P., and Gibertini, M. (1987). "Factor Structure of the MCMI Basic Personality Scales and Common-Item Artifact." *Journal of Personality Assessment, 51,* 588–594.

Reuter, E., Wallbrown, F., and Wallbrown, J. (1985). "16 PF Profiles and Four-Point Codes for Clients Seen in a Private Practice." *Multivariate Experimental Clinical Research, 7,* 123–147.

Richardson-Klavehn, A., and Bjork, R. (1988). "Measures of Memory." In M. Rosenzweig and Porter, Eds. *Annual Review of Psychology,* Vol. 39. Palo Alto, CA: Annual Reviews.

Rickers-Ovsiankina, M., Ed. (1960). *Rorschach Psychology.* New York: John Wiley.

Ritzler, B., Zambianco, D., Harder,D., and Kaskey, M. (1980). "Psychotic Patterns of the Concept of Object on the Rorschach Test." *Journal of Abnormal Psychology, 89,* 46–55.

Robe, H. (1987). Personal communication.

Rogers, C. (1951). *Client-Centered Therapy.* Boston: Houghton Mifflin.

Rogers, R. (1986). *Conducting Insanity Evaluations.* New York: Van Nostrand Reinhold.

_____, Ed. (1988a). *Clinical Assessment of Malingering and Deception.* New York: Guilford.

_____ (1988b). "Clinical Assessment of Malingering and Deception." American Academy of Forensic Psychology Workshop, Miami Beach, FL.

Rogers, R., Dolmetsch, R., and Cavanaugh, J. (1981). "An Empirical Approach to Insanity Evaluations." *Journal of Clinical Psychology, 37,* 683–687.

Rorschach, H. (1953). *Psychodiagnostics,* 5th ed., New York: Grune and Stratton.

Rosen, J. (1953). *Direct Analysis.* New York: Grune and Stratton.

Rosenbaum, G., Shore, D., and Chapin, K. (1988). "Attention Deficit in Schizophrenia and Schizotypy." *Journal of Abnormal Psychology, 97,* 41–47.

Rossini, E., and Kaspar, J. (1987). "The Validity of the Bender-Gestalt Emotional Indicators." *Journal of Personality Assessment, 51,* 254–261.

Roy, A. (1987). "Five Risk Factors for Depression." *British Journal of Psychiatry, 150,* 536–541.

Rubinow, D., and Roy-Byrne, P. (1984). "Premenstrual Syndromes: Overview from a Methodological Perspective." *The American Journal of Psychiatry, 141,* 163–172.

Rubinow, D., Roy-Byrne, P., Hoban, M., Gold, P., and Post, R. (1984). "Prospective Assessment of Menstrually Related Mood Disorders." *The American Journal of Psychiatry, 141,* 684–686.

Ruderman, A. (1986). "Dietary Restraint: A Theoretical and Empirical Review." *Psychological Bulletin, 99,* 247–262.

Rutter, M. (1987). "Temperament, Personality and Personality Disorder." *British Journal of Psychiatry, 150,* 443–458.

_____ (1988). "Depressive Disorders." In M. Rutter, A. H. Tuma, and I. Lann, *Assessment and Diagnosis in Child Psychopathology.* New York: Guilford.

Salmon, P., and Meyer, R. (1986). "Neuropsychological Assessment: Adults." In M. Kurke and R. Meyer, Eds. *Psychology in Product Liability and Personal Injury Law.* New York: Hemisphere.

Satz, P. (1987). Personal communication.

Schachter, D. (1986). "Amnesia and Crime: How Much Do We Really Know?" *American Psychologist, 43,* 286–295.

Schneidman, E. (1985). *Definition of Suicide.* New York: John Wiley.

Schwartz, M. (1987). *Biofeedback.* New York: Guilford.

Schwartz, M., and Graham, J. (1979). "Construct Validity of the MacAndrew Alcoholism Scale." *Journal of Consulting and Clinical Psychology, 47,* 1090–1095.

Scott, R., and Stone, D. (1986). "MMPI Measures of Psychological Disturbance in Adolescent and Adult Victims of Father-Daughter Incest." *Journal of Clinical Psychology, 42,* 251–259.

Seamons, D., Howell, R., Carlisle, A., and Roe, A. (1981). "Rorschach Simulation of Mental Illness and Normality by Psychotic and Nonpsychotic Legal Offenders." *Journal of Personality Assessment, 45,* 130–135.

Seltzer, L. (1986). *Paradoxical Strategies in Psychotherapy.* New York: John Wiley.

Selye, H. (1956). *The Stress of Life.* New York: McGraw-Hill.

Shacht, T., and Nathan, P. (1977). "But Is It Good for Psychologists?" *American Psychologist, 32,* 1017–1025.

Shafer, R. (1948). *Clinical Application of Psychological Tests.* New York: International Universities Press.

———— (1954). *Psychoanalytic Interpretation in Rorschach Testing.* New York: Grune and Stratton.

Shapiro, D. (1984). *Psychological Evaluation and Expert Testimony.* New York: Van Nostrand Reinhold.

Shatin, L. (1979). "Brief Form of the Competency Screening Test for Mental Competence to Stand Trial." *Journal of Clinical Psychology, 35,* 464–467.

Shemberg, K., and Leventhal, D. (1984). "Conceptualization and Treatment of Paranoid Schizophrenia." *Psychotherapy, 21,* 370–376.

Sherer, M., Kumor, K., Cone, E., and Jaffe, J. (1988). "Suspiciousness Induced by Four-Hour Intravenous Infusions of Cocaine." *Archives of General Psychiatry, 45,* 673–677.

Sherry, G., and Levin, B. (1980). "An Examination of Procedural Variables in Flooding Therapy." *Behavioral Therapy, 11,* 148–155.

Siegel, M. (1987). *Psychological Testing from Early Childhood Through Adolescence.* Madison, CT: International Universities Press.

Silver, R., Isaacs, K., and Mansky, P. (1981). "MMPI Correlates of Affective Disorders." *Journal of Clinical Psychology, 37,* 836–839.

Silverman, L. (1976). "Psychoanalytic Theory: The Reports of My Death Are Greatly Exaggerated." *American Psychologist, 31,* 621–637.

Simons, A., Murphy, G., Levine, J., and Wetzel, R. (1986). "Cognitive Therapy and Pharmacotherapy for Depression." *Archives of General Psychiatry, 43,* 43–50.

Slobogin, C., Melton, G., and Showalter, C. (1984). "The Feasibility of a Brief Evaluation of Mental State at the Time of the Offense." *Law and Human Behavior, 8,* 305–320.

Small, A., Madero, J., Gross, H., Teagno, L., Leib, J., and Ebert, M. (1981). "A Comparative Analysis of Primary Anorexics and Schizophrenics on the MMPI." *Journal of Clinical Psychology, 37,* 773–736.

Smith, C., and Graham, J. (1981). "Behaviorial Correlates for the MMPI Standard F Scale and for a Modified F Scale for Black and White Psychiatric Populations." *Journal of Consulting and Clinical Psychology, 49,* 455–459.

Smith, M., and Glass, G. (1977). "Meta-analysis of Psychotherapy Outcome Studies." *American Psychologist, 32,* 955–1008.

Smith, M., and Thelen, M. (1984). "Development and Validation of a Test for Bulimia." *Journal of Consulting and Clinical Psychology, 52,* 863–872.

Smith, R., (1976). "Voyeurism: A Review of the Literature," *Archives of Sexual Behavior, 5,* 585–609.

Smith, S., and Meyer, R. (1980). "Working Between the Legal System and the Therapist." In D. Cox and R. Daitzman, Eds. *Exhibitionsim.* New York: Garland.

———— (1987). *Law, Behavior and Mental Health: Policy and Practice.* New York: New York University Press.

Sneddon, J. (1980). "Myasthenia Gravis – The Difficult Diagnosis." *British Journal of Psychiatry, 136,* 92–93.

Snyder, S. (1986). "Pseudologia Fantastica in the Borderline Patient." *American Journal of Psychiatry, 143,* 1287–1290.

Solovay, M., Shenton, M., and Holzman, P. (1987). "Comparative Studies of Thought Disorders: 1. Mania: 2. Schizoaffective Disorder." *Archives of General Psychiatry, 44,* 13–30.

Spanos, N., Weekes, J., and Bertrand, L. (1985). "Multiple Personality: A Social Psychological Perspective." *Journal of Abnormal Psychology, 94,* 362–376.

Spitzer, R. (1988). "The DSM-III-R Reconsidered. Grand Rounds: Jefferson Hospital." Jeffersonville, IN (Feb. 2, 1988).

Spitzer, R., Cohen, J., Fliess, J., and Endicott, J. (1967). "Quantification of Agreement in Psychiatric Diagnosis: A New Approach." *Archives of General Psychiatry, 17,* 83–87.

Spitzer, R., and Endicott, J. (1978). *Schedule of Affective Disorders and Schizophrenia.* New York: Biometrics Research.

Spitzer, R., Forman, J., Nee, J. (1979). "DSM-III Field Trials: Initial Interrater Diagnostic Reliability." *American Journal of Psychiatry, 136,* 815–817.

Spotts, J., and Schontz, F. (1984). "Drug-Induced Ego States. I. Cocaine Phenomenology and Implications." *The International Journal of the Addictions, 19,* 119–151.

Srinivasan, K., Murphy, R., and Janakiramaiah, N. (1986). "A Nosological Study of Patients Presenting with Somatic Complaints." *Acta Psychiatrica Scandinavica, 73,* 1–5.

Stout, A., and Steege, J. (1985). "Psychological Assessment of Women Seeking Treatment for Premenstrual Syndrome." *Journal of Psychosomatic Research, 92,* 621–629.

Strassberg, D., Reimherr, F., Ward, M., Russell, S., and Cole, A. (1981). "The MMPI and Chronic Pain." *Journal of Consulting and Clinical Psychology, 49,* 330–226.

Streiner, D., and Miller, H. (1979). "A Table for Prorating Incomplete Form MMPI's." *Journal of Consulting and Clinical Psychology, 47,* 474–477.

———— (1981). "Prorating Incomplete Wiggins and MacAndrew Scales." *Journal of Personality Assessment, 45,* 427–429.

Svanum, S., and Dallas, C. (1981). "Alcoholic MMPI Types, and Their Relationship to Patient Characteristics, Polydrug Abuse, and Abstinence Following Treatment," *Journal of Personality Assessment, 45,* 278–287.

Swiercinsky, D., Ed. (1985). *Testing Adults:* Kansas City: Test Corporation of America.

Szasz, T. (1987). *Insanity: The Idea and Its Consequences:* New York: John Wiley.

Telch, M., Agras, W., Taylor, C., Roth, W., and Gallen, C. (1985). "Combined Pharmacological and Behavioral Treatment for Agoraphobia." *Behavior Research and Therapy, 23,* 325–336.

Teyber, E. (1988). *Process and relationship in psychotherapy.* Chicago: Dorsey.

Tomparowski, P., and Ellis, N. (1986). "Effects of Exercise on Cognitive Processes: A Review." *Psychological Bulletin, 99,* 338–346.

Trethvithick, L., and Hosch, H. (1978). "MMPI Correlates of Drug Addiction Based on Drug of Choice." *Journal of Consulting and Clinical Psychology, 46,* 180.

Tripp, C. (1987). *The Homosexual Matrix.* New York: New American Library.

Tsushima, W., and Wedding, D. (1979). "MMPI Results of Male Candidates for Transsexual Surgery." *Journal of Personality Assessment, 43,* 385–387.

Turkat, I. (1985). "Formulation of Paranoid Personality Disorder." In I. Turkat, Ed. *Behavioral Case Formulation.* New York: Plenum.

Valenstein, E. (1986). *Great and Desparate Cures: The Rise and Decline of Psychosurgery and Other Radical Treatments for Mental Illness.* New York: Basic Books.

Van Gorp, W., and Meyer, R. (1986). "The Detection of Faking on the Millon Clinical Multiaxial Inventory (MCMI)." *Journal of Clinical Psychology, 42,* 742–748.

Van Gorp, W., Satz, P., Kiersch, M., and Henry, R. (1986). "Normative Data on the Boston Naming Test for a Group of Normal Older Adults." *Journal of Clinical and Experimental Neuropsychology, 8,* 702–705.

Van Pat, P. (1984). "Sleep Disturbances." In P. Sutter and H. Adams, Eds. *Handbook of Psychopathology.* New York: Plenum.

Vincent, K., Castillo, I., Hauser, R., Zapata, J. et at., (1984) *MMPI-168 Codebook.* Norwood, NJ: Ablex.

Virkunen, M. (1975). "Victim-Precipitated Pedophilia Offenses." *British Journal of Criminology, 15,* 175–179.

Vogel, G., Vogel, F., McAbee, R., and Thurmond, A. (1980). "Improvement of Depression by REM Sleep Deprivation." *Archives of General Psychiatry, 37,* 247–253.

Vogel, W. (1985). "Interactions of Drugs of Abuse with Prescription Drugs." In A. Alterman, Ed. *Substance Abuse and Psychopathology.* New York: Plenum.

Volberg, R., and Steadman, H. (1988). "Refining Prevalence Estimates of Pathological Gambling." *The American Journal of Psychiatry, 145,* 502–505.

Wadsworth, R., and Checketts, K. (1980). "Influence of Religious Affiliation on Psychodiagnosis." *Journal of Consulting and Clinical Psychology, 48,* 234–240.

Wagner, E., and Heise, M. (1981). "Rorschach and Hand Test Data Comparing Bipolar Patients in Manic and Depressive States." *Journal of Personality Assessment, 45,* 240–249.

Wagner, E., and Wagner, C. (1981). *The Interpretation of Psychological Test Data.* Springfield, IL: Charles Thomas.

_____ (1978). "Similar Rorschach Patterning in Three Cases of Anorexia Nervosa." *Journal of Personality Assessment, 42,* 426–429.

Walker, G. (1985). "The Brief Therapy of a Compulsive Gambler." *Journal of Family Therapy, 7,* 1–8.

Walters, G. (1984). "Empirically Derived Characteristics of Psychiatric Inpatients with DSM-III Diagnosis of Schizophrenia." *Journal of Abnormal Psychology, 93,* 71–79.

Walters, G., White, T., and Greene, R. (1988). "Use of the MMPI to Identify Malingering and Exaggeration of Psychiatric Symptomatology in Male Prison Inmates." *Journal of Consulting and Clinical Psychology, 56,* 111–117.

Ward, L., and Selby, R. (1980). "An Abbreviation of the MMPI with Increased Comprehensibility and Reliability." *Journal of Clinical Psychology, 36,* 180–186.

Ward, L., and Ward, J. (1980). "MMPI Readability Reconsidered." *Journal of Personality Assessment, 44,* 387–389.

Washton, A., and Gold, M. (1987). "Cocaine: A Clinician's Handbook. New York: Guilford.

Watson, C., Plemel, D., and Jacobs, L. (1978). "An MMPI Sign to Separate Organic from Functional Psychiatric Patients." *Journal of Clinical Psychology, 34,* 398–432.

Webb, J., McNamara, K., and Rodgers, D. (1981). *Configural Interpretations of the MMPI and CPI.* Columbus: Ohio Psychology Publishing.

Wechsler, D. (1981). *WAIS-R Manual.* Cleveland: The Psychological Corporation.

Weeks, D., Freeman, C., and Kendall, R. (1980). "ECT: III. Enduring Cognitive Defects?" *The British Journal of Psychiatry, 137,* 26–37.

Weinberg, M. (1984). "The Sub-culture of Sado-masochism." *Social Problems, 31,* 379–389.

Weiner, D., and Harmon, L. (1946). "Subtle and Obvious Keys for the MMPI." (Advisement Bulletin 16.) Minneapolis: Regional Veteran's Administration Office.

Weiner, I., and Hess, A., Eds. (1987). *Handbook of Forensic Psychology.* New York: John Wiley.

Welsh, G. (1948). "An Extension of Hathaway's MMPI Profile Coding System." *Journal of Consulting Psychology, 12,* 343–344.

Westermeyer, J. (1987). "Cultural Factors in Clinical Assessment." *Journal of Consulting and Clinical Psychology, 55,* 471–478.

Wicksramasekera, I. (1976). "Aversive Behavior Rehearsal for Sexual Exhibitionism." In I. Wicksramasekera, Ed. *Biofeedback, Behavior Therapy, and Hypnosis.* Chicago: Nelson-Hall.

Wicksramasekera, I. (1988). *Clinical Behavioral Medicine.* New York: Plenum.

Widiger, T., Frances, A., Warner, L., and Bluhm, C. (1986). "Diagnostic Criteria for the Borderline and Schizotypal Personality Disorders." *Journal of Abnormal Psychology, 95,* 43–51.

Widiger, T., and Sanderson, C. (1987). "The Convergent and Discriminant

Validity of the MCMI as a Measure of the DSM-III Personality Disorders." *Journal of Personality Assessment, 51,* 228–242.

Widiger,T., Williams, J., Spitzer, R., and Frances, A. (1985). "The MCMI as a Measure of DSM-III." *Journal of Personality Assessment. 49,* 366–378.

Wiggins, E., and Brandt, J. (1988). "The Detection of Simulated Amnesia." *Law and Human Behavior, 12,* 57–79.

Wiggins, J. (1969). "Content Dimension in the MMPI." In J. Butcher, Ed. *MMPI: Research Developments and Clinical Applications.* New York: McGraw-Hill.

Wiggins, J., Goldberg, L., and Applebaum, M. (1971). "MMPI Content Scales: Interpretive Norms and Correlations with Other Scales." *Journal of Consulting and Clinical Psychology, 37,* 403–410.

Winder, P., O'Dell, J., and Karson, S. (1975). "New Motivational Distortion Scales for the 16 PF." *Journal of Personality Assessment, 39,* 532–537.

Winer, D. (1978). "Anger and Dissociation: A Case Study of Multiple Personality." *Journal of Abnormal Psychology, 87,* 368–372.

Winters, K., Weintraub, S., and Neale, V. (1981). "Validity of MMPI Codetypes in Identifying DSM-III Schizophrenics, Unipolars, and Bipolars." *Journal of Consulting and Clinical Psychology, 49,* 486–487.

Wolfson, K., and Erbaugh, S. (1984). "Adolescent Responses to MacAndrew Alcoholism Scale." *Journal of Consulting and Clinical Psychology, 52,* 625–630.

Wolpe, J. (1987). "Carbon Dioxide Inhalation Treatments of Neurotic Anxiety." *The Journal of Nervous and Mental Disease, 175,* 129–133.

World Health Organization (1979). "Schizophrenia: An International Follow-up Study." New York: Wiley-Interscience.

Yablonsky, L. (1976). *Psychodrama: Resolving Emotional Problems Through Role Playing.* New York: Basic Books.

Yerevian, B., Anderson, J., Grota, L., and Bray, M. (1986). "Effects of Bright Incandescent Light on Seasonal and Nonseasonal Major Depressive Disorder." *Psychiatry Research, 18,* 355–364.

Yudofsky, S., Williams, D., and Gorman, V. (1981). "Propranolol in the Treatment of Rage and Violent Behavior in Patients with Chronic Brain Syndrome." *American Journal of Psychiatry, 138,* 218–220.

Zeig, J., Ed. (1987). *The Evolution of Psychotherapy.* New York: Brunner/Mazel.

Zigler, E., and Glick, M. (1988). "Is Paranoid Schizophrenia Really Camouflaged Depression?" *American Psychologist, 43,* 284–290.

Zimmerman, I., and Woo-Sam, J. (1973). "Clinical Interpretation of the Wechsler Adult Intelligence Scale. *New York: Grune and Stratton.*

Ziskin, J. (1981). Coping with Psychiatric and Psychological Testimony, 3rd ed. Venice, CA: Law and Psychology Press.

Zook, A., and Sipps, G. (1985). "Cross-Validation of a Short Form of the Marlowe-Crowne Social Desirability Scale." *Journal of Clinical Psychology, 41,* 236–238.

Zubin, J. (1978). "But Is It Good for Science?" *The Clinical Psychologist, 31,* 1–7.

Zuckerman, M., Buchsbaum, M., and Murphy, D. (1980). "Sensation Seeking and Its Biological Correlates." *Psychological Bulletin, 88,* 187–214.

NAME INDEX

Abel, G., 192, 197, 200, 282, 284
Adler, M., 93, 98
Agras, W., 79, 285, 286, 288
Albert, S., 294, 295
Alden, L., 144, 249
Allison, J., 4, 5, 89, 223
Altman, J., 118
American Psychiatric Association, 10
Amolsch, T., 237
Anastasi, A., 89
Anderson, W., 39, 40, 250
Andreasen, N., 120
Archer, R., 20, 75, 291
Arkes, H., 8
Armentrout, J., 283
Aronow, E., 4
Ascher, L., 303

Baker, L., 331
Ball, H., 291
Ballenger, J., 140, 149
Balloun, K., 296
Bamji, A., 304
Barbaree, H., 282
Barkley, R., 221, 234, 239
Barnett, P., 78
Barrett, C., 32, 367
Bauer, B., 39, 40, 250
Beaber, R., 297
Beck, A., 125, 320
Beck, S., 4, 98, 110, 136
Bellak, J., 91, 105, 121, 233, 333, 339
Belli, M., 192

Bender, L., 332
Benedikt, R., 169
Bentler, P., 63, 70
Benton, A., 325
Berne, E., 182, 233
Bernstein, A., 85, 94, 100
Bertinetti, J., 77
Betman, J., 4
Beutler, L., 213
Binder, A., 239, 242, 270
Bjork, R., 324, 326
Blanchard, R., 190
Blane, H., 67, 70, 73
Blatt, S., 4, 89
Blau, T., 355
Bloom-Feshbach, J., 141, 142
Bloom-Feshbach, S., 141, 142
Boerger, A., 4
Bohn, M., 235, 236, 239, 265–270, 308, 309
Boles, J., 8
Bornstein, M., 215
Bornstein, P., 215
Boudewyns, P., 137
Brandt, J., 178, 298
Braun, P., 331
Breggin, P., 114
Breuning, S., 93
Brigham, I., 242, 247, 279, 313
Brinkman, S., 331
Brown, S., 65, 70, 274
Bruch, H., 285, 286, 288
Budman, S., 174
Buechley, R., 291
Bull, R., 296

Burger, G., 4
Burke, H., 158
Butcher, J., 4, 5, 17, 18, 20, 24, 48, 366

Caddy, G., 70
Caine, T., 6
Cantrell, J., 7
Cantwell, D., 331
Caplan, B., 324
Cappe, R., 144, 249
Carbonell, J., 265
Cargonello, J., 6
Carpenter, L., 69
Carson, R., 4, 41
Cattell, R., 6, 53, 54, 57, 58, 125
Cautela, J., 65, 197, 254
Chambless, D., 140, 218
Checketts, K., 22
Cheek, D., 171
Choca, J., 7
Clare, A., 130
Clark, C., 348
Cleckley, H., 235
Clum, G., 181, 246
Cofer, D., 118
Cohen, M., 282
Coleman, E., 189, 202
Colligan, R., 4, 18
Conley, J., 68
Cook, P., 308
Cooper, S., 4
Costello, R., 69
Cox, D., 200, 201, 202, 218
Crabtree, A., 179, 181, 182
Craig, R., 64, 68, 72
Craigie, F., 70
Crowne, D., 297
Cullen, C., 202, 340
Curran, J., 344

Dahlstrom, L., 4
Dahlstrom, W., 4, 21, 22, 107, 164
Daldin, H., 297
Dallas, C., 68
Dam, H., 121
Dana, R., 7
Dangel, R., 142
Davey, G., 202, 340
Davidson, H., 4
Davis, K., 42, 280, 308
Dawes, R., 3
Dawood, M., 129, 130, 131, 132
Dejong, R., 130
De Silva, P., 152, 155, 156, 251

Diaz-Buxo, J., 93
Didion, J., 224
Donnelly, E., 126
Donovan, J., 65, 67, 69
Dryden, W., 65, 125, 137, 249
Duckworth, J., 4
Duker, J., 4, 104
Duncan, C., 85, 91

Earls, C., 193, 283
Easson, W., 346
Eber, H., 4, 53
Eckenrode, J., 311, 314
Edell, W., 225, 227, 243
Edinger, J., 265
Edmonston, W., 168, 179
Ekman, P., 289, 296
Ellis, A., 65, 125, 137, 249
Ellsworth, R., 93
Emmelkamp, P., 137, 138, 145
Endicott, J., 297
Erbaugh, S., 5, 64, 68
Erickson, W., 283
Erlich, P., 81
Exner, J., 4, 90, 132, 136, 207, 225, 260, 318, 319, 332
Eysenck, H., 247

Fabian, M., 67
Fabry, J., 121
Fairbank, J., 157, 158
Faucett, J., 316
Faulstitch, M., 68
Fekken, C., 291, 292
Fersch, E., 284
Figley, C. A., 158
Finkel, N., 345
Finkelhor, D., 198, 312, 314
Fjordback, T., 103, 107
Fleming, M., 191
Foa, E., 140, 149
Follingstad, D., 282, 283
Fordyce, W., 169, 170
Forgione, A., 200
Fowler, R., 5, 18, 20, 27, 41, 43, 64, 123, 182, 280, 292
Freeman, W., 196
Freund, K., 206
Freud, S., 80, 165
Fuld, P., 331
Fulkerson, S., 23

Gackenbach, J., 185
Gallucci, N., 236, 239
Gardener, E., 228, 243

Gardner, D., 243
Garmezy, N., 13
Gass, C., 326, 328
Gearing, M., 236, 265, 280, 308
Gedo, J., 65
Gelles, R., 311, 312
Gil, K., 168
Gilberstadt, H., 4, 104
Gilbert, J., 70
Gilbertini, M., 7
Gillberg, C., 334–336, 339
Gillberg, I., 334–336, 339
Gittelman, R., 142
Glass, G., 3
Glasser, W., 77, 247, 306
Glick, M., 103, 108
Gold, M., 64, 76
Golden, C., 4, 225, 236, 331
Golden, R., 88
Goldfried, M., 4
Golding, S., 353
Goldstein, A., 96, 147, 279
Gotlib, I., 78
Gould, P., 105, 310, 339
Grace, W., 241
Graham, J., 5, 17, 21, 22, 24, 31,
    41, 48, 88, 229, 256
Green, R., 41, 220
Greene, R., 4, 124, 290
Grisso, T., 1, 349, 351, 354, 355,
    357
Grob, C., 200
Gross, W., 69
Guertin, W., 4
Gurekas, R., 6
Gurman, A., 93, 100
Gynther, M., 23, 24, 41, 47, 88, 135,
    291, 328

Haas, A., 156, 158
Hall, G., 199, 209
Hare, R., 234, 235
Harlow, H., 41
Harmon, L., 290
Harrow, M., 103
Hathaway, S., 17, 18, 19
Hauer, A., 283
Hawk, G., 265
Haynes, S., 107, 108, 110
Heath, D., 63, 74
Hedlund, J., 4, 23, 28, 29, 33
Heilbrun, A., 105, 109
Heinrich, T., 237
Heise, M., 117, 120
Heller, J., 136

Hendlin, H., 156, 158
Hendrix, E., 168, 201, 203
Henker, B., 335, 339
Herbert, M., 75, 84
Hersen, M., 93
Hess, A., 355
Hewett, B., 64
Higginbotham, N., 74, 79, 194, 251
Hoehn-Saric, R., 137, 143, 150
Hoffman, R., 115
Hogan, R., 101
Holcomb, W., 137
Holden, R., 291, 292
Holland, T., 4, 68, 69
Holmes, D., 296
Hosch, H., 63
Hovanitz, C., 290
Hsu, L., 4, 18
Hutchins, T., 89

IPAT Staff, 4, 53, 54, 69

Jacobsen, R., 324
Jacobson, N., 93, 100
James, W., 57
Janick, L., 286
Jarvik, M., 82
Johns, E., 6
Johnson, D., 105
Johnson, F., 199
Johnson, J., 68, 167
Johnson, M., 91
Johnson, S., 199
Johnson, V., 212, 215, 217, 218
Jordan, L., 348
Jordan-Brown, C., 290

Kabacoff, R., 4
Kalichman, S., 265, 307
Karon, B., 91, 98, 106, 238
Karson, S., 4, 55, 136, 164
Kaspar, J., 91, 339
Kaufman, A., 4, 6
Kay, S., 92
Keefe, F., 168
Keiser, T., 225, 237
Keles, A., 186
Kellam, A., 276
Keller, H., 279
Kelley, C., 4, 27, 34, 41, 42, 43, 48,
    63, 128, 184, 229, 244
Kellner, R., 161, 162, 166, 172, 175
Kelly, G., 125
Kelly, W., 156
Kembler, K., 108

Kennedy, W., 355
Kernberg, O., 228, 231, 259, 262, 278
King, G., 27, 34, 41, 42, 43, 48, 63, 128, 184, 229, 244
Kinsley, A., 211
Kirkley, B., 286
Kirman, W., 209, 281
Kish, G., 70
Kleinknecht, R., 143
Klingler, D., 4
Klopfer, W., 4
Kluft, R., 182
Klupfer, D., 122
Kolb, L., 169
Kolevzon, M., 124, 220
Kopelmon, H., 180
Koss, M., 20
Kozak, M., 140, 149, 152, 156, 173
Kraft-Ebbing, 207
Kreitman, N., 314, 316
Krishnan, R., 278, 279
Krug, S., 4, 6, 55, 62, 222, 293, 294
Kunce, J., 309
Kurlycheck, R., 348

Laboratory of Community Psychology, 351
Lachar, D., 4, 20, 68, 119, 205, 224, 232, 280, 328
Lambert, M., 120, 123
Lambert, N., 334, 336, 339
Landis, E., 162, 289, 295, 306, 307
Landman, J., 3
Lane, J., 4
Lanyon, R., 4
Lasch, C., 231
Lazar, B., 103
Lazarus, A., 124, 155
Lelos, D., 352
Leonard, K., 67, 70, 73
Lerner, P., 4
Levanthal, D., 103, 105
Levine, B., 140
Levine, S., 194, 197, 199, 201
Levitt, E., 4
Lewy, A., 115
Lieberman, R., 93
Liebowitz, M., 203
Lindenmayer, J., 92
Lipsitt, P., 352
Lo Piccolo, J., 166, 196, 214, 215
Lorr, M., 4, 6
Love, A., 169, 170, 171
Lovibond, S., 70

Low, P., 343
Lowy, D., 225, 237
Luria, Z., 212
Lykken, D., 234
Lyons, J., 114

MacAndrew, C., 5, 64, 68
Macciocchi, S., 296
Magnusson, D., 259, 262
Maher, B., 103, 106, 111, 221
Malamuth, N., 196, 207, 209, 282
Mandler, A., 113, 114, 117
Marks, P., 4, 20
Marlatt, A., 67, 70, 72, 74
Marlowe, D., 297
Martin, W., 64
Mash, E., 242, 286, 309
Mason, B., 90, 120
Masters, W., 189, 212, 214, 215, 217, 218
Matarazzo, J., 4
Matson, J., 350, 351
Mattick, R., 143, 144
May, W., 192
Mayer, S., 158
McCann, J., 91, 120
McGarry, L., 344
McGeehan, M., 81
McInerney, J., 74, 77
McKim, W., 67
McKinley, J., 17, 18
McLeod, D., 137, 143, 150
McNiel, K., 7, 8
Meehl, P., 25, 88
Megargee, E., 4, 235, 236, 239, 265–270, 280, 308, 309
Meichenbaum, D., 111, 124
Meier, M., 328, 333, 340
Meissner, W., 231, 232, 233, 243
Meister, R., 115, 172
Melton, G., 1, 355
Mester, R., 117
Meyer, R., 7, 85, 114, 162, 196, 234, 289, 295, 306, 307, 333
Miller, H., 64
Millon, T., 6, 7, 95, 175, 228, 247
Mirsky, A., 85, 88, 91, 96, 103
Mlatt, S., 139
Moldin, S., 88, 97, 103
Molish, H., 4
Money, J., 190, 192
Monahan, J., 307, 310, 314, 350, 355
Montgomery, G., 21
Moreland, K., 7

Morey, L., 4, 220, 243, 250, 260
Munjack, D., 213
Murphy, G., 314
Myers, J., 85

Nasrallah, H., 89, 94, 95
Nathan, P., 13
Nelson, B., 311, 313
Newcomb, M., 63, 70
Newmark, C., 4, 5, 89, 305, 341
Nicholson, R., 158
Nietzsche, F., 187
NIMH Staff, 113, 115, 117

Oas, P., 271, 272
O'Dell, J., 4, 55, 136
Offord, K., 18.
Ogdon, D., 4, 90
Olbrisch, M., 3, 163
Oltmanns, T., 103, 106, 111, 221
Orozco, S., 21
Orsini, D., 323, 324
Orstad, J., 7
Osgood, C., 182, 183
Oster, G., 105, 310, 339

Pallis, C., 304
Parsons, O., 67
Parwatikar, S., 298
Patalano, F., 63
Patrick, J., 7, 92, 110, 120
Pauly, I., 190
Peck, C., 169, 170, 171
Penk, W., 75
Pennington, B., 328
Peters, L., 143, 144
Peterson, R., 4
Phares, J., 65, 77, 93, 142
Phillips, D., 321
Phillips, L., 70, 90, 120, 310, 319
Piotrowski, Z., 4, 5, 6
Pollack, S., 344
Polster, R., 142
Price, W., 130, 133
Prien, R., 122
Pritchard, D., 21, 234
Propkop, C., 164, 170
Prouix, J., 193, 283

Quay, H., 234, 238, 241, 272, 274
Quevillon, R., 241, 242, 258
Quinlan, D., 105

Rabin, A., 4
Rada, R., 283

Rader, C., 284
Rapaport, D., 4, 70, 154
Reed, G., 156
Reitan, R., 122, 326
Retzlaff, P., 7
Reuter, E., 4, 6
Reznikoff, M., 4
Richardson-Klavehn, A., 324, 326
Rickers-Ovsiankina, M., 4
Ritzler, B., 91
Robe, H., 334, 336
Rogers, C., 151, 184, 247
Rogers, R., 289, 291, 295, 297, 345,
    347, 349
Rorschach, H., 4
Rosen, J., 98, 101, 106
Rosenbaum, G., 86, 91, 226
Rosenblatt, A., 22
Ross, S., 70
Rossini, E., 91, 339
Roy, A., 113, 118
Roy-Byrne, P., 130, 132
Rubinow, D., 130, 132
Ruderman, A., 80
Rumsey, N., 296
Russell, E., 326, 328
Rutter, M., 113, 121, 124, 133, 224,
    228

Salmon, P., 85, 324, 333
Sanderson, C., 7
Satz, P., 324, 331
Saunders, D., 4
Schachter, D., 178
Schneidman, E., 314–316, 320, 321
Schontz, F., 80, 81
Schwartz, M., 100, 151, 156, 305
Scott, R., 312
Seamons, D., 295
Selby, R., 20, 341
Seltzer, L., 155, 254
Selye, H., 150
Shacht, T., 13
Shafer, R., 4, 117, 154, 210, 233,
    238
Shah, S., 344
Shapiro, D., 355, 368
Shatin, L., 353
Shemberg, K., 103, 105
Sherer, M., 80
Sherry, G., 140
Shipley, R., 137, 140
Siegel, M., 4
Silver, R., 119
Silverman, L., 136

Simons, A., 98, 122
Sines, J., 42, 280, 308
Sipps, G., 10
Slobogin, C., 349
Small, A., 286
Smith, C., 25
Smith, J., 70, 90, 120, 310, 319
Smith, M., 3, 287
Smith, R., 204
Smith, S., 114, 198, 201, 345
Sneddon, J., 163
Snyder, S., 243
Solovay, M., 115
Solyom, L., 146, 147
Spanos, N., 181, 183
Spitzer, R., 10, 13, 14, 235, 297, 303
Spotts, J., 80, 81
Srinivasan, K., 166
Stava, L., 194, 197, 199, 201
Steadman, H., 274
Steege, J., 131
Stein, N., 96, 147
Stock, W., 166, 196, 214
Stone, D., 312
Stout, A., 131
Strassberg, D., 169
Streiner, D., 64
Suess, J., 91
Suziedelis, A., 4
Svanum, S., 68
Sweeney, M., 241
Swiercinsky, D., 4, 120, 227, 244
Szasz, T., 346

Taulbee, E., 4
Telch, M., 140
Terdal, L., 242, 286, 309
Teyber, E., 65, 180, 231, 281
Thelen, M., 287
Tomkin, A., 324
Tomparowski, P., 125
Trethvithick, L., 63
Tsushima, W., 191
Turkat, I., 106, 223

Vale, W., 139
Valenstein, E., 93, 121
Van Gorp, W., 7, 8, 326, 327
Van Pat, P., 185
Vincent, K., 18
Virkunen, M., 198
Vogel, G., 122
Vogel, W., 72
Volberg, R., 274

Wadsworth, R., 22
Wagner, C., 4, 117, 165, 238
Wagner, E., 4, 117, 120, 165, 238, 287
Walker, G., 274
Wall, C., 65, 197, 254
Walters, G., 290
Warburton, F., 4
Ward, J., 20
Ward, L., 20, 341
Washton, A., 64, 76
Watson, C., 4, 68, 69
Webb, J., 4
Wechsler, D., 4
Wedding, D., 191
Weeks, D., 114
Weideking, C., 190
Weinberg, M., 259
Weinberger, D., 89, 94, 95
Weiner, D., 290
Weiner, I., 355
Welsh, G., 19, 21
Westermeyher, J., 86
Wetzel, R., 314
Wicksramasekera, I., 125, 149, 203, 207
Widiger, T., 7, 87, 224, 226, 242, 243, 245
Wiggins, E., 4, 178, 298
Willage, D., 23
Winder, P., 6, 22, 55, 293
Winer, D., 181, 290
Winters, K., 119
Wittenborn, J., 118
Wolfson, D., 122, 326
Wolfson, K., 5, 64, 68
Wolpe, J., 149, 151
Woo-Sam, J., 4
World Health Organization, 88
Wrobel, T., 20, 290

Yablonsky, L., 184
Yerevian, B., 122, 125
Yudofsky, S., 282

Zeig, J., 3
Zigler, E., 103, 108
Zimmerman, I., 4
Ziskin, J., 355, 367
Zook, A., 10
Zubin, J., 13
Zuckerman, M., 65, 74, 238, 262, 272

SUBJECT INDEX

The many individual references in the text to various tests (e.g., WAIS-R, Rorschach, TAT) and interventions (e.g., systematic desensitization, assertiveness training) are not included here.

A and B therapists, 96
Adjustment disorder, 156–158
Affective disorders, 113–134
  atypical, 127
  bipolar disorder, 126
  cyclothymic disorder, 126–127
  depressive disorder, 113–134
  dysthymic disorder (depressive
    neurosis), 122–125
  manic episode (mania), 114–118
  schizoaffective disorder, 115,
    127–129
Aggression potential, 307–311 (see
    also Antisocial personality dis-
    order; Conduct disorder;
    Explosive disorder)
Agoraphobia, 137–140
Alcoholics Anonymous, 71
Alcoholism, 65–72
  Alcoholics Anonymous, 71
  Antabuse, 71
  MacAndrew Alcoholism Scale
    (MMPI), 68
  and organic dysfunction, 69
American Psychiatric Association,
    10 (see also DSM-III-R)
Amnesia, psychogenic, 178–180
  and malingering, 297–298
Amphetamine use disorder, 77–80
Anorexia nervosa, 285–288

Antiandrogens, 200
Antisocial personality disorder,
    234–238, 259 (see also
    Criminal personality)
Anxiety disorders, 135–159
  agoraphobia, 137–140
  generalized anxiety disorder,
    149–151
  obsessive-compulsive disorder,
    151–156
  panic disorder, 147–149
  post-traumatic stress disorder,
    156–158
  simple phobia, 145–147
  social phobia, 143–145
Arson, 276
Attention-Deficit Hyperactivity
    Disorder (ADHD), 334–340
  types of, 336–338
Avoidant personality disorder,
    247–249

Bestiality, 211
Bipolar disorder, 126
Body dysmorphic disorder,
    174–175
Borderline personality disorder,
    242–245
Brief reactive psychosis, 101
Bulimia nervosa, 285–288

Case preparation principles, 356–357
Catatonic schizophrenia, 96–98
Cattell Sixteen Personality Factor Questionnaire (16 PF), 53–62
  faking, 293–294
  forms of, 53
  primary scales, 55–60
   A, 54
   B, 55
   C, 55
   E, 56
   F, 57
   G, 57
   H, 57
   I, 57
   L, 58
   M, 58
   N, 59
   O, 59
   Q_1, 59
   Q_2, 59
   Q_3, 60
   Q_4, 60
  scale interrelationships, 60–62
Central nervous system impairment (CNSI), 323–334
  elderly and, 327
  hemisphere localization in, 332
  MMPI and, 326–328
  Rorschach and, 332–333
  16 PF and, 329
  TAT and, 333
  WAIS-R and, 329–331
Chemotherapeutic agents, list of, 381
Child abuse, 311–314
Civil commitment, 349–350
  prediction of dangerousness and, 350 (*see also* Aggression potential; Suicide potential)
Cocaine abuse, 80–81
Color shock, 136–137
Competency, 350–354
  to stand trial, 351–354
Conduct disorder, 238–242
Conversion disorder, 166–168, 169
Courtroom presentation, 363–369
Criminal personality, 265–270 (*see also* Antisocial personality disorder; Conduct disorder)
Criminal responsibility, 343–349
  ALI rule and, 344–345
  DSM-III-R and, 346
  Durham Rule and, 343

M'Naghten Test and, 343
Crisis intervention principles, 158
Cyclothymia, 126–127

Deception detection, 23, 25, 26
Delusional (paranoid) disorder, 108–111
Dependent personality disorder, 249–252
Depersonalization disorder, 183–185
Deposition preparation, 362–363
Depression, 113–134 (*see also* Suicide potential)
  and bipolar disorder, 126
  and cognitive behavioral techniques, 125
  and cyclothymia, 126
  and dysthymia (depressive neurosis), 122–125
  and major depressive disorder, 118–126
  and measurement scales, 27, 123
  and seasonal affective disorder, 122
  and women, 118, 129–134
Depressive disorder, major, 118–126
Depressive neurosis, 122 (*see also* Dysthymia)
Disorganized schizophrenia, 94
Dissociative disorders, 177–185
  depersonalization disorder, 183–185
  multiple personality, 181–183
  psychogenic amnesia, 178–180
  psychogenic fugue, 180–181
DSM-III-R, 3, 10–15, 219, 235, 243, 258
  axis labels, 14
  changes from DSM-III, 11, 63, 74, 106
Dyspareunia, 215, 218
Dysthymia (depressive neurosis), 122–125

Eating disorders, 285–288
ECT, 113, 355
Emotionally unstable personality, 243
Epilepsy, 279 (*see also* Central nervous system impairment)
Erectile dysfunction, 213
Exhibitionism, 200–204
  personality types in, 201
Expert witness case preparation, 361–362, 368

Explosive disorder, 279–282, 310
    (*see also* Aggression potential)

Factitious disorders, 298–302,
    303–306
Female psychosexual dysfunction,
    215, 216–218
Fetishism, 194–196
Folie à deux (*see* Shared paranoid
    disorder)
Forensic psychology roles, 344
Frigidity, 212
Frotteurism, 205–207
Fugue, psychogenic, 180–181

Gambling, pathological, 272–274
Gender identity disorders, 189
Generalized anxiety disorder,
    149–151
Global Assessment of Functioning
    Scale, 14

Heroin, 81–84
Histrionic personality disorder,
    228–230
Hypoactive sexual desire, 211,
    215–216
Hypochondriasis, 171–174,
    298–302
Hysteria, 163, 166, 228

Iatrogenic disorder, 228
Identity disorder, 245–247 (*see also*
    Dissociative disorders)
Impotence, 212 (*see also* Psycho-
    sexual dysfunctions, male)
Impulse control disorders, 271–288
Incest, 198
Incompetency, 350–354
    to make a will, 350
    to stand trial, 351–354
Induced psychotic disorder, 111–112
Insanity defense, 343 (*see also*
    Criminal responsibility)

Juvenile delinquency, 240 (*see also*
    Conduct disorder)

Kegal exercises, 217
Kleptomania, 274–276

La belle indifference, 166, 169
Late luteal phase dysphoric
    disorder, 13, 129–134
Lithium, 117

Male psychosexual dysfunction,
    211–215
Malingering, 289–306
    MMPI and, 290–293
    Rorschach and, 294–295
    16 PF and, 293–294
Malpractice, 355–356
Mania (manic episode), 114–118
    and schizophrenia, 115
Manic-depressive disorder, 125
Masochism, sexual, 207–209
Mental retardation, 340–341
Mental Status Examination, 1
Methadone, 84
Meyer Information Battery, 371–380
Millon Clinical Multiaxial
    Inventory (MCMI), 6–9
Minnesota Multiphasic Personality
    Inventory (MMPI), 17–54
    adolescent criteria, 20–24
    bias and, 21, 24, 29
    coding rules, 19
    copyright, 6
    critical items, 20
    Ego Strength Scale, 5
    F-K index, 26
    faking, 23, 25
    first consideration diagnoses and
        two-point code tables, 49–53
    Goldberg's formula for psychosis, 89
    Improved Readability Form, 20
    MacAndrew Alcoholism Scale, 5,
        68
    paranoid trough, 107
    primary scales, 18, 21
        ? Scale, 22
        L Scale, 23
        F Scale, 24
        K Scale, 18, 25
        (1) Hypochondriasis (Hs), 26
        (2) Depression (D), 27
        (3) Hysteria (Hy), 28
        (4) Psychopathic deviate (Pd), 29
        (5) Masculinity-femininity (Mf), 30
        (6) Paranoia (Pa), 31
        (7) Psychasthenia (Pt), 32
        (8) Schizophrenia (Sc), 33
        (9) Hypomania (Ma), 34
        (0) Social introversion (Si), 35
    reading level required, 19, 20
    scale interrelationships, 36–49
    secondary derived scales, 5, 29
    T scores, 18
    two-point codes, 21, 36–49
Model report format, 357–361

Multiple personality, 181–183
Munchausen's syndrome, 304

Narcissistic personality disorder,
    231–234, 258, 259
Neurosis, 135, 151, 235, 262
Neurotic triad, 135
Nocturnal penile tumescence (NPT),
    213

Obsessive-compulsive disorder,
    151–156, 252
Obsessive-compulsive personality
    disorder, 152, 252–254
Opioid use disorder, 81–84
    heroin, 81–84
    methadone, 84
Oppositional-defiant disorder,
    257–258
Organic brain dysfunction, 323 (*see
    also* Central nervous system
    impairment)
Overanxious disorder, 140–141

Pain disorder, 168–171
Panic disorder, 139, 147–149
Paraphilia, 192–210
Paranoia (*see* Delusional disorder)
Paranoid disorders, 106–112
Paranoid personality disorder,
    221–223
Paranoid schizophrenia,
    103–106
    compared to other schizophrenias,
        103
Partialism, 206
Passive-aggressive personality
    disorder, 254–257
Pedophilia, 197–200
Personality disorders, 219–263
    subclassification of, 219
Phobias, 137–147
    agoraphobia, 137–140
    simple, 145–147
    social, 143–145
Polygraph, 296, 306
Polysubstance abuse, 74–77
Post-traumatic stress disorder,
    156–158
Predicting dangerousness,
    307–321
Premature ejaculation, 212, 215
Premenstrual syndrome, 129
Prescription drug abuse, 72–74
Proverbs, 10, 91, 95, 104

Psychosis, 102 (*see also* Affective
    disorders; Paranoid disorders;
    Schizophrenia)
    atypical, 102
Psychopathic personality, 234, 235
    (*see also* Antisocial personality
    disorder)
Psychosexual disorders, 189–218
    gender identity disorders, 189
    paraphilias, 192–210
    psychosexual dysfunctions,
        211–218
Psychosexual dysfunctions, 211–218
    female, 215, 216–218
    male, 211–215
Pyromania, 276–278
Public speaking, fear of, 143–145

Rape, 197, 282–285
    personality types, 282
Report writing, outline for,
    357–361

Sadistic personality disorder, 13,
    258–262
Sadism, sexual, 209–210
Schizoaffective disorder, 115,
    127–129
Schizoid personality disorder,
    223–226
Schizophrenia, 85–100, 178, 242
    catatonic, 96–98
    developmental path, 87
    disorganized (hebephrenic), 94
    malingering of, 297
    paranoid, 103–106
    premorbid predictions of, 85
    prognostic indicators of, 92
    residual, 98
    Rorschach criteria for, 90
    undifferentiated, 94
Schizophreniform disorder, 100–101
Schizotypal personality disorder,
    224, 225, 226–228, 242
School (phobia) refusal, 140–143
Screening Information Battery (*see*
    Meyer Information Battery)
Seasonal affective disorder, 122
Self-defeating personality, 13
Self-defeating personality disorder,
    262–263
Separation anxiety disorder,
    141–143
Sexual deviation (*see* Paraphilia)
Sexual disorders, 189–218

Sexual disorders *(Contd.)*
  female psychosexual dysfunction,
      215, 216–218
    dyspareunia, 215, 218
    female sexual arousal disorder,
      216
    hypoactive sexual desire, 215
    inhibited female orgasm,
      216–218
    sexual aversion disorder, 215
    vaginismus, 215, 218
  gender identity disorder, 189
  male psychosexual dysfunction,
      211–215
    hypoactive sexual desire, 211,
      215–216
    inhibited male orgasm, 212–215
    male erectile disorder, 212–215
    premature ejaculation, 212, 215
    sexual aversion disorder, 212,
      215–216
  paraphilias, 192–210
    exhibitionism, 200–204
    fetishism, 194–196
    frotteurism, 205–207
    pedophilia, 197–200
    sexual masochism, 207–209
    sexual sadism, 209–210
    transvestic fetishism, 196–197
    voyeurism, 204–205
  Transsexualism, 189–218 *(see also*
      Gender identity disorders;
      Paraphilia)
Shared paranoid disorder *(folie à*
    deux), 111–112
Simple phobia, 145–147
Sleep disorders, 185–188
Social phobia, 143–145

Sociopathic personality, 234, 235
Somatization disorder, 162–166
Somatoform disorders, 161–175
  body dysmorphic disorder,
      174–175
  conversion disorder, 166–168, 169
  hypochondriasis, 171–174
  somatization disorder, 162–166
  somatoform pain disorder, 168–171
  undifferentiated, 175
Somatoform pain disorder, 168–171
Substance use disorders, 63–84
  abuse and dependency criteria, 66
  alcoholism, 65–72
  amphetamine use disorder, 77–80
  cocaine abuse, 80–81
  opioid use disorder, 81–84
  polysubstance abuse, 74–77
  prescription drug abuse, 72–74
Suicide potential, 314–321 *(see also*
    Depression)
  Exner's Rorschach signs, 318
  suicide notes, 320
  types of, 316
Supreme Court, 5

Tardive dyskinesia, 92
Terminal sex, 207
Transsexualism, 189–192
Transvestic fetishism, 196–197
Trichotillomania, 278–279

Undifferentiated schizophrenia, 94

Vaginismus, 215–218
Voyeurism, 204–205

Zoophilia, 210–211